D1563535

THE PHILADELPHIA CAMPAIGN, 1777–1778

THE PHILADELPHIA CAMPAIGN, 1777–1778

Stephen R. Taaffe

University Press of Kansas

Published by the University Press of Kansas (Lawrence, Kansas 66049), which was
organized by the Kansas Board of Regents and is operated and funded by Emporia
State University, Fort Hays State University, Kansas State University, Pittsburg State
University, the University of Kansas, and Wichita State University

Library of Congress Cataloging-in-Publication Data
Taaffe, Stephen R.
The Philadelphia Campaign, 1777–1778 / Stephen R. Taaffe.
p. cm. — (Modern war studies)
Includes bibliographical references and index.
ISBN 0-7006-1267-X (cloth : alk. paper)
1. Philadelphia Campaign, 1777–1778. I. Title. II. Series.
E233.T33 2003
973.3'33—dc21   2003007162

British Library Cataloguing-in-Publication Data is available.

Printed in the United States of America

10 9 8 7 6 5 4 3 2 1

The paper used in this publication meets the minimum requirements of the
American National Standard for Permanence of Paper for Printed Library
Materials Z39.48-1984.

Contents

Maps

ONE

Introduction

The previous winter's storms had swept away part of Sandy Hook's beaches, turning the remote north New Jersey peninsula into an island. Under ordinary circumstances, the octagonal lighthouse at Sandy Hook's northern tip that guided vessels in and out of New York City's harbor was the only thing of value on what one British observer called "a dismal barren spot."[1] On the morning of 5 July 1778, however, the cream of Great Britain's North American army—redcoats, German mercenaries, and loyalist provincials, some 10,000 tired men in all—flowed four columns wide down from the surrounding hills and crossed over to Sandy Hook on an improvised pontoon bridge. After a grueling hike along the island's deep dunes, the soldiers stumbled on board flatboats and rowed out to the transports waiting there to haul them and their equipment across the Lower Bay to Staten Island, from where a good many of them had departed less than a year ago on the campaign that was supposed to crush the American rebellion once and for all and restore peace and harmony to the British Empire.[2]

It had not turned out that way. Instead, although the British had won all the major and most of the minor battles, reduced supposedly impregnable fortifications, occupied the rebel capital at Philadelphia, and inflicted more casualties than they sustained, they were back where they started, with little by way of compensation for their sufferings and hardships. This in itself was difficult enough to choke down, but circumstances above and beyond the British army's eleven-month-long odyssey to and from Philadelphia had brought France into the war on the Americans' side and tilted the strategic balance against Great Britain, placing final victory further away than ever. Tallying up the ledger a month after the Sandy Hook evacuation, one dejected redcoat officer looked forward only to "the prospect of getting away from this unhappy country and receding from the sight of the disgraceful situation to which a succession of the most unaccountable mismanagement has now reduced us."3

The 1777–78 Philadelphia campaign was one of the Revolutionary War's most important, but concurrent operations in upstate New York that led to the British defeat at Saratoga have overshadowed it. Even so, in terms of numbers engaged, battles fought, and blood spilled, the Philadelphia campaign dwarfed all others. For the first and only time during the war, the main British and American armies slugged it out in the open on something approaching equal terms. Redcoats and Continentals skirmished and maneuvered in New Jersey, clashed in some of the war's biggest engagements at Brandywine and Germantown and Monmouth Courthouse, grappled along the cold, swampy Delaware River banks in complicated interservice siege operations, and struggled in the hills and woods surrounding Philadelphia. All this activity and bloodshed seems to have produced little by way of conclusive results, and the fact that the end of the fighting brought both armies back to their approximate starting points tends to reinforce this perspective. However, a closer look reveals that the campaign had a profound impact on the war's outcome by contributing to final American victory.

For the British, the Philadelphia campaign was their last chance to focus their undivided attention on suppressing the American revolt. The British army won a string of impressive tactical victories, but it was unable to deliver a knockout blow that would put an end to the rebellion. Although the war continued for another three and a half years after the British army returned to New York City, French intervention forced the British to disperse their resources throughout the world to protect their extensive empire. Indeed, North America became just another theater in an increasingly complicated world war that stretched British power and ingenuity to their limits. In addition, the strategic confusion attending the campaign played a big role in the British catastrophe at Saratoga that persuaded France to enter the war, and it helped undermine and poison the crucial relationship between British commander in chief, William Howe, and his superiors back in London. Finally, the Philadelphia campaign continued the British army's unhappy tradition of abandoning its valuable loyalist allies, thus further undermining whatever indigenous support existed for the reestablishment of royal authority. All this made it much more difficult for the British to maintain their war effort in the years following their operations to and from Philadelphia, and whatever successes they enjoyed afterward can be attributed as much to American weakness as to British strength.

For the Americans, the campaign was important as well. For one thing, they managed to survive it despite losing almost all the battles, an impressive if ironic accomplishment under any circumstances. In enduring, the Americans bought valuable time and exacted a continuing toll on Britain's finite resources. Moreover, by proving in both southeastern Pennsylvania and upstate New York that they could wage war on a sustained basis, the Americans convinced France to enter the conflict on their side, which compelled the British to abandon all their gains from the campaign, including Philadelphia, and to revert to the strategic defensive for the time being. Subsequent French naval support enabled the Americans to defeat the British at Yorktown and persuaded British policy makers to give up their hopes of destroying the rebellion. In addition, during the campaign, the American commander in chief, George Washington, solidified his control over the main American army and came into his own as a strategist. Washington used the fighting around Philadelphia as a proving ground for many of the strategic ideas he employed throughout the rest of the conflict. Similarly, many of Washington's subordinates who participated in the campaign later went on to prove themselves in subsequent fighting elsewhere. Finally, Washington's army also changed for the better by becoming a more professional force capable of standing up to the vaunted British redcoats. Thus, although the Americans gained few tactical victories, they laid the groundwork for their eventual triumph and emerged from the campaign in a stronger strategic position than their foes.

For the British to win the Revolutionary War, they had to restore royal authority throughout the rebellious colonies. On the surface, they possessed ample means to do so. Britain was among the world's wealthiest countries, with an economy capable of providing the weapons, supplies, and equipment its military required to extinguish the revolt. Most British policy makers had plenty of warmaking experience dating back to the Great War for Empire of 1754–63 with France, so they were thoroughly familiar with the complexities of formulating strategy and raising armies and navies to conduct operations thousands of miles from home. The British army was one of the world's most professional and disciplined, and it was full of veteran officers and men unlikely to be rattled by the chaos and confusion of battle. The giant Royal Navy, for its part, dominated the waves and enabled the British to deploy and supply their forces anywhere water met land. The British could also tap into substantial loyalist support present in every colony for manpower, intelligence, and supplies. In the end, however, the British were unable to translate these impressive advantages into an effective strategy that would permit them to win the war. To be sure, they faced substantial difficulties—long communications lines between Britain and the New World, the vast colonial geography extending from Canada to Georgia, and a generally hostile American population—but they overcame similar problems in conquering French Canada during the Great War for Empire. This time around, however, they had to wage war practically alone in an antagonistic international environment against an enemy with advantages hard to recognize, harder to measure, and almost impossible to overcome. The Philadelphia campaign demonstrated Britain's inability to formulate and implement a successful plan to subjugate a smaller, poorer, and less experienced opponent.

Conversely, the Philadelphia campaign sheds light on the reasons for ultimate American victory. At first glance, the Americans faced seemingly insurmountable obstacles in their efforts to gain independence. The thirteen diverse states jealously guarded their prerogatives, and they only grudgingly and reluctantly surrendered power to a Congress that never possessed enough authority to fulfill the immense responsibilities thrust upon it. Limited resources made it impossible for the Americans to build a navy capable of challenging British control of the seas, or of producing sufficient weapons and equipment necessary to sustain the tatterdemalion and heterogeneous armies they fielded. Plenty of colonial officers and men had participated in the Great War for Empire and in various conflicts with the American Indians, but hardly any had experience building armies and developing grand strategy. Moreover, the Americans initially had few contacts with European countries willing and able to supply them with the accoutrements they needed to continue the war. Finally, they confronted a powerful fifth column of loyalists present in every region that had to be identified and neutralized. In the end, however, they not only overcame these difficulties but also made virtues of some of them. For all their problems and shortcomings, the Philadelphia campaign showed that the Americans could develop and deploy sufficient forces, formulate the proper strategy, and make the sacrifices on and off the battlefield necessary to achieve independence.

The Philadelphia campaign was significant not only because of its impact on the Revolutionary War's outcome but also because it serves as a valuable tool with which to analyze various aspects of the conflict and draw conclusions. In many respects the campaign was representative of the war as a whole; it occurred in the heart of the United States in the middle of the conflict, many of the war's major players participated in it at one level or another, and both sides faced problems and challenges that haunted them before and after the fighting around Philadelphia was over. In short, understanding the Philadelphia campaign goes a long way toward understanding British and American grand strategies, the relationship between the commanders in chief and their superiors and subordinates, and the changing connection between eighteenth-century society and warfare.

TWO

Cold New Jersey Winter

AMERICAN RESURGENCE

The last American soldiers withdrew from Princeton in the afternoon of 3 January 1777, just as the British vanguard appeared on the other side of town, and not long after the smoke had cleared from the short but furious battle there that morning. Following a brief exchange of fire, the Americans faded into the icy hills, having destroyed the bridge over the Millstone River to discourage pursuit. From there the bedraggled but victorious American army tramped through Kingston, veered left, and slogged down the increasingly muddy roads to Somerset Courthouse. Along the way confused units got lost, and some of the tired and barefoot men collapsed in the snow and refused to march on despite rumors that British cavalry was close behind. The remainder, however, continued their hike up to Pluckemin, where they stopped to rest and collect stragglers. The army had left its baggage behind at Trenton, so the men scrounged for food and shelter as best they could, a hit-or-miss proposition under even optimal circumstances. Hungry and cold, they moved onward and upward, and just before sunset on 6 January, George Washington's rebel army finally reached its destination: Morristown, a small village perched on a plateau high in the north New Jersey hills, secure from any sudden British attack.[1]

In the two weeks preceding the march to Morristown, American fortunes had taken a dramatic and wholly unexpected turn for the better. Following the British evacuation of Boston in March 1776, the rebels suffered one military setback after another. In a series of battles around New York City in late summer and fall, the British and their German mercenary allies captured that strategically vital town and drove Washington's untrained and ill-equipped army headlong into New Jersey, inflicting on it a number of defeats of varying severity. About the best

6

thing that could be said about the American army was that it survived, although this was due more to British caution than to any particular military talent displayed by Washington, his officers, or his troops. By the time Washington pulled his last men across the Delaware River on 7 December 1776 to defend Philadelphia, his army was on the verge of disintegration through desertion, disease, demoralization, and casualties. Fortunately for the Americans, the British decided to put their forces into winter quarters in north and central New Jersey. This strategic blunder paved the way for Washington and his newly reinforced army to recross the river and gobble up most of the 1,400-man German garrison at Trenton in a sudden surprise attack on the day after Christmas. The Americans fell back across the Delaware with their prisoners and spoils, but within a week they were again on New Jersey soil, where a superior enemy force trapped them at Trenton. Rather than fight a losing battle against the tough British redcoats, Washington slipped around their left flank on the night of 2–3 January 1777 and plunged into central New Jersey. Next morning at Princeton the Americans shattered the British rear guard and then marched north to their Morristown refuge before the redcoats in front of Trenton could double back and catch them. Thus, in a remarkably short time, Washington threw the seemingly inexorable British advance into reverse in one of the war's most remarkable campaigns. The military gains were substantial enough, but the counteroffensive yielded another benefit as well. Before Trenton many Americans had just about given up hope, but now they took heart, and, having taken heart, they acted accordingly. One observer in Virginia noted:

> The news [about Trenton] is confirmed. The minds of the people are much altered. A few days ago they had given up the cause for lost. Their late successes have turned the scale and now they are all liberty mad again. Their recruiting parties could not get a man . . . and now the men are coming in by companies. . . . This has given them new spirits, got them fresh succours [sic] and will prolong the war, perhaps for two years. They have recovered their panic and it will not be an easy matter to throw them into that confusion again.[2]

George Washington could of course appreciate this happy turn of events as much as the next man, all the more so because he was the primary author of the recent spate of much-needed victories, but he was not the type to let success go to his head. Indeed, Washington had learned from hard experience that fortune could be fickle. Born in 1732 into a minor upper-class Virginia family, Washington from an early age craved distinction, glory, and adventure. He found all these things in the Great War for Empire, where he participated in—and survived, although the same could not be said of many of his fellow officers— Major General Edward Braddock's disastrous defeat near Fort Duquesne in July 1755. Later he commanded Virginia's forces on the colony's western frontier, an often thankless and unhappy task that introduced him to the burdens of leadership. He resigned in 1759 and returned home, where age and experience cooled his martial ardor, and he turned to life's more mundane and placid activities: marriage, overseeing his growing plantation, and public service. He shared many colonists' increasing disenchantment with Great Britain, and he was elected to both the First and the Second Continental Congress. In June 1775, Congress appointed him commander in chief of the American army, partly because of his military experience but also because some New Englanders saw it as a way to gain support from powerful Virginia.

Washington's military background and Virginia birthright got him the job, but his character made it possible for him to survive the ensuing series of defeats and disappointments. He was by nature pugnacious and impulsive, sensitive to slights real and imagined, had a terrible temper, was obsessed with his reputation, and was blessed with only an average intellect. Over the years, however, he learned to control and overcome these less admirable traits, and they only rarely got the better of him. On the positive side of the ledger, Washington possessed immense physical and moral courage, an ability to inspire intense loyalty, a sense of calm and serenity even under the greatest hardship, a deep faith in Providence and an understanding and acceptance of man's sinfulness, and a devotion to civilian control of government and rule of law. On the surface he was almost invariably stiff, distant, and correct, but he also displayed to his inner circle a certain affability and an understated and dry sense of humor. He was, all things considered, well cast for the demanding role he played, which prompted one officer to write later in the year, "Our general is a man truly made for this revolution, which could not succeed without him."3

This may well have been true, but in early 1777 Washington was more concerned about the thousands of British and German soldiers in New Jersey than his position in the pantheon of American Revolutionary heroes. He took his army to Morristown primarily because the village offered a secure resting place for his tired soldiers after their recent exertions. Once there, however, he began to perceive other, more strategically substantive, uses for the site. Not only was Morristown highly defensible and almost invulnerable to a surprise British attack, but it was perfectly situated as a base from which his army could quickly intercept any British offensive either across central New Jersey toward Philadelphia or up the all-important Hudson River. This was all to the good, of course, but in early January Washington was thinking more in terms of maintaining the initiative he had so recently seized than in responding to a hypothetical British attack. As he saw it, the battles at Trenton and Princeton had thrown the British off balance, and he wanted to take advantage of their confusion to drive them out of New Jersey altogether. However, the British did much of this work for him in early January by evacuating almost all of the state except for a thin strip of territory along the Raritan River—and, incidentally, leaving the local loyalists to the mercy of the rebels who emerged to reestablish their control and wreak their vengeance. Washington lacked the strength to assault the strongly fortified British posts there, but the more he thought about it, the more convinced he became that the very compactness of the new British position might prove to be their undoing. Confined as the redcoats were to a few square miles of New Jersey soil, Washington did not believe that they could attain enough forage for their horses unless they raided the surrounding countryside. Such efforts, however, would give American forces ample opportunity to waylay and bushwhack the dispersed British troops tramping across the snowy fields and woods gathering straw and hay. This not only would wear down and exhaust the British army but also, if successful, would prevent soldiers from collecting the forage they sought. Lacking sufficient forage, many of their horses would die, and without enough horses, Washington doubted that the British could mount a new campaign in the spring. As he put it, "The enemy's want of forage compells [*sic*] them to send out very large parties to secure it, [and] those are always beat in with some loss. Their draft and artillery horses die fast; and now that I have brought all the useful ones from their neighborhood, I think they will meet with much difficulty in advancing."[4] Washington worried that the British might respond to his efforts to short-circuit their future operations by attacking his weak and tired army at Morristown, but he was willing to run that risk in the hope of bigger gains down the line.[5]

To that end, in early January American soldiers filtered into east central New Jersey to inflict on the British the kind of damage that Washington had in mind. Large numbers of New Jersey citizens had applied for British pardons when the seemingly invincible royal army swept through the state late the previous year, but redcoat and especially German atrocities, as well as Washington's recent military successes, had changed many minds, and by early 1777 most of the state was back in American hands. New Jersey's renewed commitment to the American cause enabled Washington to use its militia to augment his regular Continental soldiers. Indeed, in mid-January New Jersey militiamen under the capable Brigadier General Philemon Dickinson—younger brother to *Letters of a Farmer in Pennsylvania* author John Dickinson—captured forty-two wagons and some 100 horses near Somerset Courthouse when the British teamsters panicked under pressure from a sudden American assault across the Millstone River. When he had enough men, and frequently he did not, Washington deployed them to impede all but the strongest British foraging expeditions, but this made them vulnerable to any unexpected British attack, so Washington warned his subordinates to travel light and keep on their toes. Throughout the winter and into spring, these American parties stripped the countryside of anything of use to the British, raided and all but isolated British outposts at Brunswick and Piscataway and Bonhamtown, ambushed innumerable foraging parties near Quibbletown and Boundbrook, and sniped at British ships bringing supplies up the Raritan River.[6]

There was, however, nothing easy or glamorous about such successes, which often involved long, grueling hikes across snowy fields and through cold woods, and short, sharp skirmishes with British and German soldiers who appeared out of nowhere to maul surprised American patrols. To make things worse, as winter wore on, the enemy adapted to this unfamiliar type of warfare. The British beefed up the size of their foraging parties and brought along more cannons to give them an advantage in numbers and firepower that the light-traveling Americans could not begin to match. They also started sweeping the countryside in efforts to snare unwary rebels. In mid-April, for example, a three-column British force under the ever-aggressive Major General Charles Cornwallis nearly trapped Major General Benjamin Lincoln's men at Boundbrook because the militia guards had deserted their posts. Lincoln and most of his troops escaped, but the British captured three cannons and many of the artillerymen, as well as Lincoln's papers and his aide. Such a continual cat-and-mouse game across east central New Jersey promised little by way of glory, but it could be every bit as dangerous as full-fledged battle. One American soldier later recalled:

No one who has never been upon such duty as those advanced parties have to perform, can form any adequate idea of the trouble, fatigue and dangers which they have to encounter. Their whole time is spent in marches, especially night marches, watching, starving, and, in cold weather, freezing and sickness. If they get any chance to rest, it must be in the woods or fields, under the side of a fence, in an orchard or in any other place but a comfortable one, lying down on the cold and often wet ground, and, perhaps, before the eyes can be closed with a moment's sleep, alarmed and compelled to stand under arms an hour or two, or to receive an attack from the enemy; and when permitted again to endeavor to rest, called upon immediately to remove some four or five miles to seek some other place, to go through the same maneuvering as before. For it was dangerous to remain any length of time in one place for fear of being informed of by some Tory inhabitants (for there were a plenty of this sort of savage beast during the Revolutionary War) and ten thousand other causes to harass, fatigue and perplex, which time and room will not permit me to enumerate.[7]

Individually, these unending skirmishes amounted to little in the big scheme of things, but Washington's intelligence network informed him that collectively they exacted a heavy toll on the British. Reports told of tired, hungry, and sick British and German soldiers in cramped, dirty garrison towns, and crowbait nags in the stables.[8] In addition, the winter's fighting provided American troops with experience they would put to good use later in the year when the stakes became higher. Finally, by pinning the British along the Raritan, the Americans denied them access to most of New Jersey's population, and in so doing they proved to the locals that the Revolution remained viable. Such efforts did not in the end cripple British attempts to mount a new campaign in the spring, but they certainly kept the redcoats and Germans off balance, on the defensive, and away from Washington's Morristown camp throughout the winter. All things considered, it was an impressive accomplishment for an army that was in a state of continuous flux.

Of equal importance, the winter's fighting demonstrated Washington's growing strategic maturity. He increasingly recognized that the key to securing American independence lay not in defeating the well-trained and well-equipped enemy armies on the battlefield—which, despite Trenton and Princeton, was unlikely to become common practice—but rather in neutralizing them as threats to the Revolution by isolating them from the population British leaders sought to control. Washington's efforts to mangle British logistics by denying the redcoats forage not only was safer than engaging them in open-field engagements the Americans probably would lose but also played to American strengths and exploited British weaknesses. Throughout that winter Washington took advantage of the militia at his disposal, local geography, and the British army's vulnerable supply lines and logistics to fight his kind of war. In effect, Washington decentralized the struggle at an operational level to dissipate and weaken British power. This pushed the contest away from a traditional eighteenth-century conflict between small professional armies toward a people's war that required popular participation. It was an approach he would continue to cultivate when spring arrived.

BUILDING THE AMERICAN ARMY

Washington's hardscrabble army contained a good many militiamen when it arrived at Morristown, but as the winter deepened, they began to melt back into the farms and towns whence they came. Each state controlled its own militia, which generally consisted of its free adult white males, and state authorities could call out part or all of it for a length of time in case of a military emergency. Many of the militiamen in Washington's army had been ordered up late the previous year to help meet the British threat along the Delaware River. They had done their jobs well enough, fighting bravely at Trenton and Princeton, but their terms of service were expiring, and they wanted to go home. Washington and his officers pleaded with them to stay a little longer, at least until promised replacements arrived, but in most instances the men refused. So, as January and February and March wore on, Washington's militia units gradually dissolved. Replacements rotated in and out from New Jersey, Pennsylvania, and New England, but seemingly without much rhyme or reason. By mid-March there were only around 1,200 militia left in Washington's army, and most of them departed by the end of the month.[9]

Washington's problems with the militia merely confirmed the jaded view he and many of his officers had developed toward the institution.[10] To be sure, the militia could and had fought well under certain conditions—it was New England militiamen who battered the British army at Bunker Hill in June 1775—but in most instances these barely trained and independent-minded men broke and ran when the long rows of cold-eyed, bayonet-wielding redcoats approached. Moreover, many states had militia laws that made it relatively easy to escape service, often by paying a fine, which after the initial enthusiasm for the war waned, reduced the quality and quantity of the men called up.[11] Those who did put in an appearance often elected their own officers, and they had little patience for military routine. Not surprisingly, Washington was increasingly reluctant to incorporate militiamen into his army unless he absolutely had to, not only because he distrusted their fighting abilities but also because he feared they would contaminate his professional Continentals with their bad habits.[12] However, Washington still believed that militiamen could perform important service in the war effort, especially if they were mustered in for a limited time and for specific purposes. For one thing, the militia played a crucial role in maintaining internal security in their states by suppressing local loyalists and watching long, vulnerable coastlines. This released scarce and valuable Continentals to join Washington's army. In addition, although the militia generally lacked the fortitude to stand up to redcoats in open battle, small groups of them could be very effective in harassing the enemy. Indeed, throughout the winter the New Jersey militia demonstrated its worth in thwarting British foraging parties and raiding British outposts.[13]

The militia was obviously an important component of the American war effort, but the Continentals formed the backbone of Washington's army. These men, often from the lower strata of society, enlisted for one to three years or the war's duration out of love for their country and in return for some sort of bounty—usually cash and the promise of land—so they had the time and opportunity to become professional soldiers capable of slugging it out with the redcoats in the open on something approaching equal terms. Unfortunately, recent campaigns had been as hard on them as on the militia, and for many their enlistments were up. By mid-March 1777, Washington reported that he had only 2,543 Continentals left at Morristown, and a good number of those were sick or otherwise unfit for duty.[14] Despite the colonies' long-ingrained aversion to standing armies, in September 1776 Congress had authorized eighty-eight battalions—or regiments; the Americans usually used the two terms interchangeably—of Continentals, and in December it tacked on sixteen more, for a total of approximately 75,000 men. Once they raised this force, many congressmen and officers were confident that it would provide Washington with the strength he needed to drive out the British and secure American independence.[15]

Voting increases in army strength was one thing, but translating the intention into reality was something else. During the winter of 1776–77, recruiting officers fanned out throughout the states to enlist the 700-man Continental battalions Congress sanctioned. Initially all appeared to be going well, and Washington and Congress received encouraging news that the units were filling up expeditiously. As winter wore on, however, Washington began to hear disturbing reports that things were not as they seemed; the new battalions were nowhere near full strength. Very few people were willing to join the army and endure all the suffering and danger that entailed, even for the sake of liberty and independence. To spur enlistments, states offered their own bounties, but this led to an expensive bidding war for the small number of men willing to put their lives on the line for cash and land, and it brought in precious few recruits. To make things worse, Washington increasingly suspected many of his recruiting officers of laziness and even fraud. Evidence indicated that some of them exaggerated the number of men they enlisted, pocketed the bounty money for these phantom soldiers, and then blamed the resulting discrepancies between recruits on paper and in the flesh on desertions. Tallying up the numbers and noting that very few Continentals were appearing at Morristown, an appalled Washington reported, "Regiments that I expected were nearly completed, by the accounts I recd [received] from some of the colonels as far back as December, upon being called upon for actual returns, have only from 50 to 100 men."[16] Such corruption, mismanagement, and ineffectiveness convinced him that he could get the manpower he needed only through rigorous conscription.[17] In fact, some states did resort to drafting men from their militias into Washington's army, but with mixed success. In the end, Washington had to make do with the system in place, but fortunately the picture was not altogether gloomy. As the snow began to melt in the northern New Jersey hills, those men who had enlisted trickled steadily into Morristown, and by mid-May Washington's army contained some 8,100 officers and men organized into five divisions of two brigades apiece. It was not as many soldiers as Washington and Congress initially hoped for or expected, but it was a beginning.[18]

Although Washington had a hard core of veterans around which to build his army for the next campaign, most of the men dribbling into Morristown possessed little or no military experience. Washington knew as well as anyone that these new recruits could not be molded into soldiers without discipline. "Nothing," he wrote, "can be more hurtful to the service, than the neglect of discipline; for that discipline, more than numbers, gives one army the superiority over another."[19] However, Washington had learned through years of hard military experience that Americans of all stations in life were notoriously difficult to control, even when they were fighting for their freedom. Small wonder, then, that alarming numbers of his men expressed their discontent with shortages of food, clothing, and pay by deserting. Most went home, but some accepted a British offer for pardon and reward if they came into enemy lines with their arms. Either way, each deserter was one fewer man on the American army's always-anemic roster. Washington did what he could to plug the leakage by imploring Congress and the states to crack down on people who harbored deserters, and even by suggesting to one of his generals that he spread false rumors that the British sold American deserters to the East India Company, but nothing had much impact. Indeed, at one point Washington complained that outgoing deserters outnumbered incoming recruits.[20]

Even worse, those who remained at Morristown often did not seem much better than those who deserted, except that they continued to grace the American commander in chief with their presence. Washington repeatedly beseeched his army to obey basic rules and regulations—to take proper care of artillery horses, to keep the camp sanitary, to appear neat and clean, and to refrain from gambling and drinking and swearing—but the fact that he had to reiterate such orders indicated that his success was at best marginal. Nor did Washington have much luck in preparing his new recruits for combat. The previous year's campaigning had demonstrated that the army needed rigorous and uniform drill, but a busy Washington left this important task to his officers instead of doing it himself. As a result, training was sketchy and uneven, and it varied greatly from unit to unit. As spring came on, most of the men still did not understand the importance of marching in tight formation, of deploying quickly into a line of battle, of maneuvering efficiently under fire, and of avoiding bunching together. Indeed, one observer wrote that in combat American soldiers excelled only at firing accurately at the enemy from behind cover before falling back. Such tactics might be effective in waging partisan war in east central New Jersey, but they were unlikely to win any upcoming full-fledged battles in open fields against the tough redcoats and Germans. Despite Washington's intentions, his army still lagged behind its British counterpart in training and discipline. Man for man, the redcoats remained supreme.[21]

In addition to their bad habits and lack of military bearing, some of Washington's new recruits brought something else with them to Morristown: smallpox. Until the twentieth century, disease regularly killed more soldiers than bullets, and smallpox was one of the greatest scourges. In fact, the mere *fear* of smallpox kept many Americans from joining the army. Washington had learned the previous winter the damage that smallpox could inflict on his army, and he resolved to prevent a recurrence at Morristown. After careful consideration, he decided to inoculate his entire force in an effort to neutralize the disease's impact. Doing so carried considerable risks. His soldiers would be out of action for approximately a month while the milder version of the affliction ran its course, and during that time the British might march on Morristown and rout the feverish American army. Moreover, many Americans remained unconvinced of the benefits of inoculation, and the idea of intentionally infecting thousands of soldiers with the often deadly contagion was certain to alarm the local citizenry. Washington, however, was determined to keep his army intact, so on 6 February he ordered all his soldiers inoculated, and soon after he recommended to the states that they do the same to their recruits before forwarding them to his army. He hoped to keep his inoculation program secret from the enemy, but he counted on New Jersey's muddy and snowy roads to discourage any British foray to Morristown should they uncover the truth. Not unexpectedly, some commanders failed to carry out their orders as rigorously as Washington wanted, and at least one community protested the inoculation of soldiers in its vicinity. Fortunately, Congress recognized the military necessity behind the inoculations and gave Washington its full support. Within a month Washington declared the experiment a success in limiting smallpox's impact, and he suggested expanding it to American soldiers throughout the states.[22]

Washington understood as well as anyone that an army was no better than its officer corps, but unfortunately this was hardly a source of comfort for the harried commander in chief. His army contained numerous quality officers who had proved their worth in previous campaigns, but oftentimes they seemed the exception to the rule. Throughout the winter and spring, Washington repeatedly complained that too many of his officers were not sufficiently attentive to their duties, did not take enough time to acquaint themselves with his general orders, and were just plain lazy. Moreover, many of them finagled furloughs and went home to visit friends and families for the winter, leaving their tatterdemalion troops on their own in Morristown. About the only things that many officers seemed to devote sufficient attention to were questions of rank and promotion, and many exerted considerable time and energy lobbying Washington and Congress for one or the other. The competition was so intense that Massachusetts congressional delegate John Adams grumbled that he had never seen anything like it, and he added, "I am wearied to death of the wrangles between military officers, high and low. They quarrel like cats and dogs. . . . Scrambling for rank and pay like apes for nutts [*sic*]."23 The trouble was that there was no standard procedure for promotion, which led to frustration, discontent, and politicking among the officers. To rectify this, Washington appointed a committee of general officers to look into the matter and make recommendations. In June the committee proposed that officers be promoted on the basis of seniority within their own regiments to the rank of captain, and then according to their seniority among all the officers from their state, with exceptions for bravery or incompetence. Washington accepted these suggestions, but this solved only part of the problem; the power to promote general officers remained lodged in Congress. In February Congress decided after much debate that it would take into account seniority, merit, and the number of generals already furnished by a state as its criteria for promotion. It was a vague and imperfect system to say the least, and several valuable officers suffered as a result. Most notably, Congress initially denied Brigadier General Benedict Arnold promotion because two of the army's major generals already hailed from his home state of Connecticut, even though by almost any standard Arnold had fought gallantly enough during the 1775–76 Canadian campaign to deserve higher rank.24

To complicate an already confused situation, Congress and Washington also had to find room in the army for scores of French officers who crossed the Atlantic to offer their services. Many of these officers turned out to be very capable men devoted to the American cause, but others were little more than incompetent adventurers. Unfortunately, oftentimes their inability to speak English made it difficult to immediately tell the difference. The crux of the problem was that Silas Deane, the American agent in Paris, guaranteed some of them certain ranks and commands, and upon reaching America these men expected Congress to deliver on Deane's promises. Congress did not want to do anything to undermine burgeoning French support for the war effort, but many delegates believed that Deane had exceeded his authority. In addition, Washington made it clear that although he welcomed much-needed artillery and engineering experts, he did not want too many of these Frenchmen displacing Americans who had already demonstrated their worth in battle. Washington understood that putting large numbers of Frenchmen in charge of American units would generate discontent among his officer corps and undermine morale. Indeed, in late May American officers heard rumors that Congress had selected recently arrived French officer Philippe Tronson du Coudray to command Washington's artillery, supplanting the experienced and effective Brigadier

General Henry Knox. Knox, Major General Nathanael Greene, and Major General John Sullivan each wrote to Congress and threatened to resign if these rumors were in fact true. They were not, but congress-men did not appreciate such public ultimatums from military men, and they notified Washington that they expected apologies from the three impudent officers. None were forthcoming, and everyone involved tac-itly agreed to let the matter drop. As for du Coudray, Congress eventu-ally appointed him to the newly created post of inspector general of artillery, but in September he drowned in the Schuylkill River after his horse jumped off a ferryboat with him still in the saddle. In the mean-time, Congress became more circumspect toward French officers, often giving them honorary ranks until they proved themselves to Washing-ton's satisfaction.[25]

In early 1777 Washington was as accustomed to matériel shortages as he was to manpower deficiencies, but in neither case did familiarity bring him much comfort. In late February he reported that his army was fast running out of muskets, gunpowder, and cannons. The rigors of recent campaigns undoubtedly depleted American stockpiles, but the fact that militiamen often took their government-issued muskets and powder home with them when their service time expired exacerbated the problem. Replacements were hard to come by, so each and every gun was important. The colonies had traditionally imported most of their weapons from Great Britain, but of course this was no longer an option once war broke out. Although several states undertook efforts to develop an arms industry, these were small-scale affairs that did not begin to meet the demand. Throughout the winter Washington and Congress did what they could to procure and repair weapons from do-mestic sources, but it was clandestine French aid that really provided the Americans with the military hardware they needed to continue the conflict. As spring approached, French vessels began docking in Amer-ican ports with shipholds full of muskets, cartridge boxes, gunpowder, cannons, flints, and gunlocks. On 18 March *Amphitrite* alone brought into Portsmouth, New Hampshire, fifty-two cannons, 12,000 muskets, and 1,000 barrels of gunpowder. In theory the French sent over suffi-cient guns and powder for every soldier in the American army—al-though one general complained that the quality of the weapons left a lot to be desired because of bad locks and springs—but even before campaigning began in earnest, Washington again complained about a lack of arms. He suspected mismanagement and even fraud. For exam-ple, one colonel drew 400 muskets for his newly recruited Connecticut regiment, but it turned out that he had enlisted only eighty men. The congressional Board of War looked into the problem of arms procurement and distribution and agreed, reporting, "Many of our soldiers have been detected in selling their necessaries; and practices of this sort it is apprehended are but too common amongst them."[26] Trying to reconcile the supply and demand, an exasperated John Adams wrote, "Eighteen thousand arms have arrived at Portsmouth and we know not what becomes of them. Other arms have arrived in Mass[achusetts]. But we know not where they are, and it is said the *Game Cock* carried 6000 into Dartmouth. Where are they?"[27] Adams did not know, but clearly many were not in the hands of the soldiers who could make the best use of them.[28]

Washington's soldiers required more than guns and powder to wage and win the war; they also needed food in their bellies and clothes on their backs. Here, too, however, the American army faced serious shortages in early 1777. Huddling in Morristown and the neighboring villages, soldiers lacked tents, shoes, stockings, shirts, entrenching tools, hatchets, tomahawks, wagons, and often even sufficient food. Fortunately, as spring came on the Commissary, Quartermaster, and Clothier departments managed with French aid to accumulate enough tents, clothing, kettles, horseshoes, canteens, forage, entrenching tools, and salted meat for 20,000 men. Washington was grateful for the effort and preliminary results, but he suspected—correctly, as events would prove—that the supply officers underestimated the army's needs. More aggravating, in the short term anyway, was the continuing corruption and mismanagement of supplies. The distribution system was faulty, so some units often had too much of one item and not enough of another, and rectifying the problem was difficult because no one was really in overall charge. Rather than navigate the uncertain labyrinth of red tape that requisitioning supplies required, many local commanders simply confiscated some or all of the equipment and supplies that passed through their bailiwicks, often leaving the intended recipient—usually Washington—high and dry. Finally, in late April a British raid on the big American depot at Danbury, Connecticut, destroyed 3,000 to 4,000 barrels of pork and beef, 1,000 barrels of flour, 80 hogsheads of biscuit, 10 barrels of saltpeter, 100 barrels of rice, 60 hogsheads of rum and brandy, 20 hogsheads of wine, 10 casks of medicines, more than 1,000 tents, 60 iron kettles, lots of hospital bedding and sheeting, 400 axes, 5 barrels of nails, 2 barrels of printing types, 2 barrels of stock locks, 100 barrels of sugar and molasses and coffee, 20 barrels of tar, and 5,000 pairs of shoes. In the end, supply officers were able to make good most of the losses before the campaign began, but in the long run the Americans could not afford such mishaps.[29]

Washington of course lamented the successful British raid on Danbury, all the more so because he had warned the Commissary department not to place such a large supply depot within reach of the far-ranging Royal Navy. Even so, he was encouraged by the stout resistance the local militia offered, which confirmed his growing belief that its most effective role was in harassing advancing British soldiers.[30] The losses at Danbury, heavy though they were, did not dampen a budding sense of optimism among many Americans as spring approached and the British remained passive and inert in their New York and New Jersey enclaves. The previous year Washington's army survived the best the British had to offer, and this time around American soldiers were better armed, clothed, equipped, and organized than ever before. Problems remained, to be sure, but as far as many congressmen were concerned, the crisis had passed.[31]

In addition to rebuilding his army, Washington also formulated a new strategy with which to conduct the next campaign. He increasingly recognized the key to victory was not winning battles or protecting territory but rather preventing the British from reimposing their authority over the American population. As such, his army served as the Revolution's shield, so preserving it was a prerequisite for independence. Rather than risk his army in battles that might lead to its destruction, Washington planned to rely on attrition to harass, wear down, and immobilize British forces. Washington hoped to use militiamen operating in small parties— organizing them into large units took too long, and they were too hard to control—to slow down advancing British troops by attacking their flanks and rear and outposts, denying them access to local sustenance, and defending well-fortified strategic positions. In addition, he wanted a hard core of Continentals capable of standing up to the redcoats when necessary, and of exploiting any opportunities the militia or other detached parties developed. In short, Washington sought to marry traditional formalized eighteenth-century European warfare based on professional troops with a partisan *petite guerre* dependent upon citizen soldiers. A good part of his strategy was based on his acceptance of some fundamental realities that were unlikely to change anytime soon—British naval supremacy and the superior redcoat discipline, for instance—but such practicality made it all the more effective and necessary.[32]

The big question on everyone's lips, as winter gave way to spring, was what the British would do next. For all Washington's success in annoying and pinning the British along the Raritan River throughout the past few months, the fact remained that these accomplishments were short-term and limited in scale and scope. Notwithstanding Washington's efforts to deprive them of enough forage, as long as the British retained both naval supremacy and their well-fortified bases in and around New York City, they could still supply their troops and go over to the offensive. Confined to the strategic defensive, Washington could do little but wait and prepare for the next British moves. Few doubted that the British would resume the offensive with the new campaigning season, but there was substantial debate over where and when the blow would fall. Washington received innumerable letters from officers and politicians speculating on possible British targets—the Hudson River, New England, and the Chesapeake Bay region were the leading contenders—that were usually in spine-tingling proximity to their own commands and constituents. Washington resisted pleas to scatter his soldiers to protect every possible British objective, patiently explaining to Connecticut governor Jonathan Trumbull, "If we divide and detach our forces to every part where the enemy may possibly attempt an impression, we shall effect no one good purpose, and in the end, destroy ourselves, and subjugate our country."[33] In fact, Washington had been predicting a British offensive across New Jersey since mid-January, and he was both surprised and grateful with each passing day that no such attack materialized because it gave him that much more time to build and equip the army he needed to resist the expected onslaught. Washington believed that the British would either directly assault Philadelphia or else first strike his army at Morristown and then descend on the American capital. However, as spring came on, American intelligence brought in increasingly bewildering information on British intentions that shook Washington's confidence in his original assertions. Various reports claimed that the British were recruiting pilots with knowledge of the Delaware River, collecting reinforcements from Rhode Island, concentrating soldiers in New Jersey, embarking men on troop transports, constructing a portable bridge, and maneuvering their naval forces in Long Island Sound. Putting it all together, Washington added British naval mobility to his calculations and for a brief time guessed that the British intended to move up the Hudson River. By June, however, he reverted to his original contention that his army and Philadelphia were the British targets, though he granted that the enemy attack might include an amphibious component. Such speculation was just that—speculation—and in fact several weeks earlier Washington admitted as much to president of Congress John Hancock, noting, "These you will please to observe are mere conjectures upon circumstances, for the actions of the enemy have, for a long time past, been so different from appearances, that I hardly dare to form an opinion."[34]

In the meantime, the war's tempo began to change as both the British and Americans braced themselves for the large-scale operations that good weather begot. In late May, Washington suspended his campaign of harassment and concentrated his army at heavily wooded and easily defended Boundbrook, some seven miles from the main British base at Brunswick. This placed the Americans in a better position either to intercept a British attack toward Philadelphia or to move quickly to the Hudson River on the off chance the redcoats headed in that direction, although deploying so many soldiers in one location stretched the American logistical system to its limits.[35] For their part, the British evacuated many of their winter outposts and gathered their army around Brunswick and Amboy. By early June, Washington was more convinced than ever that the balloon was about to go up, and he wrote to Hancock: "There remains no room to believe otherwise, than that the enemy are on the point of moving. This is confirmed by intelligence from all quarters and through so many different channels, that we must consider it certain. Whether they will move by land or water or both, cannot be ascertained, nor is their destination precisely known: but every circumstance points out Philadelphia as their object."[36]

As events would prove, the British did not function in such a straightforward or logical manner.

ALL THE KING'S MEN

On 23 February 1777, a spattering of gunfire from a hill straight ahead greeted British lieutenant John Peebles's advance detachment a few miles beyond Woodbridge, New Jersey. Peebles and his 20 grenadiers belonged to a larger force of about 1,500 men engaged in the ongoing task of collecting forage for the British army's horses and sweeping the countryside free of rebels. It was a thankless chore, but Peebles was a professional, and he understood as well as anyone that soldiering was rarely a glamorous job. At any rate, he sent word back to his commander, Colonel John "Mungo" Campbell, that he had encountered his first opposition of the day, and then he smoothly pushed his men forward through the snow and mud toward the enemy. The rebels—mostly men from Brigadier General William Maxwell's New Jersey brigade—disappeared, as they usually did under such circumstances, and Peebles resumed his advance, brushing aside knots of American resistance with an ease that befitted the grenadiers' elite reputation. On their way back to join the main British force, however, Campbell's troops ran headlong into rebels moving from a swamp to the cover of some woods. Campbell ordered Peebles to keep the Americans occupied while he took more men and tried to cut them off. Peebles deployed his troops behind a fence under increasing fire, and two grenadier companies rushed up to support him. Unfortunately, these reinforcements opened fire too soon, and by the time they reached the fence, the Americans had them in range. Redcoats began dropping fast, taking especially galling punishment from the woods to their right. In the ensuing confusion of battle, someone ordered the two supporting companies to retire, and they pulled back on the double. Unfortunately, no one informed Peebles, and enemy fire had so decimated his small unit that he suddenly realized he was the last unwounded man at the fence. Peebles expended his last cartridge and then hurried back to his company before the rebels overran his position. Once he reached comparative safety, he saw to his anger that there were plenty of redcoats around, but no one had seen fit to send them to help his exposed detachment. When they finally did advance, they managed to disperse the Americans with a heavy volley. Exhausted, the British stuffed their wounded into wagons at the road and moved out, but the rebels recognized the opportunity to snipe at the long, vulnerable enemy column and reengaged them, forcing the British to countermarch, and in the end the redcoats had to bring up artillery to keep the swarming Americans at bay. Approaching Woodbridge, the British discovered more Americans in front of them, but their ubiquitous cannons again proved their worth and scattered the enemy. It was past dark when the redcoats finally reached their base at Amboy. In the course of the expedition they suffered seventy-five killed, wounded, and missing. The next day, mulling over the high price of the otherwise insignificant skirmish, a disgruntled Peebles scrawled in his diary, "What pity it is to throw away such men as these on such shabby ill managed occasions."[37]

For the British, Peebles's skirmish outside of Woodbridge epitomized a once-promising war effort that had sputtered to a dreary and demoralizing halt. The previous year the British government had raised and equipped the largest army it had ever deployed overseas in an effort to suppress the American revolt. Under General William Howe's command, in the summer and fall of 1776 this 25,000-man force of redcoats and German mercenaries occupied New York City and defeated Washington's rebel army in almost every battle, engagement, and skirmish. By late autumn many British officers believed that the rebellion was just about over, and they were confident that they could easily mop up the remaining American resistance in the spring.[38] No sooner had the British and their German allies gone into winter quarters, however, than Washington's supposedly moribund army sprang to life. In the space of little more than a week, Washington destroyed the German garrison at Trenton and then outmaneuvered and defeated the British around Princeton before withdrawing to his Morristown lair. In the panicky aftermath of these two defeats, the British abandoned most of New Jersey for the safety of a few outposts along the Raritan River, placing them in a position that made unhappy skirmishes like Peebles's a way of life. Obviously, the war was not yet over, and would not be anytime soon. One British colonel at Brunswick wrote home, "I must own that I was once sanguine enough to think that this disagreeable war drew near to a conclusion, and that the uninterrupted success our arms had met with in the Jerseys would soon oblige the Rebels to make their submission, such, however, are the sudden turns in war, that I think we may now reckon with certainty upon another campaign."[39]

Before the British could embark on another campaign, however, they had to get through the cold New Jersey winter. There were up to 15,000 redcoats and Germans scattered between Amboy on the coast and Brunswick up the Raritan River under Major General James Grant's command. Grant's extensive military résumé included the Jacobite Rebellion, the Great War for Empire, the 1761 Cherokee expedition, and the Battle of Long Island, but none of these experiences prepared him for the dreary frustrations he faced now. Grant did not like Americans much to begin with, and the winter's events did little to sweeten his disposition toward them. Both Amboy and Brunswick were pretty towns, but their garrisons found small comfort in their beauty. The locals were unfriendly, there was almost nothing to buy, and the quarters were generally crowded, dirty, and dank. As winter wore on, the soldiers gradually took on the appearance of slack-jawed ragamuffins in their tattered uniforms and boots. To make things worse, there was precious little to do beyond the usual drudgery of soldiering. Not surprisingly, many men became ill, especially among the Germans. Food was reasonably plentiful for the troops, but not for the horses. The overconfident British had neglected to establish forage magazines when they occupied much of New Jersey the previous November and December, so they had to constantly procure it from the surrounding countryside, which led to innumerable frustrating skirmishes with roving bands of rebels intent on denying it to the enemy. Indeed, the British eventually resorted to importing forage from Staten and Long Islands, but such bulky cargo strained their supply lines and could provide only a portion of what was needed. Although the Americans seemed like a wretched and miserable lot, throughout the winter their raiding and sniping kept British and German soldiers on edge and frequently cut the communication lines between Amboy and Brunswick. Moreover, more than one officer warned that this partisan war not only drained the British army but also gave the Americans experience they would undoubtedly put to good use when campaigning began in earnest in the spring. It was, in short, a difficult time for everyone.[40]

The British commander in chief, Lieutenant General William Howe, visited the army in New Jersey twice that winter to raise morale and to have a firsthand look at the situation, but he much preferred New York City's conviviality. Born in 1729, the forty-seven-year-old Howe had plenty of military experience, having served bravely and capably in both America and Europe during the Great War for Empire. As a member of Parliament in the 1760s and 1770s, he sympathized with the colonial cause, and indeed at one point he stated he would not fight against the Americans. That was then, however, before opportunity knocked, and since succeeding Thomas Gage in command of the king's forces in America in October 1775, he had led the British army to a string of victories around New York City until the British war machine faltered at Trenton and Princeton. Opinions about Howe varied. He was a genial, good-natured, and social man who enjoyed both women and the bottle. On the battlefield he exhibited great courage—during the Great War for Empire he led Major General James Wolfe's army up the cliffs to the Plains of Abraham outside Quebec—and the fact that he had won every engagement he personally participated in attested to his tactical abilities. On the other hand, already some officers were quietly expressing doubts about their commander in chief.[41] Howe won battles, to be sure, but he lacked the incisive mind and killer instinct that made such victories decisive. He surrounded himself with second-rate staff officers, and his indolence and laziness were well known. Moreover, his strategic acumen was increasingly suspect. So far, Howe had attempted to simultaneously seize territory, beat Washington's army, and woo the Americans back into the British fold as one of the king's commissioners empowered to treat with the colonies, but none of his efforts in any of these areas had produced concrete results. Instead, British authority was limited to the New York City region and nearby Newport, Washington's army continued to exist, and the American population seemed as hostile as ever. Howe was aware that he had finite resources to expend, and his experience at Bunker Hill demonstrated the damage the rebels were capable of inflicting on the comparatively small British army. Such knowledge enlarged Howe's natural caution, and this cautiousness had already on several occasions cost him opportunities to destroy Washington's army. Howe himself seemed to sense some of these drawbacks, and as time went on his doubts about quashing the revolt increased. For all his indisputable skills in battle, William Howe was a man in over his head—and deep down he probably knew it.[42]

Happily for Howe, he did not need to worry much about the temper of the chief instrument with which he was supposed to defeat the American rebellion. In terms of quality, the British army was perhaps the finest in the world, with a reputation to match extending back to the days of Marlborough. The army recruited men for life from the lower classes, and then molded them into a well-trained, well-equipped, and well-disciplined force that had repeatedly proved its mettle on battlefields throughout the world. The British army officer corps, for its part, was composed primarily of aristocrats who bought their commissions and learned their jobs as they went along. In these circles, breeding and connections mattered more than education and ability. Fortunately, throughout the Philadelphia campaign Howe had at his disposal some thoroughly competent and experienced subordinates such as Major Generals Charles Cornwallis and Charles Grey, in whom the commander in chief showed considerable well-placed confidence.[43] Organizationally, the British army's basic building block was its 1,000-man regiments—in America, however, regiments were always well below authorized strength—each of which was theoretically divided into two battalions, but in reality the terms "regiment" and "battalion" were usually used interchangeably. Each battalion contained ten companies, including one of light infantry and one of grenadiers. The light infantry consisted of the battalion's nimblest men and was designed to act as skirmishers well suited for America's broken wooded terrain. Grenadiers, on the other hand, were the battalion's stoutest soldiers, who served as shock troops. Like other British commanders in America, Howe detached all his light and grenadier companies and organized them into separate light and grenadier battalions that became his army's largest and most elite units.

The British army in America was a multinational organization that included not only Englishmen, Irishmen, and Scots but also Germans and American loyalists. To undertake the gargantuan task of conquering the colonies, the British required a larger army than it had ever before fielded overseas. Unfortunately, recruits at home were not sufficiently forthcoming, so the British government resorted to renting soldiers from the various German states: the Hessians. Actually, Howe's Germans came not only from Hesse-Cassel but also from Waldeck and Ansbach-Bayreuth. At any given time, approximately a quarter to a third of Howe's army consisted of these German mercenaries. Generally speaking, the Germans and British got along well enough, but German officers understood that they needed to speak English, or at least have an English translator nearby, in order for them to advance up the chain of command. Despite this surface cordiality, many British officers had grave doubts about the quality of the troops the German princes conscripted and shipped across the Atlantic. To them, the Germans appeared dirty, sickly, untrained, ill clothed, undisciplined, and unmotivated, and the disaster at Trenton confirmed their misgivings. Others, however, were more generous and stated that although the Germans were not as good as the redcoats, they were capable enough soldiers who demonstrated their worth in the fighting around New York City.[44] For his part, Howe was more concerned with the German general officers than with the rank and file. In particular, Howe expressed serious doubts about the superannuated Lieutenant General Leopold Philipp von Heister, the ranking German officer in his command. Howe believed that Heister was too unsteady and timid for his important job, and he successfully lobbied London to get him recalled. Heister left America in July and was replaced by the morose Lieutenant General Wilhelm Knyphausen. Howe initially had reservations about Knyphausen as well, but the German general's skill eventually won Howe's confidence, and the two men forged a good working relationship.[45] In addition to the Germans, Howe recruited loyalist Americans, and by the summer of 1777 he had around 2,700 under arms. Some loyalist units never left the organizational charts, but others, such as the Queen's Rangers, became solid outfits that performed very well.[46]

A CURIOUS WAY TO FORMULATE GRAND STRATEGY

On 18 January 1777, the British army in New York City celebrated the queen's birthday in style with an impressive fireworks display, followed by a grand ball and a big dinner. By morning many of the officers—senior officers, that is; most of the lieutenants and captains were on duty and unable to attend—were hopelessly drunk, and a lot of them had to stumble to their quarters and barracks in the chilly morning air.[47] Among the revelers was Howe, who was not one to let a good party interfere with his official responsibilities. As it was, Howe had more than enough on his plate just then to justify an evening blowing off steam. For one thing, the British had finally stabilized their position in New Jersey after Washington's recent counteroffensive, and for a time it had been touch-and-go. For another, Howe was involved in the difficult process of putting together his plans for the 1777 campaign. Unlike some of his officers, Howe had long ago accepted that the conflict would not end that winter, and he was acting accordingly.[48] Late the previous November, back when the war was going more or less according to design, Howe recommended to his superior back in London, the American secretary, Lord George Germain, that the British next concentrate on reducing New England, the hotbed of the rebellion. Howe proposed a two-pronged assault on that region, with a 6,000-man force moving up from Rhode Island to Boston, and another 10,000 soldiers ascending the Hudson River to Albany to split the colonies in two. Howe hoped to leave 5,000 men behind to garrison New York City and its environs, and to deploy 8,000 more troops in New Jersey to keep an eye on what was left of Washington's decrepit army. If all went well, he figured that in the fall he could seize Philadelphia and perhaps Virginia. Then, once winter and substantial reinforcements arrived, Howe believed he could move on to occupy South Carolina and Georgia. As he saw things at the time, the American rebellion was on its last legs, and he crafted this campaign to deliver the coup de grâce.[49]

Within a month, however, Howe switched gears. He based his 30 November 1776 strategy on the assumption that he would receive considerable reinforcements from Europe, but he realized that such help might not be forthcoming. Just to be safe, he lowered his sights, and on 20 December 1776 he submitted a follow-up plan predicated on the 19,000 men he had on hand. Howe wanted to exploit the considerable loyalist sentiment that observers assured him existed in Pennsylvania by attacking Philadelphia.[50] He estimated that such an offensive would require some 10,000 men. With his remaining forces, he planned to garrison Newport, Rhode Island, with 2,000 men, place another 4,000 troops in New York City and the surrounding area, and deploy the last

3,000 soldiers on the lower Hudson to cooperate with any British army moving down from Canada. Howe therefore abandoned any notion of invading New England in 1777, but by now he no longer thought that attacking in that direction was likely to prove profitable or decisive. Howe believed that Washington would follow his redcoats and Germans to New England if he headed that way, but he doubted that the American commander in chief would risk his army in open battle because there was nothing there worth fighting for. Moreover, Howe was leery of the New England militia, which the previous year around Boston demonstrated that it was not a force to be taken lightly. There was considerable speculation and conjecture behind Howe's logic, but the British commander in chief knew that Germain was receptive to a strike at the American capital, and as far as he was concerned, seizing Pennsylvania was the best he could do with the limited resources at hand.[51]

The setbacks at Trenton and Princeton of course upset and disappointed Howe, all the more so because he believed he would have crushed the rebellion sooner rather than later had not Washington interfered in such an untimely and unsporting manner. Moreover, these recent setbacks had reinvigorated the American cause, making any sort of negotiated settlement all but impossible. Clearly, the nimble American army remained a potent threat to British authority, but Howe doubted that he could run it to the ground, and for this he blamed the lethargic Germans. As he explained to Germain, "I do not now see a prospect of terminating the war but by a general action, and I am aware of the difficulties in our way to obtain it as the enemy moves with so much more celerity than we possibly can with our foreign troops, who are too much attached to their baggage which they have in amazing quantities in the field."[52] These recent discouraging events, however, reinforced Howe's conviction that attacking Philadelphia was his next logical step. Washington's rejuvenated army was already in the region, inviting battle, and he still hoped to tap into Pennsylvania's reportedly large loyalist population for support.[53]

On 20 January 1777—two days after the big shindig in the queen's honor—Howe filled in the details of his latest strategic plan in another letter to Germain. Specifically, Howe proposed a dual assault on Philadelphia, with the main British army advancing overland through New Jersey, and a smaller amphibious force landing somewhere along the lower Delaware River. To carry out such an offensive toward the American capital, Howe wanted 15,000 to 20,000 reinforcements, but that was the rub. Germain stated that the British government could spare only 7,800 men for him, which by his reckoning would give Howe about the 35,000 total troops he said he needed. Indeed, in the end Germain scrounged up a scant 2,900 men, which hardly raised Howe's strength at all. Howe disputed Germain's arithmetic, and he argued that the American secretary was not providing him with nearly enough men for the kind of operations he had in mind. Mulling this over, in April Howe decided to scrap the overland attack on Philadelphia and instead use British naval superiority to move his army to the American capital by sea, even though this would cost him the opportunity to crush Washington's army between two British millstones. Howe believed that an amphibious assault would save time and avoid the dangers of crossing New Jersey on muddy roads with Washington's army hanging on his flank and rear from the nearby mountains, ready to replicate on a grander scale the miserable experiences so many British foraging parties had undergone throughout the winter. Thus, by the process of coerced elimination, Howe had his plan, but he was unhappy about the method by which he was compelled to adopt it. In fact, it increasingly seemed to him that Germain and the British Ministry were working against him, not with him. Therefore, he made sure he placed it indelibly on the record that although he was confident he could seize Philadelphia, he did not think that this would end the war, and it was Germain's fault. As Howe put it, "Restricted as I am from entering upon more extensive operations by the wont of force, my hopes of terminating the war this year are now vanished."[54]

Lord George Germain undoubtedly frowned upon reading Howe's pessimistic appraisal of the war's progress, but he was not the type to take counsel of another man's fears. Tough, efficient, headstrong, unlovable, and arrogant, Germain had attracted more than his share of controversy during his career, first as an army officer and later as a politician and policy maker. Born in 1716 into an influential family with close royal ties, he fought bravely in the Low Countries as a regimental commander during the War of Austrian Succession of 1740–48, and later on he participated in the Great War for Empire in Germany. For reasons never sufficiently explained, Germain disobeyed orders to attack the enemy at the Battle of Minden in 1759. Even then he had already made numerous powerful enemies, and they used this opportunity to successfully court-martial him for his actions; he was found guilty of disobeying orders and declared unfit for any command whatsoever in the British army. Down but not out, Germain persevered and took advantage of the public sympathy generated by his harsh sentence.

His fortunes took a turn for the better when the friendly George III ascended to the throne in 1760. Appointed American secretary in November 1775, Germain more than anyone else became the chief architect of the British war effort. As such, he was determined to crush the rebellious colonies by whatever means necessary. It was Germain who organized and equipped the army that Howe used to seize New York City, and he was eager to finish a job so favorably begun.

Unlike the increasingly gloomy Howe, Germain believed that the American rebellion was all but over. He was as disappointed as any British policy maker by the defeat at Trenton and the subsequent frustrating winter in New Jersey, but he interpreted these events as the Americans' last gasp, not as a harbinger of things to come.[55] Up until then, Germain and Howe had worked together well enough, but already the relationship was beginning to fray, especially on Howe's end. For his part, Germain worked hard to get Howe the reinforcements he requested, but British resources were limited and stretched thin, and his inability to meet Howe's unrealistic demands merely fed the British commander in chief's growing skepticism about the war effort.[56] Like Howe, Germain was confident that the British army could seize Philadelphia, but the American secretary also expected this to occur quickly enough so that Howe could support another operation in the works. Major General John Burgoyne had returned to England from a stint of duty in America with a plan to lead an army south from Canada to Albany on the Hudson River, and from there to cooperate with British forces in New York City. Burgoyne and Germain believed that taking the town would neatly sever the colonies asunder and isolate troublesome New England from its neighbors. Germain expected Howe to wrap up his mission in Pennsylvania with enough time to redeploy his army on the lower Hudson River so he could join Burgoyne upriver and take command of their combined forces. With the colonies split in two, Germain predicted that the American rebellion would rapidly wither and die.[57]

On 5 June, Howe received from Germain official word of Burgoyne's offensive. By that time he was preparing for the invasion of Pennsylvania that Germain and the king had already approved. Neither Howe nor the king's policy makers conceived of Howe and Burgoyne cooperating at this early stage, so as far as Howe was concerned the two campaigns were not interconnected. Besides, Howe did not think any British attack up the Hudson would accomplish much anyway. For one thing, Washington would surely deploy his men in the formidable Hudson Highlands forts, and prying the Americans out of there would cost the British dearly in terms of lives and time. Worse yet, Washington might interpose his army between the advancing British force and its New York City base, cutting off its supply lines. Finally, Howe doubted that seizing Albany would end the war any more than occupying Philadelphia would.[58] At any rate, Howe did not believe that Burgoyne would need much assistance. Having successfully taken Washington's measure several times, Howe was certain that Burgoyne could beat him, too, if by chance the American commander in chief moved his army up the Hudson while Howe was en route by sea to Philadelphia. Just to be safe—in terms of protecting his reputation as well as Burgoyne's army, should either become necessary—Howe jacked up the number of men he planned to leave behind in New York City to, by his count, more than 8,000 men, and he gave garrison commander Major General Henry Clinton discretionary orders to ascend the Hudson to help Burgoyne if he thought it was necessary. Having tied up these loose ends, Howe could get back to the main event: the conquest of the American capital.[59]

Major General Henry Clinton was a quarrelsome, hypersensitive, and uninspiring man, but he had enough acumen to recognize bad strategy when he saw it. Unfortunately, he combined this strategic savvy with a tactlessness that alienated those to whom he sought to give advice. Clinton had fought capably with Howe around New York City, but before that he commanded the abortive attack on Fort Moultrie in Charleston harbor in June 1776. He returned to London in part to give his side of the unhappy Charleston story but also to seek further advancement. He angled for command of the northern army in Canada, but instead the king gave it to the more junior Burgoyne, much to Clinton's chagrin.[60] In early March 1777, he met with the king, and the two men discussed Burgoyne's upcoming campaign. Clinton did not like the look of things, and he said as much. He did not oppose an invasion from Canada per se, but he believed that Howe should support it with a thrust up the Hudson River. As Clinton saw it, the Hudson was the key to winning the war; not only would seizing it render the colonies asunder, but such an effort would undoubtedly provoke Washington into committing his elusive army to a decisive battle. Clinton thought that attacking Philadelphia was a good idea, but not until after the Hudson was in British hands and Washington's army was an unpleasant memory. The king heard Clinton out but said little in reply.[61]

Clinton continued his Cassandra role in New York City after a thoroughly unpleasant voyage across the Atlantic. In a number of meetings with Howe in July, Clinton reiterated his concerns. In particular, he argued that by taking the main British army to Philadelphia by sea, Howe would in effect temporarily remove it from the strategic chessboard, which would give Washington the opportunity to strike either Burgoyne or New York City. Moreover, although Clinton expected the British to seize Philadelphia, he did not believe that Howe could conclude his offensive in Pennsylvania in enough time to conduct any other operations this campaigning season. Instead, Clinton suggested that Howe advance up the Hudson to meet Burgoyne, but Howe demurred. He had small use for the prickly general to begin with—in fact, this was a key reason he was leaving him behind to command in New York City—and his repeated, unenthusiastic, and ultimately futile efforts to reassure Clinton of his friendship were enough to tax even the genial British commander in chief's live-and-let-live attitude. But there was more to it than that. Howe had already made his plans and gotten London's approval, and it was too late to change them now. Howe doubted that Washington intended to march to the Hudson or to New York City when the British army embarked for Philadelphia, so there was no need to give Clinton all the men he demanded, especially when they could be put to better use in Pennsylvania. Indeed, he did not consider the possibility that the Americans could raise another army to confront Burgoyne. Besides, if Clinton was right about Philadelphia, then the city would fall quickly enough, thus enabling him to send reinforcements to New York City if necessary. However, in an effort to placate Clinton and assuage his fears, Howe promised to strengthen the New York City garrison before he left, which he did, but not to Clinton's satisfaction. Clinton, in short, would have to get by with 8,300 men, with the possibility of more later. Clinton did not like the fact that Howe was using his own logic against him any more than the supplementary orders Howe dispatched to him in July. In them, Howe authorized Clinton to support Burgoyne with a diversionary attack up the Hudson if necessary. To Clinton it appeared that Howe was giving him considerable responsibility but not the means to fulfill it. In fact, it looked a lot like the British commander in chief was building a record at Clinton's expense to protect himself should anything go wrong on Burgoyne's long march from Canada to Albany. Small wonder he wrote home, "I totally disapprove of the present plan of operations."[62]

In the end, of course, Howe and Clinton would be among several British generals and policy makers who would attempt to use the record to distance themselves from the disastrous events that occurred on their collective watch that year, mostly by means of shifting the blame to the handiest available target. Truth be told, however, there was plenty of fault to go around, and Howe deserved his fair share of it. In formulating his army's plans for 1777, the British commander in chief exhibited considerable unwarranted overconfidence in himself and the British military as a whole. Although to many observers it was only common sense for Burgoyne and Howe to cooperate in a joint operation down and up the Hudson River, Howe did not see it that way. Howe expected Washington to follow him to Pennsylvania, in which case Burgoyne would face minimal opposition in his march down the Hudson. Howe never guessed that the Americans would organize and deploy an entirely new army to confront an invasion from Canada. Besides, as far as Howe was concerned, defeating the rebel armies in battle was not a problem, assuming they were willing to fight out in the open. After all, he had beaten Washington innumerable times, and he believed that any British general worth his salt could follow his example. Even after Washington demonstrated surprising resilience and durability that winter and spring in the face of all of Howe's machinations, the British commander in chief unbent only enough to reinforce Clinton in New York City and give him the option to go upriver to help Burgoyne if he thought it was necessary.

Overconfidence is almost always a cardinal military sin, but, ironically enough, Howe juxtaposed his with a deep-seated insecurity about the war's final outcome. He was certain he could carry out his part of the British grand strategy and take Philadelphia, but he did not think it would bring the war to a close, and he was right. So even after he fulfilled his mission, his accomplishment paled in comparison to the catastrophe Burgoyne suffered at Saratoga. Howe contended that the shortest route to winning the war lay in destroying Washington's army, but he also admitted that this was unlikely to occur because the Americans were too agile. To be sure, at times Howe implied that he intended to use Philadelphia as an anvil upon which to smash the elusive rebel army, but when push came to shove, he gave first priority to seizing the city because he saw it as an attainable objective. To Howe, occupying territory was a key component in waging war, but he never specified—indeed, in all likelihood he probably did not know himself—the tangible gains the British would accrue from doing so as long as American armies remained in the field. Howe's strategic crime in 1777 was that he took the main British army off on a wild goose chase, and the benefits the British acquired along the way were either incidental or dearly bought.

THE NEW JERSEY INCURSIONS

From a strategic point of view, Howe's army had not accomplished much by way of winning the war since Washington chased it out of most of New Jersey in December and January. As spring came on, little changed; the British remained immobile in their winter quarters while Washington gradually rebuilt his forces without enemy interference and tormented redcoat foraging parties. Howe had reasons for his quiescence. He did not believe that his army could take the field until it received new equipment to replace that worn out and lost by the rigors of the previous year's campaigning, and such vital military paraphernalia was slow in arriving.[63] In late May, however, supply ships began docking at New York City harbor with the accoutrements Howe's army needed—tents, kettles, uniforms, boots, muskets, and dozens of other miscellaneous and mundane things that were part and parcel of eighteenth-century warfare—and soon the British started to stir. Men and matériel in increasing numbers headed up the Raritan on large flatboats or in wagons along roads swept clear of rebel snipers. The British army at Brunswick swelled in number, and it became obvious to everyone that something big was up. To round out these large-scale preparations, on 11 June Howe and his staff arrived from Amboy to complete the assemblage of nearly 15,000 British and German soldiers in east central New Jersey.

Howe was finally prepared to resume the offensive, but not toward Philadelphia—not yet, anyway. Instead, he intended to make an effort to destroy Washington's army before he undertook his long and complicated amphibious campaign toward the American capital. If he could eliminate the American army here and now, it would make subsequent operations all that much simpler, and perhaps unnecessary. Unfortunately, this was more easily said than done. The Americans were holed up in the well-fortified hills around Boundbrook, and attacking them there would be little short of suicide, even for the sturdy redcoats. Howe knew this as well as anyone, but he had developed a scheme to circumvent the formidable American defenses there that was as simple as it was clever. Howe planned to bluff a march to Philadelphia in the expectation that Washington would come down from the hills to block him and protect the American capital. Then, somewhere on the level ground toward Princeton, Howe hoped to engage the Americans out in the open in a battle in which he and his veteran soldiers could scarcely lose.[64]

To that end, in the late evening of 13 June, an 11,000-man-strong British force moved out from Brunswick in two approximately equal divisions, one under the energetic and aggressive Major General Charles Cornwallis and the other led by the aged Lieutenant General Heister, who had not yet been recalled. Howe accompanied Heister, probably to keep an eye on him, as the Germans and redcoats plodded toward the New Jersey hills. Whatever his doubts about Heister, Howe knew he could count on Cornwallis. Born into a distinguished English family and educated at Eton and an Italian military school, Cornwallis had fought in Germany during the Great War for Empire. Like Howe, he sympathized with the colonial cause, but he also emulated his boss by obeying the king's orders to go to America and crush the rebellion. He conducted himself well in the fighting around New York City, but his contempt for the rebels in general and Washington in particular played a big role in the British setback at Princeton. Even so, Cornwallis was a fine tactician and a brave if headstrong soldier well suited to serve as Howe's right-hand man.

As it was, Howe quickly encountered problems beyond one enfeebled high-ranking German officer. Marching at night was a difficult proposition under the best of circumstances even for experienced soldiers, so it was little wonder that misunderstood orders, broken-down wagons that blocked the roads, and narrow passes plagued the British and Germans from the start. On top of it all, the rebels brought Cornwallis's force to a complete halt by inconveniently destroying the bridge over the Millstone River near Hillsborough. Next morning light infantry had to engage some 200 pesky American riflemen for more than an hour until engineers repaired the bridge. Once across, British troops outflanked the rebels and chased them off. At about the same time, Heister and Howe occupied nearby Middlebush without a fight. Despite these delays and frustrations, all was going according to plan, so Howe ordered Cornwallis and Heister to stop and dig in on a line extending from Somerset Courthouse back to Brunswick, and he waited to see if Washington took the bait.

Washington was hardly surprised by Howe's long-expected offensive; indeed, he had received a steady stream of reports on the British buildup from a variety of deserters, informants, and spies scattered up and down the Raritan. In fact, Washington knew of Howe's arrival at Brunswick the same day the British commander in chief established his headquarters there. Tracking these movements, however, was much easier than discerning British intentions. Initially Washington took Howe's actions at face value and guessed that the British intended to cross the Delaware and seize Philadelphia. Even before the British march got under way, Washington called his generals to council to mull over their options. Everyone agreed that the American army lacked the strength to confront the British directly, so they unanimously recommended that for now Washington sit tight at Boundbrook, summon reinforcements from the Hudson Highlands, and await events. Washington agreed in principle, but this did not mean that he planned to remain passive and let Howe indulge his proclivity for creating mischief. Washington had no desire to openly challenge the advancing British; instead, he planned to deploy troops from his main force at Boundbrook and elsewhere to harass the British right flank and rear while recently promoted Major General Benedict Arnold collected enough Continentals and militia at Philadelphia to establish a defense line behind the Delaware. Caught between two American armies that would neither fight him on the battlefield nor leave him alone, Washington hoped that Howe's offensive would stall and collapse. With this in mind, upon learning that the British were approaching the Millstone, Washington sent Colonel Daniel Morgan and his recently created corps of several hundred riflemen to pester them. Born in 1736, the tough, rough-hewn, and earthy Morgan had served as a teamster—hence his nickname "Old Wagoner"—and met Washington during Braddock's unsuccessful attack on Fort Duquesne. The next year he was sentenced to receive 500 lashes for punching a British officer who hit him with the flat of his sword, and in 1758 enemy fire shattered half of his teeth. Despite these unlucky incidents, he not only fought throughout most of the conflict but also saw action in Pontiac's Rebellion and Lord Dunmore's War. Once the Revolutionary War began, he marched with Arnold to Quebec and was captured during the American effort to storm the city and later exchanged. He was a born leader who handled his men with a deftness rare among American officers. Morgan and his men performed well enough in their 14 June skirmish to temporarily delay and trip up Cornwallis's column, but Washington was discouraged by the effectiveness of British artillery on such units in the open New Jersey terrain. The Americans would have to do better than that to bring Howe to bay.[65]

Washington had concentrated the bulk of his army at Boundbrook before Howe's offensive unfolded, but he left one 1,600-man division under Major General John Sullivan at Princeton to obstruct any British move in that direction. Sullivan was a courageous, tactless, hypersensitive, and vain New Hampshire lawyer-turned-soldier with plenty of combat experience. He joined Washington at Boston and later served in Canada during the retreat back to New York. Captured during the Battle of Long Island in August 1776, he was exchanged in September and brought Washington the reinforcements that made it possible for him to attack Trenton. Despite Sullivan's occasional carping and a propensity for making enemies, Washington thought enough of him to entrust him with this semi-independent command in central New Jersey.[66] Sullivan planned to delay any British thrust in his direction until Washington arrived with the main army to support him. Washington, however, eventually decided to stay put at Boundbrook, and he quickly realized that doing so left Sullivan vulnerable. To prevent the British from cutting off and destroying Sullivan's isolated division, Washington ordered the New Hampshire general to fall back to Flemingtown to collect militia, and to then deploy his force in the nearby Sourland Hills to the west of Boundbrook to annoy any British advance to the Delaware from that direction. Washington's confidence was not misplaced, and by 17 June Sullivan was right where Washington wanted him, providing the commander in chief with another arrow in his quiver to use against Howe should he continue his offensive.[67]

By then, however, Washington had reassessed the situation accurately enough to suspect that Philadelphia was not Howe's goal after all. For one thing, Howe's inactivity after crossing the Millstone indicated that he was in no particular hurry to get to the Delaware or anywhere else. Indeed, the British seemed more intent on receiving than delivering any sort of attack. In addition, Washington's intelligence informed him that the British had left their tents, boats, and much of their baggage behind at Brunswick, so they could not sustain a prolonged campaign toward Philadelphia. The more Washington analyzed the situation, the more convinced he became that his army, not the American capital, was Howe's primary target. It all made sense now, as he explained in a letter to Arnold: "While we have a respectable force in the field, every acquisition of territory they may make will be precarious and perhaps burdensome. . . . I am clearly of [the] opinion, that they will not move towards Philadelphia without first endeavoring to disable us and prevent our following them."[68] The scales had at last fallen from his eyes, but Washington saw no reason to alter his troops' dispositions. If Howe wanted to destroy the American army, he would have to come to it, not vice versa. By now the Americans had had plenty of time to fortify the hills around Boundbrook, so Washington was certain that his army could repel any British assault. For added insurance, however, he ordered Sullivan to send one of his brigades to Steel's Gap, two miles from Boundbrook, to guard his right flank. Washington's confidence was further buoyed by large numbers of militia streaming in from New Jersey and Pennsylvania to supplement his Continentals. In short, all seemed to be going well, but then on 19 June Washington got word that the British were gone.[69]

Howe was disappointed that Washington refused to cooperate with his well-laid plans. The previous year the American commander in chief had repeatedly fallen for Howe's various ruses and stratagems, but in the interim Washington seemed to have developed and matured as a general, and his actions in the New Jersey mountains merely confirmed Howe's belief that destroying the rebel army was next to impossible. As Howe saw things now, he really had no good choice but to retreat. A direct frontal assault on the Boundbrook fortifications was out of the question, and efforts to maneuver the Americans out of them would be costly in terms of time, and anyway he lacked the manpower to protect his supply and communications lines back to Brunswick should he venture any further into the rebel-infested New Jersey countryside. Besides, he had already burned away a part of the campaigning season on this profitless foray. The best thing to do now was to get back to the coast and resume his original plan for an amphibious assault on Philadelphia, which he saw as his objective anyhow.[70] In short, the writing was on the wall, and on 19 June, five days after they set out to destroy Washington's army, the British marched back to Brunswick with Heister in the lead and Cornwallis bringing up the rear. So sudden was their departure that the British encountered almost no American resistance, and they were back where they started by the end of the day.

The British stay at Brunswick was brief, just long enough to complete the destruction of the fortifications they had erected there over the course of the last several months—as well as a good number of the dwellings, as things turned out—and send as much of their baggage as possible down the Raritan to Amboy. Now that Howe planned to go to Philadelphia by sea, there was no need to hold the town, so the British evacuated it on the early morning of 22 June and headed for Amboy along the coast. On a small hill overlooking the narrow bridge across the Raritan, Howe and his staff reined in their horses to watch Cornwallis's troops cross the river in retreat. If these circumstances perturbed the British commander in chief, he did not say so, even when the Americans suddenly appeared on a height on the other side of the river with several cannons and commenced lobbing shells at the backpedaling British column.[71] The rebel artillery was too far away to do much damage, but the whole episode certainly underscored British frustration over the past few days. Unfortunately, this march was not nearly as quiet as the one to Brunswick had been three days earlier, and blood began to flow more freely as the British continued their march and American riflemen emerged to engage them. The terrain between Brunswick and Amboy was full of woods tailor-made for the type of warfare at which the Americans had proved so adept throughout the past winter. At one point a British regiment shattered an American line and pursued the rebels into the woods only to run headlong into enemy cannons hidden among the trees that they then had to overcome. Later Howe himself led two regiments into battle to shore up the faltering British rear guard and drive the Americans back. The Germans burned all the houses along the road, contributing to the smoke that obscured Revolutionary War battlefields. The British forces reached Amboy late that afternoon, tired and soon to be soaking wet from an all-night downpour. Howe later claimed that the British suffered only a handful of casualties that day, but other British and German observers put their losses in the dozens.[72]

Washington was surprised by Howe's abrupt retreat—so much so, in fact, that the Americans were unable to do much more than observe from a distance the British columns marching back down the road to Brunswick. Washington was not sure why the British suddenly suspended their operations, but he gave a lot of the credit to the good militia turnout that highlighted the local population's hostility to the king's rule. He also considered the possibility that the whole expedition was just an elaborate hoax to cover a British assault up the Hudson River, but he remained convinced that his army or Philadelphia had been Howe's original goal all along. No sooner had the British army arrived in Brunswick than American intelligence informed Washington that their stay would be temporary, and this time he did not intend to let them get away scot-free. Indeed, Washington believed he had a golden opportunity to inflict substantial damage on Howe's strung-out columns slogging along the road between Brunswick and Amboy. To do so, he dispatched three brigades and Morgan's riflemen under Major General Nathanael Greene to strike the British rear guard, and he planned to follow up with the rest of the army to exploit any opportunities Greene developed. Greene was a shrewd, insightful, thoughtful, and methodical Rhode Islander with a game knee who had been with Washington since the Boston siege. He missed the Battle of Long Island due to illness, but he returned in enough time to foolishly advise Washington to try to hold on to untenable Fort Washington, whose eventual fall in November 1776 cost the Americans 2,800 casualties. Despite Greene's uneven performance, Washington continued to value his talents, and more than any other general he served as Washington's right-hand man.[73] On 22 June, however, Greene failed to justify the confidence Washington placed in him. The British had already sent most of their baggage downriver to Amboy, so they were able to move fast. By the time Greene got his lead brigade into Brunswick, the British rear guard was completing its crossing of the Raritan, and all the Americans could do was chuck some shells at them from long range. Greene's subsequent pursuit was timid and hesitant, in part because he did not want to stray too far from the rest of Washington's army, but also because of a lack of coordination among his brigades. Only Morgan's riflemen came to grips with the retreating British, and they did not possess the manpower to make it count. To top off this frustrating day, heavy rains beginning that evening prevented Washington from immediately moving the rest of his army forward to support Greene. Instead of the clenched-fist assault on the British rear guard Washington envisioned, the Americans were able to do little more than give them a brisk and ineffectual nudge. All Washington could do now was move his army to the hilly Quibbletown area and keep his eyes peeled for any more openings to punish the British.[74]

On the morning of 24 June, two days after the redcoats and Germans reached Amboy, a rebel dragoon deserted to the British with important information. He claimed that Washington had descended from the Boundbrook hills with his army and deployed it in the region around Quibbletown. Howe confirmed the report the next day. It seemed that the British retreat had provoked the very response Howe had aimed for when he led his army from Brunswick nine days earlier. The Americans were finally out in the open away from their fortifications, presenting the British commander in chief with another chance to run them in the ground, assuming he was willing to exert the effort it would require to do so. He was, even though he had already embarked one German brigade for Staten Island and was preparing to follow with the rest of his army. Orders could be changed, however, and Howe landed the Germans back at Amboy and readied the rest of his army for another go at Washington here in New Jersey. Specifically, Howe planned to strike toward Westfield to turn the American army's right flank and cut it off from its mountain stronghold as a prelude to its annihilation.[75]

On 26 June, the British marched from Amboy in two columns, one under Major General John Vaughan—Heister's recall had come through three days earlier, and he was preparing to go home—and the other under Cornwallis. Cornwallis's men marched along the coast through Woodbridge before swinging inland, while Vaughan's troops took a parallel course via Metuchen before closing up with Cornwallis later that day. Slogging in the late June heat was bad enough, but the locals had choked the wells, depriving the redcoats and Germans of water. Perhaps by way of retaliation, the troops plundered and burned many of the deserted houses along the way.[76] To add to their miseries, scattered parties of rebels sniped at them from behind rocks and trees. This was annoying, but not a serious impediment to either British column. Near Westfield, however, Cornwallis encountered stiffening resistance. There Brigadier General William Maxwell's brigade positioned itself with artillery on some small hills flanked by ravines and woods in an effort to protect Washington's left flank and cover the withdrawal of some seventy wagons. A determined German bayonet attack scattered the rebels and captured three cannons in the process, but most of the Americans, and all their wagons, got away.[77]

Howe could relish this victory as well as the next man, but it was obvious that he had lost the element of surprise. Indeed, Washington had taken alarm and was already falling back rapidly toward the hills, prepared to assume his customary hedgehog position. Defeating Washington obviously would not be as easy as it was the previous summer, and in fact this army seemed to be much more formidable than the one he so easily and repeatedly routed out of New York.[78] Having lost his latest chance to destroy the rebels, Howe decided to again return to Amboy and resume his preparations for his amphibious assault on Philadelphia. The British retreated on 27 June, unhindered by the Americans, and they reached Amboy the next day and immediately began embarking for Staten Island. Washington sent a brigade and Morgan's ubiquitous riflemen to keep an eye on them, but on the whole he did not interfere. On the afternoon of 30 June, the remaining British soldiers evacuated Amboy, thus abandoning the king's last foothold in New Jersey.

Howe's two New Jersey incursions resulted in no great battles, but they were important nonetheless. For one thing, they gave Washington an opportunity to test his new strategy, and on the whole it had served him and his cause well. Washington used the local geography to stop the British offensive without resorting to a battle out in the open with the British army that he could not have won. By doing so, he both preserved his all-important army and denied the British access to New Jersey and its population. In addition, the militia turned out with alacrity, even though it did not see much combat—this time. Washington saw some kinks that he needed to work out, such as instilling in his officers more aggressive instincts to take advantage of opportunities presented by British retreats like the one to Amboy. Also, Washington's various harassing parties lacked the firepower—specifically, cannons—to inflict serious losses on the British. For Howe, on the other hand, his two-week adventure had been a trying experience. For all his operational and tactical skills, he was unable to figure out a way to engage Washington in battle out in the open without exposing his supply and communications lines to various rebel bands intent on severing them. It seemed that Washington was maneuvering Howe into a new kind of warfare inconsistent with his training in traditional eighteenth-century tactics and strategy. His frustrations would only increase as time went on.

A BRITISH VANISHING ACT

British naval supremacy gave Howe a tremendous advantage over the Americans in terms of mobility. The Royal Navy enabled the British commander in chief to transport and disembark his troops anywhere up and down the long American coastline where water met land, leaving the rebel armies to catch up along rudimentary rutted roads choked with dust much of the year and full of mud the rest. Like most British generals, Howe was well aware of the benefits the Royal Navy provided, all the more so because his brother, the highly esteemed Vice Admiral Lord Richard Howe, commanded the British fleet in North America. General Howe had availed himself of this advantage the previous year in his assault on New York, with impressive results. He was prepared to do so again this year, and in early July, right after his unhappy adventure into New Jersey in pursuit of Washington, the British army began embarking from Staten Island for its amphibious assault on Philadelphia. Daily long lines of redcoats, provincials, and Germans trudged down to the beaches on the eastern part of the island to load first their baggage and then themselves on board transport vessels bobbing in the harbor. The British had plenty of experience with amphibious operations, but they were still among the most complicated of military undertakings. Stashing thousands of soldiers and their horses, wagons, cannons, supplies, and baggage onto small wooden vessels with enough food and water to sustain them on a voyage that might well last weeks was an extremely difficult task, so mishaps were inevitable. For example, some of the German units boarded their stinking, hot, and crowded transports in early July, more than two weeks before the expedition even left New York harbor, so they were sick, weak, and short of fresh provisions before the fleet even got under way.[79]

Despite these and other problems, by mid-July the fleet was ready to set sail, but it did not, and as the days passed, many redcoats and Germans increasingly questioned the holdup. The fact that no one but a select few knew their ultimate destination did not make the seemingly interminable lull any easier. The reasons for the continuing delay, however, were myriad. First of all, Howe wanted to wait until Clinton arrived from England to assume command of the New York City garrison. Clinton showed up on 5 July, and his persistent criticism of Howe's plans undoubtedly gave the British commander in chief reason to regret postponing his departure. Second, and perhaps as a consequence of Clinton's harping doubts, Howe hoped to get some word on Burgoyne's progress from Canada before he irretrievably moved his army away from the Hudson River and any possibility of helping his fellow general up north. On 17 July, however, Howe learned that Burgoyne had seized supposedly invulnerable Fort Ticonderoga in upstate New York with minimal losses. To Howe this confirmed his earlier assertions that Burgoyne would encounter no serious problems in his drive to Albany, certainly none that would require his army's assistance. After all, Ticonderoga was considered one of the strongest posts in America, and now that it had fallen, the rest of the campaign to Albany should be downhill. Besides, he had already given the disgruntled Clinton discretionary orders to go upriver to help Burgoyne should that become necessary. The last impediment to the British army's departure had little to do with Howe. Contrary winds kept the fleet trapped in the harbor until 21 July, when it at last weighed anchor and dropped down off Sandy Hook. Two days later the cream of the British army and its accompanying fleet, approximately 16,000 soldiers and 267 vessels, disappeared over the eastern horizon for parts and adventures as yet unknown.[80]

Howe's destination was a matter of considerable speculation not only among many of his officers and men not in the know but also for innumerable Americans in and out of the military and Congress. The fact that there was precious little hard information on Howe's whereabouts or destination to go by did not prevent Americans from engaging in endless hours of guesswork based on rumor, hearsay, and conjecture. There was certainly no shortage of potential objectives, or of reasons for targeting them. Some contended that Boston was Howe's goal because there was no other purpose for the large British garrison at Newport, Rhode Island, than to cooperate with an offensive into New England. Others, however, believed that the British were heading up the Hudson to assist Burgoyne. Such an attack would divide the states in twain and enable the British to tap in to New York's large loyalist population. Still others argued for Philadelphia and the Chesapeake region. After all, Philadelphia was the seat of Congress and an important supply depot, and it had plenty of loyalists, too, who would probably help the British. Moreover, seizing the American capital would raise British morale and demonstrate that the war was progressing toward victory. The hard truth, of course, was that no one knew for sure what the British were up to, and all most people could do was wait for the blow to fall and respond accordingly.[81]

Happily for the Americans and their cause, Washington had intelligence resources at his disposal that theoretically enabled him to do more than make educated guesses about Howe's intentions. Unfortunately, Washington's wide-ranging intelligence network did not always make his job easier. Scouts, spies, and deserters brought in information that frequently did more to muddy than clarify issues for the harried American commander in chief, forcing him to sift through and interpret innumerable often contradictory reports to separate the reliable from the unreliable. As the British fell back to Amboy in late June, Washington figured that Howe would follow the dictates of common sense and strike up the Hudson River to cooperate with Burgoyne's army marching down from Canada. He was not sure, though, and for all he knew Howe might lunge at Philadelphia, so he moved most of his army back to Morristown to be able to respond quickly to a British attack in either direction. He was well aware of British naval preparations, but he did not know their purpose. Various intelligence sources—specifically, accounts relayed secondhand to Washington from a British deserter, a loyalist-turned-patriot, and a keen-eyed observer, all of whom were recently on Staten Island and noticed that the British were fitting sheepskin-coated stalls on board their transports to prevent the horses from chafing—indicated that the British were getting ready for a trip of considerable duration. Despite this rather solid intelligence that Howe was aiming for far-off Philadelphia or New England, Washington continued to believe that the British were Hudson River–bound, especially after he received word that Burgoyne had seized Fort Ticonderoga, so on 15 July he marched most of his army to the Clove, dispatched Sullivan's and Major General William Alexander, Lord Stirling's, divisions across the Hudson, and awaited events. Even so, British maneuvers were all very confusing, and Washington wrote, "We have such contradictory accounts from different quarters, that I find it impossible to form any satisfactory judgment of the real motions and intentions of the enemy."[82] Unfortunately for him, things were about to get worse.[83]

Washington received word of the British fleet's departure from Sandy Hook the day after Howe got under way. This seemed pretty solid evidence that the British were indeed heading for Philadelphia, so he quickly recalled Stirling and Sullivan from beyond the Hudson and prepared to move his army to the Delaware River as soon as possible. At about this time, Americans captured a loyalist carrying a message from Howe to Burgoyne stating that Howe intended to make a diversion toward Connecticut and then charge up the Hudson. Washington saw it for the disinformation it was, and as a result he looked even more intently toward the American capital. Finally, reports that identified the British fleet off of Little Egg Harbor on 28 July and the Delaware Capes three days later all but confirmed his conviction that Philadelphia was Howe's objective. By now Washington had moved most of his army toward the Delaware within easy reach of Philadelphia, but he still had a hard time believing that Howe would leave Burgoyne in the lurch like this; it simply did not make much sense as far as he was concerned.[84]

The sudden disappearance of the British fleet to the east on 1 August confirmed Washington's nagging doubts about Howe's intentions. It seemed highly likely that Howe's voyage to the Delaware Capes was an elaborate ruse designed to confuse and exhaust the Americans, just the sort of thing the clever British commander in chief was likely to attempt. In response, a frustrated Washington put his tired soldiers back on the roads to the Hudson in the intense August heat.[85] The past month had certainly underscored the benefits the British gained from their naval power. As Washington put it,

The advantages they derive from having the command of the water are immense. At the same time, that they are transporting themselves from one place to another with the utmost facility and convenience, they keep our immaginations [*sic*] constantly in the feild [*sic*] of conjecture, as to the point of attack, and our troops marching and countermarching in the disagreeable road of suspense and incertainty [*sic*]. I wish, we could but fix on their object. Their conduct is really so mysterious, that you cannot reason upon it, so as to form any certain conclusions.[86]

A week passed, however, before Washington received information upon which to come to any conclusions whatsoever. In the meantime, he decided to stay put around Corryell's Ferry along the Delaware with most of his army to spare it from further exertions. Then, on 10 August, he got the surprising word that observers had spotted the British fleet off Sinepuxent Bay near the Delaware-Maryland border, heading southward. This was perhaps the most perplexing British action yet. The only objective of value in that direction was Charleston, South Carolina, which was a major center of commerce and contained substantial military stores. If that was the case, Washington had no intention to march down there to meet the British. He doubted his soldiers could arrive in time to do much to stop Howe, and in any event the diseases endemic to the region would probably put many of his troops out of action before they ever saw a redcoat over the barrel of a musket. Instead, Washington decided to march back to the Hudson and attack Burgoyne. The same day he was developing his plans, however, he learned that the British fleet was off the Virginia Capes, preparing to enter Chesapeake Bay. At first he could not figure out Howe's rationale for this, but a quick look at the map revealed the one obvious target to which the Chesapeake provided access: Philadelphia.[87]

Despite the frustrations Washington endured throughout July as he shuttled his increasingly tired soldiers back and forth between the Hudson and Delaware Rivers as part of his continuing effort to second-guess Howe's intentions, he had good reason to look back at the past six months with satisfaction. By almost any measure the American cause was in better shape that summer than it had been at almost any other time in the war so far. This was especially true of Washington's army. The previous winter it had been on the verge of dissolution through desertion, deprivation, and disease, but now it contained approximately 10,000 Continentals, as well as any number of militia that could be called up to face Howe's assault when the time came. Not only was the army numerically stronger than it had been the previous February and March, but it was also reasonably well armed and well equipped. Such successes had many fathers. Congress authorized the army's existence, the Commissary and Quartermaster and Clothier departments supplied and equipped it—with considerable clandestine French aid—and various state governors and their legislatures cooperated with it. Then there was also the army itself—the officers who led it and the men who formed its sinew and bone—which demonstrated a remarkable ability to sustain and recover from punishment inflicted by the British and Mother Nature. In short, there was plenty of credit to go around. Even so, Washington was more than anyone else responsible for the character and makeup of the force reborn in the New Jersey hills that winter. He worked hard to mold the army into a tool that he would use to wage the war, and he made sure that it remained reconciled with the people it was supposed to protect by maintaining generally good relations with Congress, governors, and locals. The American army was not an ideal instrument, and it certainly was not equal to its British counterpart in most respects, but it was a far cry from the ragged entity that tried unsuccessfully to defend New York the previous year. Whether it could do better by Philadelphia remained to be seen.

THREE

Barbarous Business in a Barbarous Country

THE BRITISH LANDING

As they trudged back and forth along the dusty New Jersey and New York roads that long, hot summer of 1777, many of Washington's soldiers undoubtedly envied their British counterparts in Howe's fleet who spent their days lounging around on their transport decks, relying on the wind instead of their aching legs to propel them to their objective. Unfortunately for Howe's approximately 16,000 British, German, and provincial troops, the reality was something else, and they suffered in ways that American landlubbers never imagined or appreciated.[1] For most of them, the omnipresent problem was simple boredom. There was little to do on board the transports except eat, sleep, read, gamble, drink, and engage in endless and generally pointless speculation as to their destination. One British officer familiar with Scripture wrote home, "I don't know whether there be any thing new upon the face of the earth, but I am quite sure that there is nothing new upon the face of the water."[2] Worse yet, the excruciating heat made life all but unbearable for the men stuffed in small, dank, smelly, leaky, lice-ridden, and rat-infested shipholds. The blazing sun even melted the pitch off the seams, and it seemed to have a similar effect on the increasingly lethargic soldiers. As the voyage continued interminably throughout July and well into August, conditions deteriorated. Some of the smaller vessels ran short of fresh water and provisions, so their officers had to row from ship to ship to procure more supplies. This sustained the men, but not the horses. As time went on, the terrible heat and a lack of forage killed 170 of the animals, forcing the crews to throw their carcasses overboard. Those not devoured by the millions of Chesapeake Bay crabs washed up bloated on the Maryland shore. Life at sea was surely tedious, but it could also be dangerous. There were almost daily thunderstorms, with lightning sometimes so fierce that it

50

killed horses, split masts, and damaged sails. Finally, there were numerous hair-raising ship collisions and near misses. It was, in short, a miserable experience for almost everyone involved.[3] One disconcerted German soldier perhaps best summed it up:

> Anyone who has a desire to experience misery and misfortune should go aboard ship. Everyone can believe me that when I am again in Europe, should the opportunity arise for another such trip, I would certainly not go. 1) There is no bread except zwieback which is spoiled or full of worms. 2) Stinking water with all possible impurities mixed in, because on this trip, from the beginning until now, we have not had one good drop. 3) The meat is miserable and frightfully salted so that it can hardly be eaten and then one nearly dies of thirst. 4) The entire ship is full of lice, and when it storms no one can think of anything else. Anyone who has never been to sea cannot understand how miserable that can be. It is nearly impossible to take a step without risk of breaking your neck or a leg. Everything has to be securely fastened and still [or] everything breaks and busts to pieces. If there is no wind the water is generally restless, which causes the ship to sway back and forth in one place in a dreadful manner. There is seldom a day when a person is satisfied, but how can I describe all of it as it is?[4]

When the British fleet departed from New York's Lower Bay, most of the men on board guessed that they were Philadelphia-bound via the Delaware River.[5] Few people were surprised, then, when on 30 July Admiral Howe's vast collection of vessels reached Cape Henlopen at the Delaware Bay's entrance. From there they proceeded up to Cape James to meet Captain Andrew Hamond and his frigate HMS *Roebuck*. Hamond had commanded a detached squadron off the coasts of Virginia, Maryland, and Delaware for a year and a half, so he was thoroughly familiar with the waters in those parts. Hamond huddled with the Howe brothers on their flagship, the man-of-war HMS *Eagle,* and pondered their options. The navy captain stated that an amphibious landing along the Delaware River was feasible but fraught with peril. For one thing, he had just received information that Washington's army had crossed the Delaware, so it might soon be in a position to oppose any landing at Wilmington or Newcastle, the most likely spots for the British army to come ashore. He went on to add that the British could disembark south of those two towns, but the terrain in that direction was full of marshes and woods intersected with innumerable creeks ready-made for a defending army. Another problem was the Delaware River itself. It was narrow and tricky, and it possessed a fast current, hardly the place to deploy or anchor large warships, vulnerable transports, and heavily laden victualers. Finally, Hamond knew that the Americans were busy constructing a fleet of their own on the river of firecraft, floating batteries, brigs, and galleys that would be extremely dangerous in the restricted channel.[6]

Hamond's report merely confirmed some doubts Howe already had about ascending the Delaware. Even before they left New York City, Howe and his brother had noted some of the problems attacking up the Delaware presented, and they had decided it might ultimately be wiser to strike at Philadelphia from the back door, meaning from Chesapeake Bay.[7] Hamond rattled off a number of advantages sailing up the Chesapeake offered: it was much easier to navigate than the constricted Delaware, the troops could land without opposition and regain their land legs in peace, the transports and supply ships would be safe because there were no American warships in the area, and once ashore the British army would still be within easy marching distance of Philadelphia. The stouthearted Admiral Howe remained willing to give the Delaware River route a try, but he told Hamond that his brother believed that a Chesapeake Bay landing would put the British far enough west to assail Washington's valuable magazines at York and Carlisle. The biggest and most obvious drawback to a Chesapeake Bay–based assault, however, was time. It would take at least a week to sail down and around the Delmarva Peninsula, and a good part of the campaigning season was already gone. Even so, the wind seemed favorable, and Howe's quartermaster assured him that the fleet had enough forage for two more weeks, so the British commander in chief opted to head south on 31 July.[8] Unfortunately, no sooner had the British started than the wind failed them by blowing either from the wrong direction or not at all. The fleet did not arrive at the upper reaches of the Chesapeake until 22 August, nearly a month after it departed from Sandy Hook.

As subsequent events proved, Howe's decision to set sail for Chesapeake Bay was a serious blunder, even though he eventually seized Philadelphia and beat Washington's army in several battles. Not only did Howe's long amphibious operation remove the main British army from the war's strategic chessboard for more than a month during prime campaigning weather, but in so doing he divided British forces in America into three weaker parts—four, counting the Newport, Rhode

Island, garrison. Howe's journey exposed both Burgoyne's advancing army and Clinton's New York City garrison to whatever combinations the Americans could deploy against them. Howe's desire to utilize British naval supremacy was commendable, but he could have accomplished many of his goals just as well by landing along the Delaware River. Hamond pointed out the difficulties with an assault up the Delaware accurately enough, but they were not intractable. Ironically, later in the year Howe faced many of the same problems he hoped to avoid when he attempted to open the Delaware to British shipping. Finally, and perhaps most important, Howe's decision to sail to the Chesapeake was a waste of time. Washington, not Howe, was waging a war of attrition, and at this stage of the conflict time was on the Americans' side. Howe's long diversion provided the Americans with time to train and equip their army, organize their government, destroy loyalist support, lobby the French for further aid, and allow for war-weariness to take its toll on the British public.

The small collection of militiamen on the Elk River bank had never seen anything like the panorama spread out before them on the cloudy and all-but-windless morning of 25 August. There, near the ferry at Turkey Point, British troop transports disgorged thousands of British, German, and provincial troops. They landed in waves, five in all, ferried from ship to shore on fifty-man flatboats five abreast. The big British navy men-of-war drew too much water to go so far up the river, but the frigates and brigs that protected the disembarkation were still larger than anything else that had ever appeared in the area. The militiamen gawked across the river for a while and then scurried away without firing a shot. Once ashore, the redcoats pushed two and a half miles inland to make way for the next group to hit the beach. By evening almost all of Howe's army was again on dry land, including the British commander in chief himself and his brother. Both men had cause to celebrate a bloodless amphibious operation that went off almost without a hitch.[9]

Once ashore, however, the British encountered problems either unanticipated or beyond their control. It rained heavily in the days after the landing, turning the area's rudimentary roads into troughs of mud. The troops' baggage had not yet been unloaded, so thousands of soldiers spent several uncomfortable days and nights out in the open without tents, soaking wet and chilled to the bone. As it was, most of the men were still wobbly from their long sea voyage, and the horses that survived the trip were in no condition to exert themselves. On 28 August the rain stopped, the glaring sun appeared, and Howe pushed part of his army a dozen miles upriver to Head of Elk village. There was almost no opposition, but the steamy hike along miry roads with nothing to eat but apples picked from the orchards that dotted the countryside caused more than enough hardship. Fortunately, the British occupied the abandoned village without a fight and moved on to take nearby Gray's Hill. They also seized nearly twenty grain-laden ships in the river, as well as a good deal of wine, sugar, and indigo. Here Howe paused again, this time to unload the transports of their equipment, supplies, and baggage, and to scour the countryside for the provisions and especially the horses his army needed to advance on Philadelphia.[10]

So far, rebel opposition had been minimal to nonexistent, but a sense of ominousness hung in the air. The countryside was almost deserted of both people and their livestock, as if emptied by the rapture. Even so, redcoats and especially Germans engaged in marauding and plundering, upsetting British officers hoping to cultivate any loyalist feeling in the area. Howe issued strict orders against such activities, but his hungry soldiers—most of their provisions remained on board the transports until 29–30 August—slaughtered and ate whatever animals they could get hold of, regardless of ownership. Perhaps a better deterrent was an armywide rumor that outraged locals who had not joined the mass exodus northward or eastward had slit the throats of two pillaging redcoats. Small wonder that one British officer commented, "It is a barbarous business in a barbarous country."[11] There was another rumor as well, one corroborated by Howe's intelligence and by redcoats and Germans out on and beyond the front lines: Washington had interposed his army between the British and the capital in his charge, and he was looking for a fight.[12]

Howe was more than willing to oblige the American commander in chief, but first he took time out to continue his growing one-sided war with Germain. Two weeks earlier, just as the British fleet entered the Chesapeake, Howe had received a letter from the American secretary dated 18 May. In it Germain expressed both his and the king's desire for a rapid and successful conclusion to the Philadelphia operation so Howe could speedily return to New York to cooperate with Burgoyne's southward drive to Albany. If all went as planned, the war might end this year. To Howe, it was obvious that Germain did not understand the situation, and he all but said as much in a reply he penned on 30 August from Head of Elk. Howe explained that, far from the walkover Germain expected, the British would have to fight hard to overcome

Washington's army and the surprisingly hostile local population before they seized Philadelphia. Indeed, *he* needed reinforcements, and until he got them there was no way he could win the war, even though his brave officers and men would, as usual, do their very best. In short, he would not be returning to New York this year, so Burgoyne was on his own.13

Having vented his spleen, Howe got back to the job at hand. By now the British army had regained its land legs and stripped the surrounding countryside of provisions and horses, so it was rested and ready to go. On 3 September the British marched from Head of Elk in two divisions under Cornwallis and Knyphausen, leaving behind a brigade under James Grant to guard the army's communications and supply lines with the fleet. The two columns reunited at present-day Glasgow, just across the Delaware border, and veered northward. So far there had been no resistance, but as the British army trudged northward, German light infantry—the jaegers—at the head of the column received scattered fire from rebel riflemen hidden behind trees and fences. Then, at Cooch's Bridge near Iron Hill—a heavily wooded prominence that provided a good view of both Chesapeake and Delaware Bays—the Germans ran into hundreds more riflemen deployed for battle. Howe looked the situation over and ordered the British light infantry to hit both American flanks while the jaegers kept up the fight from dead ahead. Unfortunately for the British, both flanking efforts failed; one got lost, and an impenetrable swamp stymied the other. In the meantime, Howe sent two British grenadier battalions and a couple cannons forward to support the jaegers, but before they made their presence felt, the Germans charged with the bayonet and broke the American line. Fighting continued in the nearby woods for another hour or so before the riflemen fell back down the road to Christiana, firing as they went. British and German losses came to about thirty killed and wounded, while American casualties were somewhat higher.14

Howe reined in his victorious soldiers around Iron Hill, partly because of another spell of heavy rains, but also to take stock. The deeper he advanced inland, the longer and more vulnerable his supply and communications lines to the fleet back at Head of Elk became, and the more men he had to detach to protect them. If the engagement at Cooch's Bridge proved anything, it proved that the Americans were no more inclined to roll over and quit south of Philadelphia than they were up in northern New Jersey, so Howe needed every soldier he could get on the firing line. Weighing his options, he decided to cut loose from his Head of Elk base and meet the British fleet at the Delaware River.

Howe's brother assured him that the Royal Navy would be there in time, but the admiral did not realize that the heavy supply ships and uncooperative winds would delay the fleet, so it did not arrive off Newcastle until 10 September, the day before Howe and Washington met at Brandywine.[15] Howe's decision, based in part on faulty information provided by his brother, was perhaps the riskiest one he had made so far in the war. Once inland, he would be on his own, without his brother's fleet nearby to resupply or rescue the army should things go awry. On the other hand, the distances involved were not insurmountable, and Howe was confident that he and his superb army could overcome any rebel challenges. To that end, Howe shipped all his surplus baggage and his wounded back to Head of Elk, closed down his base there, ordered his troops to carry only the barest necessities, and brought Grant's brigade up to Iron Hill to join the rest of the army.

The thing to do was to keep moving so the countryside could support his advancing army, and Howe did just that. The Americans were dug in somewhere in the Wilmington area, so Howe bluffed a march to Milltown, Delaware, to keep them pinned there, and then he pushed most of his men northward to skirt Washington's right flank and get between the American commander in chief and both Philadelphia and supply depots to the west. Such a maneuver had worked wonders against Washington before, most notably on Long Island back in August 1776, and Howe hoped it would prove just as fruitful this time around. On 8 September, after an impressive display of the aurora borealis entertained the troops, the British crossed White Clay Creek and plodded through the pleasant but deserted town of Newark, Delaware. Howe was in a hurry, so he kept his soldiers on the road for sixteen hours without much by way of food or water. By the time they bedded down for the night, however, the British were squarely on Washington's right flank, and next morning they struck out to take advantage of the opportunity they had created.

Unfortunately for Howe and his tired soldiers, his army was not the only one on the go the next day. So was Washington's, and throughout the afternoon and evening, redcoats and Germans caught glimpses of American troops tramping along the Delaware roads, moving northwestward to head off the enemy. After analyzing intelligence collected from deserters, local loyalists, and scouts, Howe determined that Washington was marching toward Brandywine Creek across the Pennsylvania line, so he pointed his army in that direction. Howe divided his army in two, with Cornwallis, as usual, leading one column and Knyphausen commanding the other. Knyphausen had the slow-moving baggage train and artillery in tow, but he also possessed the advantage of a road on which to march, so he reached Kennett Square by way of New Garden at nightfall. Cornwallis's men, on the other hand, trudged cross-country via Hokessin on a parallel course about two miles to the east. Not only were they closer to the backpedaling Americans, and therefore that much more vulnerable and cautious, but many light infantrymen found themselves slogging waist-deep through swampy woods in the rain. Not surprisingly, they did not reach Kennett Square until morning. By then, Howe was sure that the American army was a mere seven miles away behind the Brandywine at Chad's Ford, inviting battle. And, for the first time this year, the British commander in chief was willing to engage Washington on ground of the American's choosing.[16]

WASHINGTON INTERCEPTS

On 24 August, the day before Howe's seasick soldiers splashed ashore at Head of Elk, Washington's army paraded through Philadelphia on its way to intercept them. The American commander in chief had been reluctant to expose his troops to the variety of temptations the capital offered—even one dominated by the supposedly staid Quakers—but he ultimately decided that a show of strength might dispel rumors that his army was a ragged mob, encourage the patriots, and dishearten the loyalists. Four of his five divisions—the remaining one, John Sullivan's, was on its way south after a marginally successful raid on Staten Island two days earlier—entered the city early in the morning, strode down Front Street along the Delaware River, turned right onto Chestnut Street and past the Commons, and then crossed the Schuylkill River at Middle Ferry before proceeding to Darby to camp for the night. The American soldiers marched in one long column to the sound of fifes and drums, twelve ranks wide, with green sprigs in their hats. To enhance the army's professional appearance, Washington ordered its baggage and women to bypass the city and meet it on the other side. It had stormed the night before, and the morning was overcast and gray, but a good crowd was there to watch the soldiers tramp by. Although most observers seemed suitably impressed despite the troops' tattered uniforms, those in the know were more circumspect. For example, John Adams wrote to his wife, "Our soldiers have not yet, quite the air of soldiers. They don't step exactly in time. They don't hold up their heads, quite erect, nor turn out their toes, so exactly as they ought. They don't all cock their hats [or] all wear them the same way."[17] That might be true, but they were the best the young country had.[18]

Washington rode at the head of his army through Philadelphia with the recently arrived and newly commissioned twenty-year-old Frenchman Major General Marie-Joseph-Paul-Yves-Roch-Gilbert du Motier Lafayette at his side. Washington was friendly enough to the young French officer, but he could be forgiven if he seemed preoccupied. The knowledge that Howe would almost certainly land soon somewhere along the northern Chesapeake was undoubtedly a relief after weeks of tension-filled uncertainty, but this was merely one problem among many on the beleaguered American commander in chief's plate. In particular, American fortunes in upstate New York in the last couple of months had gone from bad to worse. On 5 July, John Burgoyne and his approximately 8,000 redcoats, Germans, and American Indians seized Fort Ticonderoga with an ease that befitted the British general's self-assurance by placing artillery on a mountain overlooking the place, rendering it untenable. The American garrison escaped, but the fall of the supposedly impenetrable fortress opened the way for Burgoyne to invade the Hudson River valley, and it alarmed Americans who had expected Ticonderoga's defenders to hold out indefinitely. As July wore on, Washington received increasingly melancholy reports from department commander Major General Philip Schuyler about conditions there. Schuyler lacked kettles, lead, cannon cartridges, muskets, and especially men. Moreover, the egalitarian New England militiamen did not think much of the patrician Schuyler, who had an aristocratic New Yorker's disdain for anything smacking of social equality, so they deserted in droves. Ticonderoga's demise caused many people to question Schuyler's competence and even loyalty. By mid-August it seemed likely that Burgoyne would easily succeed in taking Albany and carrying out his part of Germain's disjointed strategic plan.[19]

Washington was concerned about events up north, and he sympathized with Schuyler's plight. He did his best to encourage the careworn New Yorker, writing to him, "We should never despair. Our situation before has been unpromising and has changed for the better, so, I trust, it will again. If new difficulties arise, we must only put forth new exertions and proportion our efforts to the exigency of the times."[20] In fact, Washington saw opportunity where others perceived fear and gloom. As he viewed things, Burgoyne was vulnerable, strung out as he was in the north New York woods, with a long exposed supply line back to

Canada and no Royal Navy to provide support or refuge. Burgoyne's tendency to divide his army by sending out detachments on various missions further endangered him as far as Washington was concerned. In sum, Washington believed that the Americans had a chance to inflict substantial damage on the British in this corner of the war.[21]

Sensing the opportunity was one thing, but providing Schuyler with the means with which to wreak on Burgoyne the kind of havoc Washington envisioned was something else. Schuyler was short of arms and equipment, but Washington had precious little to spare for him. Nevertheless, he did what he could to send north some gunpowder, kettles, lead, and cannons, which was better than nothing at all. As for manpower, Washington dispatched two brigades of Continentals from Peekskill to Albany to join the Ticonderoga refugees, the remaining disgruntled New England militia, and other assorted troops Schuyler was rallying there. To galvanize this disorganized conglomeration, Washington ordered hard-driving Benedict Arnold and genial Benjamin Lincoln to join Schuyler. Both men were well liked in New England, and he hoped they would go a long way to compensate for Schuyler's personality shortcomings. Finally, Congress made two important decisions against Washington's better judgment that had a profound impact on Burgoyne's campaign. First, it replaced the unpopular Schuyler with Major General Horatio Gates. Congress had asked Washington to appoint Schuyler's successor, but he demurred, arguing that the northern department was more its responsibility than his. Second, Congress ordered Washington to send Morgan's elite riflemen to Albany, where the densely wooded terrain there would enhance their effectiveness. This came hard for Washington, who had relied heavily on these soldiers during the New Jersey incursions the previous June. Man for man, Morgan's corps was just about the best in his army, and it pained him to part with it on the eve of what might be the most important campaign of the war. Nonetheless, orders were orders, and Morgan and his troops headed north about a week before the Philadelphia parade.[22]

By these actions, Washington ably served the American cause and contributed to Burgoyne's defeat at Saratoga. He could have moved his entire army to northern New York to confront the British threat there, but that would have exposed the rest of the states to Howe's troops whenever they came ashore. Instead, he provided what assistance he could and obeyed Congress's instructions with alacrity, and in the end such aid proved vital in beating Burgoyne. The supplies he dispatched helped Schuyler get his logistical house in order just before Congress relieved him of his command, and both Arnold and Lincoln played major roles in organizing and fighting the army Gates inherited. Washington saw an opportunity and helped make it a reality. In stark contrast, the overconfident Howe turned his back on Burgoyne by taking his army on its roundabout voyage to Philadelphia and leaving Clinton with his vague orders. If Howe had supported Burgoyne the way Washington supported Schuyler and Gates, 1777 would not have been so unfortunate and barren for British arms and, conversely, so profitable for the American war effort.

In late August, however, American efforts to forestall Burgoyne had just begun to bear fruit, and it would take a couple months before they ripened into the victory at Saratoga. In the meantime, Washington devoted his energies to stopping Howe's offensive. Even before the British army disembarked at Head of Elk, Congress asked New Jersey, Pennsylvania, Maryland, and Delaware to call out their militias to meet the looming threat. Adhering to his strategy that had worked so well in New Jersey, Washington hoped to use the militia to harass the advancing British army's flanks and rear while he searched for an opportunity to attack it with his Continentals. Regrettably, this did not happen, or at least not to the extent Washington hoped. The battle-tested New Jersey militia was exhausted from its recent exertions and stretched thin watching local loyalists and the British near New York City, so the state assembly kept it at home for now. Pennsylvania's militia turned out willingly enough at first, but it was short of weapons and not well situated to immediately annoy the British down in Maryland. Instead, Washington ordered much of it to join his army around Wilmington. The Delaware and Maryland militias were in the best position to harass the British. Unfortunately, the Delaware militia displayed markedly little enthusiasm for the war effort, and the state's citizenry seemed more intent on avoiding, not confronting, the advancing redcoats and Germans. Maryland's militia was more enthusiastic, but it also lacked weapons and good officers, and it was hopelessly disorganized. Washington did what he could to help them get their act together by dispatching prominent Maryland officers Brigadier General William Smallwood and Colonel Mordecai Gist southward to take charge. Despite these and other efforts, however, the militia's role in the subsequent fighting was at best marginal, and it certainly did not play the major role Washington envisioned.[23]

There was not much doubt in Washington's mind that Howe's goal was Philadelphia, but he did not know how or when the British commander in chief planned to get there. At first he believed that it would take Howe some time to rest and refit his army after its long sea voyage, and to collect the horses it needed to advance, so he was surprised when the British marched in earnest only a week after they came ashore. By now Washington had gotten most of his soldiers into position around Wilmington, but he no longer had the time necessary to fully assemble and organize the region's militia. Moreover, the redcoats and Germans were traveling light, and Washington received reports that British warships and supply vessels had left the upper Chesapeake for parts unknown. Washington speculated that perhaps Howe planned to strike across the Delmarva Peninsula to the Delaware River to meet his brother's fleet there, but he guessed that the British lacked the time for such a move. As usual, Howe appeared to be operating by a system of logic peculiarly his own.[24]

Whatever Howe's intentions, Washington planned to be ready for him, and in fact he was prepared to engage the British out in the open for the first time this year. This violated the strategy he had developed and tested over the past few months, but he believed that circumstances made such a gamble necessary. Unlike northern New Jersey, the region south of Philadelphia was level and flat—Gray's and Iron Hills were just about the only exceptions—with many roads for the British to utilize. There were no easily defended mountains in the area from which Washington could safely harass the advancing British army. Moreover, the militia's lackluster turnout deprived him of an important part of his strategic luggage, increasing the burden on his Continentals. Finally, Washington was aware that surrendering Philadelphia without a major effort to protect it could lower American morale, cast doubts in the minds of the French about the viability of the Revolution, and harm his own reputation. On the other hand, there were positive reasons for fighting the British now. His 14,000-man army was reasonably healthy, numerous, well armed, and well equipped, whereas the redcoats and Germans were still recovering from their grueling sea voyage. Also, Washington was encouraged by reports of the recent American victory at Bennington, which seemed to demonstrate that boldness and audacity could reap substantial rewards on the battlefield for a commander willing to take a chance. One victory against the isolated Howe might be all that was necessary to remove this particular British threat once and for all, and maybe even secure independence. For all these reasons, Washington decided that now was the time to stand and fight out in the open.[25]

Washington deployed his army near Newport, Delaware, behind Red Clay Creek, on 30 August. By 8 September the Americans had constructed a formidable defense system of breastworks interspaced with artillery ready to blow away any enemy soldiers foolish enough to assail them. The Christiana River covered the American left flank, and Washington sent some Pennsylvania militia up to Brandywine Creek to keep tabs on any possible enemy activity in that direction. He also ordered some Delaware and Maryland militias south to strip the countryside of forage, horses, and provisions that might otherwise fall into British hands, but their effectiveness was limited by their lack of training, equipment, and numbers. To back them up, Washington dispatched his newly formed light corps of riflemen under William Maxwell to watch and harass Howe's army. The unmarried, hard-drinking, New Jersey–born Maxwell was yet another veteran of Braddock's unhappy expedition to Fort Duquesne during the Great War for Empire, a participant in the disastrous Canadian campaign, and leader of most of the American troops engaged in the free-for-all skirmish around Woodbridge the previous February. Maxwell's new conglomeration of soldiers was in no way comparable to Morgan's recently departed riflemen, but they gave a good account of themselves at Cooch's Bridge on 3 September before retreating to the Christiana River. Here as elsewhere the slow-loading riflemen's peculiar vulnerability to the bayonet and their lack of artillery proved to be their undoing, but even in defeat they provided Washington with valuable information on the British army's whereabouts.[26]

Howe's 8 September bluff toward Milltown fooled Washington, but not for long. The American commander in chief initially put his army on alert and prepared for a seemingly imminent battle, but when no British attack materialized, Washington dispatched one of Greene's brigades forward to take a look, and it reported that the main British column had marched northward. Howe was obviously reaching into his bag of tricks for one of his patented, tried-and-true efforts to turn the American flank. Washington had been victimized by such machinations before, so he decided not to wait until Howe interposed his army between him and Philadelphia. That night, around 1:00 A.M., he pulled his army out of its Red Clay Creek defenses and marched it rapidly northwestward in the light of the waxing moon. By taking the chord to the British arc, the Americans reached the Brandywine first the next day, and that evening they pushed further upriver to Chad's Ford and began to dig in. The officers and men were in high spirits, despite the exertions and uncertainty of the last few days, and were ready to test their mettle against the British redcoats. They would soon get their chance; American cavalry, reconnoitering westward toward Kennett Square, reported back that Howe's army would soon be on its way.[27]

BATTLE OF BRANDYWINE

The past nine months had been frustrating ones for William Howe, bereft as they were of the kind of praiseworthy victories he attained around New York City in the late summer and early fall of 1776. Since then Washington had outsmarted and outmaneuvered him at almost every turn. This was exasperating enough, but summer brought the interminable sea voyage to the Chesapeake that swallowed up more time than anyone anticipated. Finally, Howe had to devote his energies to his increasingly maddening strategic debate with Germain, who was unwilling to either accept the realities of the rebellion or provide him with the necessary resources with which to crush it. All this was enough to drive even an amiable man like the British commander in chief to distraction. Now, however, after months of preparation, Howe had at last maneuvered his American bête noire into position for the climactic battle he always wanted but never expected to get. Howe doubted that he could end the war in one stroke, but he might be able to demolish the American army and take Philadelphia, both of which would make squashing the rebellion easier when and if Germain finally came around to his way of thinking and gave him the troops he needed.

Now that Washington had at long last accepted the British challenge, Howe planned his destruction carefully. Up in northern New Jersey, Washington had almost always posted his army in all but impenetrable mountain strongholds, and assaulting him there would have been suicidal even for the highly skilled redcoats. Southeastern Pennsylvania and the adjacent Delaware River valley possessed no such advantageous terrain, so although the American commander in chief had deployed his army skillfully behind Brandywine Creek at Chad's Ford, his position was not invulnerable. After sifting through various intelligence reports gathered throughout 10 September, Howe decided to replicate on a smaller scale his actions from a few days earlier. Basically, he proposed to fix Washington's army at Chad's Ford with a little less than half of his approximately 14,000-man force under Knyphausen, and use the balance led by Cornwallis and himself to strike the American right flank. If successful, Howe's flanking attack would roll up and crumble the American line and open the way for Knyphausen to administer a coup de grâce from straight ahead that would obliterate Washington's army. Howe would be dividing his army in the face of the enemy, but he was willing to run that risk. For all of Washington's strategic and operational wiliness, the American commander in chief had never exhibited much finesse on the battlefield. Indeed, his victories at Trenton and Princeton were due more to surprise and numerical superiority than to any particular tactical skill. On the other hand, Howe manipulated his regiments and brigades with an orchestra conductor's deftness and precision, and the British army was undefeated when he led them into battle. Howe intended to fully exploit this golden opportunity Washington presented him.

Howe's plan was relatively simple, but it would require considerable time to implement, so the British army rose well before dawn on 11 September. Howe and Cornwallis departed at daybreak with more than half the army on their roundabout march to Washington's right flank, leaving Knyphausen and approximately 6,400 troops behind. Knyphausen's mission, easy to explain but hard to carry out, was to bull his way down the road to Chad's Ford to get into position to storm across the Brandywine when the American line buckled under the pressure Howe and Cornwallis exerted to the north. There was a chance that Washington might attack Knyphausen's isolated force, but Howe was not inclined to worry much about that. He had developed considerable confidence in his German subordinate, and he left him with most of the army's artillery, which gave Knyphausen firepower out of proportion to his numbers. Knyphausen was a sixty-year-old professional soldier who had fought with Frederick the Great in Europe. He was certainly dependable enough, but he struck many observers as gloomy, unsmiling, and morose, perhaps because he was campaigning in a strange land at an age when many of his old comrades back home were swapping war stories and contemplating or enjoying comfortable retirement.

Be that as it may, Knyphausen had his orders, and at 6:00 A.M., after Howe and Cornwallis cleared out, he jumped off from Kennett Square eastward, with the elite provincial Queen's Rangers and Major Patrick Ferguson's breech-loading riflemen in the lead. It was slow going, in large part because the Americans had placed fallen trees across the road. Then, just beyond Welch's Tavern, less than two miles and two hours from their starting point, the British encountered their first opposition of the day. It was Maxwell and his riflemen again, sent for-

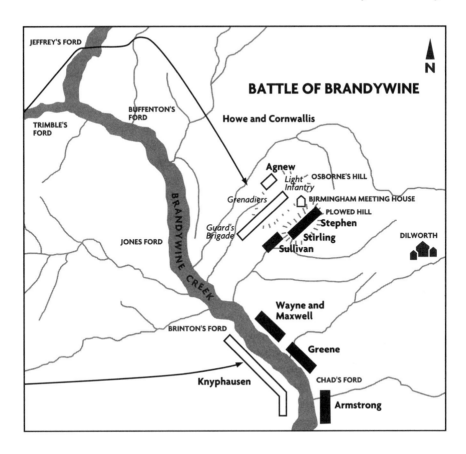

ward by Washington to annoy and slow the British advance. They deployed in marshy woods on both sides of the road to Chad's Ford and prepared to inflict at least as much damage on the enemy as they had eight days earlier at Cooch's Bridge. They opened fire on the British vanguard after luring it forward with a bogus offer to surrender. The sudden ambush rocked Ferguson's riflemen and the Queen's Rangers back on their heels, but they regrouped and, with the help of reinforcements Knyphausen rushed forward, resumed their advance. The American riflemen fired and fell back, contesting every hillock and fence down the road with increasing determination as Maxwell fed more men into the running battle. The Queen's Rangers suffered especially heavy losses as its members advanced along the exposed highway. Even so, the British made progress, and within a couple hours they finally approached the Brandywine.[28]

Unfortunately for Knyphausen and his soldiers, American resistance stiffened considerably along the Brandywine. The road to Chad's Ford wound a half mile through a swamp, with woods and tree-covered hills on each side offering a decent view of the surrounding area. Maxwell's men retreated in good order, and now he placed his 800 troops in the morass and on the nearby high ground. Two rebel batteries across the creek, one above the other, kicked into action to support them. The rest of Washington's men, dug in on the other side of the Brandywine, watched with interest as Maxwell prepared to engage a good chunk of the British army. Eschewing all tactical subtlety, Knyphausen directed the Queen's Rangers to deploy for a timesaving charge straight into the swamp. As the provincials went in with the bayonet, Ferguson worked his way around the rebel right flank. Together they flung the Americans loose and opened the way for the rest of Knyphausen's soldiers to follow down the road. The Americans, however, remained holed up in the hills on the west side of the creek, so the German general turned his attention to them. Knyphausen ordered his artillery unlimbered and into action, partly to support his advancing infantry but also to suppress heavy fire from those two American batteries. Rooting Maxwell's men out of the hills was a difficult task that caused a good many wounds, but in the end British and German professionalism carried the day. Shortly before 10:30 A.M. two British regiments broke through to Chad's Ford, driving the last rebels east across the creek. Knyphausen, having successfully carried out the first part of his mission, readied his soldiers to storm across the Brandywine when Howe and Cornwallis launched their flanking assault. For now, however, the German general was content to chuck shells at the Americans by way of letting his fellow generals up north—wherever they were—know that he was in position and ready to go.[29]

Several miles to the north, Howe, Cornwallis, and their approximately 7,500 soldiers heard the persistent boom of cannons, part of Knyphausen's running fight with Maxwell, as they trudged toward Washington's hopefully exposed flank. The rising sun had burned away the morning fog, bringing sweltering heat that did nothing to ease the difficulties of the long march. Even so, Howe's men inexorably wound their way cross-country through the woods, hills, and defiles. Fortunately, the British had the assistance of a local loyalist with intimate knowledge of the region who kept them on track. Two miles out the British vanguard encountered the first of several roving rebel patrols, but none of them were inclined to put up much opposition, despite terrain tailor-made for ambush. At 11:00 A.M., the long British column crossed the Brandywine's south branch at Trimble's Ford, and three hours and two miles later—after a rest to bring up the slow-moving cannons—the redcoats splashed into the Brandywine's upper branch at Jeffrey's Ford. The water was cold and three and a half feet deep, but once on the other side, they were not far from Washington's right flank.[30]

Quakers made up a good percentage of southeastern Pennsylvania's population, and their pacifism aroused the suspicion of both sides. For the Quakers at the Birmingham Meeting House, however, the war was about to become an intensely personal affair. The rumor mill among some of the churchwomen had it that the advancing British were killing everyone they met. As the men reassured them, thousands of redcoats and Germans suddenly emerged from the woods into the surrounding fields at the end of their seventeen-mile hike. They flooded up over steep, barren Osborne Hill, where they stopped in lines by brigades to rest and give stragglers time to come up. The redcoats discarded their surplus baggage into large piles preparatory for the bloody and gruesome work to come, and they tried to keep the innumerable rabble that accompanied eighteenth-century armies from plundering them.[31]

While the rest of the army took its ease, Captain Johann Ewald rode ahead to reconnoiter. The German officer commanded the British vanguard that day, and he was determined to refute or confirm his savvy guide's contention that the Americans had retreated from the area, and that the rebel troops on a hill behind the small village ahead constituted their rear guard. Advancing into the hamlet, Ewald's men ran into heavy fire from Americans hidden in the houses and gardens. This was more resistance than Ewald expected, so he fell back, re-formed his troops behind a nearby wall and fence, and moved forward again. This time their route took them up a hill to the right, and there they saw spread out before them 300 to 400 yards away long rows of American soldiers deploying for battle two lines deep on high ground opposite the village. The Americans waved their hats at them but did not fire, so Ewald took advantage of their generosity to scuttle down the hill and report his findings to Cornwallis.[32]

Howe probably was not surprised by information that the Americans were preparing a line of battle across the swale, news he confirmed by riding forward beyond the Birmingham Meeting House for a look of his own. After all, throughout the day his troops had seen and exchanged fire with various rebel patrols, who had surely reported their findings to Washington. The American position seemed strong enough, with artillery well placed and both flanks anchored on woods. Moreover, Howe saw reinforcements streaming forward to thicken the still-forming lines. Even so, the British commander in chief was in no hurry to roust his tired men and attack. The important thing was that Washington's army—or anyhow a good and growing piece of it—was here out in the open, and Howe was confident that his well-disciplined soldiers would win any battle under such conditions if he took the time to prepare properly. He let his men rest for about an hour and then had Cornwallis move them forward down the hill in three columns. Once there, Cornwallis and Howe—the former tall and erect on his steed and resplendent in his scarlet uniform and gold lace, the latter less impressive on a large, emaciated horse and with a sunken look about the face— carefully deployed their men in two lines within sight of the Americans across the way. They placed Brigadier General Edward Matthew's Guards brigade to the right, closest to the Brandywine, the British and German grenadiers in the center, and the light infantry on the left to the north. They kept a brigade back in reserve to watch the army's baggage, and another under Brigadier General James Agnew to support the light infantry on the left. Straight up at 4:00 P.M., Howe ordered his soldiers forward to attack.[33]

For George Washington, 11 September had been an aggravating day. On the surface, his task seemed much easier than Howe's, consisting as it did of merely preparing and waiting for the blow to fall, but the price of such passivity was a sense of frustration and uncertainty that was hard for the American commander in chief to bear. Washington had deployed his forces carefully behind the Brandywine, even though his army had reached the area only the day before. He stationed Greene's and Brigadier General Anthony Wayne's divisions at Chad's Ford, the spirited Major General John Armstrong's Pennsylvania militia downstream where they were least likely to get into trouble, and Sullivan's division on the far right of the American line. Behind Chad's Ford, in reserve, Washington positioned Stirling's and Major General Adam Stephen's divisions, as well as respected Brigadier General Francis Nash's small, recently arrived, and unattached North Carolina brigade. All things considered, Washington had chosen well, but clearly his line was most vulnerable on the right to one of Howe's patented flanking maneuvers, where any number of fords were available for British use. However, Sullivan not only had deployed most of his division at Brinton's Ford but also had sent a battalion to Jones' Ford, a mile and a half upstream, and another a mile farther to Buffenton's Ford to keep a close watch. Finally, Washington ordered his few cavalry under Colonel Theodorick Bland to patrol out beyond Sullivan's lines, even though the locals inaccurately claimed that there were no more fords within twelve miles, and that the roads leading to and from them were inaccessible.[34]

Washington's frustrations that long September day grew out of a series of increasingly contradictory and bewildering reports about the British army's whereabouts and intentions that ultimately froze the Americans in place along the Brandywine and made Howe's task much easier. Washington was of course well-informed about Knyphausen's progress toward Chad's Ford, and he even crossed the Brandywine for a firsthand look at Maxwell's running fight, during which time British riflemen might have killed him had not Ferguson had qualms about shooting an officer in the back. The big question was whether this was Howe's main effort or merely one element of a more diabolical plan to ensnare the American army. From early morning, Washington received a number of reports informing him about Howe and Cornwallis's flanking movement. One originated with Colonel Moses Hazen, a thoroughly dependable former Great War for Empire ranger whose regiment of mostly Canadian refugees Sullivan had posted at Jones' and Buffenton's Fords, and another from Bland's scattered cavalry patrols. On the other hand, other observers in the area informed Washington that they had been unable to spot any wide-ranging British force probing for his flank. After weighing the information, Washington opted to believe that Howe had indeed divided his army, and as he saw it, this presented him with a rare opportunity to defeat the British in detail. With this in mind, Washington sent Stirling's and Stephen's divisions to Birmingham Meeting House to defend his flank against any British attack in that direction just in case, and he ordered Sullivan's, Greene's, and Maxwell's soldiers to prepare to assault Knyphausen's isolated force. Some of these troops had already crossed the Brandywine and begun skirmishing with Knyphausen's men when they suddenly received orders to fall back across the creek. Major Joseph Spear of the Pennsylvania militia had appeared at Washington's headquarters and notified the American commander in chief that he had been out patrolling the upper branches of the Brandywine all morning without sighting the British. Spear's honest mistake gave Washington pause. Perhaps the reported flanking column was just a feint, and maybe Howe had reunited his force here along the Brandywine? If this were the case, an American charge across the creek in the teeth of the entire British army would be foolhardy. Better to halt Stirling's and Stephen's divisions where they were, recall the soldiers he had ordered across the Brandywine, and get ready to receive an almost certain British attack.[35]

No sooner had Washington canceled his planned assault, however, than he received disconcerting news from Bland. The cavalry colonel told the American commander in chief via Sullivan not only that the British flanking column still existed but that it was across the Brandywine and approaching the American army's vulnerable right flank. This intelligence jibed with that that of pesky local patriot Thomas Cheyney, who had appeared at Washington's headquarters with the same information and proclaimed the news long and loud to anyone who would listen. It seemed that Howe was up to his old tricks, and he might be just as successful here as he had been up in New York unless Washington reacted fast. Fortunately, Stirling's and Stephen's divisions were already in the vicinity as a result of earlier rumors of British troops on the move, so Washington ordered them to resume their march to Birmingham Meeting House. This would put about 3,000 men in Howe's way, but that might not be enough; Bland reported seeing dust stretch back for miles, indicating large numbers of British soldiers en route. To brace the new American line under construction, Washington ordered Sullivan to shift his division to Birmingham Meeting House and to assume command upon arriving there.[36]

John Sullivan was more a doer than a thinker, but his mind raced when he got Washington's orders at about 2:30 P.M. He had expected a British flank attack all along and had in fact told Washington as much that morning, but his orders and his limited authority prevented him from preparing for it, or so he argued later. Now, suddenly, after hours of contradictory reports, the British had materialized practically right behind him. This was distressing enough, but Sullivan did not know the exact whereabouts either of the British or of Stirling and Stephen. Still, orders were orders, and the New Hampshire general was not the type of man to shrink from the dangers of ignorance, so he had his men in motion in a very short time. Less than five minutes out, Sullivan ran into Hazen and his regiment falling back from Jones' and Buffenton's Fords. Hazen claimed that the bulk of the British army was right behind them, and it would in fact be here at any minute. Sullivan was not sure about that because the latest reports indicated that there were only two brigades in the British flanking column. On the other hand, Hazen had already proved his reliability once today, so Sullivan took him at his word. As they talked, the British suddenly appeared out of nowhere at the front of the American column, but fortunately they were too intent on deploying to take advantage of the opportunity to demolish the strung-out rebels. Sullivan swerved his division to the right and continued his march unhindered toward Birmingham Meeting House. Finally, approaching 4:00 P.M., Sullivan spotted the American line, and he deployed his men on a nearby hill. He rode over to consult with Stirling and Stephen, and they quickly concluded that Sullivan had posted his troops too far to the front left by about a half mile, creating a gap the British could easily exploit. He sent word for this division to fall back and reorient itself with the rest of the American line, and his Maryland and Delaware Continentals started to move out. Unhappily for Sullivan and his soldiers, as well as Stirling's and Stephen's men across the way and the cause they were all defending, the British chose this most inopportune time to begin their attack.[37]

Eighteenth-century European warfare was a highly specialized art that required considerable time and training for officers and men to master. Ideally, regiments deployed with machinelike precision from column of march into line of battle, usually in an open field that permitted easier maneuvering and communication. Soldiers stood in lines two deep close together, which made it possible for officers to shout verbal commands amid the smoke and noise and carnage that invariably cluttered the battlefield. Such proximity also permitted the men to encourage one another by word or example, promoting unit integrity and morale. Battles were intimate affairs in another respect; muskets had an effective range of only around 50 yards, so the troops had to be within that distance of their opponents to inflict much damage on them. In such close quarters, volume of fire counted more than accuracy, so officers instructed their men to load and reload as rapidly as possible, and a good soldier could get off four rounds a minute. Some engagements were decided by skilled tactics in which one side managed to tear into its opponent's exposed flank or rear, but generally victory went to whichever line was able to inflict and sustain the most casualties without breaking and running. If that did not work, one side or the other could charge with the bayonet, and in America this was a British specialty whose effectiveness was enhanced by the fact that the rebels often either did not have their own bayonets or did not know how to use them correctly. Both Americans and British employed artillery, and its impact could be substantial if used properly. However, its range and mobility were limited. Once placed, it was difficult to move the heavy cannons far or fast, and their range was approximately 400 yards. Cannoneers had to see their targets to hit them, which often exposed them to musketry from the infantry. Both belligerents also possessed cavalry to scout and patrol, but it was expensive to raise, equip, and maintain, so it rarely played a prominent role in the Philadelphia campaign. Washington especially recognized cavalry's importance to his fluid strategy, but he never had enough of it. America's geography was different from Europe's in many respects, and as time went on, each side adapted to it. In particular, both the British and the Americans developed specialized units of riflemen. The rifle's comparatively long range was tailor-made for individualized combat in the broken wooded terrain that predominated in America, but it had substantial drawbacks. Not only did it take a long time to load and fire a rifle, but scattered riflemen were very vulnerable to bayonet charges. Taken together, these weapons and tactics, primitive though they later appeared, were still capable of generating considerable casualties, making Revolutionary War battles extremely bloody affairs indeed, as both British and American soldiers near Birmingham Meeting House were about to discover.

Sullivan's division was falling back to get into line with Stirling's and Stephen's troops when the British Guards suddenly emerged from the thinly wooded forest and crossed the plain with fixed bayonets. The rearward American brigade of Maryland and Delaware soldiers was countermarching through a gateway on a narrow lane when the enemy appeared. Brigadier General William Smallwood had commanded this brigade until Washington dispatched him to help organize the Maryland militia, but before he left he complained to the American commander in chief about the low quality and inadequate training of his troops. It was small wonder, then, that they were unable to deploy into line of battle under such sudden pressure. Instead, they broke and ran for their lives. The other brigade, just behind them, managed to start to form up, but it, too, collapsed in flight. Its quarrelsome, emotional, and high-strung commander, French Brigadier General Philippe Preud-homme de Borre, was unwilling and unable to do much to stem the tide, which after the battle spawned charges of cowardice that led to his resignation three days later. Only Hazen's regiment succeeded in maintaining its integrity, and he was able to bring it into line with the other two divisions and get into action. For all intents and purposes, Sullivan's division ceased to exist as a combat-effective unit. Meanwhile, up at wooded Plowed Hill, where Stirling and Stephen had realigned their men to conform with Sullivan's planned redeployment, the New Hampshire general watched with dismay as his division vanished in almost the blink of an eye. He ordered the artillery there to open fire on the advancing British to give his soldiers time to regroup, and he and his aides galloped down to rally their division, but without much success. No sooner would they stop one group than another would run. Discouraged, Sullivan returned to Plowed Hill and resolved to contest at least this part of the field to the last.[38]

At the other end of the line, things went better for the Americans, at least at first and in comparison to Sullivan's debacle to the south. Major General Adam Stephen had just pulled his division back and placed it on Plowed Hill when the British attack commenced. Stephen had been Washington's second in command on the Virginia frontier during the Great War for Empire, but his heavy drinking had taken a toll on whatever military expertise he had developed over the years, and he had a tendency to exaggerate.[39] Fortunately, his two brigades of Virginians were ably led by Brigadier Generals William Woodford and Charles Scott—the former commanded the Virginia state militia at the rebel victory over the loyalists at Great Bridge in December 1775; and the latter, though possessing little formal education, was a tough and forthright Great War for Empire veteran who survived Braddock's disaster—and both men were determined to hold their positions at all hazards. Their soldiers greeted the British light infantry advancing across the valley and up the hill with heavy musket and cannon fire. One redcoat later remembered, "There was a most infernal fire of cannon and musketry, the most incessant shouting—incline to the right! Incline to the left! Halt! Charge! Etc. The balls plowing up the ground. The trees crackling over one's heads. The branches riven by the artillery. The leaves falling as in autumn by the grapeshot."[40] Worse yet for the British, Howe mistakenly believed that the Americans were strongest on his right to the south, so he bent his forces in that direction. As a result, Stephen's line overlapped the oncoming light infantry. Woodford had ordered Colonel Thomas Marshall's Third Virginia Regiment to a rise in the woods to cover his right flank, and he kept it there when the rest of the division redeployed to Plowed Hill. Later the Virginians fell back to a stone wall, and this isolated position gave them a perfect vantage point from which they readily pumped volleys into the British light infantry's exposed flank. The redcoats faltered and then came on again in the face of stout resistance. Stephen did not coordinate his brigades very well and Woodford was painfully wounded in the hand, but the division continued to stand fast and fight hard.[41]

Stirling's division held the center of the fractured American line on the southern part of Plowed Hill. The wealthy, vain, pompous, and self-styled New Jersey nobleman was yet another hard-drinking officer, but mild in manner and brave in battle. He had fought well as a brigade commander at Long Island, although he and most of his men were eventually captured. Exchanged soon after, he participated in the Battle of Trenton and in the subsequent winter fighting in New Jersey. There was nothing brilliant about him, but he was one of Washington's more dependable officers.[42] Stirling deployed his troops behind a series of fences and prepared to slug it out with the grenadiers and light infantry advancing and skirmishing down the east-west road. Luckily for the Americans that day, Brigadier General Thomas Conway commanded Stirling's brigade to the right of his line next to Stephen's division. Unlike so many of Washington's officers, the Irish-born French volunteer had rigorously drilled his 800 Pennsylvanians that spring and summer, and now the training paid off. Conway's soldiers held their fire until the last moment and then delivered a devastating volley against the approaching redcoats at close range, bringing the Second Grenadier Battalion to a staggering halt. Indeed, the British charge here might have collapsed altogether if Agnew had not rushed forward over the broken ground with his backup brigade to restore the line and jump-start the attack. Even so, Stirling's men continued to battle on, stalling several British assaults.[43]

For all the success Stirling's and Stephen's divisions gained, the fact remained that the attacking redcoats and Germans outnumbered them close to two to one, and soon superior British strength and discipline began to tell. On the American right, German and British light infantry worked their way around Stephen's flank and assaulted Marshall's isolated Third Virginia from two sides. After hand-to-hand fighting, the Virginians fell back from their forty-five-minute stand, losing heavily in the process. To the south, Agnew's brigade exerted increasing pressure on both Stirling's and Stephen's troops, and the grenadiers and part of the Guards brigade pushed hard against Hazen's regiment and the brigade of New Jersey troops on the far left of the truncated American line. The cumulative weight told, and first Woodford's and then Scott's brigades wavered and broke. They retreated in good order toward Dilworth until the light infantry hit their flank, throwing them into flight. Nearby, Stirling's division also came unglued, and it too fell back, covered by the New Jersey brigade and Hazen's men.[44] They fought from fence to fence and hill to hill, up through Dilworth. In addition to surrendering Plowed Hill, the Americans also lost about a half dozen cannons placed there because British fire killed so many of the horses necessary to remove them.[45]

Now that they had shattered the American line, Howe and Cornwallis sought to exploit their success to the fullest by rounding up or shooting down all the fleeing rebels within their reach. With this in mind, the British generals pointed their troops to Dilworth, through which ran the road that served as an escape valve for the defeated remnants of Sullivan's, Stirling's, and Stephen's divisions scurrying for refuge from the battle. Unhappily for many of the redcoats, instead of the easy mopping-up operation they anticipated, they encountered some of the severest combat in a day that had already surpassed the experiences of even many hardened veterans in that respect. When Washington learned that Sullivan's division had collapsed, he dispatched Greene's division and Nash's unattached North Carolina brigade to help. He himself rode over just in time to see the line crumble once and for all, threatening the destruction of his entire army. Fortunately for him, Greene's soldiers—two brigades of Virginians under former innkeeper Brigadier General George Weedon and preacher Brigadier General Peter Muhlenberg—arrived just in time after trotting four miles in a mere forty-five minutes. As Weedon's winded brigade crossed some plowed ground, Sullivan suggested to Washington that Greene deploy his men near Dilworth to strike the incautious British front and flank as they came down the road, and the commander in chief agreed. Greene hurriedly got his panting men into line, a task made all the more difficult by the soldiers fleeing from the earlier engagement streaming down the road toward Chester. As the grenadiers approached the village in the twilight, they encountered heavy fire from Weedon's brigade that threw them into considerable confusion, but they re-formed and came on again. The far-ranging Captain Ewald rode off for help and found Agnew and two of his regiments recovering from their earlier exertions, and he brought them up in a hurry to reinforce the beleaguered grenadiers. Agnew's men arrived just in time to stop Weedon's men from hitting the grenadiers on their flank and rear. Unfortunately for the British, the Virginians instead directed their fire at Agnew's troops. Rebel musketry ripped through the two British regiments, killing or wounding most of their officers in a heartbeat. Before Weedon could complete their destruction, however, the British hauled up a couple cannons to flail away at the Americans, who then broke off their twenty-minute fight in the gathering darkness and joined the retreat to Chester.[46]

To the south, around Chad's Ford, things had also gone badly for the

Americans. To oppose Howe and Cornwallis's fast-developing flank attack, Washington dispatched first Sullivan's division and then Greene's and Nash's troops, leaving only Maxwell's fought-out riflemen, Armstrong's jittery Pennsylvania militia, and Wayne's division to hold the line along the Brandywine. Wayne was a former surveyor and tanner who had served in the Pennsylvania legislature before war broke out. He fought in the Canadian campaign and later succeeded Lincoln when Washington sent that Massachusetts general up north to help Schuyler. He was an impulsive and impetuous man, and he needed all his experience and skill to confront the challenge Knyphausen was about to mount. The German general had been content to lob shells across the Brandywine after reaching Chad's Ford, but around 2:00 P.M. he noticed enemy units filing off to the right, a good indication that Howe and Cornwallis were approaching. Upon hearing the subsequent racket in that direction, Knyphausen brought his cannons down from the surrounding heights to the creek bank and deployed his troops for an attack at Chad's Ferry, near the well-defended ford. British artillery opened up a heavy bombardment, and two regiments spearheaded the assault across the creek. The British soldiers crossed the waist-deep waters in double file to the sound of fife and drums, bayonets fixed. American cannons and musket fire swept the Brandywine, but the tough redcoats kept moving, up the bank and forward toward the three batteries covering the area. Wayne's troops battled stubbornly from behind fences, walls, houses, and ditches for an hour and a half, forcing the British forces to bleed for every field and orchard they gained. In the end, however, British discipline and training carried the day, here as elsewhere on the battlefield. Wayne planted a four-gun battery on a hill next to the road to Chester to cover his retreat, and most of his men fell back in that direction, joining the rest of Washington's army in flight.[47]

The American army retreated down the road to Chester that night. Once there, officers tried to rally the exhausted men and put them in some sort of order, which sometimes worked and sometimes did not. Most soldiers fell in willingly enough, but others had had their fill of the war and kept going, across the bridge toward and beyond Philadelphia. Washington ordered the runaways in the countryside rounded up, and he had Maxwell's riflemen comb Chester for stragglers. Even so, hundreds exited the war this way, making it difficult to ascertain exact American casualties at Brandywine. One German officer noted that the British buried nearly 400 enemy soldiers on the battlefield and captured almost 500 more, and altogether American losses probably topped

1,000 men killed, wounded, and taken prisoner. Washington of course regretted the subtraction of so many troops from his ranks, but he remained focused on the problems immediately at hand, the foremost of which was stopping Howe's victorious army from exploiting its recent gains. Obviously Washington needed to refit and reorganize his defeated army, so he fell back across the Schuylkill River and on 14 September marched his tired soldiers into camp at Germantown. To delay the enemy, he reverted to the strategy he had formulated the previous winter and spring. Smallwood and Gist had organized some 1,800 Maryland militia at Oxford and Christiana, and Washington ordered them to harass the British in an effort to force Howe to divert troops to guard his new supply lines to the Delaware. Maryland militiamen had not accomplished much in the campaign so far, but Washington hoped that any opposition they could mount would buy him some time to ponder how to contest the oncoming British juggernaut.[48]

Despite the defeat along the Brandywine, most of Washington's officers and men remained in high spirits. On the whole, they had fought well against arguably the world's best soldiers, and they knew it. Moreover, many incorrectly believed that they had inflicted more casualties than they sustained. They were not inclined to assess blame, perhaps because most agreed with Washington's assertion that the day's misfortunes stemmed from faulty information that had prevented him from responding to Howe's flank attack as decisively as he would have otherwise. There were others outside the army, however, who were more interested in impugning something less abstract and more subject to punishment than an intelligence failure. For example, North Carolina congressional delegate Thomas Burke witnessed the battle, and as far as he was concerned, Sullivan's ineptitude cost the Americans any chance at victory. Specifically, Burke charged that Sullivan should have detected the British march around the American flank and reacted to it more quickly. Congress ordered an inquiry into Sullivan's conduct, but fortunately for the New Hampshire general most of the officer corps, including the commander in chief, rallied to his defense. Washington successfully argued that he could not afford to lose Sullivan, who, whatever his drawbacks—specifically, he was tactless, susceptible to flattery, impulsive, and plain unlucky—was a hard fighter committed to the patriot cause. It was simply one more problem Washington had to deal with in the days following Brandywine, and Sullivan was not the last general whose judgment and competence would be called into question during the campaign.[49]

William Howe made no immediate effort to capitalize on his victory at Brandywine. Two days after the battle he sent Cornwallis with the grenadiers and light infantry toward Chester to investigate rumors that the rebels were entrenching there—and in fact a British patrol even entered the town unopposed the next day—but on the whole the commander in chief seemed content to rest on his laurels for now, at least in a strategic sense. Howe believed that his army had plenty to do preliminary and requisite to any advance toward the American capital. The British had suffered 577 casualties at Brandywine, including 89 killed and nearly 400 wounded who needed care. There were also plenty of American wounded lying around, and Howe asked Washington to dispatch some of his surgeons to help look after them. Finally, the British army still lacked a supply line, and it was situated deep in hostile territory. As far as Howe was concerned, right now tying up these logistical loose ends had priority over pursuing Washington's battered army and occupying Philadelphia. To this end, he directed his men to scour the surrounding countryside for provisions and supplies, and on 12 September he ordered troops to Wilmington to meet up with the Royal Navy and establish a base there. The redcoats took the town the next day without opposition, and they even captured Delaware president John McKinly in the process.[50]

Such easy successes seemed par for the course these days as far as many redcoats were concerned. British and German officers were full of praise then and later for their commander in chief. Howe's tactical skill in planning and executing the flanking maneuver that won the day at Brandywine seemed self-evident, and the only regret many expressed was that they had not had an hour or two more of daylight to completely destroy or capture the rebel army.[51] Nor was such pride limited to high-ranking officers. One local Quaker later wrote,

> I was disposed to see an operation performed by one of the surgeons, who was preparing to amputate a limb, by having a brass clamp or screw fitted thereon, a little above the knee joint, he had his knife in his hand, the blade of which was of a circular form, and was about to make the incision, when he recollected that it might be necessary for the wounded man to take something to support him during the operation. He mentioned to some of his attendants to give him a little wine or brandy to keep up his spirits, to which he replied, "No, doctor, it is not necessary, my spirits are up enough without it."[52]

As the wounded redcoat's words implied, the Battle of Brandywine was by almost any conventional measurement a clear-cut British victory. Howe's army outmaneuvered and outfought the Americans at almost every turn, so when the smoke wafted away, the British not only maintained control of the battlefield, but they also inflicted substantially more casualties than they sustained despite assuming the attacker's role. In this respect, the redcoats' pride in their performance was justified. Washington rightly believed that the immediate reason for his defeat was jumbled intelligence that had prevented him from adequately tracking and responding to Howe's flank attack, but there were also deeper forces at play that day that better explained the American setback. For one thing, the redcoats and Germans were simply superior soldiers to their American counterparts. The well-trained and well-equipped British forces repeatedly overcame often heavy enemy opposition, and although they initially faltered storming Plowed Hill and driving toward Dilworth, they never broke and their persistence paid off. The Americans certainly fought bravely, but usually in a disjointed fashion that made them no match for their highly disciplined foes. In addition, British and German officers from Howe on down showed a much better grasp of tactics than did Washington and his subordinates. Howe, Cornwallis, Knyphausen, and their juniors understood their assignments—be it driving to and across the Brandywine or assaulting Plowed Hill—and they carried out their orders with commendable professionalism and aplomb. On the other hand, Washington and his officers performed in a much more muddled manner. They did not understand their tasks or know how to fulfill them. In particular, Washington was confused and befuddled by contradictory information that cost him the initiative, and Sullivan was unable to deploy his men well enough or fast enough to stop the British flank attack. No one could deny the courage exhibited by most of the American general officers—de Borre being the prominent exception—but their skill left a lot to be desired. Only Greene, Weedon, and Maxwell proved capable of both fighting and manipulating their soldiers with any degree of effectiveness, although, once positioned, Woodford, Scott, Hazen, Conway, Wayne, Sullivan, and Stirling all demonstrated considerable pluck. Finally, and ironically, the British had a better knowledge of the local geography that enabled them to divide their forces in the face of the enemy and steal a march across the Brandywine to Osborne Hill. Southeastern Pennsylvania was full of loyalists, and Howe used them tactically in a way he was never able to match strategically. Washington, however, often groped blindly in a region with which he was un-familiar, and he paid the price for his ignorance.

In a strategic sense, however, Brandywine did not advance the British war effort all that much. Howe failed to destroy Washington's army or break its morale, and as subsequent events showed, the battle did not immediately open the way to Philadelphia. Indeed, in this light Brandy-wine appears more as a missed opportunity than a conclusive victory for the British. Howe had a rare chance to engage the main American army on relatively open ground, and he neglected to take advantage of it in such a way as to make the encounter decisive. Instead, Washing-ton's army remained more or less intact, and as long as it existed, so did the cause that sustained it. Moreover, Howe would soon learn that de-spite its recent drubbing, it retained its sting, making it very difficult for the British commander in chief to disperse his men to gain control of the large chunks of American territory he needed to possess to reestab-lish the king's authority. Indeed, about the only strategic gain the British accrued from Brandywine, albeit an unintended one, was that Wash-ington afterward drew reinforcements from the Hudson Highlands, which opened the way for Clinton to go upriver and link up with Bur-goyne if he so chose. Like so many British Revolutionary War triumphs, Brandywine was a barren accomplishment that merely burned up more time, resources, and soldiers than the British could ultimately afford.

Howe may or may not have yet realized the limitations to his victory at Brandywine, but he was not the type to engage in might-have-beens anyway. Besides, he had too much to do to get his troops ready for fu-ture challenges. On 15 September, however, the British commander in chief received from an unlikely source that rarest of all gifts: a second chance. Washington and his army had recrossed the Schuylkill and were looking for another fight.

THE BRITISH OCCUPY PHILADELPHIA

Throughout its existence, the main American army had experienced more than its share of hardship, but its surprising ability to survive mismanagement, abuse, deprivation, apathy, and plain bad luck had sustained the Revolution through some of its darkest hours. Even so, its rapid recovery after the Battle of Brandywine was remarkable. Here as elsewhere its officers and men took their cue from Washington, who was no more inclined to acknowledge defeat now than he had been ten months earlier following the disastrous campaign in New York. Despite the subtraction of some 1,000 troops in its recent point-blank encounter with British military power, the basic strategic situation was relatively unchanged. Philadelphia remained in American hands, and the army was reasonably intact enough to continue to oppose its British counterpart. Both common sense and the British probe toward Chester convinced Washington that Howe planned to resume his advance to the American capital, and such foreknowledge gave him an advantage he did not mean to neglect. Washington had no intention of getting trapped between the Schuylkill and Delaware Rivers if the British undertook another flanking maneuver like the one that brought him to grief along the Brandywine. Instead, he decided to take his Continentals westward in search of an opportunity to hit the exposed British army's left flank or, if necessary, to fight it head-on again. He also deployed Armstrong's Pennsylvania militia to guard the Schuylkill fords and protect Philadelphia from straight ahead. Washington did not expect the militiamen to stop any serious enemy assault but merely to delay the British long enough to give him sufficient time to get his Continentals into a position from which they could strike. Here again, Washington was merely transferring to southeastern Pennsylvania the strategy he used so successfully in New Jersey during Howe's two incursions, only this time he posted the militia behind the Schuylkill instead of the Delaware.[53]

Washington did not waste any time, and on 14 September, only three days after the Brandywine bloodletting, the American army crossed the Schuylkill at Levering's Ford in water up to the soldiers' waists. Washington's intelligence informed him that the British were at Dilworth, probably on their way to Swede's Ford to get across the Schuylkill. The American commander in chief put his men on the road the next day and marched hard for White Horse, which he reached late in the evening. By moving fast, he placed his soldiers squarely between the British and the Schuylkill fords. If Howe wanted to get to Philadelphia, he had to deal with the American army first.

The British commander in chief sought nothing more than the chance to complete the destruction of Washington's army so promisingly begun at Brandywine, especially now that he had reestablished contact with the Royal Navy and replenished his supplies. Howe preferred to engage the Americans south of the Schuylkill away from the easily defended river if possible. Looking over his maps, Howe concluded that he could not march directly on Philadelphia because the Schuylkill was unfordable there, and he possessed no boats for any sort of amphibious assault on the place. Therefore, the only way to the American capital was via upriver fords, and he could kill two birds with one stone if he encountered and shattered Washington's army somewhere along the way. There were, however, drawbacks to this plan, the most obvious being that Howe would again have to cut loose from his supply line to go so far inland. Still, this strategy had worked once before, and Howe knew that the key was to keep moving so as to subsist on the surrounding countryside as much as possible. On 15 September, jaegers patrolling northwest skirmished with enemy detachments, and various captured Americans informed the British that Washington had indeed crossed the Schuylkill and was heading toward Lancaster. Here was the opportunity Howe had been seeking, and he issued orders for the British army to move out the next morning.[54]

The British army marched in two columns, with Cornwallis commanding the eastern one and Knyphausen the one to the west. Approaching Goshen, British patrols brought word that Washington's army was nearby toward White Horse, so Howe altered his march eastward to go after it. Both columns ran into scattered opposition from rebels sniping at them from behind trees and fences, but after the British army reunited, it came upon the American army drawn up for battle. Once again, for the second time in less than a week, Howe obtained what until recently had been a rare opportunity to fight Washington out in the open. Before he could take advantage of it, however, it started to rain heavily and violently. One German soldier reported, "I wish I could give a description of the downpour which began during the engagement and continued until the next morning. It came down so hard that in a few moments we were drenched and sank in mud up to our calves."[55] The rain fell in torrents, miring cannons in the mud, obscuring the battlefield, and flooding the fields and roads. Thus paralyzed, the British were unable to interfere as the American army rather mysteriously and certainly slowly retreated through the deluge, leaving the puzzled and inundated redcoats and Germans in possession of the would-be battlefield.

Why the Americans flinched and fell back without the dignity of a battle was anyone's guess at this point, but although Howe was undoubtedly disappointed by a second missed opportunity to run Washington to the ground, he did not neglect the opening the rebel retreat provided him. The way to the upper Schuylkill fords seemed clear now that the American army had scuttled off to parts as yet unknown. The next day the rain finally quit, so Howe put his army back into motion, but it was slow going. The Americans had used many of the same roads the day before, churning up the mud to a frightful degree. Worse yet, the excruciatingly slow-moving artillery and baggage train got lost for a time. Despite these problems, the British slogged through White Horse and on to Tredefferin. On the evening of 18 September, Howe dispatched some light infantry to seize the American supply depot at Valley Forge, which they did without opposition. Nearly 4,000 barrels of flour, several thousand tomahawks and kettles, 25 barrels of horse-shoes, and lots of soap and cannonballs and axes fell into British hands.[56] It was certainly strange that the Americans were either unwilling or unable to defend such valuable war matériel. The next day, upon hearing that Washington's army had reappeared in the area, Howe rushed reinforcements to Valley Forge, but the Americans seemed content to remain on the opposite side of the Schuylkill.

For the British, the last few days had been unpleasant and exhausting, but that was hardly out of the ordinary for eighteenth-century soldiers. The Americans, on the other hand, combined these standard miseries with additional problems uniquely their own. Washington crossed the Schuylkill with every intention to wage another battle with Howe, which was a big reason he brought his army to White Horse on 16 September. No sooner had his advanced forces started skirmishing with the enemy, however, than Washington decided that he did not like the ground on which he had deployed his troops, so he ordered them to fall back to a better position. As they did, the rain poured down. Unlike those used by the British, American cartridge boxes were made from very unseasoned leather that provided little protection from the rain for the ammunition within, so pretty soon the soldiers possessed scarcely a usable round. Under such circumstances, engaging the redcoats and Germans would be little short of suicide, so Washington pulled back to Yellow Springs before the rain ended and the British pressed forward. The march lasted twelve hours through waist-deep creeks and along roads so muddy that the tired, hungry, shoeless soldiers had to haul the cannons in relays. Once they reached Yellow Springs at 2:00 A.M., Washington discovered to his horror that almost all of his army's ammunition supply, some 40,000 rounds, was ruined. Mother Nature, it seemed, had done what the British could not, rendering the American army combat ineffective and unable to oppose the advancing enemy. Washington quickly put his troops on the road to Warwick to replenish his ammunition supply. To fill the gaping hole their departure left in the American defense system, Washington urged the popular but indecisive Smallwood to bring his Maryland militia north to harass the British, and he dispatched Maxwell's riflemen and Wayne's division to annoy the British rear if possible. So far, Smallwood's forces had not accounted for much, but Washington hoped—in vain, as things turned out—that a little more aggressiveness on their part might buy him some time. Wayne's and Maxwell's men, on the other hand, were tough Continentals who had fought well at Chad's Ford and would undoubtedly do so again. In the end, however, it was hard marching on Washington's part that prevented the British from immediately crossing the Schuylkill. Most of the exhausted American army reached Warwick on 18 September, and by the next day the soldiers were back on the road, crossing deep and rapid Parker's Ford on their way to block the British offensive.[57]

Unfortunately for Washington, he received very little help from Smallwood, Maxwell, and especially Wayne. On the surface, the thirty-two-year-old Wayne seemed ideally suited for his assignment in background and temperament; he possessed ample aggressiveness and impetuousness, and he had grown up in this part of Pennsylvania and knew the geography well. Moreover, he had suggested just such a mission to Washington earlier in the month. Wayne took his 1,500-man division from Yellow Spring to Warren, and then on the evening of 17 September to a secluded wooded spot near Paoli. After reconnoitering the nearby enemy camp at Tredefferin, Wayne reluctantly concluded that he lacked the strength to assault the British there without substantial reinforcements. Once Howe resumed his march to the Schuylkill, however, Wayne believed that he could successfully strike their strung-out and vulnerable column, especially if Smallwood and whatever Marylanders he managed to coax along cooperated with him. As he explained to Washington, "There was never, nor never will be a finer opportunity of giving the enemy a fatal blow than the present."[58] Until then, he ordered his men to sleep on their arms preparatory to the bloody work he hoped to undertake the next day, 21 September.[59]

Plenty of blood was shed within the next twenty-four hours, but unhappily for Wayne almost all of it was by his own men, and in a most grisly and humiliating manner. That evening, as Wayne finalized his plans, Howe learned—probably from local loyalists—that a good sixth of Washington's force was a mere three miles away, hovering on his right flank. The British commander in chief reacted quickly, dispatching that night Major General Charles Grey with six regiments of about

2,000 men to take advantage of this intelligence windfall and abolish the threat to his army. Born in 1729, Grey was a tough veteran of the Great War for Empire who was wounded at Minden and served at Havana. Despite the short notice and gathering darkness, Grey improvised well, and he had his men on the road by 11:00 P.M. He did not propose to merely defeat and scatter the rebels but rather to destroy them entirely. To do so, he divided his force into two columns under himself and Lieutenant Colonel Thomas Musgrave. He hoped to attack the Americans with his troops and herd them like frightened sheep into Musgrave's pre-positioned soldiers. The British general knew as well as anyone the risks inherent in such a dangerous nighttime operation, but, paradoxically enough, he believed that *reducing* the amount of firepower available to his redcoats might increase his chances of success. Grey ordered his troops to remove their flints and rely solely on their bayonets, figuring that in the dark this would ensure secrecy and prevent the confusion and friendly-fire casualties that could derail his designs.

Grey knew the general vicinity of Wayne's camp, but not its exact location and disposition. Fortunately for him, after marching down the road to White Horse, turning left, and heading toward Warren, the light infantry vanguard captured a local blacksmith and forced him to reveal that the rebels were a mere quarter mile away. The redcoats moved in, scaring off or stabbing first a couple of vedettes, then two sentries, and finally some pickets. As they emerged from the thick woods, Grey shouted, "Dash on, light infantry!" and waved his now cheering troops forward toward the stirring American camp shortly after midnight. British soldiers could see the rebels hastily forming up in front of their flickering campfires, but before they could mount any coherent resistance, the redcoats were upon them with their bayonets. For most of the Americans, it quickly became a question of running for their lives or standing and dying, and the vast majority who had the choice took the former option. The charging British drove them through the darkness in relative and haunting silence. One redcoat recalled, "Then followed a dreadful scene of havoc. The light dragoons came on sword in hand. The shrieks, groans, shouting, imprecations, deprecations, the clashing of swords and bayonets, etc., etc.; no firing from us and little from them, except now and then a few, as I said before, scattering shots, was more expressive of horror than all the thunder of artillery, etc., on the day of action."[60] The American camp caught fire, adding to the scene's eeriness as the British chased the fleeing rebels through the woods. Unhappily for Grey, the very darkness that made the British attack so successful also provided the Americans with a cloak under which to make their escape. Moreover, most of them managed to avoid Musgrave's troops and get away, eventually collecting at White Horse. When all was said and done, however, the British killed or wounded some 300 Americans, captured another 70 or 80, and sent the remaining 1,000 or so scurrying away empty-handed and in panic. In exchange, the redcoats suffered less than a dozen casualties. Grey and his men had every right to be proud of themselves and their exploit, even if they failed to completely destroy Wayne's division. In a rare and difficult night attack, and at virtually no cost to themselves, they mangled an entire enemy division in one of the war's best-conducted operations. It was a fine example of British discipline, training, and professionalism, and it earned its hard-bitten author the sobriquet "No Flint Grey."[61]

No such praise greeted Anthony Wayne when he eventually brought his shattered division across the Schuylkill to join the rest of the army. Instead, detractors charged him with gross negligence, and the fact that many of his critics came from officers within his division made such accusations all the more painful and potent. Washington had frequently warned his subordinates to guard carefully against such sudden British attacks, and indeed two days before the Paoli debacle Wayne had assured the American commander in chief that he had taken every precaution to avoid being surprised. All this was more than mortifying to a man with Wayne's pride, but Wayne was nothing if not a fighter, and he used the subsequent late October court-martial to refute his critics and defend his honor, reputation, and performance. Wayne explained that he had received warning of the British approach from a local whose acquaintance's servant had overheard British officers discussing the planned assault. In response, Wayne strengthened the vedettes and pickets, and in fact one of these vedettes had ridden into camp to alert the troops, but they did not have enough time to form up. For this he blamed brigade commander Colonel Richard Humpton, in whom Wayne had little confidence. Wayne argued that Humpton's sluggish reaction permitted the British to overwhelm his division. In the end, the court-martial cleared Wayne of the charges, and it made no attempt to fix responsibility for the debacle. So far in the war Washington's soldiers had beaten their British and German counterparts on the battlefield only under the most advantageous circumstances, so it was hardly surprising that Grey prevailed at Paoli. Indeed, even if the Americans had had more time to brace for the British assault, in all likelihood the only difference in the outcome would have been more redcoat casualties. In the murky aftermath of the battle, however, just about the only certainty—in addition to the fact that the starchy Wayne and many of his officers did not get along—was that the rebels had suffered yet another setback.[62]

Now that he had neatly eliminated the threat Wayne posed, Howe returned to the task at hand. On 20 September, just before he discovered Wayne's whereabouts, the British commander in chief pushed most of his soldiers to the Schuylkill. Unfortunately, Washington was already there on the opposite shore, with cannons and troops covering the fords, ready to bloody the waters if any redcoats or Germans were foolish enough to attempt a crossing in the teeth of such opposition. Howe pondered, and then acted in a manner that befitted his considerable tactical skills. Over the next two days the British general systematically spread his army upstream, from Fatland Ford at Valley Forge up through Bull Tavern to Gordon's Ford, where he ordered his engineers to begin construction of a bridge. Howe gambled that Washington would interpret this maneuvering as a prelude to an assault on his right flank, and he hoped the American commander in chief would respond by shuttling his soldiers upstream to prevent the British from interposing their army between his soldiers and the important American supply depot at Reading. If all went as planned, in the process Washington would loosen his grip on the downstream fords, opening the way for Howe to cross the Schuylkill and march on Philadelphia, thus leaving the American general holding the bag toward Reading. On 22 September, British and German patrols crossed the Schuylkill at Gordon's and Fatland Fords and encountered no opposition. Washington was gone, undoubtedly toward Reading to confront Howe's phantom flank assault. That evening Cornwallis led the grenadiers and light infantrymen across the river at Fatland Ford, and after moonrise around midnight, Howe followed with the rest of his army. There were no rebels in the vicinity, but that did not make the crossing easy. The water was three feet deep and ice-cold, and the troops had to march nearly 100 exhausting yards across because of a bend in the river. Once over, however, redcoats and Germans lit fires to dry off and waited for the rest of the soldiers to take their turns at the ford. At noon Grant brought across the provisions and baggage train, so the entire British army was now on the Schuylkill's east side at practically no cost. It was an impressive accomplishment that any officer could be proud of, but Howe did not rest on his laurels. Now that he had maneuvered Washington right out of the military picture, he intended to take advantage of the American general's absence to descend on the American capital. That morning and afternoon the British marched to Norristown, some six miles away, and two days later—25 September—the British army flowed southeastward along the Schuylkill in two parallel columns, one under Knyphausen along the river, and the other commanded by Cornwallis to the left. As they approached Philadelphia, the land opened up, and the huge tracts of woods disappeared. There was plenty of meat and flour to eat now from the fruitful local farms, and lots of forage for the horses. Despite stony roads and a hard, driving rain, in the evening the British army reached the heights overlooking Germantown, about seven miles from Philadelphia.[63]

George Washington had had little by way of good fortune that September. Brandywine, the abortive battle at White Horse and the subsequent ammunition shortage, Wayne's blunder at Paoli, and Smallwood's and Maxwell's inability to inflict anything more than incidental damage on the steadily advancing redcoats and Germans underscored the unhappy reality that from top to bottom the American army was inferior to its British counterpart. Washington, however, was nothing if not persistent in the face of adversity, and the fact that his hard-marching soldiers reached the Schuylkill ahead of Howe despite their detour to Warwick to refill their ammunition pouches was a testimony to his ingrained determination. Unhappily, his success was temporary. Washington made sure that his troops guarded all the upper Schuylkill fords, and he hoped to repulse any British assault across the river at the water's edge. Ironically enough, such attentiveness proved to be his undoing. Washington accurately tracked Howe's upriver probes, and he concluded that the British were trying to get between his army and his vital Reading supply depot. In response, he shifted his soldiers northwestward toward Pottsgrove, but this exposed Gordon's and Fatland Fords downriver. As Washington saw things, he had no good choice; he lacked the manpower to cover the entire upper Schuylkill, so he could defend either his supply network or Philadelphia. Washington believed that although his army could survive without its capital, it could not exist without the gunpowder and provisions Reading and Lancaster provided. On 22 September, Washington received contradictory reports of a British crossing at Gordon's Ford, and the next day he confirmed that the British had crossed the Schuylkill and were marching toward Philadelphia. Howe had outmaneuvered him yet again.[64]

Washington could have put his men on the road in an effort to overtake or catch up with the British, but he did not. Instead, he chose to rest his army, thus surrendering Philadelphia to its fate. Such passivity was not like Washington at all, but he had his reasons. For one thing, Wayne, Maxwell, and Smallwood had not yet joined his army, and until they did, the British outnumbered the Americans. Without a doubt, none of those three officers had fulfilled their orders to harass and delay the British—demonstrating among other things that implementing the commander in chief's strategic theories remained problematical—but he still needed their troops. In addition, Washington remained discouraged by the lack of accurate intelligence available to him. Southeastern Pennsylvania was rife with loyalist sentiment, and Howe's success in exploiting these people's local knowledge of the terrain had already cost the Americans dearly at Brandywine, at Paoli, and along the Schuylkill. Finally, the soldiers were simply in no shape for further exertions. American logistics were breaking down under the strain of the campaign, and the army was feeling the effect. The troops had been marching more or less continuously since before Brandywine, so it was small wonder that more than 1,000 lacked shoes, and everyone was hungry. Not surprisingly, straggling and plundering by tired and hungry soldiers was a constant and growing problem. Washington ordered his supply officers to requisition blankets and clothing from the local population for a fair price, but this was at best a stopgap measure that did nothing to solve the basic problem. The American army was exhausted, and Washington and his general officers knew it, so on 23 September he informed President of Congress John Hancock that he could no longer protect Philadelphia.[65]

Few Philadelphians were surprised by the imminent British arrival. Four days earlier, in the wee hours of the morning of 19 September, an express rider woke Hancock with word from Washington's aide Lieutenant Colonel Alexander Hamilton that it might be necessary to evacuate the city. Despite the late hour, Hancock roused members of Congress with the news, which spread rapidly until soon the moonlit streets were full of people milling about in search of information. The next day Congress resolved by unanimous consent to adjourn and meet in Lancaster, and delegates started leaving town. Thousands of others joined them with their possessions and families in tow, and one witness later recalled "wagons rattling, horses galloping, women running and children crying, delegates flying, and altogether the greatest consternation, fright and terror that can be imagined."[66] Amid the chaos, Hamilton showed up with soldiers to requisition from both willing and unwilling citizens as many shoes, blankets, cattle, and other valuable war material as possible for Washington's bedraggled army before the British occupied the city. Americans also cut the banks of the river, flooding the plain. Despite this pandemonium, the night before the British appeared passed quietly, and Philadelphia prepared for the return of royal authority.[67]

British military power was on full display the next day, 26 September, to encourage the faithful and cow the disloyal. At midmorning Cornwallis led about 3,000 British and German grenadiers and artillerymen into the city, accompanied by prominent loyalists Joseph Galloway, Enoch Story, Andrew Allen, and others. Fifes and drums played "God Save Great George Our King," the sunlight glittered off the officers' shiny swords, and the troops looked grave and resplendent in their comparatively clean uniforms. This was more than enough to impress the large crowds of mostly women and children who lined the streets to cheer the column as it wound its way to the heart of the city. For many of these onlookers the British army's presence marked an end to several years of oppression and persecution, and the promise of better times ahead. Cornwallis was not a particularly introspective man, so in all likelihood he did not dwell on such optimistic thoughts. Instead, he focused on the business at hand. He put the German grenadiers in the northern part of town and their British counterparts to the south, and he ordered engineers to begin construction of batteries along the Delaware River in case rebel warships appeared. British officers discovered lots of small arms and cannons as they settled in the city, despite Hamilton's last-minute sweep through town for anything of military value. All things considered, the occupation went smoothly, and two days later Howe visited the city and approved of Cornwallis's actions before he returned to his headquarters at Stenton House near Germantown.[68]

Philadelphia fell into British hands exactly one month after Howe's soldiers splashed ashore at Elk Ferry, and only fifteen days after Brandywine. This in and of itself spoke volumes about the British army's capabilities, but there was more to it than the time factor. In every instance the British overcame often substantial tactical and logistical obstacles to seize the American capital. Howe's redcoats and Germans conducted a complicated amphibious landing at Elk Ferry, brushed aside enemy opposition at Cooch's Bridge, won a full-scale battle at Brandywine, dispersed a serious threat to their rear at Paoli, and outmaneuvered Washington's army to cross the Schuylkill without opposition before pouncing on the American capital. At no point were the rebels able to resist British pressure once Howe applied it in earnest. In almost every instance his officers performed magnificently, be it in independent operations such as Grey's attack at Paoli or in cooperative efforts such as Knyphausen's and Cornwallis's assaults at Brandywine. Moreover, the British carried out their offense without secure or dependable supply lines, forcing them to keep moving so as to subsist their army on the fat of the countryside. Now the largest city in North America was in British hands, and Howe hoped to use it as a base upon which to build the king's authority in the region.[69]

A closer look, however, demonstrated that Howe's admittedly impressive and numerous tactical triumphs did not add up to substantive strategic gains. Howe could have used Philadelphia as an anvil upon which to fix and destroy the American army in battle, but this did not happen. Washington managed to survive Brandywine and the close run at White Horse, and after Howe crossed the Schuylkill, he deliberately turned his back on the American army and moved to occupy Philadelphia. As Howe saw it, this was his wisest course. He had no desire to pursue the Americans into the rugged terrain toward Reading, which would give Washington the opportunity to replicate his achievements in north New Jersey the previous June by deploying his troops in the well-fortified hills.[70] Trying to pry the Americans out of these all but invulnerable positions would have been costly in terms of time and casualties, with no guarantee of success. Moreover, Howe would have had to undertake this offensive without regular supply lines amid a hostile population, putting him in the same position that was at that very moment bringing Burgoyne to grief in upstate New York. Better to seize Philadelphia, establish a supply line, and rest his army before embarking on further adventures. Ironically enough, however, Howe soon discovered that occupying the American capital merely sucked him into a grinding, six-week-long operation to provision its inhabitants and garrison that made his earlier woes seem minor in comparison. Whatever Howe's rationale for his actions, the fact remained that Washington's army still existed, and now that it was no longer burdened with protecting Philadelphia, it was more elusive than ever, making it all the more potent and difficult to destroy. As long as the main American army remained intact, the British would be unable to exert their authority over any territory their army did not physically occupy, which for now included little more than Philadelphia and the surrounding region. Finally, conquering Philadelphia was not the body blow to American morale that many British officials hoped, and in fact most Americans were surprisingly blasé about the city's fall.[71] Although on the surface Howe had been remarkably successful, it was hard to see that his accomplishments brought the British much closer to final victory.

For Washington, September was a thoroughly unhappy and disappointing time. A little more than a month earlier he had marched his soldiers through the Philadelphia streets to demonstrate to its citizens that he had the power to protect them and the cause they served. Now the city was in British hands, a constant reminder to the commander in chief, and everyone else for that matter, that Howe had repeatedly outmaneuvered and outfought the American army from Elk Ferry to the Schuylkill. This was galling enough for someone with Washington's deep-rooted pride, but the details seemed equally grim. Washington's strategy was not nearly as successful in southeastern Pennsylvania as it had been up in north New Jersey the previous June. Part of the reason for this was geography. The Philadelphia region's flat terrain and comparatively expansive road network made it difficult for Washington to safely position his army in places invulnerable to British attacks. This gave Howe more opportunities to assault and destroy the American army, as at Brandywine. In addition, Washington had been unable to hinder the advancing British army as much as he hoped. The fluid military situation after Brandywine provided the Americans with several chances to wreak damage on the redcoats and Germans, but Maxwell, Wayne, and Smallwood all had failed to one extent or another in their independent missions. In fact, Washington was so discouraged with Maxwell's performance (and also, in all likelihood, by persistent rumors that the New Jersey general was intoxicated on duty—rumors that ultimately led to a court-martial that cleared him of the charges but only after a court of inquiry noted that he did drink a lot) that he eventually sent him back to command his New Jersey brigade in Stirling's division, broke up his light corps, and asked Gates to return Morgan and his experienced riflemen as soon as possible.[72] Moreover, although militiamen were an integral part of Washington's strategy, the Maryland and Delaware militias were not nearly as aggressive and experienced as their New Jersey counterpart. Throughout the campaign they were unwilling or unable to inflict on the British the large number of casualties necessary to hinder Howe's offensive. Finally, and perhaps most ominously, American logistics were clearly deteriorating by late September. The American army could survive without Philadelphia, but it needed sufficient guns, provisions, clothing, and equipment to continue the war. Altogether, it was hard to see how Washington's army could endure another rigorous campaign, especially if Howe initiated one sooner rather than later.

On the other hand, there were some good omens for the American cause if anyone cared to look. Most obviously, the American army, battered and bruised though it was, had survived to fight another day. The soldiers had battled doggedly from start to finish, and there had been no mass desertions despite all the hardships. This was of course an important factor, but Washington's strategy also played a role in the army's continued existence. If he had attempted to passively defend Philadelphia from behind the Schuylkill, the British might have trapped and obliterated his army along the Delaware River. Instead, Washington decided to take his army east of the Schuylkill in search of an opportunity to strike Howe's left flank, even though this exposed it to risky battles. Doing so not only preserved his freedom to maneuver but also gave him the option when the time came of defending either Philadelphia or his supply bases to the west. That he chose to abandon the American capital demonstrated his strategic maturity. Washington understood from hard experience that the Revolution depended more on his army's survival than on maintaining possession of any one city, even one as important as Philadelphia. By way of contrast, in 1776 he attempted to protect New York City long after it was clear that doing so put his army in jeopardy, and in the end he was lucky to escape with any troops at all. Finally, although the American logistical network was breaking down, the British had not disrupted it, so its flaws were homegrown and therefore subject to repair. Washington was down but not out.

CLOSE CALL AT GERMANTOWN

One of the reasons for Howe's success in the campaign so far was that from start to finish—that is, from the British army's Elk Ferry landing to its triumphant procession into Philadelphia—he had maintained the initiative over his American opponent. Washington spent all of September reacting to Howe's smoothly orchestrated maneuvers, and as a result he was almost always one step behind. This was no way for him to wage war, and in fact it was generally a surefire path to destruction and defeat. In this light, it was not so much surprising that the American army had lost all its battles and the city in its charge, but rather that it survived the experience at all. Washington was by nature a pugnacious man, so he understood the problem almost instinctively. After Brandy-wine he attempted to regain the initiative by first marching to White Horse and later by dispatching Wayne to Paoli, but neither effort suc-ceeded. Now, as he moved his army to Pennypacker's Mill the day Cornwallis marched into Philadelphia, Washington continued to watch and wait for an opportunity to do something soon that would reverse a strategic tide that was running swiftly against the American cause. The questions, of course, were what, where, and how.[73]

Ironically enough, Howe's occupation of Philadelphia provided Washington with the opening he sought. Howe split his army, sending part of it to garrison the former American capital and keeping the bal-ance at Germantown, seven miles away. The American commander in chief severely underestimated the British army's strength at around 8,000 men, and now that it was no longer concentrated in one place, he believed it was extremely vulnerable to the type of furious surprise attack that won the day at Trenton, when Howe made a similar mis-take and dispersed his forces. As an additional incentive, Washington's earlier pleas and orders for reinforcements were finally paying off. Irish-born Brigadier General Alexander McDougall and his 900-man brigade of Continentals arrived from the Hudson Highlands soon after the British entered Philadelphia, followed in quick succession by Small-wood's fewer than 1,000 dispirited Maryland militiamen on 28 Sep-tember and Brigadier General David Forman's 600 mostly New Jersey militia a day later. Smallwood's Marylanders had not been worth much so far, but McDougall and his Continentals were solid, and the New Jersey militia had proved its value the previous winter. Put together, Washington now had 8,000 Continentals and 3,000 militia at his dis-posal, in his mind giving him numerical superiority over the British even before Howe made the mistake of dividing his troops. Tallying up the military ledger, Washington decided to launch a surprise assault against Howe's redcoats and Germans at Germantown. If all went as planned, the Americans could cripple or destroy a good portion of Howe's army and bring the British war machine to a stumbling halt. On 28 Septem-ber, the American commander in chief met with his generals to explain the situation and discuss his scheme. Everyone acknowledged that the Americans should attack, but they were not sure about the timing. Most of the militia generals—Smallwood, Forman, and Pennsylvania's James Potter and James Irvine—favored an immediate assault, perhaps because they understood the transitory nature of the troops at their dis-posal. The impetuous Charles Scott and Wayne agreed, but the majority of those present advised Washington to wait for more reinforcements reportedly on the way. In the meantime, they suggested marching closer to Germantown so the army could quickly take advantage of any new opportunities to attack. Washington mulled this over and acquiesced, and the next day he moved his troops to Skippack.[74]

Washington was acutely aware of the value of accurate and timely intelligence, and as commander in chief he worked hard to develop and utilize informers, deserters, scouts, and spies to collect information on British intentions and movements. Throughout the campaign Washington served as his own intelligence analyst, sifting and sorting through innumerable reports for clues as to British designs. In New Jersey earlier in the year, Washington's intelligence network functioned very well in tracking the British army's whereabouts, if not necessarily its objectives. Once the war shifted to southeastern Pennsylvania, however, Washington faced some formidable problems. The region was full of loyalists who inhibited American intelligence gathering and provided Howe with valuable information that contributed to his uninterrupted string of victories in September. In addition, Washington was unfamiliar with this part of the country, so he had to build an intelligence network from scratch, something that required more than a short month to bear fruit. In early October, however, the Americans finally got an important intelligence windfall that paved the way for Washington to seize the initiative. Several intercepted letters and reconnaissance reports indicated that Howe had dispatched large numbers of troops southward in an effort to open up the Delaware River to British shipping. Encouraged by this news that Howe had diluted his forces still further, Washington decided that the time had arrived to assail Germantown. More reinforcements were on the way, including indifferently armed and untrained Virginia militia and some Continentals from Peekskill, but Washington wanted to strike while the British Germantown garrison was still weakened. His general officers unanimously agreed with his logic, so Washington set the date of the attack for 4 October.[75]

Once Washington issued his orders, the American army stirred into action. Soldiers cooked two days' provisions, received forty rounds of ammunition apiece, and combed out and transported the sick and wounded to Bethlehem to free up space for the inevitable casualties the forthcoming battle would bring. American patrols reconnoitered Germantown, gathering last-minute information for the upcoming assault. Washington's plan called for four separate columns to simultaneously assail the British garrison from four different directions. Sullivan would direct his and Wayne's divisions, with Conway's brigade from Stirling's division in front to clear the way and round the enemy left flank, down Skippack Road straight into the town. Stirling would follow behind with his New Jersey brigade and Nash's still-unattached North Carolinians as the reserve. To the east, Greene would bring his and Stephen's divisions into Germantown via Limekiln Road, with McDougall's newly arrived brigade in the lead. These two columns contained the best troops in the army—meaning the Continentals—and Washington expected them to provide the punch he needed to carry the day. As an afterthought, however, he also found roles for the militia. On the far left, next to Greene and Stephen, Washington ordered Smallwood's Marylanders and Forman's New Jersey boys to march down Old York Road and strike the British right flank. At the other end of the line, near the Schuylkill, Armstrong's Pennsylvania militiamen would perform a similar service to the left end of the British line along Ridge Road. It was a complicated and intricate plan modeled after the surprise assault on Trenton, but Washington intended to give his men plenty of time to get set. He decided to put his troops on the road for Germantown on the evening of 3 October. After a night march, the army would stop and rest for a couple hours within two miles of the British pickets. Then, at 5:00 A.M., all four columns would storm the village through the predawn darkness and, hopefully, destroy the British garrison.[76]

On 3 October, the American army lurched into motion for its fourteen-to sixteen-mile hike to Germantown, but problems developed almost from the start. Marching thousands of men—many of whom were barefoot, tired, and hungry—over unfamiliar bad roads in the dark slowed down all four columns to one degree or another. Washington accompanied Sullivan's and Wayne's divisions, and his presence undoubtedly helped keep them relatively on track, so by 5:00 A.M. they approached the British pickets at Mount Airy and prepared to attack. To the east, however, Greene's confused guide took the wrong road, so the column had to backtrack. Greene pushed his and Stephen's men hard to make up the lost time, but their troops were unable to meet Washington's schedule. The militia units on the flanks were also late. Armstrong's Pennsylvanians initially could not locate the British lines, and Smallwood's and Forman's troops had the most roundabout and confusing route of all. Washington, however, did not know about these problems because the darkness and a shortage of cavalry made it impossible for him to coordinate or even keep tabs on the other three

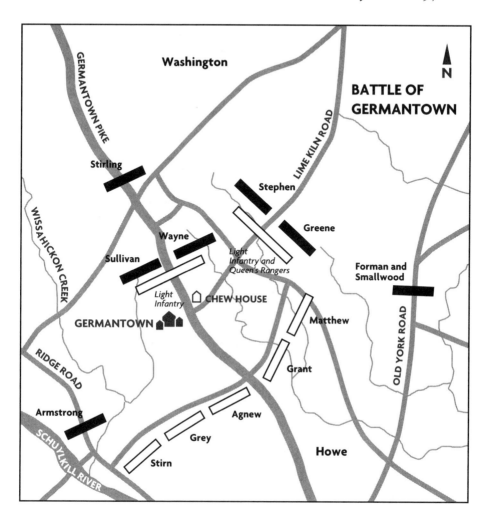

columns. Dawn revealed a dense fog covering the area, making it very difficult to discern much of anything. In any case, Conway quietly deployed his brigade and sent it rolling forward into the misty darkness just before sunrise.[77]

Howe was as aware as anyone of the obstacles the British faced in restoring their authority throughout the colonies, but he usually attributed his inability to crush the rebellion to the lack of resources at his disposal, not to any particular American moral or military superiority. Indeed, if September's events proved anything, it was that Washington had no claim in the latter area, especially now that the Union Jack flew triumphantly over the American capital. Self-assurance was an integral part of Howe's makeup, but his recent successes brought out in him a tactical overconfidence that made possible Washington's attack on Germantown. Howe garrisoned the village with 9,000 soldiers in order to protect Philadelphia while he concentrated on opening up the Delaware River to British shipping. As far as Howe was concerned, Washington's army was not much of an offensive threat after its drubbing along the Brandywine, and he figured that wide-ranging British and German patrols would sound the warning if the Americans dared to venture southeastward. In fact, Howe did not even order his troops to fortify the town because he did not want to undermine their faith in their military prowess. It was a strange sort of logic that cost the lives of many of his soldiers on 4 October. As it turned out, Washington's army was much more resilient than Howe expected, and those patrols in which he placed so much trust generally did not venture far from Germantown out of fear of ambush in the rebel-infested countryside, which in itself was evidence that the American army was by no means as played out as Howe seemed to believe.[78]

Despite Howe's blinding and misguided self-confidence, he and his soldiers at Germantown received sufficient information to alert them to Washington's intentions. In fact, on the evening of 3 October, Howe himself notified Charles Grey that British patrols had uncovered evidence of a possible American probe, and he ordered the Paoli victor to deploy some of his troops forward. Grey did so, but many British officers did not take their commander in chief's admonitions seriously, especially because rebel patrols had raided and sniped at their lines repeatedly over the past few days, so there was nothing unusual about such forays. Throughout the night of 3–4 October, more information trickled into various British and German headquarters. Before sunset a local rebel grateful to Johann Ewald for protecting his property informed him that the Americans planned to attack soon. Ewald returned to camp and notified jaeger commander Lieutenant Colonel Ludwig von Wurmb, who rode off to tell Knyphausen.[79] Wurmb also prudently doubled the pickets along Wissahickon Creek and dispatched Ewald with a patrol to confirm the warning. Just before dawn, Ewald ran into hundreds of Americans a mile from British outposts. Other patrols also seized prisoners who intimated that an attack was coming, and early in the morning a British sentry captured a rebel soldier who claimed to be part of the approaching American army. All this accumulated evidence disturbed First Light Infantry Battalion commander Lieutenant Colonel Robert Abercrombie, so he rode to headquarters at Stenton House at

4:00 A.M. to report his findings to Howe. Howe heard him out, mounted his horse, and galloped toward Germantown to look into the matter. By the time he got there, however, the American attack was just getting under way.[80]

Germantown was a narrow, two-mile-long village bisected by the north-south Germantown pike. The British line stretched east to west perpendicular to the road for about a mile. James Grant's and Edward Matthew's brigades were on the right of the pike, and James Agnew's, Charles Grey's, and German Major General Johann Stirn's brigades were to the left closest to the Schuylkill. Howe posted his two strong light infantry battalions about a half mile out in front of the village, so they caught the brunt of the initial American assault. The Second Light Infantry Battalion had just formed up to the west of the Germantown pike when its pickets ran in yelling that the rebels were right behind them. The redcoats immediately moved forward and ran headlong into Conway's advancing brigade of Pennsylvanians. Light infantry fire rocked Conway's men back on their heels, but they regrouped, pushed ahead, and broke the redcoat line. Sullivan's division arrived to back up Conway, while the light infantry received help from Thomas Musgrave's Fortieth Foot. Although outnumbered, the redcoats were tough, and their opposition convinced Sullivan to pause and align Wayne's division to his left on the other side of the pike, and to order Conway's men to file off and redeploy to his right. Once Conway's troops were in place, Sullivan pressed them and his two brigades ahead. The Second Light Infantry was already running low on ammunition, and now Americans started lapping around its left flank. The redcoats fell back, covered by Musgrave's men. To make things worse for the British, the soldiers of Wayne's division had also entered the fight, and they and their commander were determined to avenge their defeat at Paoli. American fire thinned the British line, and the redcoats retired. Many of them had never retreated before the rebels, and in fact their officers had a difficult time getting the proud men to obey their orders to withdraw. Sullivan's and Conway's soldiers swept forward in the thick fog, through the burning British camp and into Germantown, huzzaing loudly each time they overcame another knot of British resistance. There was nothing easy about it, though; the retreating redcoats fought stubbornly from behind every available fence, ditch, house, and wall as they fell back, inflicting a good many wounds on the advancing Americans in the process. Back at Germantown pike, Washington ordered Nash's North Carolina brigade to assist Sullivan, and he dispatched the

New Jersey brigade to support Wayne. As far as the American commander in chief was concerned, he was well on his way to winning his first large-scale victory since Princeton, ten months earlier. Many of the retreating redcoats would have agreed with this assessment, had they the time to analyze the situation objectively. Howe was up by now, observing the situation with his staff from under a tree, and he was dismayed at the sight of elite British light infantry backpedaling. "For shame, light infantry!" he shouted. "I never saw you retreat before. Form! Form! It's only a scouting party."[81] The light infantrymen knew better, and more than one was happy to see Howe and his aides come under artillery fire as large numbers of advancing rebels drove through Germantown herding the redcoats southward.[82]

On the northern edge of the town, however, there occurred the first of a series of events that would ultimately doom the American offensive and turn victory into defeat. After successfully covering the Second Light Infantry's retreat, Musgrave's Fortieth Foot fell back into Germantown. Musgrave—Grey's coconspirator at Paoli—realized that he needed to buy time for the rest of the army to respond to the American onslaught, so without orders he decided to hole up in his headquarters at Chew House with part of his regiment. Chew House was a large stone two-story mansion on the east side of Germantown pike, with three doors and windows on both floors. The redcoats barely made it inside ahead of the onrushing rebels, and in fact Musgrave had to unleash a last-minute volley in front of the building to discourage their pursuit. Once indoors, the approximately 120 British soldiers barricaded the entranceways, closed the shutters, and prepared for what might well be their last stand. Musgrave's impromptu fort had little impact on Sullivan's and Wayne's divisions, both of which swept by the house with scarcely a pause in their dash southward. Washington, on the other hand, stopped to survey the situation. Some of his junior officers urged him to emulate Sullivan and Wayne and simply bypass the house with his follow-up forces, but artillery chief Henry Knox was not so sure. As he saw it, it was dangerous to leave a fortified position in their rear, and he argued that the Americans should reduce it before moving on. Washington mulled over his options and agreed. He ordered the follow-up New Jersey brigade to storm the house instead of joining Wayne. Musgrave disregarded a flag of truce, so American artillery opened fire, blowing away a couple of the doors but otherwise doing no real damage to the solid stone edifice. An infantry charge likewise succeeded only in killing or wounding those Americans who managed to reach the windows in their efforts to get inside. The battle went on for more than an hour, consuming the energies of a brigade, valuable artillery, and the commander in chief.[83]

Greene was about a half hour late in undertaking his part in Washington's complicated attack, but he got his troops in line as fast as possible—Stephen's division to the west of Limekiln Road, his own two brigades and McDougall's to the east—and sent them forward. The delay gave the First Light Infantry Battalion time to brace for the shock, and the Fourth Foot rushed up to support it. Although outnumbered, the redcoats fought hard along the fence lines and across the fields, exchanging fire with Americans amid the fog and smoke at extremely close ranges. The British fell back to their camps, and once there, they by and large maintained their positions, but many American units simply went around them toward Germantown, isolating them in a pocket north of town. The fog and smoke from both gunfire and the burning fields made it increasingly difficult for officers of all ranks to coordinate their commands or see the British lines, so Greene's offensive degenerated into a confused brouhaha. American officers often discovered that they had run into enemy resistance only when they heard musket balls whiz around them, and just as frequently the fog prevented them from recognizing that the British had retreated. Most of Stephen's division veered right and marched toward Chew House, arriving in the vicinity just as the New Jersey brigade opened its attack on the structure. McDougall's brigade encountered such rough terrain to the far left that it was never able to come to grips with the British right flank as planned. Parts of Greene's and Stephen's divisions, on the other hand, made rapid but uncoordinated progress toward Germantown. Colonel George Matthews's Ninth Virginia Regiment managed to enter the town until stopped by swarming redcoats rushing forward to plug the hole in the British defensive dike. Getting out of Germantown proved considerably more difficult than getting in, and most of the surrounded Continentals eventually surrendered after the British zeroed in on their position upon hearing their premature shouts of victory. One of brigade commander George Weedon's units—the lone Pennsylvania regiment in Greene's division of Virginians—scattered a couple British battalions, seized three cannons, and just about reached Matthews's men, but eventually it had to retreat in the face of growing opposition. Muhlenberg's brigade almost met the same fate as Matthews's men in its dash forward, but he managed to cut his way through the gathering redcoat mass and salvage his unit.[84]

No one yet suspected as much, including the still-elated Washington, but the American army had shot its bolt. As it pushed southward into and past Germantown, its increasingly tired and disorganized units lost their combat integrity and effectiveness, the victims, as it were, of the law of entropy. The pea-soup fog and thick smoke that blackened soldiers' faces made it even more difficult for officers to control and direct their men in any sort of coherent fashion, let alone identify the British lines. This would not have been a major problem if the Americans had already secured their victory and needed only to mop up the tattered remnants of the British army, but this was not the case. The British line was already beginning to gel as officers sorted out their men in the fields south of Germantown. Many of the redcoats and Germans had not yet seen serious combat that day, and they had an advantage over their enemies not only in training and discipline but also in that they now knew where they and their comrades were. While Washington wasted time at Chew House, the quick-thinking Howe—he and his entourage had taken up position at the market square—prepared to unleash his regrouping soldiers on the strung-out Americans.

Wayne's division was the first to unravel, and it did so even before Howe got his counterattack under way. As they advanced southeastward through the blinding fog, the Pennsylvanians heard the New Jersey brigade's assault on Chew House, and they mistakenly believed that the British had reached their rear and cut them off. As it was, many of them were already running short of ammunition, which merely added to their apprehension. The tired and jittery soldiers began to backtrack despite their officers' best efforts to get them back in line. As they approached Chew House, they ran into Stephen's division, and in the dense fog the troops confused each other for the enemy, and some exchanged fire. The inebriated Stephen ordered a retreat, and his division began to fall back at the same time the British counterattack commenced. Under such circumstances, it was hardly surprising that Grant's brigade had so little trouble pushing the confused rebels out of that quarter of the battlefield.[85]

Across the Germantown pike, south of town, Sullivan's offensive also collapsed. Here, too, the Americans were tired, disorganized, confused, low on ammunition, and also increasingly isolated and vulnerable after Wayne's sudden disappearance. They were in no condition to effectively oppose the British counterattack launched by Grey and Agnew. Grey turned his brigade toward Germantown and pressed forward to rescue Musgrave's beleaguered men at Chew House. On his left, Agnew drove the Americans out of the upper part of the town. At about this time Francis Nash was mortally wounded on Germantown pike by a cannonball that tore off his leg at the thigh while he was sitting on his horse; he died five days later. Despite their frazzled condition, the Americans did not give way without a fight, and the redcoats had to pry or drive them out from behind houses, fences, and gardens throughout the town. The danger extended from the lowest private all the way up to Brigadier General Agnew, who was killed by a volley fired from near a Mennonite meetinghouse.[86]

Unfortunately for Washington and his Continentals, they received very little help from the militia assigned to strike the British flanks. Forman and Smallwood had such a roundabout march over such terrible roads that they never even entered the battle, thus sparing their New Jersey and Marylander boys from the honors and horrors of war that day. John Armstrong and his 1,000 Pennsylvanians did better, but not by much. Washington thought a lot of the devout old Irish-born Armstrong, a veteran of the Great War for Empire, but Armstrong had played no significant role at Brandywine, and he did little at Germantown to sustain his commander in chief's confidence in him. Certainly Armstrong faced some formidable obstacles in fulfilling his mission. Untrained militia generally lacked the stomach to assault enemy positions, and the Germans he confronted were just about the only soldiers in the Germantown garrison who took reports of a possible American attack seriously, so they were ready and waiting for the Pennsylvanians across Wissahickon Creek. The Germans gave up the bridge over the creek and took up position on a nearby hill, but they had little trouble repulsing Armstrong's halfhearted efforts to get across; in fact, they were able to easily spare men to bolster Agnew's flank when he began his counterattack. Around 9:00 A.M., Washington summoned the Pennsylvania militia, and Armstrong left behind a detachment to watch the Germans and headed for Germantown with his men. By now the Continentals had already retreated, and Armstrong was quick to follow when he came under British artillery fire. Back at Wissahickon Creek, the Germans scattered the militia remaining there, thus removing the last threat, such as it was, to the British army's left flank. The morning's affair cost the Pennsylvanians twenty casualties, a good indication of a lack of vigor on Armstrong's part.[87]

The collapse of American resistance was as sudden as it was unexpected, and no one was more surprised by this abrupt turn of events than Washington. As far as he was concerned, his army was on the verge of victory, despite the problems at Chew House. However, exhaustion, confusion, disorganization, a lack of ammunition, insufficient coordination, and the spooky fog had already half beaten his army before Howe's counterattack finished the job. American resistance melted away with the rising sun as units left the battlefield in increasing numbers. Some soldiers walked away without panic, but others ran as fast as their legs could carry them. Washington and his officers tried to rally them, but to no avail. The Americans managed to haul off their cannons and most of their wounded, but they left behind all the matériel they captured in the British camps. Cornwallis brought the grenadiers from Philadelphia on the run when he heard of the American attack, and they arrived just in time to see the British recapture their camps and the village. He and the grenadiers chased the Americans for nine miles to Chestnut Hill before he broke off the pursuit because the rebels got too great of a head start. Most of the tired and frazzled Americans reached the safety of Pennypacker's Mills that evening, putting their long ordeal behind them. One Continental remembered, "I had previously undergone many fatigues, but never any that so much overdone me as this. Had it not been for the fear of being taken prisoner, I should have remained on the road all night. I had marched in 24 hours 45 miles, and in that time fought four hours, during which we advanced so furiously thro' buckwheat fields, that it was almost an unspeakable fatigue."[88] Defeat and exhaustion notwithstanding, morale remained high. The soldiers knew that they had come tantalizingly close to beating the redcoats, and they were confident they would do better next time.[89]

The Battle of Germantown lasted only three hours, but there were plenty of casualties. Howe reported that he lost 534 men, of whom 70 were killed, including the competent Agnew. The British commander in chief's dog was among those captured, but Washington graciously returned it under a flag of truce two days after the battle. American totals were harder to ascertain, but they probably topped 1,000, including 152 killed, 521 wounded, and over 400 taken prisoner, mostly Matthews's Virginians rounded up in Germantown. Like Brandywine, the battle generated as much controversy as bloodshed. Many believed that the Americans had snatched defeat out of the jaws of victory, and there was no shortage of explanations for this unhappy outcome. Critics blamed the holdup at Chew House, the lack of ammunition, the failure of officers to keep control of their men, and Washington's complicated plan. The commander in chief himself attributed the setback to the fog and the resulting confusion, and he was not inclined to reproach any particular person for his role in the lost battle. Others in and out of the army, however, were not so understanding, and no sooner had the army reached Pennypacker's Mills than they began searching for scapegoats. There was some grumbling about Sullivan's and Greene's and Armstrong's roles, but most of the censure ultimately fell on Adam Stephen. The Virginia general's excessive drinking habits were well known, and intoxication seemed the only logical explanation for his counterproductive decisions that day. A November court-martial concluded that Stephen had neglected his responsibilities at both Germantown and Brandywine, and that he had been frequently inebriated while in command; it recommended his dismissal, and Washington agreed. Washington eventually appointed the Marquis de Lafayette to succeed Stephen as divisional commander, even though the young French officer's only real qualification for the job was his growing friendship with the commander in chief.[90]

For the British, the main topic of conversation after the battle revolved around the extent to which the army was taken by surprise. Howe then and later claimed that he received early warning of the American attack and took appropriate measures that prevented defeat. The commander in chief insisted that although the American assault drove back the light infantry, it barely dented the main British line. Others, however, believed that Washington came a lot closer to victory than Howe was willing to admit, and they credited the initial American success to the commander in chief's unwarranted complacency. Howe himself seemed to acknowledge some of this criticism, if only implicitly, by evacuating Germantown on 19 October and concentrating most of his troops in well-fortified Philadelphia.[91]

Germantown was a British victory in that Howe's army repulsed the violent American attack, but it did not contribute much toward suppressing the rebellion. Washington's army still existed, and Howe learned the hard way that it retained its sting despite all the punishment it had sustained. Indeed, the battle enlarged Howe's natural caution and erased the overconfidence he displayed throughout September. After Germantown, Howe never again presented Washington with such an opportunity to defeat his forces in detail. Unfortunately, these hard-earned lessons provided no clues toward winning the war. The redcoats and Germans fought superbly as usual, and they managed to inflict twice as many casualties as they suffered despite being taken by surprise. British and German officers maneuvered their commands with considerable skill. Musgrave and Abercrombie understood the need to delay the enemy advance long enough for the rest of the army to form up, and they made the Americans pay for every yard they gained. Agnew, Grey, and Grant took full advantage of American confusion and exhaustion to methodically clear the village in a well-timed counterattack. The problem, here as elsewhere in the campaign so far, was that such tactical triumphs did not seem to amount to much strategically.

The Battle of Germantown showed Washington and his army at their best and worst. The American commander in chief had little to lose and much to gain in attacking the British garrison. Doing so gave him the opportunity to finally seize the initiative and defeat the British in detail without exposing his army to possible destruction. Under these circumstances, Washington's actions were strategically astute. On the other hand, at the tactical level neither Washington nor his troops performed well. There were innumerable explanations for the American defeat that all contained kernels of truth, but they were all symptomatic of deeper problems that can be traced back to the commander in chief and his army. Washington's plan was surely complicated, but alternatives would not have guaranteed victory. Attacking in one or two columns instead of four would have mixed the Continentals with unreliable militia, and it would have required considerable time and luck to deploy all the men stacked up along a couple roads from march to attack formation without alerting the British. The fog undoubtedly hindered and confused the Americans, but it affected the British as well. The militia performed miserably, but their secondary role indicates that Washington did not expect much from them anyway in this kind of battle. Finally, Musgrave's brave stand at Chew House diverted Washington and the New Jersey brigade, but there were eleven other Continental brigades on the field that morning that could have taken up the slack. Despite his unquestioned courage, Washington lost control of his army before he even committed it to battle, and thereafter his role was limited to directing follow-up forces one way or another, ordering the attack on Chew House, and attempting to rally his retreating soldiers. Indeed, of the twelve Continental brigades on the field that day, only eight saw heavy fighting and contributed to the American advance: Conway's, Nash's, Sullivan's two, Wayne's two, and Greene's two. Of the other four, McDougall's did not find its way around the British right flank, Stephen's two stumbled into Wayne's men, and the New Jersey brigade got bogged down with Washington at Chew House. If Washington had maintained a firmer grasp on the battlefield, he might have utilized these soldiers more effectively and relieved some of the burden on Sullivan's, Wayne's, Greene's, and Conway's forces. In addition, Washington and his generals displayed no tactical finesse at Germantown but instead relied solely on surprise, brute force, and momentum to overrun the British garrison. As for the hungry and ill-clothed soldiers themselves, they fought with considerable enthusiasm but without sufficient discipline and skill. It was not surprising that they panicked and ran when confronted with unexpected opposition from redcoats, the fog, Chew House, or friendly fire. One officer, reflecting on the battle years later, wrote that the defeat at Germantown "must be ascribed to deeper causes: to the yet imperfect discipline of the American army; to the broken spirit of the troops, who, from day to day and from month to month, had been subjected to the most trying and strength-wasting privations."[92]

FOUR

The Delaware River

WATERY BATTLEFIELD

For William Howe, success in America was almost invariably bittersweet. Each victory he attained on the battlefield seemed merely to generate new problems for him to resolve with the limited resources Germain put at his disposal. So, although occupying New York City in 1776 delivered one of the most strategically important American towns into British hands, it also eventually sucked Howe into three frustrating campaigns in New Jersey that brought him little but grief. Similarly, seizing Philadelphia created and perpetuated a new host of strategic and logistical dilemmas for the British commander in chief. Washington's dogged army continued to exist despite the flogging Howe administered to it at Brandywine and elsewhere. There was nothing new about that, but now Howe also had to garrison, feed, and protect the former American capital, which turned out to be more complicated than anyone expected. The difficulty was that even though the British now possessed the city, the Americans still controlled its Delaware River lifeline. Unless Howe cleared the rebels from the Delaware before winter iced it over so the Royal Navy could bring food, supplies, and equipment upriver, he could not support his army and Philadelphia's inhabitants. Opening the Delaware ultimately consumed two valuable months, and doing so siphoned off substantial British resources into miserable siege operations along the river's boggy banks that diverted Howe from his primary task of suppressing the rebellion.

To protect Philadelphia from a British naval attack up the Delaware, the Americans had constructed an elaborate and ingenious interconnected defense system. At its heart were five rows of underwater obstacles called chevaux-de-frise put in place by Joseph Marsh at the behest of the Pennsylvania Navy Board. A cheval-de-frise was a large, 30-foot-long wooden bin towed to a predetermined position and then sunk and

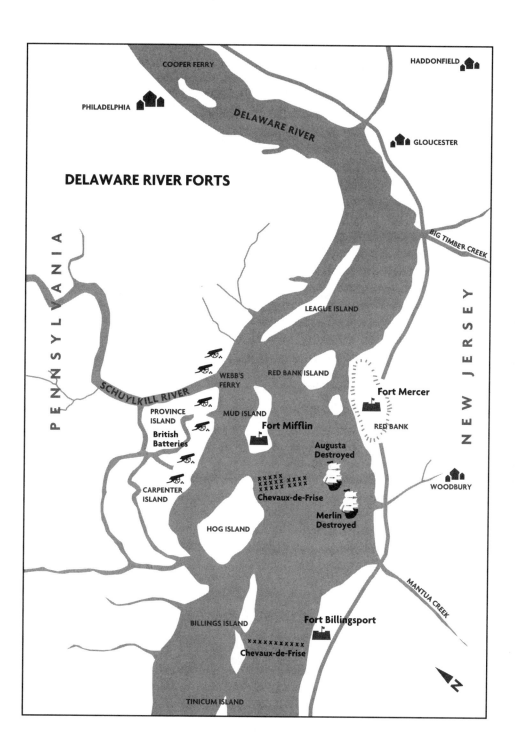

DELAWARE RIVER FORTS

COOPER FERRY

PHILADELPHIA

HADDONFIELD

DELAWARE RIVER

GLOUCESTER

PENNSYLVANIA

BIG TIMBER CREEK

LEAGUE ISLAND

NEW JERSEY

SCHUYLKILL RIVER

WEBB'S FERRY

RED BANK ISLAND

Fort Mercer

PROVINCE ISLAND

MUD ISLAND

RED BANK

British Batteries

Fort Mifflin

Augusta Destroyed

CARPENTER ISLAND

xxxxx xxxx
xxxxx xxxx
xxxx xxxx

Chevaux-de-Frise

WOODBURY

Merlin Destroyed

HOG ISLAND

MANTUA CREEK

BILLINGS ISLAND

Fort Billingsport

xxxxxxxxxxxx

Chevaux-de-Frise

TINICUM ISLAND

N

held in place on the river bottom by thirty tons of stones. Attached at an angle to each one were a half dozen long, iron-tipped wooden poles hidden at least six feet below the waterline and designed to rip the hulls off unwary approaching British warships. The Americans deployed them in rough checkerboard patterns across the main Delaware River channels, and simply locating them in the muddy water was akin to rummaging through a bag of broken glass in the dark. British vessels could not reach Philadelphia unless they cleared big enough gaps to allow them to proceed upriver, a time-consuming and dangerous process under the best circumstances.[1]

To prevent the British from taking the necessary time to eliminate these lethal underwater obstacles, the Americans also built or refurbished three forts near the five rows of chevaux-de-frise: Fort Mifflin on Mud Island, Fort Mercer at nearby Red Bank on the New Jersey shore, and Billingsport about four miles downriver. Construction began in earnest in April 1777 amid rumors that Philadelphia was next on Howe's list of targets, but there was no systematized plan. In early summer Major General Philippe Tronson du Coudray—the haughty French volunteer who prompted Knox, Greene, and Sullivan to submit their resignations when they heard false rumors that Congress planned to make him Washington's new artillery chief—inspected the works, and he was not impressed. Du Coudray recommended that the Americans concentrate their resources on Billingsport because the Delaware was narrowest there and would provide artillerymen with their best opportunity to destroy British warships attempting to squeeze through the tight channel. The French general estimated that it would require five months, thirty to forty cannons, and a garrison of 2,000 men to bring Billingsport up to snuff. The Pennsylvania Executive Council signed off on du Coudray's scheme despite misgivings about funding such an ambitious project, but its members did not want to delay the work any longer than necessary. Washington also gave his blessing at first, but in early August some of his subordinates—specifically, Colonel Joseph Reed, Knox, and Wayne—surveyed the defenses and reported back to their commander in chief that they did not like what they saw. On 10 August, Washington informed Hancock that he wanted to focus the limited American resources on Fort Mifflin, not Billingsport. Washington believed that Billingsport was vulnerable to a British land assault, and once it fell, American naval vessels could no longer remain in position there. On the other hand, warships could anchor off Fort Mifflin as long as nearby Fort Mercer stayed in American hands, and the swamps surrounding Red Bank made a British overland approach unlikely. In addition, Fort Mifflin already had three rows of chevaux-de-frise in place compared with only one at Billingsport. Washington understood that the Delaware was narrowest at Billingsport, but innumerable sandbars around Fort Mifflin limited the number of warships the British could bring to bear there, too. Finally, Washington opposed using Billingsport even as a post from which to delay any British march on Philadelphia. He was confident that he could deploy his troops in front of the American capital well ahead of the British, and he saw no reason to sacrifice its garrison to buy unneeded time. He believed that Fort Mifflin was more important than Billingsport, and Congress agreed. From that point on, New Jersey militiamen worked almost exclusively on Forts Mifflin and Mercer.[2]

Finally, the Americans also constructed and gathered a fleet of both Continental and Pennsylvania state warships to protect the approaches to Philadelphia. Under normal circumstances, this raggedy collection of fireships, floating batteries, armed brigs, sloops, schooners, more than a dozen galleys, and frigates would have been no match for Admiral Howe's powerful armada, but in the constricted Delaware River, speed and maneuverability counted for as much as size and firepower. The combination of hidden chevaux-de-frise, tricky fast-moving currents, sandbars, cannon-studded fortifications, and small pesky warships firing from hidden inlets and creeks could stymie even men-of-war, as the British would soon discover. Congress appointed Pennsylvania state naval officer Commodore John Hazelwood to command this conglomeration of vessels. The English-born Hazelwood had been a merchant sea captain before the war, and he was thoroughly familiar with the river. Many lauded his bravery and good nature, but his inability to get along with fellow officers and to motivate and maintain discipline over his often tired and unenthusiastic crews would strain interservice relations before the fighting was over. In mid-September, however, Hazelwood believed that his men were rested and ready for action.[3]

Once the British army landed at Head of Elk in late August, Washington had no plans to bolster the Delaware River defenses with his Continentals. His strategy, as usual, was to use militia to man easily defended fixed positions like Fort Mifflin while his Continentals slugged it out with the redcoats and Germans in the open when necessary. Besides, Washington believed that the decisive battles would occur somewhere west of the Schuylkill, so diverting Continentals to the Delaware would be a waste of resources. However, after Howe outmaneuvered him along the Schuylkill's upper fords and marched unopposed to Philadelphia, Washington reevaluated his position. He had not considered the possibility that the British might seize the city before they opened up the Delaware. If the Americans could maintain their grip on the river defenses long enough, they might either starve the British army into surrender or compel it to evacuate the city. Philadelphia, in short, could become a trap. Referring to Howe, Washington wrote, "I am not yet without hope, that the acquisition of Philadelphia may, instead of his good fortune, prove his ruin."[4] Washington understood that it would take more than untrained militia to hold the Delaware against the formidable combined land and sea forces the Howe brothers could deploy. Clearly, he would have to commit his precious Continentals to stiffen the river defenses, even though this violated one of his basic strategic tenets by forcing him to disperse his limited manpower. Washington thought it was worth the risk, and on 23 September he dispatched Lieutenant Colonel Samuel Smith and 200 Continentals—all he felt he could spare after the army's recent exertions—to Fort Mifflin. He urged Hazelwood to put some of his sailors in the fort, or to even flood the place if necessary to keep it out of British hands until Smith arrived. With this relatively minimal initial commitment, Washington threw down the gauntlet before Howe, and by the time the fighting was over, thousands of redcoats, Germans, Continentals, militiamen, and sailors were sucked into combat along the Delaware.[5]

On the morning of 27 September, the day after Cornwallis marched into Philadelphia and returned the city to its old allegiance, British soldiers had just finished placing two artillery batteries on the Delaware River's west bank when American warships appeared downriver. They included the thirty-four-gun *Delaware*, the eighteen-gun *Montgomery*, a sloop, and four galleys, sent upriver by Hazelwood to remind the British of American power and to secure all the shipping they could seize. The *Delaware* moved in, and the lower British battery opened fire on it at less than 400 yards. The Americans replied in kind, but only the *Delaware* was willing to close with the enemy. Unfortunately, this proved its undoing; the crewmen were so intent on engaging the British battery that they neglected the sails, and the ship ran hard aground on the falling tide. The remaining vessels lost no time in scurrying downriver, and they all made it except for one galley that crashed onto the New Jersey shore. Back upriver, the British ordered the *Delaware*'s 150-man crew to disembark—one of whom had been killed and a half dozen wounded in the half-hour battle—and grenadiers, marines, and carpenters boarded the ship, put out the small fires, and eventually refloated it, manned it, and made it the newest member of the Royal Navy. Thus, without the loss of a man, the British captured the biggest American warship on the Delaware River.[6]

Howe was of course pleased with this sudden stroke of good fortune, but he understood that seizing one rebel warship, however big, did not immediately and drastically alter the strategic situation. The American grip on Philadelphia's Delaware River windpipe remained in place, and until Howe figured out a way to loosen it, the British had to bring supplies to the former rebel capital overland from Chester, a dangerous and time-consuming task that barely met the city's and army's needs. Under these circumstances, Howe wanted to move fast, and he immediately got to work. On 29 September, only three days after Philadelphia's fall, Howe dispatched Lieutenant Colonel Thomas Stirling and two regiments to occupy Billingsport. The next day Stirling crossed the Schuylkill at Middle Ferry and trudged downriver to Chester—it was Stirling's departure that prompted Washington to attack Germantown—where the British navy ferried his troops across the Delaware on 2 October. Stirling and his redcoats marched into Billingsport unopposed in the early afternoon, but not until the post's small militia garrison spiked the cannons, set the barracks and bake house on fire, removed all the stores, and evacuated the place by water. The rear guard exchanged fire with the oncoming British across a cornfield before they boarded a skiff and headed upriver for Burlington via Red Bank. Stirling left a small force at Billingsport and crossed back over the Delaware, but a few days later Howe pulled even those troops out. The garrison may have escaped, but, with as little loss as their artillery comrades-in-arms had sustained a week ago along the Delaware River bank—that is, none at all—the British had knocked a chunk out of the American defense network, and the Royal Navy immediately got busy clearing out the first, or lower, row of chevaux-de-frise.[7]

Lieutenant Colonel Samuel Smith and his 200 Continentals arrived safely at Fort Mifflin on the evening of 26 September after a march to and across the Delaware north of Philadelphia, the same day Cornwallis triumphantly entered the American capital. The twenty-five-year-old Princeton graduate and prewar Maryland merchant had no experience with fortifications, but he did not like the look of things at all. He later described the rickety post as "a fort walled with freestone on the side opposite the Jersey shore and the approach by the river; stockaded with pine logs, 15 inches thick, opposite Province Island; and the approach from above flanked by three wooden blockhouses, mounting eight pound French guns in their upper stories. There was also an open platform, on which were mounted 18 pounders, pointing down the river, with one 32 pounder, being the only piece that pointed on Province island."[8] Smith found only sixty untrained Philadelphia militiamen garrisoning the works, and they were not inclined to obey anyone's orders, least of all his. The sailors manning the warships anchored nearby were equally uncooperative and surly, in part because many of their often fainthearted wives were behind enemy lines in Philadelphia, and in fact over the next few days they deserted to the British in large numbers, including two galley crews who took both their officers and vessels with them. Those that remained were discontented and close to panic, and Pennsylvania authorities ordered Billingsport held until the last minute because they feared its fall might completely demoralize the fleet. Moreover, there were not enough provisions and ammunition to go around. Hazelwood himself brimmed with a self-confidence Smith found hard to fathom, considering the circumstances. Finally, Smith worried that the British might seize nearby undefended Red Bank, which would enable the enemy to assail his small garrison from all sides, so he asked Washington for another 300 to 400 Continentals to man all-but-unoccupied Fort Mercer.[9]

Back at Pennypacker's Mill, Washington was dismayed by events along the Delaware. Billingsport's fall in and of itself did not greatly concern him because he did not see much value in the fort anyway, but he was unhappy with the impact that British occupation had on the timid militiamen and sailors. Washington agreed that Fort Mifflin's survival depended on Fort Mercer, and it seemed clear that only Continentals could provide a garrison capable of resisting any British attack. Fortunately, the means were now at hand to fill the demand. Brigadier General James Varnum was bringing his Continental brigade down from the Hudson Highlands, so Washington ordered him to detach two Rhode Island regiments—about 400 men—under Colonel Christopher Greene to man Fort Mercer. With Continentals in both Fort Mifflin and Fort Mercer, Washington hoped that the American stranglehold on the Delaware River would remain secure. To complete Philadelphia's isolation, the commander in chief directed Brigadier General James Potter to take 600 of his Pennsylvania militia across the Schuylkill to intercept those British convoys bringing provisions and supplies to the former American capital from Chester. Washington warned Potter against being taken by surprise, and he also suggested that he cooperate with whatever Delaware militia came forth to attack British-held Wilmington if possible. Whether the Pennsylvania militia was up to the task was an open question, but Washington had faith in the Irish-born Potter, whose humility was so refreshing in an officer corps replete with prima donnas. Either way, Washington was at least sure that his actions would keep Howe tied down along the Delaware for the rest of the campaigning season, which, while certainly not all he could have wished for, fit in nicely with his strategy of attrition.[10]

While Washington refined his strategy, the Royal Navy was hard at work near Billingsport trying to find a way through the first row of twenty-four chevaux-de-frise. No one had any experience with the underwater behemoths, and removing them was more difficult than it initially appeared. Officers dispatched their boats to look for and identify the barriers, and then the crews attached hawsers—long, thick ropes— between them and the warship and tried to pull them aside. Each cheval-de-frise weighed more than thirty tons, so progress was excruciatingly slow and full of mishaps. Hawsers snapped, anchors detached, and at one point HMS *Vigilant* even got caught on one of the obstacles. All this was frustrating enough, but almost every day Hazelwood took his flotilla downstream off Hog Island to lob shells at the British fleet, which was akin to shooting at a soldier threading his way through a minefield. Worse yet, the British warships could not reach their annoying American counterparts until they got through the chevaux-de-frise. By 10 October, the British managed to open a small gap, but in response shortly after midnight on 13 October, Hazelwood brought most of his fleet downriver in a furious night attack on the British vessels stationed outside the chevaux-de-frise. Hazelwood was low on ammunition, and his galley crews were still so disgruntled that they refused to follow their commander through the chevaux-de-frise, but they were game enough to generate plenty of terror and anxiety among the enemy. Throughout the night, British and American warships exchanged fire in the light of the waxing moon, and cannons that the rebels surreptitiously placed in recently evacuated Billingsport added their weight to the confusing melee. To compound the horror, the Americans unleashed two sets of fire rafts that lit up the night as they glided over and past the chevaux-de-frise, but the British dealt with them by dispatching boats to tow them harmlessly ashore on nearby Tinicum Island. Surprisingly, neither side suffered much damage in the nocturnal battle, and Hazelwood headed upriver as dawn broke. The persistent British returned to their job, and by the next day they had created a seventeen-foot passage in the chevaux-de-frise just wide enough to squeeze through some warships to go upriver and attack Fort Mifflin and the flotilla defending it when Howe gave the word.[11]

While the Royal Navy labored to uncover a route through the chevaux-de-frise, the British army in Philadelphia continued its efforts to loosen the American grip on the Delaware River. Occupying Billingsport had been easy enough, but now the redcoats encountered increasing resistance from both the rebels and Mother Nature. In response, Howe prudently ordered Clinton to dispatch 4,500 reinforcements from New York City for the tough fight he increasingly suspected he would soon face. Howe wanted to erect artillery batteries along the Delaware's west bank from which to blast Fort Mifflin into submission, but establishing them turned out to be extraordinarily difficult. On 7 October, British troops planted cannons near the Schuylkill's mouth at Webb's Ferry, and in the following days they pushed southwestward onto low-lying Province and Carpenter Islands across from Fort Mifflin. Hauling heavy twelve- and eighteen-pounder cannons—meaning they fired twelve and eighteen-pound shot—at night across the Schuylkill on unstable flatboats and then along flooded, muddy paths full of deep holes in the cold, pouring rain made progress extremely slow. Worse yet, the artillery crews had to set up their pieces under often intense fire from rebel galleys and floating batteries, which occasionally became so heavy that they had to temporarily abandon their positions to take cover. One artilleryman wrote, "I was relieved this evening by Captain Standish from one of the most horrid commands that ever man was upon, the whole place under water, and the battery itself knee deep [underwater], almost torn to pieces by the rebel shot, and made so badly at first that several shot have gone through, and we have no safety in it but by lying down on the platform."[12] Finally, the beleaguered artillerymen, engineers, and accompanying infantry had to contend with rebel sorties. On the morning of 11 October, Hazelwood took three galleys and a floating battery against a new British battery on Carpenter Island within musket range of Fort Mifflin. After a two-hour bombardment, the redcoats appeared on the beach and capitulated. A sudden German counterattack stopped Hazelwood from removing all his prisoners from the island, but he did collect fifty-seven of them at the cost of two killed and five wounded. The mass surrender of so many redcoats scandalized the army, but it did not stop British efforts. On the morning of 15 October, shortly after the fog lifted, the British opened fire on Fort Mifflin from their newly emplaced batteries, but except for forcing the American flotilla to move a bit upriver, it did not seem to have much effect. Howe put in an appearance the next day and complained that things were taking too long, but the fact was that the British now had both their batteries in place and a hole in the chevaux-de-frise, so they could begin their final assault on the American Delaware River fortifications.[13]

Although the British bombardment initially inflicted little damage on Fort Mifflin and its garrison, the Americans had more than their share of problems as October wore on. Hazelwood's almost daily engagements with British batteries and warships consumed the flotilla's ammunition at a fearful rate, and on 15 October the commodore warned that he had only 100 rounds left. More arrived, but supply barely kept up with demand. Hazelwood also lacked sufficient sailors to man all his galleys, and eventually he persuaded Washington to order Greene to draft his Rhode Island Continentals with seagoing experience into the fleet. More vexing, however, were personality clashes among the high-ranking officers, especially between Smith and Hazelwood. Smith asked Hazelwood to station some of his galleys near Mud Island's undefended northern tip to thwart any British amphibious assault in that quarter, but Hazelwood did not want to commit his vessels to a task he believed would lead to their destruction. Instead, Hazelwood decided to keep his warships concentrated near Fort Mercer until the British began their attack, but Smith argued that by that time it would be too late to stop an enemy landing. This increasingly bitter dispute was merely symptomatic of a larger problem in the chain of command. No one was in overall charge of the Delaware River defenses except for far-off Washington; Smith, Greene, and Hazelwood each had his own bailiwick at, respectively, Fort Mifflin, Fort Mercer, and the fleet. Unfortunately, the commander in chief merely exacerbated the difficulties. Washington originally wanted to put the experienced Prussian colonel Henry d'Arendt in charge of Fort Mifflin, but d'Arendt fell ill, so Washington sent Smith instead. Now, however, d'Arendt had recovered, and Washington ordered him to supplant Smith, although the commander in chief reassured the touchy young Marylander that this was not meant to reflect badly on him. Not surprisingly, the hypersensitive Smith and the martinet d'Arendt did not see eye to eye. D'Arendt decided to open the Mud Island dikes and flood the island's undefended northern half to hinder any British landing there, but Smith angrily and prophetically warned him that this would eventually put most of the fortifications underwater, too. Washington repeatedly implored everyone to work together for the common good, but appointing an overall commander immediately would have been more effective. The commander in chief also warned his subordinates along the Delaware that his information pointed to an imminent British attack, and in response he dispatched two Virginia regiments to reinforce Fort Mifflin. He ordered Christopher Greene to send some of his Continentals over to Mud Island and to make up the resulting deficit at Fort Mercer from the local New Jersey militia. With these piecemeal changes in place, the Americans braced themselves for the onslaught everyone knew was coming sooner rather than later.[14]

THE AMERICANS HOLD THE LINE

Inclement weather, unfriendly geography, chevaux-de-frise, and rebel warships may have slowed British efforts to clear the Delaware River, but by mid-October, Howe was finally in a position to administer the coup de grâce to American defenses and open the supply lines to Philadelphia. The last couple weeks had been difficult, but Howe could take comfort in the knowledge that throughout the campaign rebel resistance had invariably crumbled in the face of determined British pressure, be it at Cooch's Bridge, Chad's Ford, or south of Germantown. Howe and his brother planned a two-pronged attack to break the back of the American Delaware defense network. A German detachment would march overland from Philadelphia and storm Fort Mercer while the Royal Navy overcame Fort Mifflin and the American flotilla. The Germans' mission was relatively straightforward, but the navy's task was more complicated. Fortunately, Admiral Howe had brought from New York City a secret weapon to help him carry out his assignment: HMS *Vigilant*, an old East India Company vessel that the navy had refurbished the previous winter. Not only did it carry fourteen hard-hitting twenty-four-pounder cannons, but it drew only $11\frac{1}{2}$ feet of water, considerably less than the huge men-of-war. Admiral Howe hoped to use this giant floating battery to demolish Fort Mifflin at point-blank range. To get it into position, Lord Howe planned to tow *Vigilant* through the shallow and confined channel between Hog Island and the Pennsylvania shore to Fort Mifflin's more vulnerable west side. With any luck, the warship would pulverize the fort enough so that 200 British grenadiers at Province Island could storm the place if the garrison did not see reason and surrender first. Finally, to divert American attention away from *Vigilant,* Howe intended to send five warships—all that could safely maneuver in the river simultaneously—through the eastern channel to the upper level of chevaux-de-frise to engage the rebel fleet, Fort Mifflin, and Fort Mercer.[15]

Several days of heavy winds delayed the big assault, but on 23 October the Royal Navy lurched into motion. Unhappily, *Vigilant* ran aground early that morning while trying to enter the channel between Hog and Province Islands, and it remained stuck all day long. The remaining warships under Captain John Reynolds were already under way, and they swung into action in the early evening. For six hours the British and Americans hammered away at each other, and the cannon fire was audible forty miles away. The Fort Mifflin garrison and the flotilla wisely ignored the unsinkable British batteries on Province and Carpenter Islands and instead concentrated their fire on the five enemy warships maneuvering outside the chevaux-de-frise. Reynolds ordered his command to press as close to the chevaux-de-frise as possible to get at the rebel warships. In the process, the twenty-gun sloop HMS *Merlin* ran hard aground around 5:30 P.M. on a hidden bar east of the main channel. A similar fate befell Reynold's own ship, the sixty-four-gun man-of-war HMS *Augusta,* an hour and a half later as it tried to pull *Merlin* loose with a cable. Efforts to refloat both vessels under intense American fire failed, but Reynolds was confident that the next day's incoming flood tide would free them. Unfortunately, dawn brought a strong northern wind that checked the tide, leaving both warships stuck in place. The Americans also put in an appearance, sending galleys and four fire rafts after the trapped vessels and other British warships struggling to save them. The British managed to tow the fire rafts harmlessly ashore, but they made little headway with *Merlin* and *Augusta.* In fact, *Augusta* caught fire, probably because some burning wads got among the ship's hammocks. Reynolds and his crew battled the flames without success, but when the fire reached the mast, Howe finally directed them to abandon ship. The admiral worried that *Augusta*'s inevitable explosion might engulf the nearby *Merlin,* so he ordered it evacuated as well, and he brought the remaining vessels downriver. *Augusta* blew up in the early afternoon in an explosion so loud that one person compared it to 100 cannons discharged simultaneously. Shortly afterward *Merlin* followed suit, showering the water with debris. British losses in men were minimal, but the Royal Navy was now short a sloop and a precious man-of-war. As for the Americans, Fort Mifflin took a pounding from British cannons ashore and afloat, but very few defenders were killed or wounded. Among the casualties, however, was d'Arendt, who received a painful wound in the groin and was shipped back to the New Jersey shore. The Americans expended a prodigious amount of ammunition over the course of the two-day battle, but this was a small price to pay for stopping the British naval attack cold.[16]

The day before *Merlin* and *Augusta* ran aground, the Germans outside Fort Mercer underwent their own disastrous trial by fire that cost them a good deal more in terms of blood spilled than the Royal Navy experienced later. Fort Mercer was not especially important in and of itself, but it dominated Fort Mifflin, the chevaux-de-frise, and the American flotilla. British intelligence mistakenly believed that the rebels had fortified only its seaward side, so theoretically simply marching a corps of infantry there would all but seal its fate. Perhaps it was this misinformation that prompted Howe to assign the task of seizing the fort to Colonel Karl Emit Kurt von Donop. One of Donop's comrades characterized him as an experienced officer who was invariably polite and considerate toward his men, but Howe distrusted him because of his panicky reaction to Washington's victory at Trenton the previous December. Donop was aware of Howe's feelings, and he had been looking for an opportunity to redeem himself in his commander in chief's eyes. He lobbied for the job, and Howe agreed to assign it to him. Howe gave Donop considerable latitude in fulfilling his orders, but he had Cornwallis make it clear to the German officer that there better be a good reason for any undue caution.[17]

Early in the morning of 21 October, three grenadier battalions, the Mirbach regiment, and two companies of jaegers—in all, 1,500 Germans at most—marched through Philadelphia's streets to the town's upper wharf and crossed the Delaware River on flatboats into New Jersey at Cooper's Ferry. Once the cannons were over, they trudged to Haddonfield and camped that night on the heights overlooking the town. The next morning the Germans continued their march southward against scattered rebel opposition, across two small bridges over Timber Creek, and in the early afternoon they approached Fort Mercer. Reconnoitering forward, Donop was surprised to discover twelve-foot-high breastworks and palisades with sharpened stakes around the fort. The Americans were still hard at work on these landward defenses, which indicated that they were not yet complete, but of course the fortifications were not supposed to be there at all. Despite this disconcerting evidence that seizing the fort might not be the walkover Howe expected, most of the German officers retained a self-confidence born of uninterrupted battlefield victories over the past two months. Not everyone was so optimistic; one tough old artillery captain remarked, "He who has seen forts or fortified places captured with sword in hand will not regard this affair as a small matter, if the garrison puts up a fight and has a resolute commandant."[18] The Americans seemed unaware of the Germans' presence, but Donop chose not to attack immediately. Instead, he brought up his cannons, had his men gather fascines—sticks of wood bound together to fill trenches—and deployed his troops. At 4:30 P.M. Donop summoned the Americans to surrender, and upon their refusal he ordered his cannons to open fire. After a fifteen-minute preliminary bombardment, Donop directed his troops forward at around 5:00 P.M.[19]

Forty-year-old Colonel Christopher Greene was just the type of staunch commander the old German artillery captain warned of. A third cousin of Nathanael Greene, he had served under Benedict Arnold during the Canadian campaign and was captured at Quebec and later exchanged. Greene was a tough, resourceful officer unlikely to flinch in the face of adversity. He feared a siege more than anything else, so he was relieved when Donop's surrender demand indicated that the Germans planned to launch an immediate attack. Greene and his men had been hard at work on Fort Mercer's defenses ever since they arrived, ably assisted by the courageous, diligent, and mild-mannered French engineer Captain Thomas-Antoine du Plessis. The problem was that the walled structure was designed to hold up to 3,000 troops, and Greene had barely 600 men. Rather than stretch and weaken his garrison to protect the whole position, Greene accepted du Plessis's advice and abandoned the northern part of the fort. He also constructed a double row of abatis—fallen trees with their branches facing outward—a deep ditch, and a high parapet surrounding most of the occupied part of the post. Fort Mercer was a much tougher nut to crack than Donop and his Germans, not to mention Howe, expected.[20]

Donop planned to assault Fort Mercer from three sides with his three grenadier battalions. He ordered 100 men from each battalion to march 200 paces in front of each column with fascines to fill the trenches so the rest of the soldiers could quickly cross. It was a simple enough scheme based on the assumption that the rebels would not put up much of a fight. The Germans advanced in two columns to the sound of fifes and drums, supported by an artillery battery firing 200 yards from the American positions. The rebels opened fire from the fort and from some galleys offshore with cannons and muskets before the Germans even emerged from the woods, knocking dozens of Donop's soldiers down behind and along the tree line. With admirable bravery, the Germans kept moving forward. To the north, they charged through and over the gate and into the fort itself, cheering lustily. Unfortunately, they did not realize that they had entered the abandoned part of the post, and once inside, they came under galling fire from rebels behind the breastwork that delineated the occupied part of the place. Caught in a position akin to fish in a rain barrel, the Germans—those who had not been shot, at any rate—scrambled out. To the south, most of the charging Germans did not even make it across the abatis, and those that did were stopped cold at the ditch by heavy fire. Donop himself went down early at the ditch, mortally wounded by a shell that shattered both his legs. After forty minutes of this carnage, the Germans fell back.[21]

Once out of range, German officers caught their breath and pondered their options. Although they did not yet know their exact losses, they were obviously heavy. Indeed, nearly 400 had fallen, or close to one-third of those who had crossed the Delaware the day before. Clearly, they could not mount another assault or stay where they were, so retreat was the only alternative. Fortunately, the alert Ludwig von Wurmb—one of the few officers to take warnings of the surprise American assault at Germantown seriously a few weeks earlier—had the presence of mind to rush a battalion to secure the Timber Creek bridges to keep their escape hatch open. The Germans withdrew throughout that cold night along the confusing narrow roads that wound ominously through the dark woods. To compound their misery, there were very few wagons because no one had anticipated a need for them, so the wounded had to either walk or be carried by their tired comrades. The next day they met up with two British regiments rushed over to cover their retreat, and they were back in Philadelphia by evening. As for the Americans, they had suffered a scant 31 casualties in one of their most one-sided victories of the war. Some of the Fort Mercer garrison came out to strip the German dead and wounded until their officers put a stop to it. One party discovered Donop and two servants concealed behind a pine tree, and they brought the colonel inside the post, where he presently died far from home for a cause not his own.[22]

The repulses at Forts Mifflin and Mercer were the first sustained British setbacks of the campaign. Unlike the checks at the Plowed Hill at Brandywine or north of Germantown, here Howe could not rectify the situation with a quick, hard counterattack by troops already on hand. Instead, opening the Delaware would require another major effort with substantial preparatory time. The reasons for the defeats were interrelated and fairly easy to discern. British ignorance of the Delaware River's intricacies certainly played a major role. If the British had had a good understanding of the river, *Vigilant, Merlin,* and *Augusta* might not have run aground. The Americans, on the other hand, took advantage of geography to wrap their defenses around the opportunities the Delaware presented. In addition, British intelligence left much to be desired, especially in comparison to its accomplishments in southeastern Pennsylvania the month before. In particular, the British did not realize the extent of Fort Mercer's fortifications until Donop sent his Germans forward into chaos. Finally, and perhaps most important, their overconfidence caught up with them. British and German officers from Howe on down again underestimated American resiliency, and they paid the price. Redcoats and Germans could usually beat Americans in open battle, but assailing stalwart Continentals in fortifications was not likely to produce similar results. For the British it was back to the drawing board.

UNEASY INTERVAL

On 17 October, John Burgoyne formally surrendered his approximately 5,000 remaining redcoat, German, provincial, American Indian, and Canadian soldiers to Horatio Gates's army at Saratoga in upstate New York. Saratoga was perhaps the greatest and most important American victory in the war, and it yielded both immediate and long-term benefits. Defeating Burgoyne raised American morale, snapped off a thick, sharp spike in Germain's multipronged offensive to crush the rebellion, eliminated an entire British army in one fell swoop, secured New York from invasion from Canada, and eventually helped persuade France to sign an alliance with the United States against Britain. Washington received the good news at Worcester, Pennsylvania, on 18 October, four days after Burgoyne and Gates began discussing terms, and he ordered his entire army paraded in the afternoon in a celebration that included homilies by chaplains, the discharge of cannons, and three loud huzzahs to underscore everyone's relief and joy. The commander in chief was as happy as the next American patriot by this report in part because it reduced the long list of cares and concerns that weighed him down. There was more to it than that, however; Saratoga gave him the opportunity to tap into Gates's army for reinforcements to use against Howe in

Pennsylvania. As it was, Washington's own army was numerically in fairly good shape just then, despite its recent losses at Germantown. He had 8,310 Continentals and 2,717 militia with him, as well as another 650 Continentals at Forts Mifflin and Mercer and 500 Pennsylvania militiamen under Potter on the west side of the Schuylkill. This was more than the 10,000 or so troops Washington believed Howe possessed. In the week following Saratoga, more good news flowed into Washington's camp. The biggest, of course, was the British repulse at Forts Mifflin and Mercer, but Howe seemed to be retracting his claws just about everywhere because he evacuated both Wilmington and Germantown. For the first time since the previous June, the Americans appeared to be winning the war.[23]

Washington was nothing if not a military realist, and he knew full well that there were still plenty of problems to overcome before his army ejected Howe from Philadelphia and secured American independence. For one thing, the army itself was in its usual state of flux. Forman's New Jersey militiamen left in early October, and the terms of many of the Pennsylvania militia were expiring as well. By way of compensation, some Virginia militia were arriving, but sooner or later they, too, would return home. Washington was by now accustomed to such comings and goings, but that did not make managing these men any easier. He was concerned in particular with the inability of the Pennsylvania government to muster anything near the number of militiamen available for service. In fact, as far as Washington was concerned, Pennsylvania simply was not pulling its weight, which was especially galling because plenty of Virginia, Maryland, North Carolina, Delaware, New Jersey, and New England boys had sacrificed their lives at Brandywine and elsewhere to keep the British out of the state. Washington was aware that Pennsylvania had some unique problems that hindered its war effort—its weak government, its large, powerful loyalist population, its pacifist Quakers, and a capital in British hands—but it was hard to fight in a state whose support for the cause often seemed lukewarm. There were other difficulties as well that fall. The army's logistical wretchedness continued, and the soldiers were frequently short of arms, clothing, shoes, stockings, horses, and wagons. Such supply woes had already hindered military operations in Pennsylvania, and winter would only exacerbate them. To compound the problem, the army was running out of money, and on 10 October Washington warned Congress that his military chest was just about bare. Finally, Washington had to deal with rising and unrealistic expectations in Saratoga's wake.

People in and out of Congress believed that with reinforcements on hand from the Hudson Highlands, Washington should be able to engage and beat Howe. They did not understand that opportunities for fighting the British army on anything approaching even terms were few and far between after Germantown. Howe appeared to have learned his lesson, and he kept the bulk of his army buttoned up in and around well-fortified Philadelphia while he pondered ways to open up the Delaware River.[24]

Washington was also thinking about the Delaware, though he was seeking the means to keep the big river closed to British shipping. Indeed, the Delaware had now become the campaign's focal point, and it was sucking in growing numbers of British and American troops down to its soggy banks. On 29 October, Washington called a council of general officers to contemplate his army's options. The generals rejected any attack on strongly fortified Philadelphia as suicidal, and they recommended that Washington do what was necessary to maintain Forts Mercer and Mifflin until winter froze the river. This was commonsensical enough, but, as with so much in life, more easily said than done. To complicate things, Washington had learned that the British were now bringing supplies to Philadelphia via a narrow channel they had discovered around Tinicum Island to Carpenter Island, thus bypassing the American forts, fleet, and chevaux-de-frise. This alleviated their supply problems, but time was still working against them. Ice was already crystallizing on the river, and intelligence reports indicated that Philadelphia remained short of even basic necessities. However, unless the Americans could find some way to tighten the blockade on their former capital, the British would not starve as quickly as they would otherwise. Potter and his Pennsylvania militia were already west of the Schuylkill attempting without much success to intercept British overland convoys, but nevertheless Washington expanded their mission to include harassing the redcoats on their Carpenter Island terminus in an effort to interrupt their new river supply route. To help the Pennsylvanians, the commander in chief sent Captain Henry Lee and his cavalry, and he asked Hazelwood to dispatch some of his galleys to stop the British naval convoys. Neither effort was especially successful; Hazelwood balked at jeopardizing his precious galleys, and Potter's militia were too gun-shy to come to grips with the redcoats there, although they managed to keep the dikes open enough to flood Province and Carpenter Islands. Potter suggested that Washington bring his Continentals over to storm Carpenter Island and put an end to British supply efforts once and for all, but the commander in chief was reluctant to commit his army west of the Schuylkill because that would expose it to destruction and the state to further invasion. Instead, he opted to move his troops closer to Philadelphia in an unsuccessful attempt to divert Howe's attention away from the Delaware, and he increased efforts to deny the British access to the resources offered by the countryside surrounding Philadelphia. Hopefully these actions, if sustained, would isolate the British army in Philadelphia and force Howe to either surrender or evacuate the city.[25]

Washington understood that the heart of the American blockade along the Delaware remained the triad of forts, chevaux-de-frise, and warships that made it impossible for the British to bring large amounts of supplies to Philadelphia. Unhappily, maintaining the American grip on the Delaware required the commander in chief to reconcile, mediate, and arbitrate various continuing personality disputes. D'Ardent had been wounded in the big British attack on 23 October, and he recommended that Washington make Lieutenant Colonel John Green of the Sixth Virginia Regiment Fort Mifflin's new commander. Green had been in grade longer than Lieutenant Colonel Smith, but Washington opted to put the Marylander back in charge because he had been at the post since September and presumably was more familiar with its strengths and weaknesses. Green accepted Washington's decision with a selflessness rare along the Delaware, but this did not end the personnel problems. The talented, austere, and amiable Frenchman Major François Louis Teissèdre de Fleury was Fort Mifflin's engineer, and because of his expertise Washington wanted Smith to give him considerable leeway in organizing and building fortifications, but Smith did not like this much. Smith's relationship with Fleury was downright cozy compared with his continuing row with Hazelwood, which was rapidly metamorphosing into his own personal jihad. Despite their recent success in repelling the British fleet, the two continued to bicker over the flotilla's placement, as had d'Arendt and Hazelwood before the former's injury. Smith wanted Hazelwood to station galleys near Fort Mifflin to thwart a surprise British amphibious landing, but Hazelwood refused because heavy winds and swell there threatened to swamp his ships. An exasperated Smith wrote to Washington, "I am clearly of the opinion that if we had a commodore who would do his duty, it would be impossible for the enemy ever to get possession of this fort."[26] Washington pleaded for more interservice cooperation, and he attributed a good part of the squabble to misunderstandings between the two men, especially because Hazelwood insisted that he would help Smith in any way possible, weather permitting.[27]

Smith was not the only American gunning for Hazelwood; so were many of his subordinates. On 19 October, before the big British attack, Hazelwood called a meeting with his captains on board a galley, but there was not enough room there, so he decided to move it to a floating battery instead. Continental Captain Isaiah Robinson declared that there was no reason for him or his officers to attend, and they returned to their warship. Hazelwood did not understand Robinson's hostility. The commodore was a genial man, but some believed he was too good-natured for his command, and that he did not exert enough discipline over his fickle galley crews. In short, Robinson and his Continental officers simply lacked confidence in and respect for their chief. Washington, as usual, urged everyone to get along, but he was disturbed by such accusations. Fortunately for Hazelwood, he retained the support of the Pennsylvania Navy Board, which was convinced that too many Continental officers did not understand the limitations Hazelwood labored under but instead viewed the flotilla as some magic wand that could perform wonders.[28]

The dissension did not end there. Washington asked New Jersey for 2,000 militiamen to supplement the Delaware River defenses, but nowhere near that many turned out. A lack of patriotism in the heavily Quaker southern half of the state was part of the problem, but there was more to it than that. State Brigadier Generals David Forman and Silas Newcomb were responsible for organizing and commanding the militia, but they did not get along. Forman ranked Newcomb, but Newcomb did not see it that way. Newcomb refused to obey Forman's orders on all matters big and small, and he claimed that he was not even answerable to the New Jersey Council of Safety. Washington had confidence in Forman, who had suppressed a loyalist uprising at Monmouth the previous November, and he believed quite rightly that Newcomb was a fussy, lazy, and incompetent man who could not instill discipline among the few militia who showed up. In early November, an exasperated Forman finally mounted his horse and rode to Princeton to complain to the assembly, council, and governor. There some assemblymen accused him of improper actions in recent elections, which so infuriated him that he resigned his commission. As for Newcomb, Governor William Livingston had as bad an opinion of his abilities as everyone else, and he successfully pressured the general to resign in early December. But by that time the damage had been done, and New Jersey's militia, so helpful the previous winter around New York City, contributed little to the defense of Forts Mercer and Mifflin.[29]

Washington's troubles with his truculent subordinates extended beyond the Delaware River. Burgoyne's surrender and Henry Clinton's decision to withdraw his troops back down the Hudson after an eleven-day foray up the river in early October convinced the American commander in chief that only Howe's Philadelphia-based army posed much of a threat to the Revolution right now, so he wanted to concentrate as many troops against it as possible. On 30 October, he sent his aide Lieutenant Colonel Alexander Hamilton to Albany to hurry the transfer of troops from Gates's now-dormant army south to Pennsylvania. Unhappily, extracting the soldiers proved exceedingly difficult. Gates initially insisted on keeping two large Continental brigades because he feared that Clinton might again ascend the Hudson. Hamilton persuaded him to give up one, but that was simple compared with getting all the troops downriver. Transportation snafus, sickness, shortages of almost everything, and a mutiny by two brigades that refused to march until they received assurances about back pay slowed progress. Finally, popular but incompetent Hudson Highlands commander Major General Israel Putnam wanted to hold on to some of these Continentals, and he proved so obstinate and evasive that Hamilton wrote his boss, "I owe it to the service to say that every part of this gentleman's [Putnam's] conduct is marked with blunders and negligence, and gives general disgust."[30] Washington had to send Putnam repeated orders to release most of his Continentals, and these events went a long way toward explaining his decision to ease Putnam out of his command the next spring. In the end somewhat fewer than 5,000 Continentals eventually joined the main American army at Whitemarsh, but Washington afterward lamented that they arrived too late to save Fort Mifflin.[31]

In late October, Washington decided that the detrimental squabbling along the Delaware had gone on long enough, and it was time to take stronger steps to put an end to it. With this in mind, he dispatched Brigadier General James Varnum and the rest of his brigade to the Delaware, and he gave Varnum the authority to arbitrate disputes among the officers in the forts and on the warships. He also warned Varnum that his men were more important than the forts. Organizationally, Varnum's appointment made sense; half of his brigade was already there, so deploying the rest would strengthen the defenses without further mucking up the chain of command. In other aspects, however, Varnum's selection was surprising because he hardly seemed the type to pour oil over troubled waters. He was born in 1748 and had been expelled from Harvard before graduating first in his class from Rhode Island College in 1769. Varnum was in fact a stiff, impatient, and tactless man, and fellow Rhode Islander Nathanael Greene wrote, "He is as unfeeling as he is unpolite. That gentleman has the least gratitude of any person I ever saw that claims so much. Thank God the liberties of America are not in his power."[32] Despite these personality traits—or perhaps because of them—Varnum got results. He and his men arrived along the Delaware on 3 November, and within a week he pressured Hazelwood to agree to place his galleys north of Fort Mifflin, his floating batteries and armed boats next to the chevaux-de-frise, and Continental vessels—specifically, the brig *Andrew Doria* and the sloop *Fly*—near the Schuylkill. He also quickly dismissed the New Jersey militia as useless and did not include them in his calculations. Now that he had his quarrelling ducks more or less in a row, he could concentrate on stopping the British.[33]

Varnum did not intend to passively stand by while the British prepared for another go at his defenses, so on 5 November he dispatched Captain James Lee with a couple cannons to a hill two and a half miles downriver from Fort Mercer near Mantua Creek to take potshots at British warships near Billingsport. Over the course of several hours that afternoon, the impromptu battery and some of Hazelwood's galleys damaged both the man-of-war HMS *Isis* and the small frigate HMS *Pearl*. Indeed, the shattered *Isis* ran aground on Tinicum Island until freed by the rising tide, and Varnum believed that Lee could have sent the warship to the bottom of the river with *Augusta* and *Merlin* if Hazelwood's galleys had been more aggressive. Despite this success, Varnum and Hazelwood still had plenty of problems. Both men lacked ammunition, medicine, and clothing, and as a result there was an increasing number of sick soldiers and sailors as the weather turned colder. Hazelwood was also desperately short of seamen to man his galleys, not so much because of casualties but rather due to illness and more than 250 desertions. Varnum asked Washington for more of almost everything, and he even had his officers confiscate clothes from the local population to cover the backs of his almost naked soldiers. Most worrisome of all, however, was growing evidence throughout early November that the British were getting into position for another giant assault. American intelligence collected reports that redcoats with fascines were crossing Webb's Ferry in large numbers, that there were floating batteries at the Schuylkill's mouth, that the British had reoccupied Billingsport and set up cannons there, that transports with reinforcements from New York City were lying downriver, and that engineers were placing more artillery on Carpenter and Province Islands. Something big was about to happen—and soon. [34]

Unlike Washington, Howe did not have to deal much with bickering subordinates who hindered his military operations, but he had more than enough problems of his own. The British commander in chief faced a race with time, not just in the broad, grand strategic sense but also in a more immediate way that threatened to wreck his army sooner or later. Washington's hovering troops made procuring provisions from the surrounding countryside very difficult, and the Delaware River fortifications blocked ships from docking at Philadelphia's wharves. Howe was bringing supplies and equipment into Philadelphia every few days both overland from Chester and, increasingly, upriver at night on flatboats around Tinicum Island to Carpenter Island, but they were stopgap solutions. These routes avoided rebel defenses, but they were slow, dangerous, and risky, and neither route provided enough long-term succor for the British garrison and the city's inhabitants. Besides, winter's snow and ice would render both routes inoperative within a few weeks. Already the army and Philadelphia's residents were feeling the pinch. Flour, vegetables, and meat were in short supply, and fences were rapidly disappearing into fireplaces for warmth. Moreover, there was demoralization to go along with deprivation. On 3 November, the army learned of Burgoyne's surrender, and many feared that this victory would reinvigorate a rebel cause recently wilting in the heat of Howe's successful offensive. Even before official word of Burgoyne's fate arrived, one artillery officer wrote, "This is such a capital stroke against us that it is doubtful whether we [will] ever subdue them."[35] Be that as it may, it was fairly obvious to everyone that the British had to seize Forts Mifflin and Mercer, destroy the rebel fleet, and remove the chevaux-de-frise before the Delaware River iced over, or else they would face the unwelcome choice of starvation or ignoble retreat, either of which would probably cost Britain the war.[36]

Time being of the essence, Howe immediately began planning another assault on the Delaware River defenses. Ice was already forming over parts of the river at night, so he would have only one shot, and he wanted it done right this time. As he saw it, the key to success was more firepower to demolish Fort Mifflin stone by stone, board by board, and man by man if necessary. The navy had plenty of heavy thirty-two- and twenty-four-pounder cannons, so Howe had his brother ship them upriver on flatboats around Tinicum Island with the supplies and equipment. This took time, as did setting the guns in place. It rained throughout late October: a cold, sleety, windy rain that put already soggy Province and Carpenter Islands well under water and swept away the bridge at Middle Ferry. Redcoats waded to and installed their new batteries on platforms in icy mud and waist-deep water, often under heavy American fire. Even the gun platforms were knee deep in water. Downriver, the fleet struggled to widen the gap through the lower chevaux-de-frise, but without much success, even when the warships shifted tactics and tried to overturn the underwater obstacles. Rebel fire from the galleys and the pesky Mantua Creek battery made a difficult job even worse, as did accumulating evidence that the chevaux-de-frise were more numerous than the British originally thought. Nevertheless, the work went on, albeit slowly and not without considerable grumbling on Howe's part. On 28 October, British troops reoccupied Billingsport to provide cover for the warships at the lower chevaux-de-frise, and upriver the redcoats gradually manhandled the big guns into position. By 10 November, they were ready, and that morning British batteries on Province and Carpenter Islands opened fire on Fort Mifflin with fourteen heavy cannons. The big attack had begun.[37]

IRRESISTIBLE FORCE AND THE UNMOVABLE OBJECT

Fort Mifflin had never been especially well laid out or aesthetically pleasing, but it rapidly lost whatever of either attribute it possessed as the big British guns brought their weight to bear. British fire knocked out the American cannons one by one, battered the barracks and officers' house on the fort's west side, and demolished the three dilapidated blockhouses. The only refuges for the soldiers were in a pen or behind a nearby stone wall next to a palisaded embankment with an intervening ditch. Troops scurried there from their labor details until a cane-wielding Fleury periodically rousted them out and back to work. But no matter where the soldiers sheltered themselves, they had to deal not only with enemy fire and the almost as formidable Fleury but also with rain and mud so deep that it muffled the sound of exploding British shells. Starting on 10 November, the British bombarded the fort around the clock, hindering nighttime efforts to repair the day's damage. Sentinels yelled, "Shot!" whenever they spotted shells following parabola-shaped arcs in the sky, and everyone ducked for cover. The unending racket and danger made it impossible for anyone to catch any more sleep than a catnap. All this was hard enough to tolerate, but the approximately 500-man garrison was also chronically short of clothing, shoes, stockings, and provisions. Years later, one Connecticut Continental remembered, "Here I endured hardships sufficient to kill half a dozen horses."[38]

As the hours stretched into days, the cumulative effects of the British bombardment took a physical and psychological toll on the garrison's officers and men. The beleaguered Smith had asked Washington to relieve him of his command even before the British batteries opened up in earnest, and hours of ducking and dodging shells amid the disintegrating, waterlogged fortifications did little to change his mind. As Smith increasingly saw things, if Washington's goal was to protect the chevaux-de-frise, the Americans could do that just as well from nearby Fort Mercer as from Fort Mifflin, so there was no need to expose the garrison to all this hardship. In the end, however, it was the British, not Washington, who removed him from the fort. On the morning of 11 November, a spent British shell injured Smith in the left hip and wrist as he finished scribbling a note to Varnum. He fell heavily to the ground, covered in bricks from a demolished chimney, and rolled out the door. A doctor bled him and sent him to the New Jersey shore for good, and command devolved on Lieutenant Colonel Giles Russell. Smith was not the only or highest-ranking jittery officer along the Delaware. At first Varnum did not believe that the British bombardment was making much of an impact, and in fact casualties had been very low so far, but a visit to the fort shortly after Smith went down convinced him otherwise. Varnum told Washington that he did not fear an amphibious assault, but rather that the constant shelling would simply break the garrison's will to resist. He did not think that the men could endure for two more days.[39]

Washington undoubtedly scowled upon reading Varnum's increasingly pessimistic reports. As far as he was concerned, Fort Mifflin was the linchpin of the Delaware River defenses, and holding on to it was the key to unraveling Howe's army. Even so, he was loath to second-guess the man on the scene, and he certainly did not want the large garrison and all its artillery to fall into British hands, so on 12 November he gave Varnum authority to abandon the fort if absolutely necessary. In the meantime, however, Varnum had had a change of heart. On the night of 12–13 November, he rotated a new garrison into Fort Mifflin under Major Simeon Thayer. Thayer was a tough veteran of both the

Great War for Empire and the Canadian campaign, and he had no intention of giving the place up. He believed that his troops could withstand any bombardment, so the British would have to storm the island to take it. Encouraged by Thayer's resolution, Varnum told Washington that they would try to persist. Unhappily for the Americans, within hours the British played a card that trumped everything Washington, Varnum, Thayer, or their soldiers possessed.[40]

By now frost covered the landscape every morning, and parts of the Delaware were iced over a half inch thick. Winter was clearly just around the corner, and with it starvation or humiliating retreat for the British army unless it punched its way through the American defenses. Time being of the essence, the Howe brothers eschewed all subtlety and instead called for the sudden, massive, and overwhelming application of firepower on Fort Mifflin from ship and shore. The British obviously could not sink the fort like an enemy warship, but they could certainly try to do the next best thing and simply blow the place and everyone in it to smithereens. The army's batteries on Province and Carpenter Islands had already opened up, but heavy winds kept the fleet from carrying out its part of the design for five long and frustrating days. Finally, the morning of 15 November dawned fair and moderate, thus presenting Admiral Howe the opportunity to join the fight. Howe planned to bring *Vigilant* and the sloop HMS *Fury* up through the Hog Island channel and anchor them to the right of the army's batteries, within point-blank range of Fort Mifflin. At the same time, he hoped to send another half dozen warships upriver. The men-of-war HMS *Somerset* and *Isis* would pound the fort from head-on and protect *Vigilant* from enemy galleys, while the smaller *Pearl, Roebuck,* and HMS *Liverpool* would move into shallower waters to engage American batteries on the New Jersey shore.[41]

The Royal Navy's offensive, however, nearly came undone before it even got under way. The night before the attack, *Roebuck*'s commander Captain Andrew Hamond—the same man whose information helped persuade the Howe brothers to invade Pennsylvania via the upper Chesapeake—rowed to *Somerset* to get final orders from his superior, Captain George Ourry. To Hamond's surprise, Ourry had no specific instructions, and in fact he wanted Hamond to provide him with a pilot to take his man-of-war up to the upper chevaux-de-frise. Sensing trouble, Hamond went to see Howe in his flagship. Howe was outraged that Ourry had not bothered over the past two weeks to take soundings and chart the tricky river, and he considered relieving him of his command.

Even under ordinary circumstances Royal Navy vessels frequently ran aground in the narrow river, and the hulks of *Augusta* and *Merlin* were constant reminders of what might happen the next day under fire if no one knew where to safely station his warship. Howe did not have the time to postpone the assault, and anyway his brother was depending on him, so he told Hamond to give Ourry one of his pilots to carry out the operation.[42]

Around midmorning British warships took the stage and opened fire to play their role in the drama unfolding along the Delaware River. The American flotilla and batteries responded in kind, and the air reverberated with the sound of discharging cannons and exploding cannonballs. Shortly thereafter *Vigilant* and *Fury* warped through the shallow Hog Island channel, stationed themselves less than 300 yards from Fort Mifflin, and fired away. All day long the British hurled shells at the fort, and *Vigilant* gradually worked its way to within speaking distance, enabling it to blow to pieces almost any man-made object from close range. Indeed, sharpshooters even sniped at individual Americans from the ship's rigging. Unfortunately for the British, the injuries were not all one-sided. *Vigilant, Isis,* and *Roebuck* all sustained heavy damage to their masts, yards, and rigging, and in fact 34 cannonballs went through *Isis* alone. On Province Island the Howe brothers—the admiral had come upriver via flatboat—Cornwallis, Grant, and other high-ranking officers watched the bombardment with interest. Most observers had a hard time believing that anyone could survive this holocaust of fire, and indeed the entire island seemed aflame. Howe had 400 redcoats from the Guards brigade ready to board flatboats and storm the island, and as the day wore on, some suggested that it might be time to unleash them to put an end to this business here and now. Howe disagreed, and he remarked that he was pretty sure those rebels still alive would abandon the post after dark.[43]

For most of the British officers and men on the scene, the bombardment of Fort Mifflin was an interesting if macabre spectacle, but for the approximately 500 Americans on Mud Island it was an experience nothing short of horrific. The soldiers' nerves were already stretched taut by unending shelling from British batteries on Province and Carpenter Islands, but *Vigilant*'s approach toward Fort Mifflin's undefended southwest corner posed an immediate and dire threat. Thayer recognized the danger right away, and he organized a detail to drag over and manhandle into position a thirty-two-pounder cannon to take on the looming British warship. The Americans fired fourteen rounds at *Vigilant* without success before British grapeshot swept the crew away. *Vigilant,* joined by *Fury,* systematically pounded the fort to pieces, and soon it was impossible for the garrison to even man most of its cannons. Worse yet, ammunition ran low, and Thayer ordered a blue distress flag hoisted to alert the American flotilla as to his plight. The British assumed the rebels were surrendering and ceased fire until Thayer had the American flag heaved back up, but a British shell immediately tore the flag raiser in two. In the meantime, Fleury had discovered some cartridges that enabled the Americans to resume fire with their few cannons still in action, but by early afternoon the ammunition was gone and all the guns were dismounted or destroyed.[44]

So far, Thayer's calmness and encouragement under worse than trying conditions went a long way toward bolstering his soldiers' spirits, but his brave example did not compensate for the garrison's declining ammunition supply. Thayer called a council of his officers in what was left of one of the blockhouses to ponder their options. They all agreed that unless they received more ammunition, the jig was just about up. As if to underscore their predicament, British cannonfire ripped into the blockhouse and knocked down a piece of timber that wounded Fleury and killed former Mantua Creek battery commander James Lee. Thayer understood that *Vigilant* was the big obstacle to any resupply efforts, and he wanted the American warships to destroy it. Hazelwood led a half dozen galleys over to Mud Island to engage the British warship, but once there his captains had second thoughts and refused to go on because of the danger. An outraged Varnum and Greene offered to man the galleys with their own troops, but Hazelwood turned them down. As far as he was concerned, going after *Vigilant* would be suicidal, and his galleys and crews had suffered enough damage and casualties that day.[45]

Varnum had been in command along the Delaware for only a couple weeks, but surely they were among the longest and most difficult of his life. As he saw things, Fort Mifflin was now untenable, and he had no desire to expose its garrison to further suffering or, worse yet, capture, so he decided to abandon the place that night. Besides, all was not lost; Varnum had started to come around to Smith's position that perhaps the post really was not all that necessary to protect the chevaux-de-frise as long as the Americans maintained control of Fort Mercer and the New Jersey shore. Or so he rationalized to Washington when he broke the news to the commander in chief. Fortunately for the Americans, the evacuation went relatively smoothly, despite the constant British shelling. Thayer and a rear guard burned everything that British fire had not already destroyed, but they left the heavy cannons behind, as well as a drunken German soldier. One Continental, viewing the scene around him, later wrote, "When the firing had in some measure subsided and I could look about me, I found the fort exhibited a picture of desolation. The whole area of the fort was as completely plowed as a field. The buildings of every kind [were] hanging in broken fragments, and the guns all dismounted, and how many of the garrison sent to the world of spirits, I knew not. If ever destruction was complete, it was here."[46] With that, he and his comrades dodged British fire, threaded their way through the mud over to the wharf in the flame-lit darkness, and boarded the three bateaux that took them across the river to safety.[47]

That night redcoats spotted American galleys on the move, but instead of coming after the British warships still on station, they docked at the Mud Island wharf. Large fires consumed what was left of the fort, and shortly thereafter *Vigilant* signaled that the rebels were gone. Howe had been right after all. Early the next morning marines landed, tore down the rebel flag, and raised the Union Jack. The British suffered only six killed and nineteen wounded throughout the daylong battle, but one quick look at Fort Mifflin's stout fortifications and the two chains surrounding the island indicated that they would have lost many more men if they had tried an amphibious assault. Picking through the debris, redcoats discovered nearly thirty cannons that the Americans had been unable to move, as well as one left-behind rebel nursing a hangover. A British officer wrote a week later, "Took a ride to see Mud Island, which is prodigiously shattered and torn to pieces and leaves a spectacle very much to the honor of those that defended it."[48] He was not the only one with grudging praise for the enemy; another noted, "They [the rebels] certainly defended it with a spirit they have shewn [sic] no where else to an equal degree during the war. I went on shore to survey this celebrated place. Nothing surely was ever so torn and riven with cannonballs. A more dismal picture of ruin can scarce be conceived."[49]

THE NEW JERSEY SHORE

In seizing Fort Mifflin, Howe believed that he had knocked the keystone right out of the American Delaware River defensive arch, and now he moved swiftly to kick over the remaining upright stones. Admiral Howe assigned navy captain William Cornwallis—Charles's brother—the task of removing the upper chevaux-de-frise, and he got to work at once. Fortunately for him, rebel deserters informed the British about a gap in the underwater obstacles protected only by a chain. Once the British removed it, transports could carefully pick their way through the narrow passageway to dock at Philadelphia. By 28 November, Howe was confident that he could bring up as many vessels as necessary to resupply the city before the river froze over completely, but he warned that clearing all the chevaux-de-frise would have to wait until the next year. In the meantime, shortly after midnight on 18 November, General Cornwallis and 2,000 troops marched from Philadelphia down to Chester, and early the next morning they crossed the Delaware to Billingsport on small craft and flatboats. There they joined the 4,500 recently arrived British and German soldiers that the competent and jovial Major General Thomas Spencer Wilson had brought to the Delaware in response to Howe's 8 October call for reinforcements from New York City. Two days later, approximately 4,200 men pushed toward Fort Mercer to put an end to this long and miserable operation.[50]

Despite Fort Mifflin's loss, Washington still hoped to maintain his grip on the Delaware.[51] Both Varnum and Smith had argued that as long as the Americans controlled Fort Mercer, they could continue to protect Hazelwood's flotilla and prevent the British from removing the chevaux-de-frise. On 18 November, Washington sent Major General Arthur St. Clair, artillery chief Henry Knox, and French volunteer Brigadier General Johann de Kalb on a quick inspection trip to the Delaware, and the three officers agreed that Fort Mifflin's fall did not automatically doom the defensive system along the river. The game, in other words, was not yet up, at least not as long as the Americans possessed Fort Mercer. Washington was more than happy to drag out the fighting along the Delaware a little longer, but doing so would require another infusion of Continentals. Varnum's command was just about worn to a frazzle, and it was in no condition to carry the main burden any longer, so Washington dipped into his pool of recently arrived units from Gates's army and ordered Brigadier General Jedediah Huntington's brigade to reinforce it. At about the same time that Washington was finalizing these plans, however, he learned that Cornwallis and his troops had left Philadelphia for the New Jersey shore in what was obviously another effort to seize Fort Mercer. Washington recognized the threat this presented, but he also saw an opportunity. Howe had divided his army again, providing the Americans with the chance to defeat the British in detail, assuming Washington could get enough men into New Jersey to do the kind of damage he envisioned. To be sure, Washington would be splitting his army, too, but he was willing to take that risk for the possible gains. So, in addition to Huntington's brigade, Washington also dispatched Nathanael Greene's division, Brigadier General John Glover's brigade, Henry Lee's cavalry, and Morgan's riflemen. He put Greene in charge, and he gave the Rhode Islander considerable discretion in fulfilling his orders. When Greene brought all his scattered forces together in New Jersey, he would have around 7,000 troops under his command, hopefully enough to cripple or repulse the wily and hard-fighting Cornwallis.[52]

Washington hoped to use Fort Mercer as bait to lure Cornwallis into the trap that Greene would then spring, but events rapidly outran his plans. Both Varnum and Christopher Greene tracked the British buildup at Billingsport, and they surmised its obvious purpose. Neither officer believed that the Fort Mercer garrison could withstand a siege without substantial help from the main army, but the visiting St. Clair, Knox, and de Kalb doubted that Washington could send enough assistance in time. Weighing their options, Varnum and Greene concluded that preserving their soldiers was more important than holding on to the fort. On 19 November, Varnum met with Greene and discovered that the Rhode Island colonel had already given orders to evacuate the place because his information indicated that the British were across Mantua Creek. Engineer du Plessis sprinkled gunpowder around the post and prepared the magazine for destruction, and the troops got ready to leave. At this point, however, Varnum and Greene had second thoughts; neither man wanted to abandon the fort without explicit orders from Washington, and they were unsure about British movements. Temporizing, they blew up the magazine and pulled most of their men out except for a small rear guard that remained until the next day—21 November—when it fell back just ahead of the British vanguard and followed the rest of the Americans to Mount Holly and Haddonfield.[53]

Despite the confusion attending Fort Mercer's evacuation, Varnum succeeded in saving his brigade for future battlefield use. Hazelwood was not as fortunate. Greene's decision to abandon Fort Mercer caught the commodore off guard, and in fact he did not learn about it until the next morning. The American flotilla depended on the New Jersey shore for refuge and supplies, so it could not remain there once Fort Mercer fell. On 19 November, Hazelwood huddled with his officers on board the sloop *Speedwell* at Lads Cove, and they agreed that the best thing to do was to try to run upriver past Philadelphia with the first good wind. Unfortunately, the next two days were calm, leaving most of the fleet stuck in place. The thirteen galleys, on the other hand, were not limited by wind power, so Hazelwood sent them and some armed boats upriver just before daybreak on 20 November, and they slipped undetected past the city's batteries. In the meantime, Varnum withdrew from Fort Mercer with its stores and supplies, leaving the remaining warships in the lurch logistically. Hazelwood mounted his horse and went in search of provisions for his sailors, and in his absence his nervous officers decided to ascend the river the next morning before the British seized the New Jersey shore. This time the British were more alert, and cannon fire from their batteries and the former American frigate *Delaware* drove a schooner ashore and set it aflame. Other vessels managed to make it through the gauntlet, but the wind died down before some of the bigger warships could get under way. Instead, the Americans set fire to them—eleven in all, including the brig *Andrew Doria* and the sloops *Race Horse* and *Fly*—and their burning hulks drifted downriver past Gloucester Point. American naval power along the lower Delaware was no more.[54]

While Varnum, Christopher Greene, and Hazelwood played out their long saga around Red Bank in ignorance of the new role assigned to them, Nathanael Greene struggled to implement Washington's plan to maul Cornwallis. The Rhode Island general brought his division down to Burlington along the Delaware River on 21 November—the same day Hazelwood's ships went up in flames and Fort Mercer finally fell into British hands—but mismanagement and a shortage of scows delayed his crossing for a day. Once in New Jersey, Greene pushed forward to Mount Holly and linked up with Varnum and Huntington, but he soon had cause to regret leaving the main army. New Jersey militiamen came and went with bewildering speed, so merely tabulating their constantly fluctuating numbers was difficult, and Greene quickly dismissed them from his calculations. On paper Greene had nearly 7,000 soldiers at his disposal, but gathering them in one place so he could employ them effectively was almost as difficult as making heads or tails out of the New Jersey militia. Varnum's and Huntington's brigades were on hand at Mount Holly, but no one knew where Glover's brigade and Lee's cavalry were, and Greene especially missed the latter and its ability to inhibit British foraging. Neither unit showed up until 25 November, and only after considerable anxiety about their whereabouts on Greene's part. Most troublesome of all, however, was Greene's almost paralyzing indecision that was reminiscent of his hesitation in pursuing the British after their first New Jersey incursion the previous June. He had expected Fort Mercer to still be in American hands, but Varnum and Christopher Greene's evacuation disrupted Washington's plan on which his mission was based. Estimates of Cornwallis's strength varied widely, and Greene was not sure to what extent he should jeopardize his command in coming to grips with the enemy. In a note to Washington he wrote somewhat plaintively, "For your sake for my own sake and for my country's sake I wish to attempt everything which will meet with your Excellency's approbation. I will run any risque [sic] or engage under any disadvantages if I can only have your countenance if unfortunate."[55] Not until 25 November did he advance against the British, but by then it was too late.[56]

While Greene was wringing his hands and pondering his plight, Cornwallis carried out his assignment with his usual thoroughness, professionalism, and aplomb. The British marched into Fort Mercer right after Christopher Greene's rear guard left, and the Royal Marines spent 22 November demolishing the place while the bulk of the army camped nearby in and around Woodbury. From there they headed up to Gloucester on 25 November, their mission complete. Crossing the Delaware required three days, but the only opposition they faced was a strong American probe on the evening of 25 November that cost the Germans and redcoats fifty casualties, and heavy sniper fire from the woods as the last British troops left the town on board flatboats.[57]

News of Cornwallis's return set off alarm bells in Washington's head. American intelligence had indicated that the British garrison in Philadelphia was demoralized and weak, so throughout November Washington again seriously considered assaulting the city, especially after Cornwallis's departure drained away more redcoats and Germans. Washington polled his generals, but there was no consensus. Stirling, de Kalb, Wayne, Scott, and Woodford favored an attack of some kind, but Armstrong, French engineer Brigadier General Louis Duportail, Brigadier General John Paterson, Brigadier General Enoch Poor, Smallwood, Knox, Greene, and Sullivan all believed that assailing the city was too risky. After carefully reconnoitering the Philadelphia defenses, Washington reluctantly agreed that the British fortifications were too strong. Remaining idle outside of the city came hard for the pugnacious commander in chief, but he continued to believe that patience was the right policy. When Cornwallis recrossed the Delaware, however, it suddenly occurred to Washington that Howe was now in a position to do to him what he had hoped to do to the British: defeat him in detail. Once

Cornwallis rejoined the rest of the British army, Howe could attack and destroy Washington's weakened army at Whitemarsh with his entire force while Greene marked time in New Jersey with his five brigades. Moreover, Washington's agents in Philadelphia warned that Howe was preparing for just such an expedition. The American commander in chief immediately ordered Greene and his troops back to Whitemarsh as soon as possible. Greene had already pushed Varnum's and Huntington's brigades toward the British camp at Gloucester, but they found the defenses there too strong to inflict much damage. Lafayette assaulted the British pickets with some militia and riflemen on the evening of 25 November, and after a back-and-forth skirmish across the woods and swamps he broke off contact. Greene regretted that his foray had achieved so little, but he rapidly embarked his men from Mount Holly across the Delaware, and by 1 December all his troops were at Whitemarsh. With that, the Americans surrendered their last chance to hold on to the New Jersey shore and interfere with the British supply route to Philadelphia. Howe had finally secured the river for British use.[58]

YET ANOTHER HOLLOW BRITISH VICTORY

As with Brandywine and Germantown, clearing the Delaware River was a British tactical triumph but a strategic cipher. Tactically, the operation did credit to British arms. Reducing Forts Mifflin and Mercer required interservice cooperation between the army and navy, engineering aptitude, navigational skills, persistence, courage, and determination. The British overcame dogged American resistance, miserable weather, disadvantageous terrain, and peculiar and stout rebel defenses in a timely enough manner to enable them to hold on to Philadelphia and thus retain their only tangible gain that year. Officers and men as usual fought bravely and professionally, from Stirling's seizure of Billingport to Cornwallis's march on Fort Mercer. Their only major setback—the failed navy/German assault of 22–23 October on Forts Mifflin and Mercer—was due mostly to overconfidence and intelligence failures, but the British did not let this defeat discourage them from trying again, and in their second attempt they learned from their mistakes and succeeded in their mission with minimal casualties.

Even so, British victory along the Delaware did not amount to much strategically. Howe managed to open up the supply lines to Philadelphia, but this did not bring the British any closer to suppressing the rebellion. Conquering Forts Mifflin and Mercer failed to fulfill any of the prerequisites for winning the war: destroying Washington's army, seizing large amounts of American territory, and reestablishing royal authority over significant numbers of Americans. Indeed, in strategic terms the Delaware River operation was a soggy cul-de-sac for the British that diverted them from the road to victory. With the notable exception of the German repulse at Fort Mercer, the campaign cost little blood, but it was enormously expensive in terms of time. In fact, it took the British twice as long to secure Philadelphia's supply lines as it had to seize the city in the first place. In so doing, Howe burned away another two months in a war in which time was working against him. Few redcoat and German officers, including Howe, expected so much opposition along the Delaware, and certainly the British had little choice but to wage the operation if they wanted to keep Philadelphia, but this complication resulted from poor strategic planning and choices Howe made months earlier.[59] Had Howe landed along the Delaware in the first place instead of disembarking at Head of Elk, it probably would have taken the British longer to occupy Philadelphia because Washington would have had the added advantage of the river defenses at his disposal to slow the British advance, but it also would have provided Howe with more opportunities to destroy an American army limited in its freedom to maneuver by its commander's desire to protect the capital in its rear. Instead, a relatively small number of Americans held up the British juggernaut for two months without significant risk to Washington's all-important army. Summing up the frustrating reality, one Philadelphia resident wrote, "Thus by American perseverance and the fort's situation a British army of 12,000 men and a fleet of 300 sail had been detained in their operations near seven weeks by a power far inferior to theirs and which has always appeared contemptible in the eyes of men who have uniformly despised the Americans as a cowardly insignificant set of people."[60]

For their part, the Americans could take pride in their performance throughout the operation. They created their ingenious Delaware River defense system on a shoestring budget and with minimal aid from professional military engineers, but they were shrewd enough to make full use of the local geography and available resources. Their defenses were not perfect, and indeed the British eventually exploited some of their flaws—for example, they found a hole in the upper chevaux-de-frise and took advantage of poorly designed Fort Mifflin to compel the rebels to evacuate it—but the fortifications and obstacles were good enough to stymie the formidable British army for two months. Most of the American soldiers and sailors fought well despite terrible weather and shortages of almost everything, and those at Fort Mifflin withstood as long as possible the heaviest concentration of firepower ever brought to bear on the North American continent up to that time. Most of the officers displayed considerable skill, resourcefulness, and tenacity, and it is hard to find fault with Thayer's courage at Fort Mifflin or Christopher Greene's at Fort Mercer. Perhaps most important, they did so without needlessly sacrificing their men, thus preserving them for future use. There were exceptions of course; Newcomb was just plain incompetent, and for all his bravery Hazelwood lacked the personality to enforce discipline over his jumpy crews. The biggest problem for the Americans, however, was conflict among the officers, which caused considerable tension between the army and navy in particular. Many observers during and after the campaign roundly criticized Hazelwood's failure to engage the British as closely as army officers wanted, but it is worth remembering that the tiny American flotilla took on part of the largest and most skillful navy in the world day in and day out for eight weeks, and sometimes army officers did not understand the navigational, climatic, and logistical limitations it labored under. These personality conflicts were inevitable in any stressful large-scale operation, but Washington was ultimately responsible for letting them fester as long as they did. In the end, however, the Americans' steadfastness won the admiration of even their opponents, who were perhaps in the best position to judge.[61]

Strategically, the Americans gained from the campaign even in defeat. In an ideal world, they would have held on to the forts and forced the British to evacuate Philadelphia, surrender, or starve. This did not happen, but Washington got the next best thing. The American commander in chief successfully used the fighting along the Delaware to buy time as part of his war of attrition. By doing so, he all but ran out the clock on the campaigning season, and he did so without putting his main army at risk. In fact, until Nathanael Greene and Huntington crossed the Delaware, Washington foiled the British with a maximum of only 1,600 Continentals and some ineffectual militia. By stalling the British for another year, Washington opened the door to the possibility of an improved military situation the next spring. On the other hand, events along the Delaware further demonstrated some of the problems Washington had in implementing his strategic designs, especially in his use of the militia. Theoretically, militiamen should have manned Forts Mifflin and Mercer and raided British supply lines to Philadelphia while the Continentals grappled with Howe's army, but the militia was not up to the task, here as elsewhere in the campaign. On the whole, however, Washington's actions in the fall of 1777 were a fine example of his strategic acumen, and they moved the Americans closer to independence in fact as well as in name.

FIVE

Winter Quarters

Long after sunset on 4 December, 12,000 redcoats, Germans, and provincials marched out of Philadelphia in two heavy columns under Cornwallis and Knyphausen. The soldiers slogged northward without baggage trains through the frosty, cold, dark, and windy night. Within three miles, Cornwallis's vanguard encountered and dispersed scattered rebels sniping from behind fences and trees, while in the distance American cannon fire punctuated the darkness, sounding the alarm. In the morning, British light infantry crested Chestnut Hill, ten miles from the city, and gawked at the American camp at Whitemarsh. No sooner had the redcoats surveyed the panorama before them than Brigadier General James Irvine and 600 Pennsylvania militia emerged from the woods to engage them. The British easily repulsed the ragged militiamen and captured the wounded Irvine in the process.[1]

Howe came up the next day, and he did not like the look of things. The Americans were posted on several hills extending four miles along Whitemarsh Creek, with abatis on both flanks and artillery covering the access roads through the swampy wooded plain that separated them from the British on and around Chestnut Hill. Clearly, any assault on these stout works was bound to fail, which of course was why Washington chose to make his stand here. Howe hoped to lure Washington into a decisive battle, but, except for sending out Irving's hapless Pennsylvanians, the American commander in chief seemed content to remain behind his fortifications, hedgehog-like, and leave the next move to the British. Howe examined the American position all day and finally decided that if he could not coax or pry the rebels out, he would try to maneuver them into a position from which he could destroy them. At 1:00 A.M. on 7 December, the British fell quietly back through Germantown, then trudged cross-country to Jenkinstown in an effort to turn the American left flank.

Along the way they burned the villages through which they passed, creating a conflagration so fierce that it was hard for the soldiers to breathe. Near Jenkinstown, Howe detached Charles Grey's brigade, the Queen's Rangers, and some light infantry to probe for an opening. If all went as planned, Howe would bring the rest of the army up to exploit any opportunities Grey developed. Both Howe's and Grey's columns encountered Morgan's recently arrived riflemen deployed on steep, wooded Edge Hill. After a series of bewildering skirmishes in the thick woods, the riflemen drew back to the main American position, ably supported by Mordecai Gist's Maryland militia. Meanwhile, the remainder of the British army rested while Howe scouted out the American left flank, but it appeared just as strong here as along the rest of the line. Instead of attacking, Howe concentrated his army at Edge Hill and bedded down for the night. As far as the British commander in chief was concerned, he had exhausted his options, and without baggage and tents he could not long remain where he was. The next day the British retreated back to Philadelphia with little opposition, reaching the city around 9:00 P.M. Howe's fruitless foray cost his army nine killed, sixty wounded, and thirty-three missing.[2]

Washington was neither surprised nor dismayed by Howe's sortie. His intelligence network within Philadelphia had warned him of the planned march before it materialized, and his pickets outside the city quickly alerted him once the British army got under way. Both the American commander in chief and his troops were ready for action and confident of victory. A good percentage of his 15,000-man force consisted of hard-bitten Saratoga veterans flushed with victory and eager to deal Howe the same treatment they had administered to Burgoyne in upstate New York. Moreover, the American army had been at Whitemarsh since 2 November, so the men had had plenty of time to construct fortifications strong enough to repel anything Howe could throw at them. The Americans were as usual hungry and ill clothed, and the soft loamy ground made everyone even dirtier than normal, but they were keyed up and prepared to fight. When Howe appeared in front of Whitemarsh, Washington followed his standard strategy and sent militia units and riflemen out to harass the enemy while his Continentals prepared for the heavy work that would be required to repel an all-out British assault. To everyone's surprise, however, the suddenly skittish Howe abruptly retreated back to Philadelphia after poking and prodding the American lines for several days. Indeed, the British withdrew so unexpectedly that detachments Washington sent to nip at their heels could not catch up with them. The operation—if it could be called as much—was over, and the Americans suffered little more than fifty casualties. In return, Washington and his soldiers could take comfort in the knowledge that despite their trials, tribulations, and losses, they had survived their third campaigning season.[3]

For William Howe, his short Whitemarsh adventure merely confirmed his growing belief that suppressing the rebellion was next to impossible under current conditions. Despite his string of tactical successes that culminated in his occupation of the American capital, it was increasingly obvious that the traditional strategy he employed based on winning battles and seizing cities and territory was not working, and victory seemed as far away as ever. In fact, the British commander in chief was not an especially introspective man, so although his failures undoubtedly needled his conscience, there was little evidence that he made much of an effort that year to transcend conventional thinking to understand the unique circumstances into which he had been thrust. Howe had attempted to use eighteenth-century strategy to defeat a modern society, and it simply had not worked. By now he believed more than ever that the key to victory was to destroy Washington's army in a climactic battle, and he did not think he could do so unless and until he received at least 10,000 more soldiers from Britain. He did not explain how these reinforcements would enable him to lure the American commander in chief into a decisive action, or how they would permit him to occupy the territory necessary to reestablish large-scale royal control, or how they would enable him to reduce to submission a democratized and participatory society motivated to revolt on the basis of ideas peculiarly its own. Instead, he sought to fix responsibility on others for his strategic myopia. He denounced Burgoyne's ineptitude at Saratoga for raising American morale and Washington's troop strength, but mostly he blamed Germain's lack of support. Howe interpreted the American secretary's failure to provide the soldiers he demanded as a lack of confidence in him born out of Germain's incompetence. Without a doubt Germain deserved his share of censure for British strategic blunders that year, but Howe's accusations demonstrated incredible parochialism on his part and an inability to understand the limitations under which the British war effort labored. Germain's unrealistic expectations for rapid and easy progress merely exacerbated Howe's frustrations. On 22 October—the same day Greene repulsed the Germans outside of Fort Mercer, and the day before *Merlin* and *Augusta* went aground in what became an exasperatingly miserable campaign to open the Delaware—Howe asked to be re-lieved of his command. More than a month later, just before he marched off to Whitemarsh, he reiterated his request. The war had claimed its biggest victim to date, and the fact that the wounds were psychological rather than physical scarcely reduced their importance.[4]

Information traveled slowly across the Atlantic, so Germain did not learn of Howe's request until 1 December, five weeks after the British commander in chief penned his missive. Such news came at a bad time for Lord Frederick North's ministry, arriving as it did just before Par-liament received word of the Saratoga catastrophe. Burgoyne's defeat invigorated the opposition, which sought to use the disaster as a club with which to beat the ministry out of power. North's heart had never been in the war, and in fact one of the king's duties was to periodically prop up his first minister and persuade him to continue in office, where his considerable parliamentary abilities kept His Majesty's friends in control. As for Germain, his wife's death in January diverted his atten-tion from state affairs, but by now the American secretary had plenty of grievances both big and small against Howe. The heart of the mat-ter, however, was that Germain did not believe that Howe was prose-cuting the war vigorously enough, and the commander in chief's ill-tempered complaints merely fed the American secretary's suspicions. North hated strife, but it was increasingly apparent to him and the king that either Germain or Howe had to go, and Howe's resignation made the choice that much simpler. Even so, the king took his time to mull over the implications and fit them into the generally dismal military sit-uation as the old year ended and the new one began, but finally he gave his assent. On 4 February, Germain wrote to Howe that His Majesty had approved his application, and he could return home as soon as his replacement arrived.[5]

VALLEY FORGE

Unlike his British counterpart, Washington had no intention of resign-ing until the war was won. He, too, had his problems with superiors with unrealistic expectations, but in this instance Congress's decentral-ized power structure worked to his advantage in that no one obdurate person could determine his fate. At about the same time Howe repeated his request for relief, Washington was thinking hard about a winter campaign. Most of his general officers opposed one. As they saw it, the army desperately needed to rest and refit after the buffeting it had sustained in the course of the past three months. The soldiers were increasingly short of shoes, stockings, clothes, tents, and much else, and there was little likelihood that the army's wobbly logistical system would adequately meet their needs anytime soon. Moreover, undertaking a new campaign was problematic. In the previous winter, Howe had scattered his troops throughout New Jersey, and their vulnerable garrisons and frequent foraging expeditions provided the Americans with plenty of opportunities to harass and waylay them. This winter, however, it looked like the British army would remain buttoned up tight in Philadelphia, and attacking the well-defended city was out of the question. Even so, there were a number of militia generals—Armstrong, Potter, and Irvine before he fell into British hands—who favored doing *something* aggressive, but most of the Continental officers were convinced that right now the army was in no shape for further exertions, and Washington eventually concurred. Many congressmen in York disagreed with the commander in chief and preferred a major winter campaign, if for no other reason than that success might free them from the high-priced, cramped, dull jerkwater Pennsylvania town in which they had taken refuge. In early December a congressional delegation visited the army at Whitemarsh for a firsthand appraisal of the situation. The delegates talked to Washington and his officers and took a good look at the army's wretched condition before concluding that committing it to battle now would be foolhardy, and they reported as much to the rest of Congress. With this political protection in hand, Washington redirected his efforts toward locating satisfactory winter quarters for his bedraggled soldiers.[6]

As things turned out, going into winter quarters was not as easy as it sounded. There were three possible locations for the army to pass the season—Wilmington, the Lancaster-Reading region, and west of the Schuylkill—and each had its advantages and disadvantages. There was plenty of housing for the army in Wilmington, it was close enough to Philadelphia for the Americans to keep an eye on the British there, and it was within reach of New Jersey. On the other hand, staying there would uncover the important supply depots to the west, and the army would be vulnerable to a sudden British attack. The Lancaster-Reading area was quiet and close to the American logistical nexus, but it was full of refugees whom soldiers would displace, and it was too far from Philadelphia to permit the army to control the surrounding region and its population. Wintering west of the Schuylkill would maintain the lines of communication with New England, and it was reasonably near the British, but supplying the troops there would be difficult. Washington's generals were divided in their counsel. Greene, Wayne, Scott, Duportail, John Cadwalader, and Potter favored Wilmington; Lafayette, de Kalb, Knox, Woodford, Weedon, and Muhlenberg wanted to go to Lancaster-Reading; and Stirling, Armstrong, Maxwell, Smallwood, and Irvine supported wintering west of the Schuylkill.[7]

Washington wanted to rest his army, but he also believed that he needed to protect—or, more critically, control—the large number of Americans and their property around Philadelphia from British foraging or seduction. After weighing his options, he decided on an imperfect compromise. He ordered most of his Continentals into winter quarters west of the Schuylkill, but he sent his few cavalry to New Jersey and a division under the indecisive Smallwood to Wilmington to prevent the British from drawing supplies from those regions. For all his faults, Smallwood was popular in his assigned area, many of his troops were fellow Marylanders, and he outranked the more effective Mordecai Gist. As during the last winter, Washington hoped to use local militiamen to annoy the British, but past experience with the lackluster Pennsylvania militia persuaded him that he would probably have to commit some Continentals to help them out. He understood that his dispositions still left New Jersey relatively unprotected, but he did not want to divide his army any further, and he knew as well as anyone that waging war meant making such hard choices.[8]

On 11 December, three days after Howe fell back from his unproductive lunge at Whitemarsh, Washington put his army on the road toward the Schuylkill. Sullivan's division had the lead, and as soon as it reached Matson's Ford that afternoon, the New Hampshire general directed his troops across the bridge there. Wayne's division, next in line, was halfway over when some of Potter's Pennsylvania militiamen suddenly appeared on the run and claimed that large numbers of redcoats were on their way. Sullivan reined in his impulsive nature and ordered all the Americans back across the bridge, which he then destroyed. By the time Washington came up, the British had seized the heights across the river, and the Continentals had taken refuge in some nearby woods. The American commander in chief sent his cavalry out to scout, and from their reports he guessed correctly that they had bumped into a large British foraging party. Cornwallis and several thousand redcoats were out scouring the countryside for supplies and provisions when they accidentally encountered and scattered Potter's men after a surprisingly stubborn fight. Washington regretted the missed opportunity to maul a big part of the British army, but he did not let Cornwallis's unwelcome appearance interfere with his plans. The next day he took his army upriver, and on the snowy, cold night of 12–13 December, it crossed the Schuylkill on a bridge of thirty-six wagons set up end to end and held together by boards and planks. It was grueling work, and by the time the men reached the Gulph, the army was in deplorable shape. One despondent surgeon scrawled in his diary over the course of several days there:

> This Gulph seems well adapted by its situation to keep us from the pleasures and enjoyments of this world, or being conversant with anybody in it. . . . I am sick, discontented, and out of humor. Poor food, hard lodging, cold weather, fatigue, nasty clothes, nasty cookery, vomit half my time, smoked out of my senses, the devil in it, I can't endure it, why are we sent here to starve and freeze? There comes a soldier, bare feet are seen through his worn out shoes, his legs nearly naked from the tattered remains of an only pair of stockings, his breeches not sufficient to cover his nakedness, his shirt hanging in strings, his hair disheveled, his face meager, his whole appearance pictures a person forsaken and discouraged.[9]

Six days later, on 19 December, the army moved again, this time to its winter quarters: Valley Forge.[10]

Washington chose Valley Forge, located along the Schuylkill's right bank less than twenty miles from Philadelphia, because of its proximity to the former American capital, and because it was easily defensible against any British attack. Once there, his approximately 12,000 troops erected long rows of fourteen-by-sixteen-foot huts capable of holding a dozen men apiece, with officers' quarters behind them. When they finished this, the soldiers got to work fortifying the camp with redoubts and building a bridge over the Schuylkill. As the days passed, conditions at Valley Forge deteriorated. The weather was not that bad for winter, but all the other problems plaguing the army made it seem worse than it really was. There were chronic and worsening shortages of all kinds of clothes—shoes, stockings, shirts, coats, and hats—and blankets. Wearing the same tattered outfits week after week led to frostbite, encouraged lice, and spawned typhus, and a lack of kettles made it difficult to produce soap necessary to alleviate the itch and bring the disease under control. At one point the clothing scarcity rendered 3,000 soldiers unfit for duty. Food was also in short supply; the men went days at a time without meat, and there were almost never any vegetables. Firecake—burned flour and water—was the standard staple, and a poor one at that. Despite its declining numbers due to desertions and disease, the army consumed huge amounts of food; from December to February, it used up 2.25 million pounds of beef, nearly 2.3 million pounds of flour, a half million gills of rum and whiskey.[11] The horses suffered even more than men because both armies had picked the surrounding countryside clean of forage the previous fall, so they died by the hundreds. As usual, the troops neglected proper sanitation, which became a real problem in spring when the melting snow exposed carcasses and improperly located latrines. Throughout the late fall and early winter, soldiers had stoically accepted their plight, but as they whiled away their days in their miserable camp, discontent increased. The men muttered, "No meat, no meat," and "No bread, no soldiers" to their officers to convey their frustration. The desertion rate ballooned, and there were mounting instances of renegade soldiers plundering the locals. In February an entire regiment walked to Brigadier General John Paterson's headquarters and threatened to depart en masse, but Paterson defused the crisis by permitting them to temporarily leave camp to buy meat with what little money they possessed. Indeed, as the old year ended and the new one began, some officers expected the army to disband altogether, and Washington warned that it was in no shape to take on the British right then. That it did not collapse was primarily because of the soldiers' devotion to their cause. Most of them came from the lower classes, and many undoubtedly saw their bounties as a means with which to climb up the socioeconomic ladder, but such practical motivations did not negate their patriotism that burned all the more brightly for the sacrifices they had already made. Like soldiers throughout history, they made do. Snowball fights, games, theatricals, drinking, and religion helped pass the time one way or another. Some men deserted, and others fell sick and died, but most remained to carry on the war.[12]

On 22 December, shortly after he arrived at Valley Forge, an anxious Washington wrote new President of Congress Henry Laurens, "It is with infinite pain and concern, that I transmit Congress the inclosed copies of sundry letters respecting the state of the Commissary's department. If these matters are not exaggerated, I do not know from what cause, this alarming deficiency or rather total failure of supplies arise; but unless more vigorous exertions and better regulations take place in that line, and immediately, this army must dissolve."[13] This was no small matter, and Washington had already been forced to cancel efforts to confront a British foraging expedition because he lacked provisions for the men. The biting irony was that the army was starving in the midst of one of the country's most fertile and productive regions, but military and government authorities seemed incapable of getting food from the prosperous civilians to the troops who were fighting and dying for them.

In fact, the army's logistical woes were both multiple and complicated. Some were easy to identify but hard to immediately fix. Both armies had already skimmed over the Valley Forge region the previous September just before Howe crossed the Schuylkill, so supplies had to come from far away. Winter's onset brought rain and snow that turned the roads into impassable sloughs of mud for high-priced wagoners bringing their cargoes to relatively remote Valley Forge, and some of them simply abandoned their freight wherever convenient rather than push on to camp through the interminable muck. And, as usual, local commanders continued to commandeer supplies and equipment earmarked for Washington's army. Other problems, however, grew out of the ingrained nature of American government and society. Congress lacked the power to tax, so not surprisingly its currency gradually lost much of its value, and it would eventually become all but worthless. Under such conditions, persuading farmers to sell their produce for this increasingly useless script, or, worse yet, for promissory notes, was extremely difficult. Moreover, the British in Philadelphia often paid gold for food, and when push came to shove, some of the area's hard-pressed farmers often sacrificed their patriotic ideals for material gain, while their loyalist counterparts were more than willing to take the king's money. The logistical system in place for acquiring and distributing provisions, supplies, and clothes was not very effective. Most of the overworked purchasers were civilians compensated on a percentage basis instead of by a straight salary, which led to considerable corruption and confusion on top of the usual wastefulness of war. Many of these men were technically civilians, so they were not subject to the strict military discipline that might have kept them in line. Finally, there was poor leadership in the relevant departments. Quartermaster General Thomas Mifflin resigned on 8 October 1777, but he had pretty much given up his duties long before that, and he did not visit the army after the war moved to Pennsylvania. Commissary General William Buchanan and Clothier General James Mease were similarly lackadaisical; Washington eventually wrote to the latter, "I am now to inform you that the complaints against your department have become so loud and universal, that I can no longer dispense with your presence in camp to give satisfaction on the many subjects of discontent that prevail in the army from that source, and to relieve me from those difficulties in which I am involved in by your absence."[14] Taken together, then, it was small wonder that about 2,000 soldiers died at Valley Forge that winter of disease, cold, exhaustion, and hunger.[15]

Desperate times called for desperate measures, and as the winter wore on, Washington was increasingly willing to take extreme actions to preserve his army. Although Congress gave him the power to impress supplies in the Valley Forge region, the American commander in chief was initially reluctant to alienate the local population by doing so, and he tried to limit such treatment to loyalists and the ever suspect Quakers. However, as time went on and conditions at Valley Forge deteriorated, Washington changed his mind. Detachments under Nathanael Greene spread out toward the Delaware River and into New Jersey to scour the countryside and seize provisions, forage, and livestock for the army, or to destroy them to keep them out of British hands. Washington ordered his subordinates to leave enough for families to get through the winter, and to hand out receipts, but this was small comfort for those who lost most of their possessions to soldiers who were supposed to be fighting for their liberties. Not surprisingly, many of the locals hid their cattle and horses in the woods, making the region look emptier than it truly was. Such widespread foraging was merely one stopgap effort among many that Washington undertook that winter. When lazy and incompetent Commissary General William Buchanan warned him that he could no longer support the army, Washington wrote to the New England deputy commissary general, Henry Champion, and to governors and leaders in Maryland, New Jersey, New York, Connecticut, Delaware, and Virginia to explain the army's plight and ask for whatever immediate help they could provide. Such efforts had a cumulative and positive effect. Greene was convinced that his foraging expeditions prevented the army from disbanding. Champion, New Jersey governor William Livingston, and New York governor George Clinton proved especially helpful in procuring and dispatching livestock to the army. By late February the crisis had eased, but both officers and congressmen recognized that the fundamental problems remained unresolved, and many doubted that the army could function much longer under such a flawed logistical system. Greene wrote ominously, "The quarter master general, commissary general, and clothier departments are in such a wretched condition that unless there are some very great alterations in those departments, it will be impossible to prosecute another campaign."[16]

As if Washington did not have enough problems trying to maintain his army that winter, he also had to deal with his proud and prickly officer corps. The winter's trials and tribulations did not prevent many officers from continuing their efforts to gain favor and promotion—or to prevent others from gaining advancement at their expense. Some artillery officers, for example, protested Thomas-Antoine du Plessis's promotion to lieutenant colonel as unmerited, but Washington recognized the French engineer's value at Fort Mercer and defended him. Most seriously, there was a complicated dispute within the Virginia line among Brigadier Generals William Woodford, Peter Muhlenberg, Charles Scott, and George Weedon over seniority. Washington respected all four men for the bravery each demonstrated at Brandywine and elsewhere, and he urged them to remain in the army no matter what the outcome of their dispute. Congress and Washington kicked the problem back and forth between each other, and eventually Congress ruled in favor of Woodford. Unfortunately, Weedon put pride before patriotism and headed for home. He was not the only one leaving. Now that the fighting was over until spring, officers clamored for extended furloughs to visit their families and take care of neglected business. Washington denied innumerable requests, but a good many officers managed to finagle their way home anyhow. This irked the commander in chief because he needed every officer he could get to help him keep the army together. Indeed, at one point all his brigadiers were absent from Valley Forge for one reason or another except for Enoch Poor, Paterson, and Varnum.[17]

Revolutionary warfare by its very nature disrupts and warps social, political, and economic norms, and by the end of 1777 this often brutal reality began taking a toll on Washington's officer corps. Prices for even the most basic necessities skyrocketed as the conflict went on, making it difficult for officers to support their families back home on their fixed and increasingly meager incomes. Destitute wives frequently pleaded for their husbands' return, and in response a growing number of officers resigned their commissions. Commenting on rising prices, Washington's general officers noted, "This [inflation] has already had a pernicious effect, and caused a considerable number of valuable officers who have found themselves unable longer to subsist in the army to resign their commissions. Many others are complaining of the hardship occasioned by the former regulations and unless a remedy is applied, will follow the example of others by quitting the service."[18] In March, Nathanael Greene noted that hundreds of officers had left the army since it went into winter quarters, and one officer observed that fifty officers in Greene's division resigned on one late December day alone.[19] Washington understood that the loss of so many battle-hardened veterans was bound to damage the army when campaigning began in earnest in the spring, although he also blandly noted that it was a good way to get rid of some of its more incompetent members. To remedy the problem, some officers wanted to adopt the British army's system of paying officers half their salary for life after the war. Washington initially was not enthusiastic about this idea, but he eventually endorsed it as the only realistic way to preserve the officer corps. Such talk, however, disturbed many congressmen because it went against the American grain. Delegates worried that half pay might create a type of peacetime standing army that would threaten American liberties, that it would be too expensive, and that it would infringe on the states' right to appoint their own officers to their own units. In the end, however, Congress bowed to military necessity—to an extent—and on 15 May passed a resolution calling for half pay for seven years after the conflict ended. This was a lot less than what most officers wanted, but it sufficed to keep many in the army and to maintain it as a fighting force.[20]

Americans have mythologized Valley Forge as an inspiring example of American bravery, fortitude, and sacrifice. There is a good deal of truth to this, but in many ways the army's experiences there were mild compared with its ordeal at Morristown in the winter of 1780–81. Valley Forge, however, was unique because of what came before and after it. Trenton, Princeton, and congressional legislation authorizing a large army of Continentals generated considerable optimism among many Americans that Washington would be able to win the war in 1777. Washington's army had not fulfilled these hopes, and instead it had suffered defeats and lost Philadelphia. Such disappointment made winter quarters all the more depressing. Moreover, winter focused attention on the army's serious and seemingly intractable logistical problems. Not only did thousands of soldiers die as a result of these difficulties, but hundreds of disgruntled officers resigned their commissions. Out of the ashes of Valley Forge, however, rose a new well-trained army capable of standing up to the British redcoats in open battle, and it was this force that would eventually win the war and secure American independence.

THE CONWAY CABAL

Discontent was widespread that winter, infecting not only the army's soldiers and officer corps but some in and out of Congress as well. Cooped up in York without many of the amenities their former capital had offered, some delegates could not help but look unhappily upon the military picture that had painted them in their internal exile. Brandy-wine, Paoli, Germantown, and Philadelphia's occupation were all unpleasant markers along a road that seemed headed in the wrong direction. More and more prominent policy makers and a number of officers were increasingly inclined to trace the army's problems not to apparently incompetent subordinates like Sullivan and Wayne, but rather to the man at the very top of the chain of command: Washington. Some of those who visited the army observed and bemoaned its lack of discipline, its large number of stragglers, its obvious need for reorganization, and its quarreling officer corps. Its record that fall seemed to speak for itself as conclusive evidence of its commander's failings. Summing up the growing sentiment among some congressmen, one wrote, "We want a general; thousands of lives and millions in property are yearly sacrificed to the insufficiency of our commander-in-chief. Two battles he has lost for us by two such blunders as might have disgraced a soldier of three months standing: and yet we are so attached to this man that I fear we shall rather sink with him than throw him off our shoulders. And sink we must under his management."[21] Congress's high turnover and low attendance rates further undermined Washington's support because so few of the remaining delegates had had a hand in his selection, and they therefore felt little personal responsibility to support a man they did not choose. To many it seemed that the country and the army charged with securing its independence could and should do better than Washington. No one was willing to express these sentiments publicly yet, but the small number of congressmen remaining at York made it easier for such unhappy people to make their voices heard behind the scenes.[22]

Moreover, by early winter those dissatisfied with Washington had a successful general with which to unflatteringly compare him. Horatio Gates's tremendous victory at Saratoga seemed to show that a skillful general could train and fight an army capable of beating—indeed destroying—the British. A cursory evaluation of each officer's recent record appeared to indicate that Gates had the magic touch necessary to do to Howe what he had done to Burgoyne. Placing the two generals side by side, one delegate wrote, "The one on the pinnacle of military glory, exulting in the success of schemes planned with wisdom and executed with vigor and bravery, and above all see a country saved by their exertions. See the other outgeneraled and twice beaten, obliged to witness the march of a body of men only half their number through 140 miles of thick settled country, forced to give up a city the capital of a state, and after all outwitted by the same army in a retreat."[23] There were some serious flaws in such analysis, not the least of which were unfounded assumptions about Gates's military abilities and leadership. That winter, however, it was easy for some to portray Gates as a winner and Washington as a loser, and it seemed to many only logical to consider putting the war's direction in the hands of the general who had had the most recent success.[24]

The sun still hung in the sky on 28 October 1777 when Colonel James Wilkinson strode into a Reading, Pennsylvania, tavern. Born in 1757 in Maryland, Wilkinson had abandoned his medical practice to go to war. He accompanied Benedict Arnold to Canada before becoming Horatio Gates's deputy adjutant general during the Saratoga campaign. Despite his youth, he had risen rapidly through the ranks, although this was more a tribute to his deep-seated ambition than to any real military ability. In fact, Wilkinson was a flashy, sly, querulous, and thoroughly unscrupulous man whose actions did considerable damage to his country. On that late October day he was on his way to York to deliver official word of Burgoyne's surrender to Congress, but he decided to take a detour and visit his girlfriend. In the Reading tavern he met Major General Lord Alexander Stirling, one of Washington's few high-ranking officers who had escaped public and congressional censure that defeat-plagued autumn. Wilkinson, Stirling, and the general's staff officers passed the day conversing and drinking. As was often the case in Stirling's presence, the wine flowed freely, as did the talk. In his inebriated state Wilkinson told Major William McWilliams that while perusing Gates's correspondence he had uncovered an interesting letter from Brigadier General Thomas Conway. According to McWilliams, Wilkinson quoted Conway as writing, "Heaven has been determined to save your country, or a weak general and bad counselors would have ruined it." The "weak general" referred, of course, to Washington, and presumably the "bad counselors" were his ranking subordinates—men like Stirling. McWilliams informed his boss, who did not think much of Conway anyway. Stirling in turn immediately clued in the commander in chief when he returned to the army at

Whitemarsh. In response, Washington penned an icily brief note to Conway on 9 November:

> Sir: A letter which I received last night, contained the following paragraph. "In a letter from Gen[era]l Conway to Gen[era]l Gates he says: 'Heaven has been determined to save your country; or a weak general and bad counselors would have ruined it.'"[25]

Brigadier General Thomas Conway furnished his name to the confusing and peculiar series of events that followed and went down in history as the Conway Cabal. He was a forty-four-year-old Irish-born French officer whom Silas Deane dispatched from Europe to help the Americans win their independence. His fluent English gave him an advantage over other foreigners who offered their swords to Congress, so in May 1777 Washington put him in command of a brigade that he turned into the best-drilled unit in the army. He fought well at Brandywine at the Plowed Hill, and he had a good reputation in Congress and among officers such as John Sullivan and, at least at first, the Marquis de Lafayette. On the other hand, others saw him as an insolent, ambitious intriguer who rubbed people the wrong way, although many of the harsher characterizations came after the battlelines were drawn in the power struggle to come. Some praised his brigade's performance at Germantown, but Brigadier General John Cadwalader claimed that during the battle he and Colonel Joseph Reed found Conway cowering in a farmhouse because his horse had been wounded in the neck. Whatever the truth in these allegations, they helped convince Washington to strongly recommend to Congress against Conway's promotion to major general. As the commander in chief wrote to one delegate on 17 October, "General Conway's merit, then, as an officer, and his importance in this army, exists more in his own imagination, than in reality: For it is a maxim with him, to leave no service of his own untold, nor to want any thing which is to be obtained by importunity."[26] Washington also argued somewhat hypocritically that Conway was not senior enough to deserve promotion, although the commander in chief would later prove willing to give the inexperienced and youthful Lafayette responsibilities he did not earn. At any rate, Congress did not initially advance Conway for many of the reasons alluded to by Washington.[27]

Conway's career in the army was therefore clearly on the skids by the time Washington learned one of the particulars of his correspondence with Gates, and it appeared that he would soon go the way of other foreigners, like de Borre, who were unwilling or unable to adjust to the American way of waging war. In fact, on 20 October, Virginia delegate Richard Henry Lee assured Washington that Conway sought promotion solely so he could return home with honor. At about this same time, however, Congress undertook several initiatives that raised suspicions among some that there was a conspiracy afoot to remove Washington from his command, and Wilkinson's drunken confession substantiated such fears. Thus, to some, Wilkinson's otherwise unimportant indiscretion became the smoking gun that proved that a struggle was under way for control of the army. For one thing, the mere exchange of letters between one of Washington's most disgruntled generals and his chief rival indicated to many that there was some sort of planning between the two men. Moreover, on 17 October, Congress established a new Board of War to oversee army activities, and on 27 November it put Gates in charge. Not a few observers believed the board's real purpose was to humiliate and emasculate Washington. In early November, Congress also decided on Gates's recommendation to promote Wilkinson, and a month later it not only elevated Conway, too, but also appointed him to the newly created inspector general position. This outraged dozens of Washington's officers over whose heads Wilkinson and Conway were advanced, and some speculated that such an irregular procedure was compensation for some underhanded service the two men had performed or promised to perform. Finally, later in the winter Congress authorized an invasion of Canada, and initially there was talk in York of putting Conway in charge. In the end, Lafayette got the job, and not much came of it, but perhaps some delegates pushed for Conway because they wanted to reward him or groom him for more important commands. Put together, then, it seemed to many of Washington's supporters that shadowy and sinister forces in and out of Congress were setting plans into motion to separate the commander in chief from the army he had directed for more than three years.[28]

Not surprisingly, Washington and the officers closest to him reacted most strongly to the alleged conspiracy because they had the most to lose. These men had no doubts that a plot existed, and they saw it as a mortal threat to the American cause because they thought so little of its instigators' motives and abilities. Washington's officers had been stung by the unfavorable comparisons between the northern and southern armies, and as far as they were concerned, Philip Schuyler, Benjamin Lincoln, and Benedict Arnold deserved most of the credit for victory at Saratoga, not Gates. From this perspective, it was not surprising that these men were inclined to close ranks and think the worst of Gates on the slimmest of evidence. Conspiracy theories ran deep in the American psyche, and indeed a sincere and widespread belief among many colonists that the British government was scheming to strip them of their liberties contributed to the Revolution itself. As far as Washington and his supporters were concerned, Wilkinson's drunken and indiscreet talk not only prematurely revealed the plot's existence but also exposed some of its perpetrators. Chief among them were Conway, Gates, Wilkinson, and, at its head, former quartermaster general Major General Thomas Mifflin. The high-ranking and vain Mifflin was popular and influential in some circles, but he had not performed well as quartermaster general, and he was supposedly angry with Washington because the commander in chief had not heeded his advice the previous spring to deploy more troops in New England. Once Washington's allies had identified the suspected conspirators, they moved to discredit them by, in their minds, showing the alleged plotters for what they were. In dozens of letters that winter to influential friends and policy makers, Washington and his supporters denounced these men as intriguers and malcontents whose selfish ambition would ruin the war effort and the Revolution unless they were stopped.[29]

The truth of the matter was that no conspiracy against Washington existed—except in the minds of the commander in chief and his allies. There were certainly prominent people who griped about Washington's recent lack of success and compared him unfavorably with Gates, but there was no secret plan among them to remove him from his command. There were logical and innocuous reasons behind Congress's actions that Washington's supporters incorrectly interpreted as threads to the conspiracy. Congress formed the new Board of War to help the commander in chief, not to shear him of his power. The old board consisted solely of delegates who lacked sufficient time and expertise to make it very useful; Congress hoped that putting professional soldiers like Mifflin and a staff on it would increase its effectiveness. Delegates expected the board to find and fix problems with the various departments, thus freeing Washington from the logistical busywork that took up so much of his time so he could focus on beating the British. Gates had successfully held an important independent command and could thus best understand Washington's problems, so it only made sense to put him in charge of the board. Congress advanced Wilkinson mostly to please Gates, and it made Conway inspector general because his primary duty would be training troops, and for all his faults the French officer had a proven track record in this area, as British soldiers who stormed the Plowed Hill could testify. Besides, the delegates did not know about Conway's alleged insidious correspondence when they promoted him. Finally, the proposed invasion of Canada was many things—including bad and unrealistic strategy—but it had nothing to do with grooming or rewarding Conway. Therefore, Washington and his supporters prepared to disgrace fellow officers whose only sins were that they complained or listened to others complain that the war was not conducted as well as they wished.[30]

In his battle with the alleged conspirators, Washington was fortunate to have the assistance and allegiance of President of Congress Henry Laurens of South Carolina. Elected unanimously on 1 November to replace John Hancock, Laurens was a sensible, worldly, judicious man highly esteemed by his colleagues. Gout plagued him throughout the winter of 1777–78, and in fact he often propped himself up and placed both feet and legs on baskets to conduct business before hobbling home on crutches over the snow and ice. Laurens did not want to be president, but he was determined and resigned to do his duty. Washington was pleased with his selection, all the more so because Laurens's son John was one of Washington's aides, who served as a valuable conduit between the two men. Before he became president, Laurens recognized the dissatisfaction many delegates had with the commander in chief, and he believed that it had some merit. However, frequent correspondence with his son, Washington, and some of the commander in chief's subordinates gave him a more sympathetic view of the army's problems, and it also made him more susceptible to their conspiracy theories. Laurens used his influence to gather information on Washington's supposed enemies, to keep congressional allies informed about the army's progress and problems, and to prevent anyone from disrupting the war effort by challenging the commander in chief's authority. On 8 January, Laurens informed his son that he had discovered a cabal against Washington outside the army and strongly implied that Mifflin was at its head. He promised to cover Washington's congressional flank so the commander in chief could concentrate on beating the British. Four days later, however, Laurens had second thoughts; he reassured Lafayette that although there were those who opposed some of Washington's actions, that was part and parcel of representative government, and the malcontents lacked the power to injure the commander in chief. Laurens explained, "But I think the friends of our brave and virtuous general, may rest assured that he is out of the reach of his enemies, if he has an enemy, a fact which I am in doubt of. I believe I hear most that is said and know the outlines of almost all that has been attempted but the whole amounts to little more than little tattle, which would be too much honored by repeating it. . . . In a word, Sir, be not alarmed; I think it is not in the power of any junto to lessen our friend without his own consent."[31]

As for Conway, Laurens saw him as small potatoes, and he was sure that sooner or later the inveterate French officer would destroy himself with his own words. On 27 January, Laurens succeeded in viewing a copy of Conway's infamous letter to Gates courtesy of fellow delegate Daniel Roberdeau. Several weeks later, Washington's aide Colonel John Fitzgerald passed through York on his way home to Virginia to fill in Laurens about the alleged conspiracy's details, and the president showed him the extract he had copied, which Fitzgerald sent along to Washington on 16 February. Conway had actually written to Gates, "What a pity there is but one Gates! But the more I see of this army the less I think it is fit for general action under its actual chiefs and actual discipline. I speak to you sincerely and freely and wish I could serve under you."[32]

Given these circumstances, it was no surprise that Washington and his supporters so easily succeeded in cowering or disgracing the officers they targeted for condemnation. The accused plotters' initial response to these conspiracy charges was to run for cover and attempt to demonstrate their innocence, but their often clumsy efforts to prove a negative usually served to deepen their guilt in their enemies' eyes. Horatio Gates was a fifty-year-old former British officer who had served in America and the West Indies during the Great War for Empire before retiring to Virginia. He was usually a generous and cautious man, and hardly the type to engage in cabals. His only sin was that he was a successful general who received an unsolicited letter from one of Washington's most vocal critics. Word spread through the army about Conway's supposed remarks, and on 3 December, Gates learned about the developing scandal from Mifflin. Naturally enough, Gates's initial reaction was outrage that someone had pilfered his private correspondence, and he focused his attention on uncovering the culprit. He questioned his military family, and Wilkinson disingenuously suggested that perhaps Gates's aide Lieutenant Colonel Robert Troup had inadvertently blurted something to Alexander Hamilton during the latter's visit to Albany. When Gates learned the truth about Wilkinson's drunken gossiping from Conway, he angrily reprimanded him. Gates explained to Washington that he and Conway were not friends, and in any case the French officer's letter did not contain the purported sentence. Gates admitted that Conway had criticized the army, but he noted that officers did that sort of thing all the time in their private correspondence. Washington, not about to let Gates off the hook so easily, responded that Gates's account did not ring true to him. Washington suggested that releasing the relevant correspondence was the best thing Gates could do to clear his name and bring this unpleasant episode to an end—unless he had something to hide. Gates desperately wanted to appease the commander in chief, but he also believed in protecting Conway's privacy. In the end, Gates simply assured Washington, "I solemnly declare that I am of no faction."[33] Washington replied that he was satisfied with Gates's explanations, as he well might be now that his chief rival was so eager to placate him, but in a letter to another officer several weeks later he indicated that he still had his suspicions despite Gates's protestations: "G[ate]s has involved himself in his letters to me, in the most absurd contradictions. . . . I have a good deal of reason to believe that the machinations of this junto will recoil upon their own heads, and be a means of bringing some matters to light which by getting me out of the way some of them thought to conceal."[34]

Gates at least managed to survive the episode professionally, though at the price of surrendering any ambitions he may have harbored to succeed Washington, but the same could not be said of the man who gave his name to the whole sordid affair. Conway was well aware that most of Washington's officers—but not all; Sullivan remained grateful until the end for Conway's performance and support at Brandywine and Germantown—despised him as a malcontent and a coward, and he was angry that Congress had promoted junior foreign officers like de Kalb over his head. He left Whitemarsh in November under the assumption that his military career in America was over, and Washington wished him Godspeed back to France. Congress's surprising decision to promote him and appoint him inspector general, however, offered him the opportunity for resurrection, or at least for a stay of execution. Unfortunately for him, his letter to Gates—or, more accurately, Wilkinson's inebriated and erroneous retelling of it—destroyed whatever slim chances he had for redemption. Conway did not keep a copy of the letter, so he was unsure of whether he had used the incriminating phrase, but he knew full well that he had criticized the commander in chief and the army. In an awkward series of letters to Washington in November, December, and January that were at once beseeching and condescending, he explained that his comments were meant to be constructive, and anyway officers frequently communicated with each other in such an open and blunt manner. He also complained truthfully enough that Washington's supporters were out to dishonor him, and he cynically compared the commander in chief to Frederick the Great. Washington was already predisposed to believe the worst about Conway, and the French officer's mordant letters did nothing to change his mind. As far as he was concerned, even if Conway's purported quotation was not exact, the general gist of it was probably on target. Indeed, the exchange so angered him that he forwarded the correspondence to Congress for its scrutiny. At the same time, he coolly and deceptively insisted to Conway that he had nothing to do with his subordinates' efforts to discredit him, and that he would treat him with all professional courtesy. Conway discovered otherwise when he visited Valley Forge just before the new year to talk to Washington about his responsibilities as inspector general. He received such a frosty reception there that he realized he could not adequately fulfill his duties, so he returned to York and stepped down. The next month Conway finally got a copy of his letter, and he wrote to Washington on 27 January to assure him that the alleged damning phrase was not accurate and that he was not part of any cabal, but the commander in chief remained unmoved. Conway thought about publishing the letter to clear his name, but Henry Laurens dissuaded him because it might alert the British to discord in the American camp, although as a matter of fact they were already aware of it. In the meantime, Congress sent him to New York to get him out of the way, but later that spring Conway wrote to Laurens and threatened to resign unless he received an independent command. To his surprise, the crafty Laurens submitted the letter to Congress, which took advantage of the opportunity to rid itself of the troublesome Frenchman by accepting his resignation forthwith on 28 April. Strife followed Conway out of the army. Cadwalader had accused him of cowardice at Germantown, so Conway challenged him to a duel that they fought on 4 July. Cadwalader severely wounded Conway in the face, and for a while it looked like the French officer might not survive. While on his supposed deathbed, Conway wrote one last letter to Washington to apologize for all the trouble he had caused. He eventually recovered, however, and returned to France later that year.[35]

As for the Conway Cabal's inadvertent instigator, he, too, paid a price for his actions. Wilkinson's undeserved promotion generated considerable resentment among his fellow officers, and his subsequent efforts to conceal his role in divulging part of Conway's correspondence with Gates by denying it and shifting the blame to Robert Troup did little to change things. He later asserted that he did not remember uttering the damning phrase in the Reading tavern, which may or may not have been true. When Stirling learned about Wilkinson's claims, he asked for a copy of Conway's letter to Gates to settle the issue once and for all, but Wilkinson indignantly refused to participate in such an underhanded scheme, stating, "I may have been indiscreet, my Lord, but be assured I am not dishonourable."[36] This was open to debate, and in fact shortly beforehand one of Stirling's friends had presciently written of Wilkinson to the New Jersey general, "If he betrayed the confidence of his patron he may do the same by his country, and from the opinion Mr. Gates seems to have of such a character, I think he will not hereafter chuse [*sic*] to have him near his person."[37] Gates was indeed furious when he learned of Wilkinson's role in the growing scandal, and he censured his onetime aide. Wilkinson already knew that Gates had zeroed in on him as the culprit, and even before he got Gates's angry letter, he challenged his former patron to a duel, writing, "My Lord shall bleed for his conduct, but it is proper I first see you."[38] The two men met privately in York on the morning of 24 February, just before the encounter was to take place, and the affable Gates managed to soothe Wilkinson's ruffled pride enough to cancel the planned shoot-out. A month earlier Congress had appointed Wilkinson secretary to the new Board of War, and he and Gates agreed that they ought to devote their energies to their new jobs. Wilkinson then traveled to Lancaster to spend a couple weeks with his girlfriend before heading to Valley Forge on 16 March. Much like Conway earlier, Wilkinson encountered so much hostility from the officers there that he decided to resign his commission and step down as secretary to the board. Before he left camp, Washington invited him to dinner, where the commander in chief spoke freely about the conspiracy he believed was afoot. Wilkinson disclaimed any complicity; in fact, he was quick to condemn Conway in the strongest terms. None of this bought him Washington's support or respect, and he left the army soon after.[39]

By the time Wilkinson slithered away from Valley Forge, Washington and his supporters believed that the alleged plot had all but collapsed. Thanks to Wilkinson's drunken blabbering and Stirling's alert response, Washington and his friends successfully nipped the nonexistent threat in the bud by smearing the supposed plotters with charges of conspiracy, malevolence, and discord. Conway had resigned as inspector general, was on his way to internal exile in New York, and within two months would leave the army; a chastened Gates was eager to assure everyone from Washington on down of his loyalty to the commander in chief; and, finally, accused ringleader Mifflin denied any role in a cabal, and he professed to want all such infighting to end. Nathanael Greene was closer to the truth than he knew when he noted, "The late faction that has been the subject of much speculation for sometime past vanishes like a mist before the warming beams of the sun in a summer's morning. It begins to be a doubt whether there ever was any such thing if the party charged were to be credited."[40] Certainly the fact that no such conspiracy against Washington existed made it relatively easy for the commander in chief and his friends to triumph in their one-sided power struggle, but there was more to it than that. The Conway Cabal must be analyzed in the context of the times. American fortunes were at a low point that winter, which undoubtedly motivated murmurings of discontent with Washington. Those same conditions also made the commander in chief and his supporters touchier and quicker to take offense than would have been the case otherwise. Indeed, it is unlikely that Washington and his allies would have been so concerned about conspiracy reports if the Americans were winning the war, but of course under those conditions there probably would have been no such rumors in the first place. Most of Washington's officer corps rallied around their commander in chief because they saw attacks on him as an attack on the army as a whole, and Congress's strange decision to promote Wilkinson and Conway merely reinforced this inclination. There were many officers besides Conway who were frustrated with some of Washington's actions—Anthony Wayne and Johann de Kalb being two of the most prominent—but in the end they sided with their commander in chief or remained silent. This in itself was a testament to Washington's ability to inspire loyalty among most of his subordinates. Similarly, even those delegates who had expressed dissatisfaction with Washington saw no advantage to speaking out publicly against him and risking charges of dissension. Washington and his allies sincerely believed that a plot existed, and there is no evidence that they manufactured it as a way to increase their power, though this was in fact a result of the episode. Indeed, months after the supposed conspiracy had run its course, Washington wrote to a friend,

That there was a scheme of this sort on foot, last fall, admits of no doubt; but it originated in another quarter; with three men, who wanted to aggrandize themselves; but finding no support, on the contrary, that their conduct and views, when seen into, were likely to undergo severe reprehension, they slunk back, disavowed the measure, and professed themselves my warmest admirers. Thus stands the matter at present. Whether any members of Congress were privy to this scheme, and inclined to aid and abet it, I shall not take upon me to say; but am well informed, that no whisper of the kind was ever heard in Congress.[41]

The Conway Cabal had a profound impact on the Revolutionary War. The incident secured Washington's position as commander in chief by demonstrating to everyone in and out of the army the high political and professional costs of challenging—or, more accurately, being perceived as challenging—his authority. Congress continued to question Washington's decisions and even on occasion to overrule him, but after the winter of 1777–78 there were no more rumblings about removing him. Washington's enhanced status benefited the war effort because he now had more freedom to formulate strategy and deal with officers without constantly looking over his shoulder at a Congress ready to displace him at a moment's notice. Had Washington been unsure of Congress's support, he might have been reluctant to undertake such risky plans as the march to Virginia in 1781, or to confront Charles Lee after the Battle of Monmouth Courthouse. The episode turned Washington into the untouchable and indispensable man, a dangerous combination for a young republic struggling to secure its independence and freedom. The Conway Cabal also solidified Washington's bond with his officer corps, and thereafter much, but certainly not all, of the backbiting and discord that characterized this group disappeared. This undoubtedly made for a more effective army in the years to come, but it also increasingly separated the officers from the society they were charged to protect. Indeed, the officer corps gradually developed the mind-set of a standing professional army in a society that historically viewed such a force as a threat to liberty. Although Washington's actions and behavior during the Conway Cabal were hardly exemplary, he acted out of a sincere desire to do what was best for the army and the country, and in the end his better nature consistently asserted itself to the country's benefit. Even so, the cabal and its consequences were risky business for a country that prided itself on being a nation of laws.

THE BRITISH IN PHILADELPHIA

While Washington's troops starved, froze, and bickered at Valley Forge, William Howe's 16,800-man British army settled into Philadelphia for a far more pleasant and harmonious winter. A year earlier many redcoats and Germans had suffered in squalid New Jersey towns vulnerable to rebel sniping and raids, but this time around they had at their disposal the finest city in America. Philadelphia possessed paved streets lit by lanterns at night, two-story brick houses to quarter many of the soldiers, and an often sympathetic largely Quaker population. Once the Delaware and Schuylkill Rivers iced over, the local citizens and their protectors—or, from another point of view, occupiers—hunkered down until spring, and the British were content to enjoy the diversions the former American capital offered. Indeed, it was often easy to forget about Washington's annoying army and the unpleasant war that brought them there. For the enlisted men, winter quarters provided a respite from campaigning, and soldiers turned to life's simpler and coarser pleasures: drinking, gambling, and whoring. Because the officers had more money, freedom, and status at their disposal, their entertainment was usually more sophisticated, if not necessarily more wholesome. Some spent their leisure time reading and studying, but many more courted the local girls or attended the numerous parties, plays, assemblies, concerts, and clubs organized for their amusement. The theater put on mostly comedic plays once a week, and proceeds went to a charity for soldiers' widows and orphans. Army and navy officers served as actors, and while a few observers applauded their thespian skills, others condemned some of their roles as undignified. For those with less artistic tastes, taverns with public rooms were open every evening except Sundays. Some of the rooms were devoted to chess, but gambling was the primary activity, and large numbers of officers indulged in this pastime, including the commander in chief. Both officers and men took advantage of any opportunity to celebrate. For example, on 17 March an Irish grenadier impersonated Saint Patrick and led a drunken procession through the city streets in celebration of the holiday. Finally, there was scandal to keep the tongues wagging. Sixteen-year-old Mary Fygis accused Captain Alexander Campbell of using her to deliver messages to the rebels. Campbell was a brave and honorable officer without a motive for treason, but there did not seem to be any reason for the girl to lie either. Fortunately for Campbell, he had an airtight alibi, and on 11 March a court-martial headed by Thomas Musgrave acquitted him. Another trial two weeks later condemned the girl, who subsequently recanted her story, and the British exiled her from the city.[42]

Some people then and later compared British winter quarters in Philadelphia with the Carthaginian stay at Capua during the Second Punic War because in both instances luxury, indulgence, and debauchery corrupted and softened the occupying army while its enemies grew stronger through their virtuous suffering. Indeed, there is some basis for the analogy. Gambling certainly got out of control that winter, with up to $50,000 changing hands in some instances. As was usual with gaming, there were more losers than winners, and many otherwise good officers were forced to sell their commissions to pay off their debts and return home. Their replacements were not necessarily as qualified to assume their positions, and one person speculated that by the end of the winter, gambling had erased all the hard-earned experience the officer corps had collectively accrued over the past two years. Some officers, like Knyphausen, recognized the negative impact this had on the army and tried to discourage it, but it was a tough sell when even Howe took his turn at the tables. Lassitude also contributed to a rise in dueling among officers with so much time on their hands that they could engage in petty personal disputes over honor. Many soldiers fell in love with locals that winter, and when the British evacuated the city in June, some of them deserted rather than leave their newly found sweethearts behind. Winter quarters was supposed to provide the troops with the opportunity to rest and prepare for the next year's campaigning, but it was an open question whether the British army really emerged from Philadelphia as fit as it should have.[43]

Confidence in Philadelphia's defenses and knowledge of the American army's weakened condition reinforced widespread British complacency that winter. British engineers constructed fourteen strong 50-man redoubts to ring the city from the Delaware to the Schuylkill to prevent a repetition of the rebel assault on Germantown, with fresh garrisons rotated in daily. Besides, British intelligence indicated that Washington's army was in no condition to attack anyone because it lacked basic necessities and was desperately short of manpower. In fact, 1,134 soldiers and 354 galleymen deserted to the British that winter, more than enough to indicate serious problems in the rebel ranks. Howe even received somewhat inaccurate information that Washington and Congress were quarreling. Put together, then, there seemed to be an opportunity for the British army to march on Valley Forge and destroy Washington's decrepit force, but Howe was so fixated on his own comparatively minor problems that he did not recognize it. The British commander in chief believed that the Valley Forge defenses were too strong to assail, and that his army did not have sufficient forage to march there. When the snow melted, Howe continued to balk; a failed attack might inspire the rebels to continued resistance and dash British peace proposals, and he figured that the next campaign would maneuver them away from well-fortified Valley Forge anyhow. So Howe squandered yet another opportunity to eradicate the American army, and Washington did not have to contend with a British offensive on top of all his other woes. It was possible that a wintertime British foray from Philadelphia might have ended in frustration as at Whitemarsh in December, or even in a repulse, but it was equally possible that Howe could have crushed the American army right then. Doing so probably would not have ended the war, but it certainly would have been a step in the right direction. One thing was clear, and that was that remaining in Philadelphia would not bring the conflict to a close anytime soon. A German officer who remembered that the army's primary job was waging war wrote in disgust, "I think that General Washington and all his soldiers, who suffer from lack of almost everything, have gained enough honor this winter by staying throughout this winter in huts so close to us. Do not let anyone ask me why we tolerate this!"[44]

Now that he had submitted his request for relief, Howe showed little inclination to engage in any more strategic thinking or planning. As a result, the British war effort in America stagnated that winter, the victim, as it were, of Howe-induced strategic inertia. Neither the king nor Germain liked this one bit; they wanted Howe to aggressively prosecute the war until his replacement arrived. Not surprisingly, their efforts to prod the British commander in chief into action merely provoked another unprofitable strategic dispute that led nowhere. London policy makers were considering using British naval power to bring the rebels to their knees through a reinvigorated blockade that would cut the Americans off from outside sustenance. As part of the new plan, Germain and the king believed that the British should concentrate on raiding New England seaports in an effort to destroy nests of American privateers there that preyed on British commerce. Howe, however, wanted no part in what he believed was a bad strategy that would not end the rebellion. He estimated that such operations would require 4,000 troops, and any damage they inflicted would not be worth the risks involved. He noted that the New England coastline was foggy and difficult for warships and troop transports to navigate, and putting redcoats ashore there would stretch British logistics and expose the troops to some of the same militiamen who had brought Burgoyne to grief the previous autumn. Instead, he said that he intended to keep his soldiers concentrated in Philadelphia to take advantage of any opportunity to attack and destroy Washington's army, although his reasoning was more than a little disingenuous in light of his failure to march on Valley Forge that winter. He also turned down suggestions that he open a campaign in the southern states. Howe claimed that conducting a successful offensive in that direction would require substantial loyalist support, and he had by now lost faith in the loyalists' abilities to contribute much to British army operations. Howe's response reached London on 1 June, but by then the military picture had changed so drastically as to render the king's proposals irrelevant for the time being.[45]

Despite the surface placidity that prevailed in Philadelphia that winter, the fact remained that it was an occupied city surrounded by rebel territory, and this hard reality distorted many otherwise normal facets of life. The civilian population declined to 21,800 because so many evacuated the place before Howe arrived, but the British army garrison and thousands of transients swelled the total to over 55,000 people. The military governed the city through loyalist Superintendent General of Police Joseph Galloway, and except for minor cases heard by three magistrates, civil courts disappeared. There were widespread shortages of even the most basic goods until the British opened up the Delaware River in November, but within weeks the markets filled up, and in mid-January one observer noted that only firewood and flour were hard to come by. In fact, over the course of the winter soldiers and civilians alike bought and presumably consumed 293,120 gallons of rum, 3,716 gallons of brandy, 39,520 gallons of molasses, and 42,847 bushels of salt. Even so, prices remained very high because filling the demand was such a risky and costly proposition. Loyalists slipped through the shaky rebel cordon into Philadelphia from the Pennsylvania interior and southern New Jersey to sell iron, foodstuffs, livestock, liquor, and lumber to the army and to the city's inhabitants. British officials were especially grateful for the timber because the army alone consumed 800 cords a week. Forage was in even shorter supply, and as they had done the previous winter, British soldiers swept the countryside in search of hay for their horses. They encountered opposition along eastern Pennsylvania's and southern New Jersey's roads and fields, but it was not as serious as it had been the previous winter. British officers were by now accustomed to such partisan warfare, and they made sure to operate in large, spread-out detachments capable of overcoming all but the stoutest resistance. In addition, Howe concentrated his forces behind Philadelphia's redoubts, so the rebels lacked opportunities to torment small, isolated British outposts and their supply parties as they did the previous winter. For Howe's redcoats, Germans, and provincials, this was merely another reason to be grateful for a winter in the American capital.[46]

Twenty miles up the Schuylkill, across eastern Pennsylvania's frozen woods and fields at Valley Forge, Washington lamented British good fortune. He had hoped to duplicate the previous winter's successful campaign in east central New Jersey by bushwhacking British foraging parties and impeding trade between Philadelphia and the surrounding countryside. This time he did not expect such efforts to cripple Howe's ability to undertake operations next spring, but he still wished to wear down British strength as part of his strategy of attrition. Unhappily, doing so proved impossible. As usual, Washington planned to rely on militiamen to harass and annoy the British around the former American capital while his Continentals recovered and rested from the last campaign's exertions, but the Pennsylvania militia was not up to the task. In late December, Pennsylvania militia commander John Armstrong estimated that he would have the 1,000 troops north of the Schuylkill necessary to carry out Washington's strategy, but expiring enlistments and difficulty in calling up replacements reduced the force to only around 100 by the end of the winter. This was hardly sufficient to stop the locals from bringing their goods to Philadelphia, let alone to successfully waylay large British foraging detachments. To make things worse, in January, Brigadier General James Potter of the Pennsylvania militia went west, and the state government replaced him with the young, inexperienced Brigadier General John Lacey. Lacey did his best under very trying conditions, but he lacked the manpower and leadership skills for such a difficult assignment. Washington was realistic enough to realize that it was impossible to completely sever all trade between Philadelphia and the neighboring region, but as winter wore on, he was angered and dismayed by reports that people were coming and going from the former American capital almost at will. Both Washington and a visiting congressional committee worried such interaction not only might hurt American logistics by draining much-needed resources away from Valley Forge but also might economically tie large numbers of Pennsylvanians to the British government, which was a first large step toward winning their political allegiance. In response, Washington resorted to increasingly heavy-handed measures to stop the illicit commerce. On 1 February, he ordered Lacey to dismantle the region's mills by removing waterwheel spindles and sawing off their spikes to keep the locals from producing the grain the British needed, and after 27 February he permitted his soldiers to keep whatever they seized from people illegally trading in Philadelphia. Unfortunately, none of this had its intended effect, and traffic between the former American capital and the countryside continued unabated. Instead, constant skirmishing and foraging by British and American soldiers gradually depopulated, desolated, and impoverished the region around Philadelphia, and law and order vanished as lawless gangs terrorized the people unfortunate enough to get caught between the British and the Americans.[47]

A NEW AMERICAN ARMY

On 26 September 1777, the same day Cornwallis entered Philadelphia in triumph, the Americans received one of their most valuable wartime assets. It was not a weapon, at least not exactly, but rather a man: Friedrich Ludolf Gerhard Augustin von Steuben. The German-born Steuben had served in the Prussian army in both staff and line positions during the Great War for Empire, in the process acquiring a thorough understanding of eighteenth-century warfare. Discharged as a captain at the end of the conflict, Steuben fell on hard times and accumulated considerable debts over the course of the next fourteen years. He unsuccessfully sought employment in a number of European armies until he encountered Benjamin Franklin in Paris in September 1777. The savvy Franklin saw something worthwhile in the down-on-his-luck forty-seven-year-old German, so he dispatched him to America with a letter introducing him inaccurately as a Prussian army lieutenant general. Steuben disembarked at Portsmouth, New Hampshire, traveled to Boston, and then headed south to present himself and his credentials to Congress in York. On 27 February, he met with Washington at Valley Forge. Washington was his formal and cordial self, despite the burdens he labored under that winter. By now the American commander in chief had come across enough foreign officers whose performance did not live up to their résumés to know that all that glittered was not gold, but he was impressed with Steuben's obvious military expertise, and even more impressed with his uncommon generosity. Steuben was as ambitious as the next man, but he allayed Washington's skepticism with his willingness to serve as a volunteer major general in any capacity the commander in chief saw fit until he proved himself enough to warrant a regular commission. Washington initially toyed with the idea of making him a quartermaster, but he ultimately decided that Steuben could best serve his newly adopted cause by drilling Continentals. This was the inspector general's job, but Washington did not want to exacerbate tensions stemming from the ongoing Conway Cabal by asking Congress to assign Steuben to the position, so instead he gave the German an inspector general's mandate and authority, but without the title. With his marching orders in hand, Steuben got to work.[48]

Washington understood better than anyone that insufficient training was one of his army's greatest weaknesses. Many of the officers and men had plenty of combat experience, but this did not mean that the army functioned as a professional eighteenth-century military force. Throughout the past three years, the British had repeatedly demonstrated their superiority in close-order marching, rapid deployment, open-field maneuvering, mass volley firing, and hand-to-hand combat. Time and time again, British discipline won the day, from the Plowed Hill at Brandywine to the midnight brouhaha at Paoli to the foggy streets and fields at Germantown. For all its pluck and resilience, the American army was in comparison sluggish, unresponsive, and ineffective in its full-scale engagements with its British counterpart. The busy Washington lacked the time to oversee the rigorous training of his soldiers, so he delegated the task to his subordinates. Some of them, such as Conway, took the job seriously and drilled their men meticulously, but most did not have the ability or the inclination to do so. In fact, a good many officers were more interested in securing promotions or furloughs than in parading their men in the cold. Moreover, there was little consistency in what training did occur, so units big and small deployed and maneuvered according to their officers' own peculiar methods. Washington wanted Steuben to establish a precise and uniform system of drill for his army, and to do so quickly because the campaigning season was just around the corner.[49]

Steuben was willing to do just that, but not at the expense of prudence and forethought. Watching the scruffy Continentals go through their paces, he quickly concluded that standard European drill would not suffice. Because this was a different kind of army, full of independent-minded freemen and plagued with short-term enlistments and frequent turnover, Steuben crafted a new drill that took these realities into account. Taking his cue from Washington, he emphasized simplicity and uniformity in the hope of teaching the troops to do a few important things very well. He organized a 100-man model company and personally trained them, setting an example for an officer corps that frequently disdained such mundane work. There was nothing easy about it; Steuben's English was poor and his temper short, but both improved rapidly over the next few weeks with the help of translators and a growing understanding and appreciation of American society. The men themselves were amused by his multilingual cussing but impressed with his efforts, and he attracted an audience that watched with interest as he put his company through its paces. Washington created brigade inspectors to carry Steuben's training throughout the rest of the army, and soon Valley Forge echoed with the clomp of boots and the barking of commands as the Continentals drilled and paraded in one form or another from dawn until midafternoon. By spring, entire divisions were maneuvering against each other in rudimentary war games, preparing for the bloody work to come.[50]

As the snow melted at Valley Forge, the American army continued to drill and march with increasing precision and uniformity. Almost all observers were impressed both with the results and with the architect of these efforts. One person stated that he watched fifteen regiments maneuver as well as any redcoats; another wrote more expansively, "I continue to be pleased with the appearance of everything here. Discipline seems to be growing apace and America will be under lasting obligations to the Baron Steuben as the father of it. He is much respected by the officers and beloved by the soldiers who themselves seem to be convinced of the propriety and necessity of his regulations. I am astonished at the progress he has made with the troops."[51] Some, however, worried about Steuben's broad authority, and others resented the German officer's roughshod methods, which left little room for commanders to improvise. However, such sentiments were rare, and they were not indicative of the pride and professionalism that Steuben instilled in both officers and men. By way of reward for his labors, on 5 May Congress appointed Steuben army inspector general with the rank of major general. Few then or later doubted that the German officer richly deserved the promotion. Steuben found an American army that already possessed the combat experience, pride, and dedication necessary to become a formidable fighting force; his contribution was to systematically train it to work together as a single cohesive unit. As such, Steuben served as midwife at the birth of a new professional American army, one that became capable of standing up to the redcoats in an open field of battle with a reasonable chance of success.[52]

Steuben could drill the Continentals all he wanted, but they would not be worth much in battle if they did not have food in their bellies, guns in their hands, and clothes on their backs, and all this was by no means certain. By the time Washington's army reached Valley Forge, the American logistical system was fast collapsing, and that winter it broke down completely. Only drastic and emergency measures saved the American army from starvation and dissolution, but Washington understood that such stopgap procedures would not work when campaigning began in earnest in the spring. Washington wanted to revamp the American logistical apparatus but lacked the authority to do so unilaterally without Congress's consent. Congress had gradually become aware of serious problems in the Commissary, Quartermaster, and Clothier departments toward the end of 1777, and on 3 January, Laurens warned that the entire supply system was approaching a crisis, though in fact the crisis was already upon them when he penned those words. In response, on 10 January, Congress established a committee to travel to Valley Forge to investigate the supply difficulties, consult with Washington, and recommend solutions in time for the next campaign. When the committee arrived in late January and set up shop at William Moore's house a couple of miles north of Washington's headquarters, its members were shocked and appalled by the sorry state of the American supply network and the army's dire straits. It uncovered multiple instances of greed, corruption, mismanagement, incompetence, and bottlenecks. Committee member Joseph Reed reported to Laurens that 6,000 spades, shovels, and tomahawks, as well as innumerable tents and uncounted yards of cloth, lay unguarded in a local farmer's barn. Abandoned valuable wagons dotted the countryside. The Commissary department could not get salt from New England, and without salt it could not begin stockpiling provisions for the 30,000 men the committee hoped it could feed by summer. Not surprisingly, the committee quickly agreed with Washington that the logistical system needed to be overhauled, but this was more easily said than done. Congress had already planned to divide the Quartermaster department into four branches, but the committee disapproved because no one would be in overall charge, and this would lead to more confusion and graft. Instead, it recommended increasing the quartermaster general's power and giving him two assistants appointed by Congress who would split a 1 percent commission with their boss, and Congress agreed. As for the Clothier department, the committee recommended that the states take over outfitting their own troops, though Congress did not put this plan into effect until the upcoming campaign was over.[53]

There were innumerable and intractable problems with American military logistics, a good many of which began with incompetent or negligent leadership. Washington had lost faith in both Commissary General William Buchanan and Clothier General James Mease—although, ironically, Washington refused Mease's offer to resign in December, probably because he had no handy replacement—and the Quartermaster General position had been vacant since Thomas Mifflin quit in October. Congress concentrated first on finding a quartermaster general, but this turned out to be more difficult than expected. Some suggested the deputy quartermaster general, Colonel Henry Lutterloh, but the committee rejected him because its members did not think he possessed enough energy or talent for the post. Others advocated Major General Philip Schuyler because he had administrative ability and experience, and as a former army commander he could understand Washington's travails. However, some New England congressmen continued to harbor a grudge against the aristocratic New Yorker for his actions in upstate New York during Burgoyne's invasion, so they vetoed the idea. Instead, the committee finally and reluctantly turned to Nathanael Greene. The Rhode Island general possessed considerable military knowledge, and Washington had a lot of faith in him and his judgment. The normally accommodating Greene hesitated to accept because he did not want such a thankless, unglamorous, dreary, and difficult job; he finally agreed on 2 March on the conditions that he did not have to surrender his line rank and that he could choose his two chief subordinates. As for Buchanan and Mease, the former resigned in April and was replaced by hardworking Connecticut businessman Jeremiah Wadsworth, who forged a good working relationship with Greene. Mease did not step down until August, after the 1778 campaign was well under way.[54]

Greene got to work at once to put the American logistical house in order in time for the spring campaign. He established or refurbished a chain of magazines and supply depots at Head of Elk, along the Schuylkill to the Susquehanna, around Trenton, and from the Delaware to the Hudson for the army to draw upon. He also repaired the broken roads to Valley Forge to make it easier for wagons to bring supplies to camp. To combat theft, he authorized branding the army's livestock, and he tapped into Maryland as a source of horses and wagons to ease the burden on war-ravaged Pennsylvania. He paid his deputy quartermasters by commission to motivate them, despite the opportunities for corruption this presented, and he compensated citizens the army did business with in printed certificates redeemable in a short period of time to limit inflation's impact on them. Unlike his predecessor, Greene had the advantages of better weather, a good relationship with Washington, and Congress's willingness to sacrifice economy and spend whatever was necessary to supply the army, so he got results. By mid-May, Washington noted that both the Quartermaster and Commissary departments were still not up to par because of the neglect and incompetence under which they had suffered the previous winter, but they were in good enough shape to permit the army to wage war that spring.[55]

For all its miseries, Valley Forge marked one of the American army's most important turning points. That winter's events transformed the army physically and psychologically from top to bottom into a professional eighteenth-century military force. The Conway Cabal and shared deprivation forged the officer corps into an increasingly distinct and separate part of American society. Disgruntled or fainthearted officers unwilling or unable to cope with the pressures of war resigned their commissions and went home, leaving behind a hard kernel of devoted men who saw themselves as a unique and vital part of the American war effort. Despite an American society that frowned on such things, the officer corps became increasingly professional, a not uncommon occurrence in revolution. As for the soldiers, they, too, became professionalized by the isolation, suffering, and training they experienced at Valley Forge. More and more, the army consisted of lower-class men who enlisted for comparatively longer terms, which made them much different from the militia. Even the logistical system fell into the hands of professionals as Congress retreated from overseeing its day-to-day operations. As spring came on, Washington had to decide how he planned to use his new army. Should he continue to adhere to his patient strategy of attrition by avoiding big battles with the British and relying instead on cooperation between the Continentals and the militia to gradually wear the British army down? Or should he change his strategy and instead test his well-trained army in a straight-up battle that might defeat and destroy the British army, thus bringing the war to a quick and successful conclusion? As May turned into June, such questions became less and less academic.

SIX

A Brand-New War

A WORLD WAR

The Revolutionary War did not take place in an international vacuum but instead was part of a broader multipolar Eurocentric world. Eighteenth-century foreign policies were usually geared toward maintaining a balance of power in which no one country was strong enough to dominate the rest. For more than 100 years, Great Britain had played a crucial role in upholding this balance of power, and in the process it had accumulated innumerable colonies around the world and become perhaps the wealthiest nation on earth. In fact, London policy makers believed that their empire and their commerce went hand in hand, together generating the prosperity and military resources Britain used to outlast and defeat France in the Great War for Empire. By 1763, Britain's extensive domain included not only England, Ireland, and Scotland but also chunks of India, parts of the west African coast, several valuable sugar-rich West Indies islands, Florida, Nova Scotia, former French Canada, and of course the thirteen North American colonies. The empire was something all Britons could be proud of, and if such pride often slipped into arrogance, it was that very conceit that helped them repeatedly triumph over their enemies. Britain's success, however, created resentment and unease among other European great powers that looked suspiciously upon its growing strength. This, along with London's unwise and shortsighted foreign policy decisions in the 1760s and 1770s, led to Great Britain's diplomatic isolation; thus it entered the Revolutionary War without any major European allies.

As France nursed its wounds and its anger after the Great War for Empire, its policy makers kept a wary eye open for any opportunity to knock the upstart British down a peg or two. The French were well aware of Britain's problems with the colonies, so they were quick to grasp the possibilities the American rebellion offered. If British prosperity depended on its commerce with its empire, then breaking the political links between London and its North American colonies might undermine British power and enable France to regain its military and economic superiority. Even so, getting involved in such a family squabble was risky; French finances were shaky, its military was not yet ready for war, and the rebels' commitment and determination were uncertain. As it was, the Americans were more than willing to accept the French clandestine aid that flowed across the Atlantic in 1776 and 1777, but they did not push for a military alliance until after their disastrous defeats around New York City. Throughout 1777, American commissioners in Paris lobbied for France's entry into the war, but the French hesitated in part because they questioned American resolve. Victory at Saratoga and Washington's determined resistance around Philadelphia, however, cleared up such doubts and convinced the French that the Americans were in their war for the long haul. On 6 February 1778, the United States and France signed treaties of commerce and alliance that bound the two countries to wage war together until American independence was won. French recognition of the United States made conflict with Britain inevitable, and by mid-June the two countries were at war.[1]

Howe's resignation placed British strategic planning in the ministry's hands, and in the winter of 1777–78 Germain and his colleagues—primarily the king, First Lord of the Admiralty Earl of Sandwich, and adviser and Great War for Empire hero Lieutenant General Jeffrey Amherst—worked hard to prepare for the next campaign. Even before the Franco-American alliance, the ministry had decided to reorient its strategy in response to the Saratoga disaster and Howe's inability to crush the rebellion. Subjugating America through direct military conquest had obviously failed, and further efforts along those lines were increasingly beyond Britain's limited means. Indeed, Amherst estimated that doing so would require 30,000 or 40,000 more troops, and nowhere near that many were available. In light of these unhappy realities, British policy makers crafted a new strategy to win the war for Howe's replacement, Lieutenant General Henry Clinton. Speaking for the ministry, Germain wanted Clinton to try to bring Washington into a decisive battle as soon as possible, while at the same time the British attempted to negotiate American readmission into the empire on generous terms. If this carrot-and-stick approach failed, Germain proposed to undertake efforts to isolate and reduce New England, which he believed was the heart of the rebellion. To do so, he planned to first secure British bases in North America by strengthening Canada, Halifax, Newport,

New York City, St. Augustine, and, if possible, Philadelphia. Once the British had firmly anchored themselves along the coast, Germain intended to use the Royal Navy and troops released from chasing Washington's army over hill and dale to blockade and raid New England seaports. Germain hoped that depriving New England of its overseas trade and destroying its privateers and shipbuilding industry would not only protect British commerce but also paralyze the region's war effort.[2]

Ambitious though this strategy was, Germain saw it merely as ancillary to the second part of the ministry's grand design. More than 12,000 British and German reinforcements would be available for service in America by the early autumn, and Germain wanted to use them to conquer the supposedly vulnerable southern states. This would protect and utilize the region's reportedly large loyalist population, and it would enable the British to destroy or capture the raw materials there that the rebels used to purchase the military supplies, equipment, and weapons from abroad that they needed to sustain the conflict. Germain believed that Clinton could deploy 2,000 soldiers in conjunction with troops from Florida to assault Savannah, Georgia, in October. Once Georgia was returned to its old allegiance, 5,000 British troops could then seize Charleston, South Carolina, and open a route through the state northward. At the same time, diversionary attacks on Cape Fear, North Carolina, and into Virginia and Maryland would unlock communications with local loyalists and devastate the region's valuable rice, indigo, and tobacco crops. If all went as planned, the British would eventually occupy the territory south of the Susquehanna River, and this, combined with the vigorous naval war against New England, would hopefully make it impossible for the rebels to continue the war.[3]

The Franco-American alliance rendered much of Germain's strategy largely academic in the short term, although the British later attempted to implement various components of the plan. The British were well aware of Franco-American negotiations, and in fact their intelligence network quickly learned of the treaties' details. British policy makers understood that war with France was now merely a matter of time, and they feared the consequences. France was one of Europe's most powerful nations, with a large army and a revitalized navy that contained fifty-two men-of-war. This was shy of the sixty-six men-of-war the Royal Navy possessed, but the British recognized that their numerical superiority would vanish in an instant if France's ally Spain also joined the conflict, which was possible because the Spanish also harbored grudges left over from the Great War for Empire and from Britain's seizure of Gibraltar during the War of Spanish Succession earlier in the century. France's inevitable entry into the war on the Americans' side would change the conflict's strategic dynamics in all sorts of ways detrimental to Britain. For one thing, it would transform what had been an unpleasant but manageable regional conflict into a world war that might threaten Britain itself, and it would force the British to disperse their limited resources around the globe to protect their extensive, valuable, and on the whole weakly defended empire. For example, there were only 1,800 mostly sick redcoats garrisoning the West Indies, hardly enough to repulse a determined French attack. Reinforcing these and other possessions would require men, equipment, and matériel that would have to be diverted from suppressing the American rebellion. Scarier still, Britain's lack of allies would enable the French to devote their full attention to a naval war instead of worrying about a continental threat. The French might deploy their naval power in North American waters to scatter or destroy the British fleet there that protected and succored redcoats and Germans engaged in crushing the rebellion. The British army was divided into various detachments up and down the American coast at Halifax, Newport, New York City, Philadelphia, and St. Augustine, so French naval superiority could cut the army's supply and communications lines, rendering it as defenseless as a man with a shattered spine in the face of a determined American attack. Finally, the Franco-American alliance would undoubtedly hearten and encourage the rebels, thus jeopardizing British efforts to negotiate their readmission into the empire.[4]

On 13 March the French government officially notified the British of France's commercial treaty with the United States, which was tantamount to formal recognition of the Americans' status as an independent country. The British recalled their ambassador from the Versailles court that night, and the two countries careened toward war. Imminent conflict with France forced the British to reformulate their strategy, and on 21 March, Germain dispatched new orders to Clinton. The ministry instructed the commander in chief to load 5,000 soldiers from his Philadelphia garrison on board transports for an immediate attack on the French West Indies island of St. Lucia before the hurricane season began. It also wanted another 3,000 troops sent to reinforce St. Augustine and Pensacola in Florida. Once Clinton made these detachments from his 16,000-man army, he would not have sufficient men to hold on to Philadelphia, so Germain directed him to abandon the former American capital and take his troops by sea to New York City, from where he was to await results of British peace proposals. Germain also gave Clinton discretionary orders to evacuate New York City for Halifax and Newport if necessary. Once Clinton had consolidated British forces in America, and assuming negotiations with the rebels failed, he could undertake operations against the New England coast.[5]

On 29 March, a little more than a week after the American secretary sent Clinton his latest orders, Earl of Carlisle, former West Florida governor George Johnson, and Northern Department undersecretary and spymaster William Eden met with Germain, North, and several other British policy makers to discuss their peace mission to America. The young, wealthy, and foppish Carlisle was officially in charge of the proposed commission because of his connections with Opposition leader Charles Fox, but Eden provided its brains and impetus. The ministry also made the Howe brothers members, but North correctly doubted that Sir William would acquiesce now that the king had accepted his resignation as commander in chief. If this indeed proved to be the case, Clinton was to take his place. As Britain lurched toward conflict with France, London policy makers were increasingly willing to put an end to the American war in order to concentrate their resources against their old and dangerous rival. With this in mind, the ministry was prepared to offer the rebels extremely generous terms that amounted to self-rule within the empire. On 19 February, Parliament had renounced its right to levy direct taxes on the colonies and to station soldiers there without the Americans' consent. To sweeten the pot, the ministry ordered the commission to guarantee Congress's continued existence, the sanctity of colonial charters, and the Americans' right to maintain their own armies. In return, the British would get little more than an end to the war, the power to regulate colonial trade, and continued preferential access to American markets for their manufactured goods. All these concessions represented a complete capitulation to colonial prewar demands, but they would maintain the empire. Most in the ministry, however, doubted that the rebels would accept such terms now that they had declared their freedom and struck an alliance with France. The king thought that nothing short of independence would satisfy them, and he was not prepared to grant this because he believed that the dissolution of the empire would reduce Britain to a second-rate power. He wanted the war prosecuted with the utmost vigor while the commission spun itself out. For his part, Germain predicted that this evidence of British accommodation was just as likely to drive the Americans closer to France as to end the war. No wonder Germain saw little reason to divulge the ministry's latest strategic plans to Carlisle during a last-minute meeting the day before the commission set sail. Instead, the American secretary merely cryptically suggested that Carlisle go to New York City instead of Philadelphia because the former American capital might not be in British hands by the time he got there.[6]

The Franco-American alliance made an already atypical war all the more bizarre for British policy makers, and the ministry's 1778 strategy reflected the conflict's peculiar and thorny nature. For three years the British had tried unsuccessfully to crush the American rebellion, and now they faced an additional enemy determined to permanently sever their economic relationship with the colonies upon which many believed British prosperity and power depended. From this perspective, concentrating British resources on France made sense. War with France posed all sorts of unpleasant strategic scenarios to the British, but it also offered opportunities to pick off valuable French overseas colonies like sugar-rich St. Lucia to help pay for the conflict's expense. Besides, in this instance the best defense seemed to be a good offense; British strength in the West Indies was minimal, so merely scattering reinforcements among their various possessions there would not improve their overall security. On the other hand, a sharp and sudden blow against a key island like St. Lucia would throw the French off balance and secure the British the strategic initiative that might end the French threat sooner rather than later. But there may have been more to it than that. War with France was familiar, comfortable, and simple compared with the appalling complexities and frustrations presented by the attempt to suppress the American rebellion. With the French, winning battles and occupying territory mattered—or anyhow it had in the past—and doing both was likely to bring about results that seemed unattainable in America. The price of focusing on France, however, was forfeiting any immediate chance of military victory over the rebels. The British would also be surrendering the short-term strategic initiative in America to Washington, who had already shown on several occasions that he would be quick to grasp and use it in ways invariably harmful to the British. Moreover, any cooperation between a French fleet and Washington would greatly increase the American army's potency. Even so, the ministry believed that at this point war with France was the overriding priority.

Besides, although the British were clearly relegating the American war to secondary status, they were not abandoning all efforts to suppress the rebellion, assuming the Carlisle Commission failed. Instead, they sought to make a virtue of necessity by using their limited resources more wisely. Germain's strategy toward New England in particular had much to recommend it, if Clinton could undertake it. Instead of trying to occupy large tracts of territory and annihilate Washington's army—both of which seemed next to impossible to accomplish—Germain wanted to isolate and destroy the resources upon which Washington's army relied. This in and of itself was a marked improvement over Howe's pedestrian thinking. Also to his credit, Germain saw little point in cultivating ineffective loyalist sentiment in New England, which freed the British to conduct the vigorous and heartless war necessary to demolish enemy resources and gain victory, although whether America would be worth possessing when the smoke cleared was an open question. On the other hand, this strategy had plenty of flaws. Germain believed that Washington would disperse his army to confront British coastal raids, but keeping his forces concentrated was one of the American commander in chief's chief strategic tenets, and he had so far successfully resisted all political pressure to do otherwise. If the past three years had proved anything, it was the peril of dismissing or underestimating the persistent Washington, but Germain seemed prepared to do just that. In addition, no matter how powerful the Royal Navy was, it was unlikely that it could enforce a tight blockade on New England, transport and land enough raiding expeditions from New Hampshire to Connecticut to inflict real damage on the rebel infrastructure, protect the British Isles and communications lines around the world, combat the big French fleet, and eventually support British army operations in the southern states and elsewhere. Finally, many British policy makers incorrectly assumed that the Americans would prefer to return to the British Empire rather than establish an independent nation tied to France. Be that as it may, the ministry's leaders believed they had done their best under bad circumstances, and throughout the summer of 1778 they anxiously awaited the results of their efforts.

THE BRITISH EVACUATE PHILADELPHIA

Despite his faults, most British officers personally liked the congenial William Howe, and as his tenure as commander in chief wound down in the spring of 1778, some of the army's staffers wanted to show their appreciation for the man who had led them to so many battlefield victories over the past three years. The result of their efforts was a going-

away party that probably surpassed any other celebration ever seen in
Philadelphia. The so-called Meschianza—a derivative from the Italian
word for "medley"—was primarily the brainchild of Captains John
Andre and Oliver De Lancey, who organized a bash that reflected and
befitted their flamboyant and grandiose natures. It cost British officers
a staggering 3,312 guineas, not counting the hours of manpower the
army and navy devoted to its preparation, but it was worth it as far as
most of its 730 invited participants and their guests were concerned. At
3:30 P.M. on 18 May, the Howe brothers, high-ranking British and German officers, and some of the city's most prominent and beautiful citizens assembled at Philadelphia's upper wharf and embarked on
decorated barges and flatboats. A band played "God Save the King,"
and onlookers cheered from the shoreline and from the warships anchored in the river as the fleet sailed down the Delaware. After landing
at the city's lowermost wharf, the revelers proceeded to a mock tour-
nament where two officers representing the fanciful Knights of the
Blended Rose and the Knights of the Burning Mountain jousted to a
draw for the ladies' favor amid the sound of blaring trumpets. The company then walked between a procession line drawn from all the army's
regiments to a mirror-adorned house for tea, coffee, and dancing.
Around 9:30 P.M. there was a fireworks display, and a couple of hours
later the crowd retired to a specially built 100-foot-long hall that seated
1,040 people to eat and drink the finest foods and wines. Throughout
the night the partyers knocked back innumerable toasts to the king, the
royal family, the army and navy, the noble ladies of Philadelphia, the
festival's organizers—and of course to William Howe. They were still at
it when dawn broke, and many had to fight the morning sun's glare as
they stumbled home. Six days later, Howe left Philadelphia for England,
never to return. Despite the good feelings generated that night, then and
later some British and German officers criticized the event as frivolous,
excessive, and ultimately counterproductive to the war effort. One
wrote, "It cost a great sum of money. Our enemies will dwell upon the
folly and extravagance of it with pleasure. Every man of sense, among
ourselves, tho' not unwilling to pay a due respect [to Howe], was
ashamed of this mode of doing it."[7]

Meanwhile, the war continued, and as winter gave way to spring, its
intensity around Philadelphia increased with the rising temperatures.
Rebel units pushed closer to the city in a renewed effort to isolate it
from the surrounding region. In response, the British dispatched more
troops into the countryside to protect their foraging and woodcutting

parties, as well as local loyalists. Doing so, however, was often dangerous work; Americans in the woods and fields sniped at and harassed
patrolling redcoats and Germans with growing frequency. Chasing
these small rebel parties through the lawless no-man's-land outside
Philadelphia was about as effective as hunting down individual bees in
the midst of a swarm. Howe understood this, and although he was
loath to march to Valley Forge to eliminate the queen bee Washington
represented, he was willing to strike at any subsidiary hives he identified. In early May, Lieutenant Colonel Robert Abercrombie and 700
light infantry, rangers, and cavalry surprised young and ineffective
Brigadier General John Lacey and his 600 Pennsylvania militiamen in
their Crooked Billet camp about seventeen miles from Philadelphia.
Abercrombie scattered the hapless militia and inflicted over 100 casualties at the cost of only 9 men. On 7 May, Major John Maitland led
the Second Light Infantry up the Delaware on flatboats accompanied
by several galleys, an armed schooner, and a brig to assail the remnants
of the American navy on the river at Bordentown. Washington had long
suspected that the British might undertake such an attack, and he had
repeatedly urged the Navy Board to scuttle the warships there rather
then expose them to enemy capture, but to no avail. In fact, his intelligence network warned him of the impending sortie, so he ordered
Maxwell to take a detachment to Bordentown to intercept the British.
Unfortunately for the Americans, a heavy rain delayed Maxwell, so
Maitland had little trouble destroying forty-four rebel vessels of various
sizes, including the frigates *Washington* and *Effingham*, and valuable
stores of tent poles, pegs, tar, and pitch.[8]

Howe could take pride that spring in these and other engagements
that kept the rebels off balance and demonstrated the superiority of
British arms. Such good fortune, however, was somewhat marred, if not
counterbalanced, by controversy generated by the aborted British strike
at Barren Hill a couple of weeks later. On 18 May—Meschianza day in
Philadelphia—British intelligence learned that several thousand Continentals under Major General Marquis de Lafayette had left Valley
Forge, crossed the Schuylkill at Fatland Ford, and taken up position at
Barren Hill. American intentions were unclear, but next morning
Howe—presumably nursing a hangover—grasped another chance to
defeat the rebels in detail. He decided to send James Grant and 5,000
troops to cut Lafayette off from the Schuylkill, and then follow up with
more men. At the very least Howe planned to destroy the exposed detachment and its impudent young commander, but he also hoped that

he could maul the entire American army if Washington attempted to rescue his subordinate. Late in the evening of 19 May, Grant's column marched toward Lafayette's left flank via Whitemarsh and Abington Hill in a grueling roundabout hike. Unfortunately for Grant and the British, by the time they approached Barren Hill at daybreak, the American rear guard was scuttling back across the Schuylkill, its getaway complete. Grant had no choice but to pull back to Chestnut Hill to meet Howe and his two follow-up brigades, and the entire force retreated to Philadelphia as empty-handed and red-faced as a snark hunt victim. British losses were minimal, but many officers criticized Grant for his slowness, his excessive caution, and his failure to secure all the Schuylkill fords before he moved toward Barren Hill. Many officers disliked him anyway for his arrogance and ambition, although he had Howe's confidence and friendship. In fact, Howe himself later admitted that he did not want to run any undue risks as his tenure as commander in chief ended, so he was not inclined to put too much blame on his friend and subordinate for the missed opportunity.[9]

Incoming British commander in chief Lieutenant General Henry Clinton was among the Meschianza's guests of honor, but in all likelihood he did not enjoy himself nearly as much as did Howe. The good-natured Howe and the dour Clinton certainly possessed very different personalities, but the responsibilities they currently labored under undoubtedly reinforced each man's natural disposition. Howe would soon be on his way home, freed from the burdens of leadership that had tormented him for the past three years. Clinton, on the other hand, was about to inherit all of Howe's old intractable problems, as well as many new ones stemming from France's imminent entry into the war. Born in 1730, Clinton spent his formative years in New York during his father's tenure there as the colony's royal governor. Like many of his fellow high-ranking officers, he cut his military teeth in Germany in the Great War for Empire on his way up the chain of command. After the war he served in Parliament, and he suffered from depression after his wife's death in August 1772. Shipped over to America with Howe and Burgoyne in 1775, he saw action at Bunker Hill and a year later commanded the abortive Charleston expedition before rejoining the main British army for its assault on New York City. He fought well on Long Island, but his unsolicited and generally unwelcome advice irked Howe, who sent him to occupy Newport to get him out of the way. After a trip home to defend his actions outside of Charleston harbor and to unsuccessfully lobby for command of the Canadian army, he returned to

America to take charge of the New York City garrison while Howe attacked Philadelphia. Clinton wanted no part in the uncoordinated strategy Howe, Germain, and Burgoyne cobbled together that year—and Howe wanted no part of Clinton, which was why he left him behind in New York City—but some later faulted his failure to drive up the Hudson to Albany to relieve Burgoyne's beleaguered army. Shunted to the war's backwater, criticized for his role in a campaign he thought was a bad idea from the start, convinced that his superiors did not appreciate him enough, and believing that he could not contribute much to victory with the limited resources at his disposal, Clinton repeatedly asked to be relieved of his command. Instead, on 4 February the ministry appointed him Howe's successor, mostly because he was the senior officer in America, and Amherst did not want the post. Clinton possessed a keen strategic mind, but this did not compensate for his significant shortcomings. He was in fact vain, plagued with self-doubt, cautious, hopelessly uninspiring, and so hypersensitive and quarrelsome that he sooner or later bickered with almost everyone with whom he came into prolonged contact. None of these character weaknesses boded well for a man about to confront some of the most complicated and tricky military problems an officer could face.[10]

Clinton arrived in Philadelphia on 8 May on the frigate HMS *Greyhound*, and the next day he received Germain's 21 March directive. To Clinton, such seemingly defeatist and impractical orders were a disturbing introduction to his new command. The ministry had clearly opted to pursue a negotiated settlement with the rebels while it concentrated British resources against the French. Since this was the case, there was little glory to be won in America, so Clinton's climb to the top of the military ladder had come to naught, at least as far as advancing his career and promoting his reputation were concerned. Worse yet, Clinton did not believe that implementing Germain's plan right away was strategically sound or logistically possible. Admiral Howe currently lacked the warships necessary to convoy all those troops to the West Indies and Florida; in fact, there was no guarantee that he could even maintain control of the seas in the face of the French fleet reportedly on its way from Toulon. Weighing the risks, Clinton decided to first take his entire army back to New York City, and then dispatch from there the various expeditions to St. Augustine, Pensacola, and St. Lucia. Here too, however, there were problems. Clinton did not want to abandon the army's baggage or Philadelphia's large loyalist population, but there was not enough shipping available to bring everyone and everything to New York City in the one trip necessary to permit him to carry out his other operations. In addition, Admiral Howe stated that he would have to embark the army and its hangers-on from Newcastle, forty long, vulnerable miles from the former American capital. It was also possible that bad weather might delay the fleet's journey as it had the previous summer, thus again temporarily removing the British army from the strategic chessboard and giving Washington the opportunity to attack and capture New York City before Clinton arrived to reinforce the place. The more he thought about it, the more Clinton concluded that the thing to do was to march the British army to New York City overland through New Jersey. This would place the army beyond the reach of any French warships attempting to seize the vulnerable troop transports. Moreover, it would free up enough room on the transports for the loyalists and much of the army's equipment, and Clinton could embark them from Philadelphia instead of Newcastle because the army would not leave the city until the fleet was under way. There was also the off chance that somewhere along the way Washington might engage the British army in a full-scale battle that would enable Clinton to destroy it in one fell swoop. Clinton doubted that the canny American commander in chief would take such a risk with the possibility of French assistance just around the corner, but it was worth a try.[11]

Rumors that the British intended to abandon Philadelphia in the spring spread through the army even before Clinton arrived and read Germain's latest directive. As the gossip hardened into fact, many British and German officers responded to London's orders with disgust and dismay born out of their ingrained self-confidence and parochialism. As officers like Charles Grey saw it, they had beaten Washington's army before and could do so again, if only they had the opportunity. The problem was a lack of will on the part of unspecified others above them—usually meaning Howe, although few wanted to directly and openly criticize a man most genuinely liked—not a lack of means. The decadent winter quarters might have corrupted and bankrupted many officers, but by spring the army itself was well fed, equipped, clothed, and ready for battle, if only someone would lead them to Valley Forge to whip Washington once and for all. Instead of abhorring French participation, many officers welcomed it as a way to finally hit back at the country that had been aiding the rebels for the past two years. Turning the American war over to diplomats for a negotiated settlement that would probably give the rebels more than they deserved was galling, and it seemed clear that there were few laurels to be won in this part of the world. It was not surprising, then, that that summer some British officers such as Cornwallis asked to come home. The rank and file had no such option, but the possibility that their days in America were numbered impacted them as well, and as spring came on, there was a marked increase in desertion by men who for whatever reason did not want to leave.[12]

Philadelphia's imminent evacuation was more of a blow to the British army's pride than anything else, but for the city's loyalists it represented something much worse. More than 4,300 people had taken a loyalty oath to the king since Howe's army showed up, and many others had been equally public in their allegiance to the Crown. On 21 May, when Howe told magistrate Samuel Shoemaker that the British army was leaving, he blandly suggested that the loyalists make the best deal they could with the rebels. Word of this conversation spread rapidly through the close-knit loyalist community, and Clinton confirmed it the next day. Many loyalists had faithfully supported the king before and during Howe's occupation, but now fate—or, more accurately, London policy makers and their jittery reaction to the Franco-American alliance—had rewarded their devotion with two equally unpleasant options: they could leave Philadelphia for the unfamiliar confines of British-occupied New York City, or they could remain behind and take their chances with the vengeful rebels. Either way, they would likely lose their hard-earned property and status, which was not what they had expected the previous September when they so joyfully lined the streets to welcome the redcoats to town. This latest unhappy news confirmed for some loyalists their growing conviction that Howe had not done nearly enough to suppress the rebellion. Joseph Galloway, for one, remained convinced that the majority of Pennsylvanians backed the king, but Howe's refusal to sufficiently tap into this deep pool of support had contributed to the predicament the British and loyalists now confronted. For neither the first nor the last time in the war, the British were leaving the loyalists in the lurch, and each occasion further undermined indigenous backing for their war effort. Small wonder, then, that there was so little enthusiasm among the loyalists for the king's 4 June birthday celebration.[13]

The ministry's new strategy embittered not only the British army in America and the loyalists but also the Carlisle Commission. On 16 April, Carlisle, Eden, and Johnson embarked from England on the man-of-war HMS *Trident*. After a delay made all the more irksome by the fact that fellow distinguished passenger Charles Cornwallis—he was returning to America from a winter leave with a promotion to lieutenant general—used his authority to find rooms on board for his aides at the commissioners' expense, they set sail five days later. As *Trident* approached the American coastline, on 27 May it encountered the brig HMS *Stanley*, whose captain informed them that Howe and Clinton were at Philadelphia, not New York City, so the commissioners decided to stop there to confer with the outgoing and incoming commanders in chief. Before they left Britain, Carlisle, Eden, and Johnson were optimistic about their mission because their information indicated that many rebels, including some high-ranking officers, were ready for peace. Their journey up the Delaware lasted only two days, but it was an eye-opener for all three men. The rebels controlled the riverbanks, and their eagerness to take potshots at the passing *Trident* indicated that they were still full of fight. Worse yet, when the commissioners arrived at Philadelphia on 6 June, they discovered 400 mostly loyalist-laden transports bobbing in the river and the British army preparing to evacuate the city. Their shock was compounded by a sense of betrayal because Clinton informed them that the ministry had decided upon its new strategy before the commission left England, so Germain had intentionally kept them in the dark. Carlisle, Eden, and Johnson believed that their success required an aggressive and active British army with which to threaten the rebels if they refused their generous proposals, but they would lose all credibility once the Americans realized that the British army was retracting its military claws. In this fellow commissioner Clinton agreed. Taking stock, they decided to move fast before the military situation deteriorated further, so on 9 June they officially informed Congress of British terms. They held nothing back because they were in no position to engage in prolonged negotiations, and they figured that laying all their cards on the table from the start would place the onus of refusing such a good deal squarely on Congress.[14]

Rumors that the British were prepared to negotiate peace had filtered into America throughout the spring, and most rebel leaders were skeptical even before they learned the details. Washington speculated that the British were trying to divide the Americans with the siren song of peace and was not altogether confident that Congress would see through the ploy. In this instance, however, Congress did not disappoint the commander in chief. The delegates debated the British offer in mid-June, but there was no sentiment to accept it. By now too many Americans had invested too much blood, sweat, and tears into their Revolution, so proposals that might have placated them three years ago held no attraction now. Besides, the United States had just signed an alliance with France, and repudiating it under these conditions would be dishonorable. On 17 June, Laurens informed the Carlisle Commission that Congress would enter into negotiations to end the war only if the British first explicitly recognized American independence or withdrew their forces from the states. The commissioners had no authority to do either, and their mission sputtered to a discredited halt in New York City by the end of summer, especially after Johnson's unsuccessful efforts to bribe several congressmen became public. Most in the ministry were not all that surprised, having had little faith in the mission to begin with, and on 23 August the king emphasized that the British should continue their efforts to implement their latest strategy.[15]

In Philadelphia, Clinton was determined to do just that, although he knew better than anyone the multiple risks transforming the ministry's complicated directives into action entailed. Evacuating an occupied city in the face of an enemy army was among the trickiest of military problems, but the possibility that a French fleet might appear out of nowhere to disrupt Clinton's plans by blowing British transports and warships out of the water was too horrifying to contemplate. There was no chance that the British could conceal from the Americans the large-scale preparations necessary to withdraw their army and their loyalist supporters; nevertheless, Clinton hoped to confuse Washington as to the ultimate purpose of these machinations by persuading the American commander in chief that the British intended to strike Valley Forge first. With this in mind, the British continued to improve the redoubts surrounding the city until the last minute, even damming the creeks in front of them to create a moatlike effect in an effort to convince the Americans that they were not yet abandoning the city. Inside Philadelphia itself, however, there were no doubts that the British were leaving soon. Grief-stricken loyalists scurried to sell all but their most precious possessions before they boarded the packed transports crowding the river, which created a gloomy atmosphere on the streets. Jubilant rebel sympathizers counted the days until liberation, and loyalists condemned the British army for hanging them out to dry. On 24 May, the British began embarking their heavy baggage, artillery, stores, sick and wounded, and about 3,000 loyalists for the voyage to New York City, an arduous and time-consuming task that taxed everyone's patience. Transports daily descended the river to make room for others taking their place. At the same time, the British destroyed anything of military value that they could not take with them. On 14–15 May they burned superfluous shipping in the stocks, and 130 flatboats, one galley, and a frigate went up in smoke. Unfortunately, high, dry winds spread the flames to two nearby stables and a house as well. Redcoats also spiked forty unserviceable cannons, demolished the city's fortifications, shot lame horses, dismantled the bridges, and threw surplus munitions into the river. By 17 June the only British still in Philadelphia were the infantry, and next morning at daybreak they marched four miles down the Delaware across from Gloucester Point, where flatboats guarded by the aptly named *Vigilant*—the same vessel that delivered the coup de grâce to Fort Mifflin the previous November—ferried them across the river to the New Jersey shore. Philadelphia, the object of so much British sweat and blood, was back in rebel hands before the last redcoat left Pennsylvania soil.[16]

Clinton divided his army into two divisions for its trek through New Jersey, one under recently arrived Cornwallis and the other commanded by the ever-dependable Knyphausen. The British march bisected the state, through Moorestown, Mount Holly, and Bordentown. Heavy storms cooled the air and kept the dust down the first couple of days, but after 21 June a blistering, sultry sun baked the sandy roads, and thunder echoed ominously in the distance as the redcoats, Germans, and provincials hiked northeastward. Many of the locals abandoned their homes and drove off their livestock as the British approached, making the countryside seem strangely empty. But it was not; rebels filled the wells, felled trees across the rutted roads, and destroyed the bridges over the region's numerous small creeks, all of which slowed the winding British columns to a crawl. Repairing the broken roads and bridges was hard, tiring, thirsty work, and many soldiers fell out with fatigue. Others seized opportunities to desert; one officer estimated that at least 200 Germans alone left the army this way. Desertions among the Germans in particular became such a problem that in an effort to stop the practice, Knyphausen spread the false rumor that the troops would be returning home after they reached New York City. The British took more draconian remedies to keep their men in line by hanging a captured deserter along the road for the passing troops to see and contemplate. Other soldiers participated in plundering, despite Clinton's strict orders against it. The Germans were as usual the worst perpetrators, but the British were hardly innocent. It was redcoats, not Germans, who ransacked Freehold's church and city hall on 26 June. Such extracurricular activities, however, became increasingly risky as time went on and rebel resistance steadily grew. Militia, riflemen, and Continentals popped up on the hillsides and in the woods to snipe at the long British columns, and advancing redcoats and Germans engaged in frequent skirmishes along New Jersey's roads and creeks.

On 23 June, a British detachment seized the stone bridge over Crosswicks Creek intact after a sharp skirmish during which a rebel sniper wounded a redcoat officer near the conspicuously dressed Clinton. The next day the British occupied Allentown, forcing the new commander in chief to determine the army's route once and for all. Clinton had considered taking his troops to New York City via the Raritan River, but British intelligence indicated that Washington had crossed the Delaware with his army, and that Horatio Gates was bringing more rebel troops down from the Hudson. Like most British officers, Clinton was confident that his soldiers could beat any number of Americans in a fair fight, but he did not want to expose his long 1,500-wagon baggage train to attack from two directions. Mulling things over, he decided to head toward Sandy Hook, and from there embark his army across the Lower Bay to New York City. To that end, he put Knyphausen and James Grant in the lead with the baggage train and kept Cornwallis's division between it and the hovering rebels, and on 25 June the army pushed on toward Freehold. Knyphausen arrived there the next day, and Cornwallis's covering force halted a mile behind them at Monmouth Courthouse. Approximately 200 troops fell out from heat and exhaustion that day, and a terrific thunderstorm that night turned the roads into mud, so Clinton decided to give his army a rest. Besides, he had received reports that Washington's army was close at hand, and he still harbored hopes of defeating it in a decisive battle. He got his fight the next day.[17]

CONFUSED AMERICAN RESPONSE

Eighteen days after the profligate Meschianza, the American army at Valley Forge also celebrated, but for a better cause and in better taste than their British counterparts in Philadelphia. In late April the French frigate *La Sensible* had docked in Falmouth with dispatches announcing that the French government and the American commissioners at Versailles had signed an alliance on 6 February. Rumors of the Franco-American treaties reached camp on the last day of April, but Washington waited until he got official word from Congress before he ordered a fete for 6 May. That morning, soldiers paraded with Steuben-instilled precision, chaplains preached this new evidence that God was on the right side, and Washington reviewed his resilient army with a pride born of three years of shared suffering and survival. Thirteen cannons boomed three salvos, followed by running fire and cheers from one end of the American line to the other. In the afternoon the commander in chief invited his officers to a dinner at which the assemblage drank innumerable toasts to the French king for this recent evidence of his wisdom and support. As the feast went on, however, Washington gradually replaced Louis XVI as the immediate object of the officers' affections. When the American commander in chief left, officers yelled, "Long live General Washington!" and applauded him until he rode out of sight. The troops had no such fancy supper to generate enthusiasm, but the gill of rum the commander in chief ordered for each of them served just as well to help motivate them to join their officers in cheering Washington as he passed by.[18]

While the indolent Howe waited for his successor in Philadelphia with a drink in one hand and dice in the other, Washington prepared for the next campaign. Despite Burgoyne's disaster at Saratoga, the British were still a formidable foe. Howe's army remained unbeaten and intact, and the Royal Navy gave the British the mobility to strike anywhere along the long exposed American coastline. Redcoats occupied Canada, Halifax, Newport, New York City, Philadelphia, and St. Augustine as springboards for further invasions. Throughout the winter, Washington was convinced that Howe would march on Valley Forge to assault his depleted army as soon as the snow melted, and late March reports that the British commander in chief was augmenting his strength with soldiers from Newport and New York City reinforced this view. Washington believed that his duel with Howe would determine the war's outcome, so he needed every soldier he could get to resist the expected British offensive. Jittery politicians continued their efforts to disperse his army to protect every nook and cranny vulnerable to enemy attack, but Washington repeatedly explained to them that keeping his forces together was the only way to achieve ultimate victory and secure independence. Even so, he understood that any quick resolution to the war in the United States' favor was unlikely as long as the Americans remained on the strategic defensive.[19]

No British offensive materialized that spring, and, except for dispatching various foraging and raiding expeditions, Howe seemed content to remain ensconced in his Philadelphia stronghold. Washington did not dwell on the reasons behind Howe's inactivity, perhaps because experience had taught him that his British counterpart was just plain inscrutable in this area. Instead, he wanted to take advantage of enemy passivity to seize the strategic initiative and attack the redcoats in one of their lairs. Doing so before had enabled him to wrest New Jersey back from British control in the winter of 1776–77, and it nearly had knocked the props out from under Howe's army at Germantown the previous October. Such assaults against the remaining British bastions, if successful, offered a quick and victorious resolution to the war. It was also risky, but Washington was aware of important nonmilitary factors working against the strategy of attrition he had generally followed. War-weariness and economic hardship were clearly taking their toll on Americans in this their fourth year fighting the world's most powerful country. Time was proving to be a double-edged sword, and it was not clear which side would succumb first to its blows. Besides, defensive warfare went against Washington's grain, and he constantly chafed under the strategic confines that inadequate American resources imposed on him.[20]

Unfortunately, his options were limited. Scanning his maps and reading his reports, Washington concluded that he could attack New York City, remain on the defensive, or assail Philadelphia. All three possibilities had important pros and cons. Assaulting New York City would move the conflict away from war-torn and loyalist-ridden Pennsylvania, but it presented all sorts of unfamiliar military and logistical problems. Washington estimated that he would have to dispatch up to 6,000 soldiers from Valley Forge and call out the New Jersey, New York, and Connecticut militias to help the Continentals in the Hudson Highlands carry out the proposed mission. Moreover, seizing the city would entail complicated amphibious and siege operations in which the Americans had little experience. Remaining on the defensive would permit Washington to continue to build, train, and equip his troops, but keeping his forces dormant for that long would enable the British to retain the strategic initiative and demoralize Americans in search of decisive action. Small wonder, then, that Washington preferred an attack on Philadelphia, but the devil in the details rendered such a maneuver problematic too. Storming the well-fortified city would result in an American bloodbath, so taking it necessitated a more systematic approach. Washington, who figured that he would need 20,000 troops to successfully invest the place, would have to call out 5,000 militiamen who were unlikely to display the patience prolonged siege operations required. He would also need large numbers of cannons that probably would not be available. Moreover, British control of the seas would permit them to resupply the city at will unless the Americans could find some way to sever Philadelphia's link with the Royal Navy. Occupying Billingsport on the Delaware River would serve this purpose, but Washington guessed that he would have to deploy 8,000 soldiers to hold this bottleneck. Only the local militia could provide these extra men, and its performance over the past nine months was enough to give him pause. Finally, dividing the army so as to encircle Philadelphia would present the British with the opportunity to defeat the Americans in detail. All in all, none of Washington's prospective undertakings seemed to promise the sharp and crippling blow he hoped to deliver.[21]

There had been no word from the commissioners in France since the previous May, and until *La Sensible* arrived at Falmouth at the end of April, the Americans had filled the information vacuum with lots of frothy speculation and gossip. Some believed that war between Britain and France was inevitable; others doubted it would happen at all. For his part, Washington speculated that an Anglo-French conflict was likely, but he did not think it would come as soon or as easily as did others. News of the Franco-American treaties interrupted Washington's military planning and provided him with a new piece to fit into the already complicated strategic puzzle. Without a doubt French entry would help the American war effort, but no one knew how, where, or when this prospective assistance would be forthcoming. Washington hoped that the alliance would encourage Americans to further exert themselves for the cause; he was realistic enough about human nature, though, to worry that having a new ally to share the burden might instead breed complacency and laziness among the war-weary population. He predicted that events in Europe would put a crimp in British operations in America, but he was not inclined to rely too much on a new alliance whose benefits were as of yet all potential. As far as he was concerned, this remained the Americans' war to win or lose.[22]

On 8 May, Washington held a Congress-mandated conference at Valley Forge with some of the American army's highest-ranking officers—Gates, Greene, Stirling, Mifflin, Lafayette, de Kalb, Armstrong, Steuben, Knox, and Duportail—and asked their opinions on the upcoming campaign. He admitted that he did not know much about the current situation in Europe beyond the fact that the United States and France had signed an alliance, but he guessed that France's inevitable entry into the war would constrain British operations in America by limiting the number of available reinforcements. The council mulled over the options Washington provided them, and next day it unanimously recommended that the army "remain on the defensive and wait events; without attempting any offensive operation of consequence, unless the future circumstances of the enemy should afford a fairer opportunity than at present exists, for striking some successful blow; in the mean time employing our utmost exertions, to put the army in the most respectable state possible, both with respect to numbers, appointments and discipline, and to establish and fill our magazines with arms, military stores, provisions and necessities of every kind.[23] The officers believed they had good reasons for recommending this passive defensive strategy. As Washington himself admitted, assaulting New York City or Philadelphia would require large numbers of men and matériel that the army probably could not accumulate. Moreover, the cost of failure could be catastrophic if the proposed operations resulted in the destruction of the main American army. Finally, the generals pointed to the new Franco-American alliance to justify their caution: "If we hold our own and keep the enemy on the defensive, without effecting any thing more, it will have rather a good than a bad appearance in Europe. . . . We have the chance of events, resulting from the important treaties lately concluded between France and America, which may oblige the enemy to withdraw their force without any further trouble to us."[24] Washington reluctantly agreed, so the American army sat back to await events— meaning the British and the French—or some other as yet unanticipated opportunity to inflict substantial damage on Howe's army.[25]

Washington was discouraged that he could not seize the strategic initiative, but he and his officers had made the right decision. An American assault on or siege of Philadelphia or New York City would almost certainly have failed, given the unfavorable geography, the paucity of resources, the militia's limitations, the strong fortifications around each city, the enemy's skill, and the Royal Navy's ability to resupply the otherwise isolated British army. The irony was that, for the short term anyway, the very Franco-American treaties so many Americans lauded put Washington in this strategic straitjacket. Before the alliance, the British were willing to deploy their forces inland in an effort to destroy rebel armies and occupy territory. This gave the Americans opportunities to waylay vulnerable British columns far from their naval support, and it had paid big dividends in New Jersey in 1776–77 and in upstate New York in 1777. France's imminent entry into the war, however, reinforced the recent British inclination to fortify enclaves along the American coast and use them as bases from which to raid and blockade the states. Unless the British changed their strategy—which they would not do until 1780—or made a political decision to end the war, there was no way to pry them out of their strongholds without significant French naval support necessary to isolate and reduce these citadels. In short, Washington could still use his risky strategy of attrition to win a long war, but a quick and decisive victory was in French hands. Unfortunately, although France's entry would disperse British resources around the globe, the same pressures and demands of waging world war would make America merely one of many regions competing for scarce French military resources.

Remaining on the defensive did not imply inactivity on Washington's part; in fact, the American commander in chief had plenty to do even without the burdens of planning an offensive. The American army was always a work in progress, and throughout the spring Washington struggled to ready it for action. Recent personnel and climactic changes eased its logistical problems, but there remained shortages of innumerable items, including shirts, bayonets, and cartridges. Washington devoted much of his time toward raising the men—or, more accurately, toward persuading Congress and the states to do so—he needed to prosecute his next campaign. He hoped to have 40,000 Continentals, but nowhere near that many appeared. Neither bounties to stimulate volunteers nor conscription worked very well, and only New Jersey and Maryland came close to fulfilling their quotas. Virginia, for example, recruited only 1,242 men of its 3,500-man allocation. Worse yet, the quality of the new troops continued to leave much to be desired. Congress prohibited enrollment of former British redcoats because of their proclivity for desertion, but many recruiting officers signed them up anyway. One detachment full of ex-redcoats lost all but 13 of its 60 recruits on the roads from Boston to Valley Forge. On 4 April, Congress authorized Washington to call out up to 5,000 Pennsylvania, New Jersey, and Maryland militia, but he was reluctant because doing so would require considerable time and money for minimal results. Indeed, he noted that hardly any of the 1,000 Pennsylvania militia he wanted to cordon off Philadelphia had turned out. Washington even undertook efforts to enlist 400 American Indians as scouts to intimidate the enemy, but the British remained unexpectedly buttoned up in Philadelphia when the first ones arrived on 14 May, so he sent them home because there was so little for them to do. Fortunately, as spring wore on, more recruits streamed in, and by mid-May there were 14,000 troops at Valley Forge.[26]

Without discipline and organization, these 14,000 soldiers were little more than an unorganized mob. While Steuben transformed the new recruits and veterans into a well-trained military machine, Washington struggled to arrange them into coherent units. The cavalry was in deplorable shape even though Washington had excused most of it from winter duty in an effort to rest it for future operations. It lacked men, horses, and equipment—and leadership. For this Washington blamed the officers, whom he thought were more interested in joyriding through the countryside than in looking after their men and mounts. In addition, disease, desertion, and battle had reduced the numbers of most of the infantry battalions far below their authorized strength of 700 men, and it was extremely unlikely they could ever all be brought up to par. Some brigades had as many men on furlough as present for duty. Large numbers of skeletonized regiments hindered the army's performance by cluttering up and slowing down the chain of command, reducing the combat power of brigades and divisions, and providing employment for too many superfluous and often incompetent officers. Moreover, the disparity in numbers among the battalions caused problems in camping, marching, and guard details. The obvious solution was to consolidate some of the regiments, but this was more easily said than done. Displacing officers would generate resentment, and politicians liked the patronage large numbers of units provided. In January, Congress established a committee to look into army reorganization, but Washington was unable to put its recommendations into effect until November, long after the campaign was over. In the meantime, he told his brigadiers to form their brigades into battalions of 80 to 111 men apiece until Congress made such action official.[27]

Washington had difficulties enough with his officer corps even without the disruptive prospect of a drastically reorganized army, though they were more manageable than in the past. As usual, officers bickered over rank, promotion, and placement, and politicians intervened in subtle and not-so-subtle ways to advance their favorites. The army lost approximately 300 officers the previous winter through disease, resignation, and reassignment, and the problem continued into spring. Washington had been unhappy with Hudson Highlands commander Major General Israel Putnam for quite some time, and he was not alone in his sentiments. Putnam was brave and popular but also incompetent. Washington was convinced that his ineptitude unnecessarily delayed the transfer of Gates's troops to his army at Whitemarsh after Saratoga, and that the holdup contributed to Fort Mifflin's fall and the end of American efforts to keep the Delaware closed to British shipping. Rather than dismiss the patriotic Putnam outright, Washington eased him away from his command by granting him permission to visit his family in Connecticut, then replacing him with Alexander McDougall. It pained Washington to part with the brave, zealous, modest, and talented McDougall, but Washington wanted a reliable officer in charge of the strategically vital Hudson Highlands.[28]

John Sullivan also left the main army that winter. The bluff, hypersensitive New Hampshire general felt unappreciated for his efforts and over the course of the past year had frequently complained to Washington about the indignity he had endured as the army's highest ranking officer without an independent command. During the summer and autumn he was too busy fighting the British and defending his actions on various battlefields to prosecute his private campaign; once the army went into winter quarters, though, he quickly picked up his quill and resumed his petitions to the commander in chief with the same stubbornness he displayed at Brandywine. Now, however, he also sought a furlough to visit his family and take care of neglected private business. Sullivan undoubtedly tried Washington's patience, but the commander in chief valued him for his loyalty and stoutheartedness, so he went out of his way to praise and reassure him in ways he never did for the more secure Greene. Despite Sullivan's entreaties, Washington refused to part with him, especially because that winter the troops were in such dire straits and there were only two other major generals in camp to help run the army. In February, however, when Major General Joseph Spencer resigned as commander in Rhode Island, Washington saw an opportunity to finally placate and reward his persistent subordinate. On 10 March, he ordered Sullivan to Rhode Island to replace Spencer, and Sullivan was very happy for both the independent command and the opportunity to see his family along the way. Sullivan's departure meant that the stalwart Stirling was the only original divisional commander remaining from those who had begun the last campaign in June 1777.[29]

McDougall's and Sullivan's departures were counterbalanced in terms of stature gained and controversy generated by Charles Lee's arrival six weeks later. The English-born Lee served as a British army officer during the Great War for Empire, where he saw action in both America and Portugal. Put on half pay in 1763, he fought as a mercenary in Poland before retiring to Virginia in 1773. There he became an ardent patriot, whose military experience and enthusiasm for the cause motivated Congress to appoint him a major general on 17 June 1775. He participated in the siege of Boston, unfairly claimed credit for successfully repelling the British assault on Charleston in June 1776, and then returned north to contribute to the disastrous campaign around New York City. During the retreat through New Jersey, Washington repeatedly urged Lee to join the main army with the detached troops under his command, but Lee dallied, and on 13 December a British cavalry patrol captured him in his exposed headquarters at Basking Ridge, New Jersey. As a former redcoat officer, Lee and others feared that the British would put him on trial for treason, but Howe and the ministry ultimately decided to treat him as a prisoner of war. British forbearance came in spite of rather than because of Lee's personality; he was a strange, rash, boastful, bad-tempered, arrogant, and narcissistic man who was alternately charming and offensive. He certainly seemed to know what he was talking about, at least at first, which prompted one British officer to call him a "sensible fool." His conduct as a prisoner was, to say the least, peculiar. He believed that neither side could win the conflict, and he presented himself as a reasonable middleman who could bring the rebels and British together for a negotiated settlement. In fact, for unclear reasons, he even drew up military plans for both Howe and the Americans. This was odd—or, more critically, treasonous—behavior for a prisoner of war, but it was also Lee's way. His vast ego knew few equals, and the disdain he held for many extended to Washington and his chief subordinates, all of whom he considered incompetent. Indeed, he wrote to Laurens, "I am well and hope [I] shall always be well with General Washington—and to speak again vainly I am persuaded (considering how he is surrounded) that he cannot do without me."[30]

Washington either did not know of or chose to overlook Lee's low opinion of him. Despite the grief Lee subjected him to during the New York City campaign, he continued to value the captured officer's military abilities, and he became a driving force behind efforts to secure his release. In April the British and Americans agreed to exchange Lee for Major General Richard Prescott, whom a small party of rebels had seized in a daring raid on his Newport billet in 1776. On 5 April, Washington, his main lieutenants, and their aides rode four miles out from Valley Forge to welcome Lee. The returning hero arrived with his usual retinue of dogs yipping behind him. Washington dismounted and greeted Lee warmly, then escorted him past the troops drawn up to pay their respects. That evening Washington hosted an elegant dinner for the newly paroled officer, and the next morning he delayed breakfast because Lee slept late. Washington hoped that Lee would be an asset to the American cause, but others had their doubts, though the Lee mystique caused many to keep their opinions to themselves. Greene, for one, worried that the remnants of the imaginary Conway Cabal might poison Lee's mind against the commander in chief. As it was, Lee needed no such encouragement; a year and a half in British captivity had not changed his mind about the rebel army or its commander, and a cursory look at the troops convinced him that they were in worse shape than ever before, despite Steuben's efforts. In fact, Lee argued that any attempt to mold freedom-loving Americans into professional European soldiers capable of standing up to the British was bound to fail, and that only an army based on the militia could secure independence for America. Shortly after his arrival at Valley Forge, Lee traveled to York to lobby Congress for a promotion to lieutenant general. Congress had already heard rumblings of Lee's collaborative behavior in British hands, so he got a frosty reception from various delegates. Nonplussed, Lee returned to Valley Forge and assumed command of Greene's old division.[31]

American intelligence picked up evidence that the British planned to evacuate Philadelphia soon after Clinton opened Germain's 21 March orders authorizing him to do so. As May wore on, it became increasingly obvious to everyone that the days of British control of the city were numbered. Washington received reports that women and children were embarking on board transports in the Delaware River, that British officers were removing the sick from hospitals and weapons from arsenals, and that a prominent loyalist business was closing up shop. The British continued work on their redoubts surrounding the city, but Washington saw this for the feeble ruse it was. Unfortunately for the American commander in chief, such a conclusion was merely one part of a more complicated conundrum he had to unravel. Clinton's destination, timetable, route, and overall intentions remained unclear. Would the British leave the city by land, or sea, or both? Would they strike at Valley Forge before they departed, or at Smallwood at Wilmington, or neither? Would they go to New York City or withdraw from America altogether? If their destination was New York City, would it merely be a prelude to an offensive up the Hudson River? Sifting through his innumerable and often contradictory reports, Washington gradually and accurately surmised that New York City was their destination because of information that the British were preparing houses in the city for refugees. He figured that part of the British army would quit Philadelphia by sea, and that the rest would march overland through New Jersey to South Amboy, then head for New York City.[32]

Washington believed he had deciphered Clinton's immediate plans, but he was not certain, and therefore he was reluctant to shift his whole army into New Jersey to interrupt the possible British march. Doing so would expose Valley Forge's valuable supplies and its nearly 4,000 sick rebel soldiers to a British sortie that could kick the blocks out from under the American war effort before the campaigning season even began. He felt that he had to wait for the British to make the first move, even though he recognized that this would give them sufficient head start so that it would be almost impossible for him to catch them. Instead, he hoped to simply harass them in New Jersey while he advanced his army as rapidly as possible to the Hudson Highlands to block any subsequent British attack in that direction. Therefore, he concentrated much of his army around Valley Forge, ordered Greene to establish the supply depots necessary to feed the troops as they headed northward, and detached part of Maxwell's brigade—the rest of it was already there—to Mount Holly to cooperate with Philemon Dickinson's New Jersey militia in pestering the British when and if they plowed through the state. He lamented that he was not in a position to inflict more damage on the exposed British trek he foresaw, but he explained to Dickinson,

> If this [march through New Jersey] be their real design, it is much to be regretted that our present situation incapacitates us from giving them so much annoyance as we possibly might in the other case. The number of sick in camp and its vicinity as well as our stores [that] must be guarded, renders it highly imprudent to make any considerable detachment previous to the actual commencement of the enemy's march, as the remaining part of the army would be exposed to a sudden attack from their whole force. And little can be hoped from pursuit after their departure considering the distance and the ground which they will have gained in their first march.[33]

Washington left no stone unturned in his efforts to keep tabs on the British that spring. On 18 May, he dispatched 2,400 picked troops under Major General Marquis de Lafayette to cross the Schuylkill to gather information on British whereabouts and intentions and to exploit any openings he might uncover. The twenty-one-year-old Lafayette was the scion of a powerful and wealthy French noble family. He had crossed the Atlantic the previous year to offer his services to the American cause, and his enthusiasm, commitment, apparent modesty, friendliness, good temper, and generosity won him many friends. These included Washington, who treated him as an adoptive son. If Lafayette's relationship with the commander in chief was not as tight as he often claimed, it was good enough to secure him command of Stephen's old division. In fact, Lafayette had almost no experience leading large numbers of troops in action—he was an observer at Brandywine, where a redcoat bullet winged him in the thigh and put him out of action for Germantown, and he directed 300 men in a skirmish along the Delaware the previous November—but Congress's reluctance to offend such an influential voice in the French court and Washington's friendship compensated for these deficiencies.

Lafayette accepted his advancement and assignment as no more than his due, and after sunset on 18 May he crossed the Schuylkill and marched ten miles to a crossroads on Barren Hill. Disregarding Washington's admonition that he stay mobile to prevent detection, he took up position on the hill and sent out patrols to establish contact with the British. He might have saved himself the trouble; British intelligence discovered his expedition before it even left Valley Forge, and Howe rapidly designed a trap to crush the young Frenchman between two columns. Lafayette unwisely assumed that Pennsylvania militiamen would patrol the roads toward the Schuylkill and warn him if they encountered any British approach, but they did not. Fortunately for the Americans, an army surgeon stumbled upon Grant's troops and sounded the alarm at dawn on 20 May. Lafayette did not panic. Instead, he verified the information before he rapidly and skillfully withdrew his men in good order across the Schuylkill at Matson's Ford, his rear guard splashing over when the British vanguard was a mere half mile away. The British did not press the issue, so Lafayette was able to return to camp unmolested a couple of days later. At Valley Forge, the rest of the army was under arms and ready to march within fifteen minutes after Washington learned that Lafayette was in danger, a tribute to Steuben's training. In fact, the troops could take pride in the manner in which they conducted themselves in the course of a week of maneuvering against the British, but the same could not be said of their commanders. Washington could have accomplished his objectives without exposing some of his best soldiers to destruction, and Lafayette's unwise actions created the crisis that permitted him to demonstrate his admirable coolness under pressure. Washington did not see it this way, and he wrote afterward, "Upon the whole the Marquis came handsomely off, and the enemy returned [to Philadelphia] disappointed and disgraced."[34] Another officer, however, came closer to the truth when he wrote, "It was a very luckey [sic] affair on our side, that we did not loose [sic] our whole detachment."[35]

On 15 June, a woman who washed clothes for the Carlisle Commission learned that the British intended to evacuate the city in a few days, and she relayed the information to Washington's headquarters through her son. The next day three captured British deserters confirmed the intelligence. The balloon was about to go up, so on 17 June Washington met with his generals—Lee, Greene, Arnold, Stirling, Lafayette, Steuben, Smallwood, Knox, Poor, Paterson, Wayne, Woodford, Muhlenberg, Jedediah Huntington, and Duportail—to brief them on the situation. Washington predicted that the British would march through New Jersey with approximately 10,000 British and Germans, and he noted that the American army had around 11,000 troops ready for action, not counting Dickinson's militia and Maxwell's 800-man brigade already across the Delaware. Washington, who still had many doubts about Clinton's intentions, decided that once the British abandoned Philadelphia, he would push his army to the Delaware and then take a fresh look at the situation. The next morning, after Washington learned from a man who had shouted to some Philadelphians across Middle Ferry that the British were gone, he put his army in motion. A detachment under Colonel Henry Jackson headed for Philadelphia to take possession of the city, and along the way soldiers scooped up scores of enemy deserters hiding in cellars and hogsheads. Patriots were already streaming back to the city, and this, combined with the shattered houses and torn-down fences, gave it a somewhat unkempt appearance. But it was American property again, and on 7 July Congress reconvened there and ended its nine-month exile.[36]

While Congress prepared to reassemble in Philadelphia, Washington's army left Valley Forge and pushed northeastward to keep pace with its British counterpart. On 20 June, the American vanguard reached the Delaware River at Corryell's Ferry north of Trenton, and over the course of the next two days the whole army crossed the big river. Moving 11,000 soldiers and their baggage, equipment, and artillery over any large body of water on rickety flatboats was difficult enough even under the best of circumstances, but the same heavy rains that slowed Clinton's march also hindered American efforts. As Washington's troops slogged along the steamy Pennsylvania and New Jersey roads to and from the Delaware, Maxwell's brigade and Dickinson's 1,200-man militia struggled to impede and harass the British advance by sniping at enemy soldiers, felling trees across the roads, filling up wells, and destroying bridges. This was all well and good, but Dickinson had a hard time believing that this alone accounted for the sluggish British march, and he reported as much to Washington. Indeed, the British had covered less than forty miles in the past week, leading Washington to speculate that perhaps Clinton was trying to lure the Americans into a trap. On the other hand, the commander in chief also recognized that the dilatory British advance presented him an opportunity to overtake and inflict some serious damage on Clinton's slow-moving columns. On 24 June, as the American army paused in Hopewell township, five miles short of Princeton, to take a breather from the heat and rain, Washington took advantage of the break to seek the counsel of his generals. Some, such as Anthony Wayne, wanted to act more aggressively, but Lee argued forcefully and persuasively against such action. He did not believe that the American army was capable of standing up to the redcoats, so any confrontation was bound to end in a defeat that would be all the more unfortunate and unnecessary now that significant French aid was in the offing. Some of Washington's officers already doubted Lee's abilities and judgment, but no one was willing to speak out against him yet. Instead, the council recommended that Washington dispatch another 1,500 men to cooperate with Dickinson and Maxwell while the rest of the army acted according to circumstances. No one wanted to provoke a full-fledged battle, but hopefully these reinforcements might make the British bleed more as they crossed through New Jersey, although no one explained exactly how this process would work. It was an imperfect compromise that accomplished little more than to commit the army piecemeal to an uncertain mission. No wonder Washington's aide Alexander Hamilton later wrote that the conference "would have done honor to the most honorable society of midwives, and to them only."[37]

Hamilton was not the only one who thought so. Talking among themselves, many of Washington's generals regretted their timid and halfhearted recommendations. Greene, Wayne, and Lafayette each wrote to Washington to urge more aggressive action. Greene lamented that they were missing an opportunity to strike the vulnerable British column because of unfounded and exaggerated fears of failure, adding that he was confident that the army could win any big battle that might ensue. Lafayette said that he, Greene, Steuben, Duportail, Wayne, and Paterson all wanted to send more troops after the British. Washington needed little persuading, and the next morning he issued new orders. He had already dispatched Morgan's riflemen and 1,500 men under battle-tested Charles Scott to pursue the British, but now he upped the ante by directing the ever-aggressive Wayne to join them with another 1,000 troops. He put this advanced corps—Maxwell, Morgan, Scott, and Wayne—under Lafayette's command. Washington instructed the young Frenchman to hit the British rear if he found an opening, and he promised to support Lafayette with the rest of the army. On 25–26 June, Washington moved his army from Kingston to Cranbury amid the cheering of the locals while Lafayette got into position at Hightstown. Lafayette's job was more demanding than Washington's succinct instructions implied; he was not sure of Clinton's exact whereabouts, he lacked provisions, and coordinating his far-flung and disparate command was no easy task. In fact, a frustrated Hamilton wrote to his chief about conditions on the bleeding edge of the American advance, "I found every precaution was neglected; no horse was near the enemy, or could be heard of till late in the morning, so that before we could send out parties and get the necessary information, [the British] were in full march, and as they have marched pretty expeditiously we should not be able to come up with them during the march of the day. . . . We are entirely at a loss where the army is, which is no inconsiderable check to our enterprise."[38] The burden of independent command made Lafayette jumpy and apprehensive, but he was not about to give up. At this point, however, Washington yanked the rug right out from under his favorite.[39]

By right of seniority, Lee should have led the advanced corps, but he turned down the assignment because he did not agree with its mission. However, when he learned that Lafayette's new command consisted of 5,000 troops, or almost half the army, his pride and ego overcame his principles, and he asked Washington for the job. Washington, who did not want to offend Lee or Lafayette, crafted another peculiar compromise. He put Lee in charge of the advanced corps and reinforced it with two additional brigades, but he ordered him to refrain from interfering if he discovered that Lafayette had already decided to commit his troops into action. As it was, Lafayette had already determined against any such attack for now, and he cheerfully agreed to serve under Lee. On 27 June, Lee took control of the tip of the American army's spear at Englishtown.[40]

On the evening of 26 June, American intelligence located the British army near Monmouth. The next day the American advanced corps concentrated at nearby Englishtown, and Washington brought up the main body three miles behind it at Manalapan. The two armies were now less than five miles apart, but Washington feared that Clinton might get away unscathed because the British were only a day's march from the safety of the easily defended hills around Middletown. If he wanted to strike a blow, he had to do so very soon. With this in mind, on 27 June Washington met with Lee, Wayne, Maxwell, Scott, and Lafayette to plot strategy. Washington instructed Lee to attack the British rear guard the next day if possible, and he promised to bring up the rest of the army in support. Maxwell, Wayne, Scott, and Hamilton all later testified that Washington's orders were discretionary, but they also asserted that their chief clearly wanted aggressive action even if it led to a big battle with the entire enemy force. As Wayne subsequently and convolutedly put it, "The idea I conceived from General Washington's conversation was, that we should attack the enemy, and that he should be near to support us with the main body of the army, which, in its consequences, must, if we were pushed, inevitably, I think, have brought on a general action."[41]

Lee, however, saw things differently. As far as he was concerned, the Americans should avoid any major engagement with the superior British army, and he believed that recent conferences at Valley Forge and Hopewell confirmed this policy. He was unwilling or unable to see that Washington had gradually changed his mind over the past week. Lee was ready to attack the British column, but only if he could do so without provoking a full-fledged battle, whereas Washington was now prepared to run that risk. After his meeting with Washington, Lee conferred with his subordinates, but he had no orders for them because he claimed that the current military situation was too fluid to make any concrete plans. Instead, he merely told them to stay on their toes and— with unconscious hypocrisy—to avoid disputes over rank. In fact, Lee was more interested in receiving than delivering an attack, and he half expected one from Clinton. Washington thought otherwise. Because he continued to worry that Clinton might slip away that night or first thing in the morning, he directed Lee to dispatch troops to delay any possible enemy march long enough for the Americans to overtake them before they reached Middletown, and to attack if he had the chance. Lee relayed the commander in chief's instructions to Morgan's 600 riflemen, Dickinson's 800 militia, and Colonel William Grayson's 600-man detachment, but he was more interested in the opportunity that seemed to be unveiling before him. In the wee hours of the morning, Dickinson reported that the British army was in motion, providing Lee with an opening to hit their rear guard without bringing about the big clash he dreaded.[42]

THE BATTLE OF MONMOUTH

Eighteenth-century battlefields were usually bewildering places for the troops engaged there. Accurate information was a prized commodity, but it often was hard to come by. Primitive communications, heavy, dense smoke from thousands of discharged muskets and cannons that limited vision, tired and scared soldiers pushing close together for mutual protection, and unfamiliar terrain made directing and maneuvering regiments and brigades under fire akin to playing blindman's bluff with a buzz saw. American and British officers were very familiar with Carl von Clausewitz's fog of war long before the German military theorist put quill to paper, but many of them also recognized that discipline, training, experience, clear orders, and a tight chain of command helped to compensate for the chaos inherent in warfare. Unfortunately for the Americans, instilling these attributes was no simple chore, and on 28 June, Washington paid a price for his failure to train his officers as rigorously as Steuben trained his men.

As a veteran of numerous battles extending back to Long Island, William Grayson understood the difficulties that carrying out even seemingly simple directives often entailed, but he was undoubtedly a frustrated man early on 28 June. At 3:00 A.M., Lee ordered him to take his and Scott's brigades—but not Scott himself, who stayed behind to command other units—down toward Monmouth to help keep an eye on the British and sound the alarm if they suddenly pulled up stakes. But he did not get his troops under way for another three hours because he could not locate a guide to help him navigate the unknown New Jersey countryside. David Forman finally rounded one up for him, but the sun was rising fast when he crossed the bridge over the West Ravine and ran into New Jersey militia scuttling hither and yon. A British patrol had surprised and scattered them in the woods, and Dickinson was doing his best to rally them on a nearby hill when Grayson rode up to meet him. Grayson deployed a regiment and posted a couple of cannons near the ravine, and together the two men brought some order to the chaos as the British withdrew. The sudden British attack convinced Dickinson that, far from retreating, the British were advancing in strength, probably in an effort to crumple the advanced corps as it marched down from Freehold. When Lee arrived soon after, Dickinson explained the situation and his concerns to him. Lee pulled Grayson's men back across the ravine, but he angrily dismissed Dickinson's fears. Washington's aide John Laurens, who had been out reconnoitering that

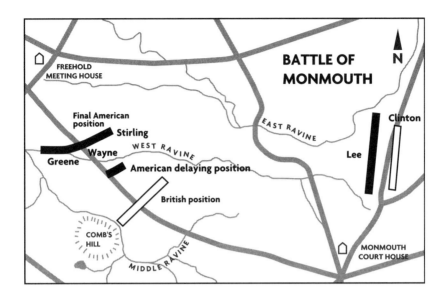

morning, told Lee that the British were pulling out from Monmouth, and some of Dickinson's own subordinates agreed. Dickinson replied heatedly and mistakenly that this was not the case, and he warned Lee against exposing his advanced corps to destruction by moving it over the narrow bridge that provided the only easy access across the swampy West Ravine. After their argument the rest of the advanced corps— minus Morgan's riflemen, who were hovering on the British right flank about three miles away—filed up the road after their six-mile hike through Englishtown and past Freehold. Eager for action, the men waited to see what Lee would do.[43]

Patience was not an integral part of Charles Lee's makeup, so the contradictory intelligence Dickinson and others delivered on British whereabouts and intentions rapidly exhausted whatever scant reserves of forbearance he possessed. He angrily declared that he would no longer rely on such exasperatingly incongruous reports but would instead move ahead and determine for himself whether or not the British were still at Monmouth. To that end, he ordered Wayne to take command of the 600 or so troops up front, and the impetuous Pennsylvanian led the advanced corps two miles eastward onto open ground in plain view of the Monmouth Courthouse. Wayne scattered some British cavalry there without much trouble, but he could see nearly 1,000 more redcoats deploying to the north. Aggressive as always, Wayne wanted to go after them, but Lee put at his disposal only two regiments of 200 men apiece under Colonels Richard Butler and Henry Jackson. Undaunted, Wayne pushed on beyond the swampy East Ravine toward the Middletown road and came under British cannon fire. Jackson's regiment had fallen behind because its men had to take time to gather sufficient cartridges, creating a gap between it and Butler that the British spotted and sought to exploit with a furious cavalry attack. With Steuben-instilled instinct, Butler's men formed and coolly broke the charge at forty paces with well-directed fire. Despite the setback, the British line on the Middletown road continued to thicken, so Wayne stopped Butler's advance, deployed Scott's, Grayson's, and Maxwell's arriving troops around them, and waited for further orders from Lee.[44]

Lee had his reasons for limiting Wayne's offensive power to a mere two regiments, though he chose or neglected to fully communicate them to Wayne, Scott, Grayson, or Maxwell. American scouts confirmed that the British had abandoned their camp from the night before, so Lee believed that the 1,500 to 2,000 men confronting Wayne constituted the rear guard Clinton had undoubtedly left behind to keep the Americans at bay while the rest of his army made its getaway. With this hard intelligence in hand, Lee grasped the opportunity to strike the blow Washington wanted without provoking the big battle he was convinced the inferior American army could not win. Lee planned for Wayne to apply moderate pressure to fix the British rear guard in position while he swung the rest of his advanced corps southward near Monmouth Courthouse to cut those isolated redcoats off from the rest of Clinton's army. Lee deployed Wayne's brigade—now under Colonel Henry Beekman Livingston while its commander undertook the other duties Lee assigned him—part of Scott's brigade, and a re-formed New Jersey militia brigade to assault the British left flank preparatory to its destruction. While these units got into position, Lee spotted large numbers of redcoats streaming down the Middletown road toward Monmouth Courthouse in two columns, with their cavalry out front driving the small number of American horsemen at Lee's disposal ahead of them. Clinton was not retreating, not anymore anyway, but instead was showing every indication that he intended to do to the American advanced corps what Lee hoped to do to the British rear guard—gobble it up before the rest of the army arrived to reinforce it. The hunter, it seemed, had become the hunted. Lee reacted to this startling news by ordering Scott to secure the hinge between Wayne's detachment and the rest of the advanced corps, and by directing Lafayette to take three regiments to protect the American right flank.[45]

Unfortunately for the Americans, Lee's efforts to realign his advanced corps to challenge the unexpected British onslaught proved their undoing. Lee commanded Lafayette's troops to fall back to Monmouth and re-form there, but their confused efforts to do so opened the cataract that undermined the entire American line. There was not enough room at first for all the regiments to deploy, and some of the officers clearly did not understand Lee's intentions. Worse yet, Lee and Lafayette each issued orders that did not always mesh. Some units successfully got into position, but others kept retiring westward across the fields and through the woods. The concurrent noisy artillery duel and the stifling heat that gave the battlefield a hazy shimmering gloss did not help matters. Little by little, and in spite of Lee's best efforts, the American right began to unravel. Across the way, Wayne and Scott looked on quizzically. They sent to Lee for orders and received no reply, but the aides they dispatched to have a look reported that their comrades-in-arms were withdrawing. The British continued their slow advance, and redcoats started to probe Scott's increasingly exposed right flank. As the battle-hardened Virginian interpreted things, his options had narrowed to retreat or destruction, so on his own initiative he chose the former. Once Scott pulled out, Wayne's entire line caved in. Wayne ordered Butler's exposed regiment to give ground before it became surrounded, and Grayson and Maxwell followed suit with their units. Their withdrawal merely accelerated the retreat already under way on the right. Despite the setback, the Americans did not flee in panic but instead remained in formation as they marched away. Lee, furious at this unanticipated turn of events, blamed Scott's decision to fall back without orders; "Then, by God, you have ruined me!" he exclaimed when he met Scott. Thus, without firing scarcely a shot, the advanced corps removed itself from the field.[46]

Henry Clinton did not intend to fight at Monmouth. He certainly wanted to engage and hopefully annihilate Washington's army somewhere on his way across New Jersey, but he doubted that his shrewd American counterpart would risk battle in this boggy and cut-up part of the state. On the evening of 27 June, he received intelligence that the American army was nearby, so he positioned Cornwallis's division between Knyphausen and the baggage train just in case Washington reached deep into his bag of tricks in an effort to interfere with the British march. The next morning, however, the reconnoitering Queen's Rangers found only 1,000 rebels in the vicinity—mostly Dickinson's harum-scarum New Jersey militia—whom they easily scattered in the

woods, although the militiamen rallied so rapidly that the veteran loyalist unit placed discretion ahead of valor and withdrew. Disappointed
but not surprised at Washington's absence, Clinton put Cornwallis's division on the road for Middletown at around 10:00 A.M. No sooner
had the redcoat column gotten under way, though, than large numbers
of rebels poured across the ravines and onto the Monmouth plain. Clinton recognized them as Washington's advanced corps, but he guessed
incorrectly that his exposed baggage train was its target. The British
commander in chief did some quick calculations as he watched the
rebels come closer. He estimated the American army at 20,000 men, but
he noticed that the advanced corps had isolated itself from the main
body by crossing the ravines, thus providing him with an opportunity
to crush it before the rest of Washington's troops came up. Besides, he
figured that attacking it was the best way to protect his baggage train.
Clinton turned Cornwallis's men around, dispatched the light infantry
to confront the oncoming rebels, deployed three brigades and the
grenadiers nearby, and sent to Knyphausen and Grant for reinforcements. A sharp cavalry attack had failed to make much of an impression on the enemy, but Clinton got better results when he hit the
vulnerable American right flank and seized the high ground on the east
side of the East Ravine. In fact, the rebels gave way without much of a
fight, and soon their whole line collapsed. Clinton did not stop to contemplate his good fortune but instead pushed his men westward in pursuit of the backpedaling rebels.[47]

At Manalapan, Washington put his army on the road as soon as he
received Dickinson's message that the British were in motion. He sent
Lee orders to attack Clinton's rear guard unless there was good reason
not to, promising to support him as quickly as possible. He was in a
hurry, and in his desire to make haste he even commanded his men to
chuck their packs and blankets to increase their pace. Along the way
Hamilton returned with word that Lee was about to engage the enemy,
and on his advice Washington detached part of the main body under
Greene toward the right to protect that flank. Shortly thereafter, however, evidence mounted that things were not going according to plan.
Within two and a half miles of Monmouth, Washington encountered a
frightened fifer, who told his commander in chief that Lee's corps was
retreating. Washington threatened to have the man whipped if he continued to spread such demoralizing rumors, but knots of backtracking
soldiers down the road confirmed the story. Approaching the West
Ravine, Washington met entire units falling back in good order or sit-

ting down along the roadside, with angry officers condemning Lee's un-necessary withdrawal. Washington had seen more than his share of military debacles in the course of his three defeat-studded years as commander in chief, but familiarity did not mask the anger, frustration, and disappointment he invariably felt in such circumstances. Whatever his emotions, he kept his mind focused on the issue at hand as he crossed the West Ravine and rode onto a field to survey the situation with his spyglass as British shells landed around him. He was unsure what to do; he did not know the ground, Lee was nowhere to be found, and the British were only fifteen minutes away. Fortunately, Lieutenant Colonel David Rhea volunteered that he was familiar with the area, and he asserted that the army could make its stand behind the West Ravine. Wayne arrived, and he agreed. Washington liked the idea, too, but he needed time to bring up the main body, re-form the advanced corps, and deploy everyone behind the defile. Livingston was already rallying some of his men nearby, so Washington sought to use this kernel of resistance to his benefit. He instructed two regiments under Lieutenant Colonel Nathaniel Ramsay and Colonel Walter Stewart to form with Livingston at the base of a hill behind a rail fence and a swamp, backed them with a couple of cannons, and explained to the soldiers their mission. Although all of them certainly understood that Washington was asking them to barter their lives for time, they nodded and got into line. With this done, Washington turned his attention to other matters.[48]

Consulting with Lee was among the other matters vying for Washington's immediate attention. The former British officer rode up at the head of another column of backtracking troops, and a frustrated Washington asked angrily, "What is all this?" Lee did not quite hear the question over the shells falling around them, so he hesitated and stammered, "Sir? Sir?" until Washington repeated himself and expressed astonishment at this "unaccountable retreat." Lee thought that he had done a fairly good job salvaging the advanced corps from the trap he believed Clinton had baited for him. He responded to Washington's irate query by blaming contradictory intelligence, battlefield confusion, superior British cavalry, and insubordination among too many officers. He singled out Scott in particular for condemnation, and he reminded his boss that he had always opposed attacking the British army. Washington replied that Lee should never have taken command of the advanced corps if he was unwilling to obey orders. The argument was necessarily brief, since the British were fast approaching, so Washington directed Lee to help Livingston, Ramsay, and Stewart delay the British while he positioned the main body. Lee did as he was told, and afterward Washington sent him back to Englishtown to collect stragglers.[49]

While Lee and Washington argued, Livingston, Ramsay, and Stewart readied their men for the British storm sweeping toward them over the Monmouth plain. Redcoat cavalry came on first, but well-directed American fire broke their charge before they got within forty paces of the rail fence over which the rebels leveled their muskets. Clinton rapidly increased the pressure on the impromptu American line by sending the grenadiers and a battalion from the Guards brigade to push through the cornfield and into the swamp as American cannon fire rained around them. "Charge, grenadiers!" Clinton cried, "Never heed forming!" Indeed, the redcoats rapidly lost unit cohesion in the marsh, but they got through it and over the fence. By now, however, the three regiments had bought Washington enough time to build his new line, so Lee brought the troops back across the West Ravine bridge in good order, even though many of the men wanted to stay and continue the fight. Despite the haste Clinton imposed on him, Washington had improvised well, so his position was a good one. He put Stirling in command of the left flank facing some open ground, and Wayne took charge of the center behind a swamp. Greene had headed off to the right earlier in the day with part of the main body, but with soldierly instinct he marched to the sound of the fighting when he learned that Lee was in trouble, arriving in enough time to bolster and direct operations on the right along the ravine and in some woods. With their ducks more or less in a row, the Americans braced themselves for Clinton's next move.[50]

Clinton had problems of his own with which Washington could have sympathized, had he known about them. This was the first time the British commander in chief had led this particular army into battle, and it was not nearly as easy as Howe made it appear. When the fighting began in earnest, Clinton sent to Grant and Knyphausen for reinforcements; the two officers failed to send them, though, probably because they believed they would need the men to hold off Morgan's sniping riflemen. As it was, Morgan's efforts amounted to little more than incidental harassment thanks to the efforts of the jaegers, but the British First Brigade spent the battle standing at arms, useless. Moreover, Clinton did not use all the troops he had at hand. He kept the Fourth Brigade and the German grenadiers behind the East Ravine, and the Fifth Brigade farther back in reserve. As a result, he waged the battle primarily with the Guards, grenadiers, some light infantry, and the Third Brigade. Finally, despite the courage he displayed in repeatedly exposing himself to rebel fire, Clinton did not control his soldiers especially well. The light infantry in particular slipped the leash and attacked more aggressively than he wished, which contributed to their difficulties that day.[51]

By afternoon the temperature at Monmouth topped ninety degrees Fahrenheit, and throughout the day scores of thirsty men on both sides succumbed to heatstroke. The noisy cannonade that lasted for two hours and constituted the war's heaviest artillery exchange was equally distracting. Here Mary Ludwig Hays—later dubbed Molly Pitcher—won her reputation by serving a cannon after her husband was wounded. Fortunately for Clinton, the soldiers he did commit to action were among the best in the British army, men who had successfully taken the rebels' measure many times over the past three years and were more than willing to do so again. The British charged the American lines with the bayonet, and there was especially heavy fighting around a barn where Wayne had drawn up his troops. Washington ordered Greene to send William Woodford's Virginia brigade to seize unoccupied Comb's Hill, about a mile south of American lines overlooking the British left flank. Cannons subsequently placed there and by Stirling on the American left helped tip the scales and forced the redcoats back. This gave Clinton pause, and, having paused, he reconsidered. His troops were exhausted, he had succeeded in protecting his baggage train, and it was obvious that he was not going to destroy the surprisingly effective rebel army today, so he ordered a withdrawal behind the East Ravine. Disengaging in the face of the enemy, however, proved as difficult as storming American positions. Most of the troops who were supposed to cover the exposed light infantry on the British right flank mistakenly fell back first, leaving their comrades exposed. At about this time Washington launched a limited counterattack with New Hampshire and Virginia troops under Colonel Joseph Cilley. Continentals and the retreating redcoats slugged it out in an orchard and along the edge of a swamp, but in the end two cannons provided the firepower the British needed to get away. Encouraged that Clinton was pulling in his horns, Washington ordered Woodford's, Enoch Poor's, and Brigadier General Thomas Clark's brigades to assault both British flanks, but bad terrain delayed them from getting into position before dusk put an end to the day's fighting. Intending to resume the battle the next day, Washington had his men sleep on their arms.[52]

By the time Washington's exhausted soldiers roused themselves the next morning, however, the British were long gone. Clinton withdrew his men around midnight, except for some forty to fifty redcoats too badly wounded to move, and the British army reached Middletown late the next day. Clinton harbored hopes that Washington would provide him with another opportunity to destroy the American army by chasing him into the tangled northeastern New Jersey hills, but when no pursuit materialized, he concentrated on getting his soldiers to Sandy Hook and across the Lower Bay back to Staten Island before the French fleet reportedly on its way made an appearance. Washington had no desire to advance into the hot, barren, and waterless region around Middletown with his tired and blown troops, so he instead sent Morgan's corps and Maxwell's brigade to keep an eye on the enemy column, discharged the New Jersey militia, and marched the remainder of his army northward toward the Hudson River. By 3 July, American troops were bathing in the Raritan River in an effort to wash off the accumulated grime of sixteen days of hard marching and fighting.[53]

Washington was quick to declare victory at Monmouth because the Americans retained control of the battlefield. Clinton put British losses at 65 killed in battle, 59 dead from heatstroke, 170 wounded, and 64 missing, for a total of 358 casualties. American losses were probably about the same, though Washington tallied them at only 196, including 59 slain. Afterward the issue among most Continental officers was not whether they won the battle—almost all thought they had—but whether their victory should have been more decisive. Many argued that they missed a golden opportunity to mangle a large portion of the retreating army, and for this they blamed Charles Lee. The consensus among the officer corps forged soon after the guns cooled was that Lee's timidity, his inability to control his troops, and his failure to carry out Washington's orders prevented the advanced corps from mangling the British rear guard. As Joseph Cilley wrote, "It is my opinion that if he [Lee] had behaved well we should have destroyed the major part of Clinton's army."[54] Two days after the battle, Wayne and Scott formally complained to Washington about Lee's conduct. The American commander in chief was not inclined to pursue the matter, having committed more than his share of battlefield blunders and seen many of his other subordinates do the same, but Lee forced the issue by writing Washington a series of insulting letters in which he demanded a court-martial to clear his name. Washington granted Lee's request and added with scathing sarcasm no less effective for being grammatically suspect: "As soon as circumstances will permit, you shall have an opportunity either of justifying yourself to the army, to Congress, to America, and to the world in general; or of convincing them that you were guilty of a breach of orders, and of misbehavior before the enemy, on the 28th inst[ant], in not attacking them as you had been directed, and in making an unnecessary, disorderly, and shameful retreat."[55]

Lee's court-martial—headed by Stirling, who had accumulated considerable experience in this role—met on and off throughout the summer of 1778. Officers once cowed and intimidated by Lee's reputation and acidic tongue used the opportunity to denounce him. Like Conway and Gates before him, Lee learned to his sorrow that attacking Washington was tantamount to attacking the army, so the officer corps lined up solidly against him. He did not understand until too late that the trial was as much about Washington's credibility as his own, and under such circumstances there could be only one outcome. On 12 August the court found Lee guilty and suspended him from the army for a year because he had disobeyed orders by not attacking the British, had retreated without sufficient cause or skill, and had insulted Washington in insolent letters he penned after the battle.[56]

As Lee certainly suspected, the officer corps willingly offered him up as a scapegoat for several unwise command decisions Washington and others made before and during the Battle of Monmouth that turned the engagement into such a brouhaha. The commander in chief favored an aggressive response to the British march through New Jersey if possible, but at Hopewell Lee initially persuaded him and his chief subordinates, against their better judgment, to try to do so without endangering the army. In his efforts to square this circle, Washington committed his forces to an unclear mission in a piecemeal fashion, he muddied the chain of command by replacing the inexperienced Lafayette with the unenthusiastic and intractable Lee as advanced corps commander, and he failed to make clear to Lee that he was willing to risk a major battle with the British army. If Washington had acted more decisively, he might have inflicted the kind of damage he envisioned. Fortunately for the Americans, Washington redeemed himself by rallying the backtracking advanced corps, choosing a new line from which to fight, and deploying his main body there in enough time to resist the oncoming British. Had he failed, Clinton probably would not have destroyed the nimble American army, but he certainly would have injured it so badly that it could have carried out subsequent operations only with difficulty. Moreover, in seizing and using the unoccupied high ground overlooking the British positions, Washington displayed more tactical ability than he had demonstrated at Brandywine or Germantown. Finally, in sidestepping defeat at Monmouth and successfully condemning Lee for the mishaps that did occur there, Washington avoided more damage to his military reputation and further cemented his relationship with his officer corps.

Lee's military sins were not as extensive as his fellow officers maintained, but he, too, deserved his share of blame for the American army's performance at Monmouth. He undertook an assignment he did not believe in so as to gratify his own ego, and he failed to communicate his plans to his chief subordinates because he had so little confidence in their abilities. Without adequate direction from above, senior officers such as Wayne, Scott, and Lafayette tried to fill the command vacuum by acting on their own initiative, but in so doing they merely added to the confusion Lee's reticence created. On the other hand, it is doubtful that Lee missed an opportunity to crush the British rear guard. Clinton himself later noted that if Lee had not fallen back when he did, the British would have smashed his advanced corps at the East Ravine long before Washington's main body arrived to support it. The advanced corps' helter-skelter withdrawal, therefore, probably saved the American army from a potentially crippling defeat. Even so, Lee could claim little credit for this fortuitous retreat because it happened against his orders to stand fast near Monmouth. If anyone deserved the credit, it was Scott and Wayne, both of whom in giving ground without orders did the right thing for the wrong reasons. The officer corps as a whole fought valiantly as usual, and once Washington exercised his firm grip over the battlefield, Wayne, Knox, Greene, and Stirling—as well as men of lesser rank such as Cilley, Ramsay, and Stewart—exhibited a greater ability to maneuver their troops than they had hitherto shown. In the end, however, the enlisted men were the only group on the American side that warranted unconditional praise. At Monmouth they did everything their officers asked of them in an efficient and timely manner that was a tribute to Steuben's training. In contrast to Brandywine and Germantown, they did not break and run even under the heaviest pressure, but they instead successfully withstood ferocious assaults by the flower of the British army. Monmouth showed the enlisted men as the professionals they now were; it was their officers' amateurish actions that cost the Americans whatever chance they had at a decisive victory.[57]

Not surprisingly, Clinton disputed Washington's claims of victory at Monmouth. As he saw things, he had successfully repelled an American effort to shatter his army and his baggage train as he transferred both across the hostile New Jersey countryside. Under such circumstances, the fact that Washington maintained control of the battlefield meant little. Publicly he praised his army's performance, but in private he criticized what he saw as his officers' slipshod and unprofessional methods. He later wrote,

> Every officer in the army was a general—and not only gave his opinions, but acted, with an independence destructive of all order, subordination, and discipline. . . . What I call gallantry in public was in fact indecent, ungovernable impetuosity, . . . which might have engaged me, in such a country, with half the army worn down with excessive heat and fatigue, [and] with Washington's whole army arriving fresh from Englishtown. Both Lord Cornwallis and I saw many instances that day, both in conversation and conduct, that alarmed us.[58]

There was more than a grain of truth in his petulant observations. Certainly Knyphausen's and Grant's refusal to send Clinton reinforcements and the light infantry's unauthorized over-the-top assaults were symptomatic of a lack of discipline infecting the officer corps. However, Clinton himself merited censure for the British army's substandard showing. He committed only part of the troops at his disposal to the battle, and in relying on a series of frontal assaults, he displayed little tactical imagination. The British rank and file fought well as usual, but their efforts did not compensate for their officers' failings.[59]

Monmouth was a consequence of British and American grand strategies, and it should be interpreted in that context. Here as elsewhere, Washington preferred to use Continental and militia detachments to harass the enemy as part of his long-established strategy of attrition rather than risk his army in a big engagement with the redcoats that hard experience showed he was unlikely to win. Unfortunately for him, Dickinson's militia, Morgan's riflemen, and Maxwell's Continentals had little success in their efforts to nibble away at Clinton's troops as they marched through New Jersey, so Washington eventually decided to commit his army to battle rather than permit the enemy to escape unscathed. In the end, the British suffered losses at Monmouth, but not so many as to hinder their ability to conduct future operations. Considering Washington's goals, the fact that the Americans maintained control of the battlefield carried little strategic weight, although it permitted them to claim a tactical victory that was worth something in the court of public opinion. Monmouth also rid the American army of Charles Lee and served as a bloody graduation exercise for the Steuben-trained rank and file, although these were not on Washington's agenda when he led his army into the battle. For Clinton, Monmouth was a hurdle he had to overcome to successfully redeploy his forces to New York City. In parrying Washington's thrust, Clinton preserved the British army for future operations against both the French and the Americans. From this perspective, Monmouth was a British strategic victory, even though for once the British did not have the satisfaction of driving the Americans from the battlefield.

SEVEN

Conclusions

T he Revolutionary War in America continued for another three and a half years after the British embarked from Sandy Hook, but the two main armies never again met in a major engagement even though they remained in close proximity near New York City. Instead, the critical fighting shifted southward, culminating in the Franco-American victory at Yorktown in October 1781. Although the war did not return to the Philadelphia region, the 1777–78 campaign around the American capital had a profound impact on the conflict's outcome and influenced subsequent developments. France's nascent involvement increased dramatically with the arrival of its army and naval forces to aid the Americans; both Clinton and Washington continued their efforts to implement strategies developed or refined in 1777–78 until Yorktown prompted the ministry to finally accept the British general's resignation; and many of the officers who played prominent roles at Brandywine and Germantown and Monmouth Courthouse—Cornwallis, Clinton, Greene, Wayne, Lafayette, Morgan, and Steuben, for instance—eventually found their way to battlefields in the Carolinas and Virginia. From this perspective, the Philadelphia campaign served as a crucible that helped forge the war's outcome, and thus conclusions about the fighting there are relevant for understanding the war as a whole.

STRATEGIES

George Washington was the person most responsible for victory in the Revolutionary War, and as such he deserves to be called the first great American strategist. Unlike most of his opponents, he understood both British and American strengths and weaknesses and the societies that produced them. Washington transcended traditional eighteenth-century military thinking to fashion a strategy that accommodated American social, political, and economic realities. Having learned through hard experience around New York City that the Americans could not overcome British military and economic advantages on the battlefield, Washington instead turned to attrition to exhaust the enemy's will and resources. He recognized that he needed time to implement attrition, not unattainable battlefield victories, so he sought to control the campaign's pace whenever possible through the skillful use of geography, mobility, and fortifications. Outmaneuvering Howe in east central New Jersey, operating west of the Schuylkill River, deflecting British forces toward the Delaware River, and maintaining the American army's position at Whitemarsh all cost the enemy more in time than in casualties, but for Washington the former was more important than the latter. In the end his actions around Philadelphia bought enough time and credibility to help bring France into the war, and it was French assistance that made it possible for the Americans to secure their independence how and when they did. Washington's strategy might have eventually succeeded on its own, but it would have taken much longer and cost the country much more socially, economically, and politically. Washington's approach rarely worked exactly as he wished—Germantown and Monmouth Courthouse proved this—but it made the American army a more formidable and successful foe than its defeat-laden record indicated.

Washington realized that his army was the sword and shield upon which the Revolution depended. As long as it existed, the British could not safely disperse their troops and occupy the vast territory necessary for them to reestablish their power throughout America. Instead, the threat Washington's army presented forced the British to keep their redcoats and Germans concentrated and limited their authority to little more than the ground upon which their soldiers stood. Because safeguarding his army was a prerequisite for victory, Washington rarely exposed it to the direct confrontations out in the open with its superior British counterpart that might have led to its destruction. From Morristown and Boundbrook he resisted Howe's efforts to tempt him down from his mountain strongholds, he sacrificed Philadelphia to protect the vital depots that supplied his troops, and he evacuated the Delaware River forts to conserve their garrisons. Such efforts at self-preservation, however, did not imply passivity. Although the British assumed an offensive role throughout the campaign, Washington seized every opportunity to wrest the initiative from them without exposing his army to damage it could not afford to sustain, and both Germantown and Monmouth flowed directly from his aggressive nature. Washington made his share of mistakes along the way, but in the long run his sins of commission hurt the American cause much less than Howe's strategic and operational lethargy damaged his.

As commander in chief, Washington faced the unenviable task of reconciling a small professional army with a large, untrained citizen militia. Fortunately for the American cause, he was savvy enough to recognize that he needed both Continentals and militia to successfully implement his strategy. Indeed, he saw the two as complementary entities working in tandem. Washington understood the militia's limitations, but instead of trying to convert the militia into something they were not and could not become, he accepted them for the part-time, ill-disciplined citizen soldiers they were and employed them accordingly. He used the militia to harass British columns in New Jersey and Pennsylvania, provide internal security against local loyalists, garrison strongpoints along the Delaware and Schuylkill, and cut off both large and small British posts. None of these tasks required them to tackle and withstand large numbers of redcoats out in the open, and they freed up the professional Continentals for Washington's use elsewhere. The militia was not a unitary actor, so its effectiveness varied from state to state and from year to year. Leadership, numbers, morale, and organization also played a role. The New Jersey militia performed well in east central New Jersey in 1777 under Philemon Dickinson's capable direction, but later in the year it contributed little to the defense of the Delaware because of Silas Newcomb's poor leadership and an unenthusiastic turnout by the locals. Similarly, the Pennsylvania, Maryland, and Delaware militias completely failed to impede Howe's advance to Philadelphia or to isolate the city from the surrounding countryside once it was in British hands. When the militia did its job, however, it provided Washington with opportunities to strike at detached, isolated, and vulnerable British troops as part of his strategy of attrition.

Washington wanted his Continentals to stand up to the redcoats when necessary, but their inability to consistently live up to his expectations hindered his efforts to implement his strategy. Insufficient instruction, inexperience, poor organization, inadequate leadership, and substandard diet and equipment all contributed to their problems on the battlefield. They generally fought well from behind prepared positions such as Whitemarsh, Fort Mercer, and Fort Mifflin, but Germantown in particular demonstrated that they lacked the training, discipline, and tactical proficiency necessary to overrun and destroy British troops. As the campaign progressed and Steuben's schooling took hold, the Continentals acquired enough skill to withstand redcoat attacks out in the open as at Monmouth, but for the rest of the war taking the tactical offense against the enemy remained a hit-or-miss proposition that hindered Washington's efforts to wear out the British.

At the same time, Washington was flexible enough to temporarily disregard his strategy if political, military, and geographic circumstances warranted. At Brandywine he fought Howe's army in a big engagement out in the open to protect the symbolically important American capital at Philadelphia. Shortly thereafter, he deliberately divided his force by dispatching Continentals to the Delaware River in an effort to sever British supply lines. Finally, at Monmouth he willingly risked battle with Clinton's army because he believed he had a chance to inflict substantial losses on it. In all three instances he failed to achieve his objectives, but they all demonstrated that he was not shackled by the chains of strategic consistency.

On the surface Washington's strategy appeared cautious because it avoided the direct encounters with British military power that might have annihilated his army in one day. A closer look, however, revealed that his strategy carried grave risks that were no less severe for their gradual nature. A strategy of attrition by definition took a long time to take effect, and during the Philadelphia campaign public disillusionment and resource depletion increasingly undermined the American war effort. Many impatient civilian policy makers did not understand Washington's strategy, and he had to resist their efforts to disperse his forces to defend every locale in America or to engage the British in one giant Götterdämmerung. Washington also worried that British enticements such as the Carlisle Commission might seduce the Americans into a peace short of independence. However, generating the resources necessary to continue the conflict was the bigger problem. Maintaining armies required large numbers of men, equipment, and supplies that American economic and political structures were increasingly unable to provide. Indeed, by the end of 1777, Washington's logistical system broke down completely. Reorganization and increasing French aid provided relief, but as the war went, on the Americans could not field the forces necessary to conclusively defeat the British. If Washington's strategy of attrition permitted the Americans to survive year after year, it was French assistance that provided the extra push that brought the British down at Yorktown.

There were also more immediate military factors that worked against Washington's strategy throughout the Philadelphia campaign. The Americans needed broken and remote terrain behind which to deploy their forces with minimal fear of successful British attack. Northern New Jersey, Pennsylvania west of the Schuylkill, and the lower Delaware River possessed the swamps, rivers, and hills that were conducive to a policy of attrition, so Washington was able to stymie British efforts in these regions. Southeastern Pennsylvania, on the other hand, was flat and open enough to enhance British mobility and reduce Washington's opportunities to securely position his army. Indeed, this unfriendly geography contributed to Washington's decision to fight Howe along the Brandywine. Moreover, to apply his strategy, Washington needed opportunities to waylay and wear down British forces. He had plenty of chances to do so throughout 1777 in east central New Jersey and southeastern Pennsylvania, but imminent French entry into the war changed all this. The ministry's decision to withdraw British forces into their well-fortified coastal enclaves removed them from Washington's reach, making American victory increasingly dependent on the French naval support necessary to pry them out of their citadels. Finally, Washington's strategy required both the militia and the Continentals to fulfill their assignments, which they often did not do. Despite these disadvantages, on the balance Washington's strategy was undoubtedly the best available because he based it on an accurate appreciation and acceptance of American society, politics, economics, and geography.

Unlike Washington, the British never understood the society over which they sought to reestablish their authority. Howe's thoroughly unimaginative strategic thinking was geared toward waging a typical eighteenth-century European conflict. Throughout the Philadelphia campaign, he concentrated on seizing territory and destroying Washington's army in a climactic battle. He succeeded in occupying the rebel capital and beating his opponent in a string of engagements big and small, but doing so brought him no closer to victory. Howe never fully realized that he was waging war against a democratized and politically conscious society motivated by a desire for independence and liberty. To suppress the rebellion, he had to nullify the idea that gave birth to it, but he could never figure out a way to do so. He attempted at various times to cultivate loyalist sympathy and to sweet-talk rebels back into the fold, but neither effort went to the heart of the dispute between the mother country and its wayward colonies. In the end, Howe resorted to incessant demands for more and more troops to implement a clearly bankrupt strategy. His resignation came as a relief to almost everyone, including himself.

The ministry took control of British planning after Howe submitted his resignation and French intervention became increasingly likely. Germain and his colleagues' new strategy was an improvement over Howe's conventional thinking, but it was not effective enough to secure victory. Their decision to make significant concessions to the rebels via the Carlisle Commission, to concentrate British forces in well-defended coastal enclaves, and to undertake a naval war against New England's resources demonstrated a growing awareness that neutralizing the Americans' ability and willingness to wage war one way or another was a key to victory. Unhappily, they also continued to grasp at old straws. They hoped to bring Washington's army into a decisive battle, and they planned to undertake the conquest of the supposedly loyalist-filled southern states, two chimeras that never had and never would pan out. The biggest problem with this strategy, however, was its timing. The terms the Carlisle Commission offered were three years too late, and French entry promised to encourage the rebels and to disperse the resources the British needed to effectively prosecute their war against America. Although the British were surprisingly successful in their efforts to execute their new strategy, at least at first, in the end Germain and his associates were a day late and a dollar short.

ON THE BATTLEFIELD

The efforts by British policy makers to carry out their flawed plans at the operational level met with mixed results during the Philadelphia campaign. Washington's strategy of attrition almost invariably thwarted and befuddled Howe, and the British army occasionally maneuvered like a blindfolded child flailing away at a piñata. Howe's New Jersey incursions, for example, not only wasted considerable time but also demonstrated clearly Howe's inability to come to grips with Washington's way of war. Such uncertainty bred caution, which further undermined Howe's efforts. His decision to land at Head of Elk instead of along the Delaware River and his refusal to attack Valley Forge were motivated in large part by a desire to play it safe. Prudence certainly had its place in his war with his opponent, but in these instances it prompted Howe to waste both time and opportunities the British could not afford to lose.

Ironically enough, however, Howe combined this cautiousness with a breezy tactical overconfidence that also occasionally cost him and his men. For all of his strategic insecurities, Howe was always supremely confident that he could beat the rebels if they would only stand up to his army out in the open. Such self-assurance without a doubt contributed to his unquestionable skill on the battlefield, but it also led him to underestimate the American army, which brought him considerable grief at Germantown and along the Delaware. On the other hand, Howe did occasionally maneuver adroitly, especially when he managed to get Washington to fight the British kind of war in the process. His decision to cut loose from his supply lines after he disembarked at Head of Elk and during his march to the upper Schuylkill fords required considerable nerve, and both contributed to Philadelphia's fall. Unfortunately for Howe, Washington rarely gave him such chances.

As for Clinton, he played little role in formulating British strategy in the winter of 1777–78, but he effected his first instructions very well. He recognized right away that he lacked the means to implement the ministry's orders, but he did not become paralyzed by indecision. Instead, on his own authority he resolved to take his army from Philadelphia to New York City by land before dispatching expeditions to Florida and St. Lucia. It seemed commonsensical in retrospect, but Clinton took an enormous risk in running the American gauntlet through New Jersey, and his success was a tribute to the firm grip he kept on operations that spring.

Whatever its strategic or operational problems, the British army performed magnificently on the battlefield throughout the Philadelphia campaign in almost all circumstances. At Brandywine it outflanked and overran the well-placed Americans, at Paoli it surprised and scattered Wayne's luckless soldiers in the middle of the night, at Germantown it repelled Washington's sudden violent attack out of the fog, along the Delaware it erected and manned dozens of heavy cannons in the water and muck to fire on Fort Mifflin, and at Monmouth it fought off the swarming rebel army. With the exception of the German repulse outside of Fort Mercer and the drawn battle at Monmouth, the British army won every major engagement during the campaign, and it did so in a hostile countryside and despite its multinational composition. Training, experience, and morale certainly contributed to the British army's triumphs, but there was more to it than that. British officers repeatedly displayed a firm grasp of tactics that permitted them to outmaneuver their enemies and cut through the inevitable confusion of battle in a way the rebels never equaled. Howe in particular combined simplicity of purpose with tactical finesse to repeatedly bend the Americans to his will. Moreover, British officers adjusted to the demands of warfare in America by, for example, augmenting their light infantry units and adding more firepower in the form of artillery to deal with rebel partisans. For their part, the British army's rank and file—not only the redcoats but also the Germans and provincials—rarely faltered or broke in battle; when they did, as at Germantown, they quickly rallied, reformed, and resumed the attack. The British made their share of mistakes on the battlefield, but their resiliency enabled them to repeatedly recover from the shock of momentary defeat to wrest the initiative from the Americans. Unfortunately for them, such superb tactics could not overcome their leaders' defective strategies that ultimately rendered all their victories barren.

The American army was surprisingly successful in its contest with its better-trained and better-equipped opponent in the Philadelphia campaign. The Americans possessed a number of advantages that Washington cleverly exploited to implement his strategy on an operational level. Many British officers had spent considerable time in America, but it was the Americans who best married their strategy with the local geography, despite occasional and costly mistakes at Brandywine, Germantown, and Paoli. Washington used his knowledge of the surrounding terrain to torment the British in New Jersey in the winter of 1776–77 and to outmaneuver Howe during his two incursions into the state the following summer. The Americans also took advantage of their familiarity with the Delaware River to establish the intricate defense network there that so confounded the British. In addition, Continentals marched with a celerity that frequently put the British to shame. Washington's fast-moving army headed off Howe's efforts to outflank it at Red Clay Creek, reached the upper Schuylkill fords before the British despite a long detour to Warwick to replenish its ammunition supply, and overtook Clinton in his excursion through New Jersey. Such efforts did not completely compensate for British naval mobility, but throughout the Philadelphia campaign Washington almost always managed to interpose his army between the redcoats and their immediate objective. Finally, the Americans grew adept at constructing defensive works so formidable that the British did not attempt to test their strength. Continental positions at Morristown, Boundbrook, Red Clay Creek, Whitemarsh, and Valley Forge served as dams to block, delay, or deflect British advances.

On an intellectual level, Washington and his men could take pride in their strategic and operational achievements if they so chose, but during the Philadelphia campaign they never had the emotional satisfaction of chasing the redcoats from the field of battle and engaging in the backslapping and hollering that accompanied victory. Indeed, with some minor or qualified exceptions—the German repulse at Fort Mercer, for example, or the inconclusive contest at Monmouth—the American record throughout the campaign was one long litany of tactical defeats of varying severity. The reasons for such ill fortune were myriad. The untrained militia that made up such a large percentage of American forces played a vital part in Washington's strategy, but they were completely incapable of standing up to the tough enemy in open battle. Instead, Washington assigned them subsidiary roles, but they failed to accomplish much even then. At Germantown, for instance, the New Jersey and Maryland militias did not even find the British lines, and their Pennsylvania counterparts did little better. On the other hand, the Continentals performed increasingly well on the battlefield as the campaign progressed, but they still generally came off second best against the redcoats. Although they fought gamely at Brandywine and Germantown, in each case they ultimately broke and ran. Part of the problem was insufficient training and experience, but both time and Steuben rectified these difficulties sufficiently so that they earned a draw or better at Monmouth. In the final analysis, however, Washington and his officers were most responsible for their army's tactical ineptitude. The American commander in chief was undeniably a brave and unruffled general who usually deployed his men fairly well, but he never maneuvered his troops with the rapier-like skill Howe demonstrated again and again. In fact, his tactics were generally unimaginative and predictable, as were those of most of his subordinates. Contradictory intelligence reports at Brandywine paralyzed him, he developed an overly complicated plan for the assault on Germantown, and at Monmouth he imparted unclear orders to a convoluted command structure he had created. From this perspective, it was just as well that Washington avoided set-piece battles.

SUBORDINATES

An army is no better than the officers who command it. Fortunately for Howe and later Clinton, they both had at their disposal innumerable high-ranking subordinates of quality. These men bickered over the distribution of glory, rank, reputation, and command as much as any

234 The Philadelphia Campaign, 1777-1778

other group of ambitious people, but long-established rules governing such things and the 3,000-mile gap between them and London policy makers prevented these disputes from hindering the army to the same extent it did Washington's. Most prominent British and German officers had experienced the Great War for Empire in Europe or America, so they were thoroughly familiar with the horror and chaos of battle. More important, they were also used to directing and maneuvering large numbers of men. Throughout the Philadelphia campaign, British and German officers demonstrated an ability to think on their feet and act on their own initiative. At Brandywine, Agnew hurried his men to Dilworth to save the beleaguered grenadiers from the beating Weedon administered, and at Germantown, Musgrave threw his troops into Chew House to buy time for the rest of the army to re-form. In neither instance did these men have orders to act as they did, but they each saw a problem and undertook efforts to solve it without direction from above. Such enterprise could cause difficulties. At Monmouth, for example, light infantry officers acting on their own attacked more aggressively than Clinton wanted and exposed themselves to Cilley's sharp counterattack, but on the whole initiative was one of the British officer corps' greatest strengths.

Moreover, British officers also performed well on independent missions. Knyphausen skillfully brought half the British army to the Brandywine in the face of increasing resistance, Grey formulated and executed a brilliant plan to surprise Wayne's division at Paoli, and Cornwallis deftly swept the Delaware's east bank clean of rebels after Fort Mifflin fell. There were exceptions of course, Donop's Fort Mercer fiasco and Grant's bumbling attempt to snag Lafayette at Barren Hill being two of the most obvious, but they were just that—exceptions—and not the norm.

The British officer corps' biggest problem was that it shared Howe's strategic myopia. Most of Howe's high-ranking subordinates believed that seizing territory and winning battles would bring the war to a victorious conclusion. Cornwallis agreed with Howe's wrongheaded decision to land at Head of Elk instead of on the Delaware, and throughout the winter of 1777-78, Grey assumed that a quick march to Valley Forge to disperse Washington's army there would put an end to the rebellion. Like their boss, they did not understand that suppressing the American revolt required more than traditional eighteenth-century strategic concepts.[1] There was undoubtedly something to be said for the superiority many of these men felt toward the enemy that enabled them to overcome or repulse the rebels at almost every opportunity, but such disdain was a two-edged sword that cost the British Empire dearly.

During the Philadelphia campaign, Washington's chief subordinates were almost as much a burden as a blessing to the careworn American commander in chief. This was especially true of the militia commanders. Except for Dickinson, none of them—Armstrong, Potter, Irvine, Smallwood, Forman, Newcomb, and Lacey—did much to help Washington wage his war. No doubt these men labored under great difficulties in keeping together their ill-trained, undisciplined, poorly motivated, and badly equipped soldiers, but they rarely demonstrated the driving leadership skills necessary to overcome the militia's inherent problems and to motivate their troops to put their lives on the line. It was perhaps not surprising that Armstrong recoiled from assaulting the dug-in Germans at Germantown, but most militia commanders displayed a marked reluctance to even engage the British in the kind of skirmishing Washington called for, which made both these soldiers and Washington's strategy that much less effective. As a result, Washington was unable to effectively harass Howe's army as it marched to the Schuylkill, or to sufficiently seal Philadelphia off from the surrounding countryside.

Nor did Continental officers provide Washington with much solace. Most rarely griped about their commander's strategy—although this could be chalked up to either agreement or ignorance—but often many of them seemed as concerned with reputation and personal advancement as with winning the war, and Congress's proximity and unclear rules for seniority and promotion encouraged such bickering and politicking. Indeed, during the Philadelphia campaign, there was scarcely a general who did not resign or threaten to resign unless his grievances were met, including Washington favorites Greene, Knox, and Sullivan. Competition frequently divided the officer corps into cliques and factions that undermined the American war effort. Lee's differences with the rest of the officer corps, for example, almost proved ruinous at Monmouth. The Conway Cabal demonstrated that Washington could deal with such problems adeptly—if not exactly honorably—but they remained an unwelcome distraction.

Such infighting might have been tolerable if Washington's subordinates had performed well on the battlefield, but this was often not the case. Although many Continental generals were veterans of the Great War for Empire, they had little experience commanding large numbers of troops. Most Continental officers fought courageously but not necessarily skillfully, especially when called upon to maneuver their men in the pandemonium of combat. At Brandywine, Scott, Woodford, Conway, and Stirling held out longer than expected from prepared positions against Howe's flanking assault, but Sullivan's confused gyrations showed his inability to reconcile conflicting intelligence, unfamiliar terrain, and insufficiently trained troops on the battlefield. Similarly, Sullivan, Wayne, and Greene had no trouble leading their troops in a headlong charge into Germantown, but they could not cope with complications growing out of the fog and increasing enemy resistance. There were exceptions, of course—Greene and Weedon maneuvered well at Brandywine, and Morgan maintained tight control over his riflemen during the first British incursion into New Jersey and later at Whitemarsh—but on the whole, Continental officers rarely demonstrated the certainty and decisiveness that characterized British tactics. American officers as a group lacked the ability to cut through the fog of battle and direct their men where they were most needed. Although they gradually gained experience over the years, most never possessed the same confidence, expectation of victory, and hauteur that motivated British officers to take battlefield setbacks as personal affronts to be avenged immediately.

Although Washington's strategy called for concentrating his Continentals as much as possible, on occasion during the Philadelphia campaign he dispatched detachments to carry out various missions. Unfortunately, those subordinates he entrusted to command such independent expeditions rarely lived up to his expectations. Greene was too cautious in his pursuit of Howe during the British retreat from Brunswick and later against Cornwallis along the Delaware, Wayne failed miserably at Paoli, Lafayette was lucky to escape destruction at Barren Hill, and Lee's bumbling at Monmouth nearly cost the army its advanced corps. Here, too, the inexperience that bred either timidity or recklessness was mostly to blame, and the Americans were lucky that the British did not defeat them in detail more often than they did.

Fortunately for the American cause, many of these officers proved willing and able to learn from their mistakes, and in this sense the Philadelphia campaign served as a priceless training ground for officers. Wayne, Greene, Lafayette, and Sullivan made their share of mistakes in 1777–78, but they all went on to give valuable service in subsequent campaigns and battles. Conversely, Washington used the fighting around Philadelphia to weed out officers who repeatedly demonstrated an inability to obey orders or get things done. In this sense, Stephen and

Lee, as well as lesser lights like de Borre, were among the campaign's biggest casualties. Such on-the-job training was certainly expensive for the soldiers who paid in blood for their inexperienced or incompetent commander's mistakes, but it was the only school available, and its graduates helped win the war.

SCHIZOPHRENIC AMERICA

In some ways the Revolutionary War was the world's first modern conflict, not militarily or technologically but in political terms. For the first time, a largely democratized and participatory society united by a common set of values—not by nationality or race or a charismatic leader—waged war to defend and implement its ideas. America was the most politically conscious society on earth, and the universality of its beliefs enabled the Revolution to transcend class, religion, region, and ethnicity to unite the majority into a cohesive force capable of resisting British power. Unquestionably, America's large population of loyalists and black slaves indicated that not everyone agreed with or had the opportunity to agree with the Revolution, but enough did to place the source of American resistance squarely in the hearts and minds of the populace, not in some small elite that the British could easily capture, co-opt, scatter, or destroy. On the other hand, in some respects the war was a conflict from an increasingly bygone era. Political power in America was not situated in a centralized body—Congress's authority was limited and uncertain throughout the war—but was dispersed among the various states. Although this localism was gradually disappearing in Europe, it was sufficiently alive and well in America that the war effort did not depend on any one city, region, state, or group of people for its survival.

To win this kind of war, the British had to either break the Americans' will to resist or offer them an alternative idea that would entice them back into the empire voluntarily. Throughout the conflict, the British tried a little of both, but with neither were they successful. The diffuse nature of American power and limited British resources made it impossible for the redcoat generals to use the coercion necessary to reestablish their authority over all the remote farms, villages, towns, and cities from New Hampshire to Georgia. Conversely, efforts to seduce the Americans back into the empire did not go to the heart of the issue, were unenthusiastic, or were too little too late. The Philadelphia campaign symbolized the dilemma the British faced. During the campaign they won almost all the battles, occupied the rebel capital, and seized chunks of territory, but it was never enough to overcome American society's peculiarly schizophrenic nature. Most American policy makers, however, almost innately understood the people they represented; thus, they waged war secure in the knowledge that their revolution grew out of the population they represented and led.

Biographical Afterword

William Alexander, Lord Stirling, continued his loyal if undistinguished service to the American cause that included temporary command of the army when Washington was away consulting Congress and president of the court that condemned John Andre to death for his role in Benedict Arnold's treason. He died of gout in January 1783, just as the war officially ended.

John Armstrong spent more of his remaining years in politics than in the military, including two terms in the Articles of Confederation Congress. He died in 1795. His son and namesake was secretary of war during the War of 1812.

Benedict Arnold took charge of Philadelphia after the British left, and there his ostentatious living, high-handed ways, and close association with prominent loyalists alienated many. Feeling increasingly disgruntled and unappreciated, he opened a correspondence with Henry Clinton in 1780 in which he eventually offered to surrender his new West Point command to the British in exchange for rank and money. Exposed by the capture of go-between John Andre before he could betray the vital Hudson Highlands fortress in his charge, he fled to British lines. His treason rocked the Continental army to its very foundations and made him the country's most famous and hated traitor. He later commanded British raids into Connecticut and Virginia, but Clinton never really trusted him. After the war he became a merchant in Britain, and he died in 1801 a despised and depressed man.

Frederick, Earl of Carlisle, made public anti-French remarks that prompted Lafayette to challenge him to a duel, but Carlisle breezily dismissed him. He returned to Britain in November 1778, later served as

Lord Lieutenant of Ireland, and became a patron of the arts. Lord Byron was his nephew. He died in 1825.

Joseph Cilley campaigned with John Sullivan against the Iroquois in 1779 and retired from the army in January 1781. After the war he served in the New Hampshire legislature and as a major general in the state's militia. He died in 1799.

Henry Clinton marked time after concentrating British forces in New York City by conducting various raids, quarreling with others, and periodically asking the ministry to relieve him of his burdensome command. In late 1779, he undertook the conquest of the southern states. After successfully besieging Charleston and capturing more than 5,000 Continentals there, he left Cornwallis in charge and headed back to New York. The two men's subsequent personal and strategic disagreements contributed to the British disaster at Yorktown. Clinton resigned in 1782 and returned to Britain to wage a public and largely ineffective public relations battle with Cornwallis over responsibility for that decisive British defeat. He reentered Parliament in 1790, and in 1794 the ministry appointed him governor of Gibraltar, where he died the following year.

Thomas Conway returned home after his duel with Cadwalader and rejoined the French army. He fought bravely in India and eventually became governor general of all French forces there. Unfortunately for him, his royalist sympathies forced him into exile when the French Revolution began, and he died around 1800.

Charles Cornwallis participated in the siege of Charleston, and afterward Clinton put him in charge of British efforts to subdue the southern states. His independent attitude, direct correspondence with Germain, and single-minded strategic views ultimately poisoned his relationship with the British commander in chief. Aggressive as ever, he beat Horatio Gates at the Battle of Camden and secured both Georgia and South Carolina for the Crown. Unfortunately for him and his cause, he overextended his forces by chasing and fighting his old opponent Nathanael Greene through North Carolina and Virginia. Washington's Franco-American army captured him and his troops at Yorktown in October 1781, but most people in and out of the British government blamed Clinton for the fiasco. He was later appointed governor-general of India, where he instituted many far-reaching and positive reforms. He afterward became viceroy and commander in chief in Ireland, and he negotiated the Peace of Amiens with France in 1802. He died in 1805 while serving a second time as India's governor-general.

William Cornwallis fought in the West Indies for the rest of the war and afterward served in India. During the Napoleonic Wars, he helped blockade the French coast, and he died in 1819.

Philemon Dickinson continued as New Jersey's militia commander until the end of the conflict. During the war he ran unsuccessfully for New Jersey governor three times against William Livingston, and he later served as the state's senator. He died in 1809.

Thomas-Antoine du Plessis returned to France in 1779 and later supported the revolution there. His own soldiers killed him in Santo Domingo in 1791 during the island's brutal wars.

Johann Ewald served capably throughout the conflict and surrendered with Cornwallis at Yorktown. He returned to Hesse in 1784 and gained a reputation as a military expert. He was employed by Denmark throughout the Napoleonic Wars, and he died in 1813.

Patrick Ferguson was wounded at Brandywine, and while he recovered, Howe disbanded his breech-loading rifle unit for reasons that remain unclear. He later served at Charleston, and he was killed in 1780 leading his loyalist soldiers at the Battle of King's Mountain.

François Louis Teissèdre de Fleury fought at the Siege of Newport and later received a rare congressional medal for his courageous actions at Stony Point. He left for France in September 1779 but returned to America with the French army and participated in the Yorktown siege. He was executed during the Reign of Terror, although some accounts place him alive in 1796.

David Forman spent the rest of the war ruthlessly rooting out loyalists in and around Monmouth County in New Jersey. Afterward he moved to Maryland, then Tennessee, and he died of a stroke at sea in 1797 after a British privateer captured his vessel.

Joseph Galloway returned to Britain after the Americans reoccupied Philadelphia and waged a bitter public relations campaign against Howe, whom he believed had squandered innumerable opportunities to win the war. His efforts to regain his extensive American landholdings failed, and he died in 1803.

Horatio Gates was appointed by Congress to command the Southern Department in July 1780 against Washington's wishes. Shortly thereafter, Cornwallis crushed his army at the Battle of Camden. He retired to his farm amid allegations of cowardice, but two years later he rejoined the army just before the war ended. He later served in the New York legislature for a term, and he died in 1806.

George Germain continued as American secretary until discredited by the defeat at Yorktown. He resigned in February 1782, retired from public service a year later, and died in 1785.

Mordecai Gist fought bravely at the Battle of Camden with his Maryland Continentals, most of whom were killed, wounded, or captured. He retired to South Carolina in 1783 and died in 1792. His grandson Brigadier General States Rights Gist was killed at the Battle of Franklin in November 1864 defending the cause his name implied.

James Grant commanded the successful British assault on St. Lucia in December 1778, rose to full general in 1796, and served in Parliament from 1787 to 1801. He died in 1806 at the age of eighty-six.

William Grayson resigned his commission to serve on the Board of War, and he later became one of Virginia's first two senators. He died in 1790.

Christopher Greene later commanded a regiment of black Rhode Islanders at the Siege of Newport. He was killed in May 1781 by loyalist partisans in a skirmish between the lines in front of New York City.

Nathanael Greene endured two more years as quartermaster general until his resignation in 1780, after which Washington appointed him to succeed Gates as Southern Department commander. Despite extremely limited resources, in a brilliant campaign he outmaneuvered Cornwallis and then freed almost all of the Carolinas from British control, even though he never won a single battle. After the war he fell on hard financial times, so he moved to Georgia in an effort to recoup his fortunes. He died there of sunstroke in 1786.

Charles Grey returned to Britain after leading a number of raids with the same skill he showed at Paoli. The ministry appointed him commander in chief in America in 1782, but the war ended before he could take up his duties. He later fought against the French and became a full general. He died in 1807.

Alexander Hamilton quit as Washington's aide after a petty dispute in July 1781, assumed command of a battalion, and fought bravely at Yorktown. He later participated in the Constitutional Convention, contributed to the *Federalist Papers,* served as Washington's secretary of the treasury, and became army inspector general during the Quasi War with France. His political career declined with the Federalist party's, and he was killed by Aaron Burr in a duel in 1804.

Moses Hazen fought throughout the conflict and rose to command a brigade at Yorktown. Afterward he settled in Vermont and died there in 1803.

William Hazelwood became commissioner of purchases in 1780 when Pennsylvania disbanded its navy, and after the war he returned to private business. He died in 1800.

Leopold Phillip von Heister died soon after he returned to Hesse, in November 1777.

William Andrew Hamond fought the French navy in America and the West Indies, and he later became an admiral. He died in 1812.

Richard Howe resigned soon after his brother, but he remained in command long enough raise the Franco-American Siege of Newport. Recalled to service in March 1782, he relieved besieged Gibraltar, was later First Lord of the Admiralty, and defeated a French squadron at the Battle of the Glorious First of June in 1794 in the French Revolution's first Anglo-French naval engagement. In 1797 he persuaded British sailors at Spithead to end their dangerous mutiny. He died in 1799.

William Howe survived a halfhearted parliamentary inquiry into his performance as commander in chief, was later promoted to full general, and commanded troops in the British Isles during the French Revolution. He died in 1814.

William Irvine later served on the western frontier as Fort Pitt's commander, and after the war he was a land agent and Pennsylvania congressman. He died in 1804.

Henry Knox remained Washington's faithful and capable artillery commander throughout the war. Afterward he served as secretary of war both for the Articles of Confederation Congress and in Washington's administration. He died in 1806.

Wilhelm Knyphausen commanded Clinton's German troops until declining health forced him to retire in 1782. He was a military governor when he died in 1800.

John Lacey abandoned military pursuits for political and business ones. He served in the Pennsylvania government, and after the war he moved to New Jersey and became an iron manufacturer. He died in 1814.

Marquis de Lafayette participated in the Siege of Newport before returning to France as a hero to lobby for more aid to the United States. Once back in America, he served as an intermediary between French and American forces, and in 1781 Washington sent him to Virginia to confront Cornwallis's rampaging army. Although outnumbered, he managed to keep Cornwallis busy enough that Washington's army and French forces could get into position for the Yorktown siege. He was a moderate in the French Revolution and was persecuted and imprisoned for his political positions. In 1824 he made a triumphal tour of the United States and was acclaimed everywhere he went by a grateful nation. He died a decade later.

Henry Laurens resigned as president of Congress in December 1778, but the delegates later chose him as emissary to the Netherlands. Captured on his way across the Atlantic, he suffered declining health in British hands until he was exchanged for Cornwallis. He died in 1792, ten years after his son John was killed in a minor skirmish in South Carolina.

Charles Lee was haunted by the Monmouth controversy and his own tart tongue. Both John Laurens and Anthony Wayne challenged him to duels because he impugned their honor in his statements about Monmouth. Laurens wounded him, which prevented him from fighting Wayne. He retired to his Shenandoah Valley farm and wrote an insulting letter to Congress that prompted that body to dismiss him from the service in January 1980. He died in 1782.

William Maxwell fought with his brigade in Sullivan's campaign against the Iroquois before resigning in July 1780. He was later elected to the New Jersey legislature, and he died in 1790.

Alexander McDougall fought throughout the conflict, although illness periodically put him on the sidelines. After the war he served in the Articles of Confederation Congress and in the New York legislature, and he later organized and became the first president of the Bank of New York. He died in 1786.

Thomas Mifflin finally resigned from the army in February 1779, but he later became president of Congress and governor of Pennsylvania. He died in 1800.

Daniel Morgan resigned in the summer of 1778, ostensibly for health reasons but in fact because he was angry that Washington did not appoint him to command the newly created light infantry brigade. He declined Congress's orders to return to duty when the British invaded the southern states, but after the Battle of Camden he rejoined the army. At the Battle of Cowpens in January 1781, he won the most brilliant American tactical victory of the war. A month later, however, poor health forced him to quit again. After the conflict he prospered as a landowner, politician, and devout member of the Presbyterian Church. He died in 1802.

Peter Muhlenberg served throughout the conflict in both the northern and southern theaters. After the war he became a successful Pennsylvania politician, and he died in 1807.

Thomas Musgrave went with Grant to St. Lucia, and from there he was invalidated home, though he later returned to America as the last commander of the British garrison in New York City. He subsequently served in India and became a general. He died in 1812.

Charles Scott was captured at Charleston in May 1780 and sat out the rest of the conflict. After the war he participated in successive campaigns against the American Indians in the Ohio region. He also served as governor of Kentucky, and he died in 1812.

William Smallwood fought at the Battle of Camden in July 1780, but he later refused to serve under the foreigner Steuben and spent the rest of the war in Maryland raising troops. Afterward he was that state's governor. He died in 1792.

Samuel Smith fought at Monmouth, and after the war he remained in the Maryland militia and rose through its ranks to become a major general. He also served as a congressman, senator, and secretary of the navy in the course of his long political career. During the War of 1812, he commanded the American defenses at Baltimore. He died in 1839.

Baron von Steuben later served in Virginia, but civilians there responded to him without the enthusiasm Continental officers and men displayed. After the war he became an American citizen and popular New Yorker who was continually in and out of debt. He died in 1794.

John Sullivan's desire for independent command turned to ashes in his mouth when he failed to take British-held Newport in conjunction with a French naval squadron in the summer of 1778. The next year, however, he carried out a successful campaign against the Iroquois, but illness forced him to retire in November 1779. He was then elected to Congress and remained Washington's faithful ally in politics as in war. After the conflict he was active in New Hampshire politics and later served as a federal judge. He died in 1795.

James Varnum fought at the Siege of Newport before resigning in March 1779. He subsequently commanded Rhode Island's militia, and after the war he served first in the Articles of Confederation Congress and then as a judge in the Northwest Territory. He died in 1789.

George Washington remained commander in chief for the rest of the war. He had little luck getting at the well-defended British coastal enclaves until 1781, when he led a Franco-American army southward to capture Cornwallis's soldiers at Yorktown in conjunction with a French fleet. He wanted to retire to his Virginia plantation, but the American public would not let him. He attended the Constitutional Convention, served two terms as the United States' first president from 1789 to 1797, and was called back into military service at the beginning of the Quasi War with France in 1798. He died in 1799.

Anthony Wayne served with distinction throughout the war as perhaps the American army's best combat leader. He learned his lessons from Paoli sufficiently so that in 1779 he successfully stormed the well-defended British post at Stony Point along the Hudson River in a nighttime bayonet attack that killed or captured most of its garrison. Later he put down a dangerous mutiny by the Pennsylvania Continentals, fought capably under Lafayette in Virginia, and ended up campaigning in Georgia. After the war he fell on hard times until President Washington appointed him commander of the twice-vanquished western army. He whipped it into shape, decisively defeated the American Indians at the Battle of Fallen Timbers, and imposed on them the Treaty of Greenville. He died in 1796.

George Weedon returned to Virginia after his resignation, but he later commanded the Virginia militia during the Yorktown campaign. He died in 1793.

James Wilkinson married his Reading girlfriend. He served as clothier-general from July 1779 until March 1781 before quitting amid accusations of corruption. After the war he fought with Wayne at the Battle of Fallen Timbers and rose to command the American army. He subsequently conspired with Aaron Burr to detach the western part of the country, but he escaped blame by turning in his erstwhile partner. He campaigned unsuccessfully along the Canadian border during the War of 1812. He eventually penned his memoirs in defense of his controversial career, but he omitted the fact that he had been in Spain's pay for much of it. He died in 1825.

William Woodford was captured with most of his brigade at Charleston in May 1780, and he died in captivity six months later.

Notes

CHAPTER 1. INTRODUCTION

1. Ambrose Serle, *The American Journal of Ambrose Serle, Secretary to Lord Howe, 1776–78,* ed. Edward H. Tatum (San Marino, Calif.: Huntington Library, 1940), p. 240.

2. Archibald Robertson, *Archibald Robertson: His Diaries and Sketches in America, 1762–1780,* ed. Harry Miller Lydenberg (New York: Arno Press, 1971), pp. 178–79; John Peebles, *John Peebles' American War: The Diary of a Scottish Grenadier, 1776–1782,* ed. Ira D. Gruber (Mechanicsburg, Pa.: Stackpole Books, 1998), p. 195; John Charles Philip von Krafft, *Von Krafft's Journal* (New York: New-York Historical Society, 1882), pp. 50–52; Johann Ewald, *Diary of the American War: A Hessian Journal,* trans. and ed. Joseph P. Tustin (New Haven, Conn.: Yale University Press, 1979), pp. 136–38; Bruce E. Burgoyne, ed., *Enemy Views: The American Revolutionary War as Recorded by the Hessian Participants* (Bowie, Md.: Heritage Books, 1996), p. 263.

3. James Murray to David Smyth, 10 August 1778, James Murray, *Letters from America, 1773 to 1780: Being the Letters of a Scots Officer, Sir James Murray, to His Home During the War of American Independence,* ed. Eric Robson (Manchester: Manchester University Press, 1951), p. 56.

CHAPTER 2. COLD NEW JERSEY WINTER

1. Charles Willson Peale, 2–6 January 1777, "Journal by Charles Willson Peale," *Pennsylvania Magazine of History and Biography* 38 (1914): 281–85; Benjamin Tallmadge, *Memoir of Col. Benjamin Tallmadge* (New York: Thomas Holman, 1858), p. 18; William Howe to Lord George Germain, 5 January 1777, *Correspondence of Charles, First Marquis Cornwallis,* vol. 1, ed. Charles Ross (London: John Murray, 1859), p. 28; Thomas Rodney, 3–6 January 1777, *Diary of Captain Thomas Rodney, 1776–1777* (New York: Da Capo Press, 1974), pp. 37–41.

2. Nicholas Cresswell, 7 January 1777, *The Journal of Nicholas Cresswell,*

1774–1777 (Port Washington, N.Y.: Kennikat Press, 1968), pp. 179–80. Others agreed that Trenton reinvigorated the colonial cause. See Enoch Anderson, *Personal Recollections of Captain Enoch Anderson* (New York: Arno Press, 1971), p. 29; Philip Schuyler to George Washington, 30 January 1777, *The Papers of George Washington: Revolutionary War Series,* vol. 8, ed. Dorothy Twohig (Charlottesville: University Press of Virginia, 1998), p. 192; William Ellery to Nicholas Cooke, 4 January 1777, *Letters of Delegates to Congress, 1774–1789,* vol. 6, ed. Paul Smith (Washington, D.C.: Library of Congress, 1980), p. 30.

3. Marquis de Lafayette to Duc d'Ayen, 16 December 1777, *Lafayette in the Age of the American Revolution: Selected Letters and Papers, 1776–1790,* vol. 1, ed. Stanley J. Idzerda (Ithaca, N.Y.: Cornell University Press, 1979), p. 192.

4. Washington to James Livingston, 8 February 1777, *Washington Papers,* vol. 8, p. 275.

5. Washington to John Hancock, 7 January 1777, *Washington Papers,* vol. 8, pp. 9–10; Washington to a Committee of the Continental Congress, 12 April 1777, *The Papers of George Washington: Revolutionary War Series,* vol. 9, ed. Dorothy Twohig (Charlottesville: University Press of Virginia, 1999), pp. 126–27; Washington to Heath, 5 January 1777, *Memoirs of Major-General William Heath, by Himself,* ed. William Abbott (New York: William Abbott, 1901), pp. 97–98; Washington to Hancock, 12 January 1777, *Washington Papers,* vol. 8, p. 47; Washington to Hancock, 14 January 1777, *Washington Papers,* vol. 8, p. 64; Washington to Hancock, 17 January 1777, *Washington Papers,* vol. 8, p. 89; Washington to Schuyler, 18 January 1777, *Washington Papers,* vol. 8, p. 99; Washington to Schuyler, 19 January 1777, *Washington Papers,* vol. 8, pp. 101–2; Washington to Robert Morris, 19 January 1777, *Washington Papers,* vol. 8, p. 107; Washington to Pennsylvania Council of Safety, 19 January 1777, *Washington Papers,* vol. 8, pp. 107–8.

6. For a good analysis of partisan fighting in New Jersey that winter, see Mark V. Kwasny, *Washington's Partisan War, 1775–1783* (Kent, Ohio: Kent State University Press, 1996), pp. 113–38. See also Nathanael Greene to Cooke, 10 January 1777, *The Papers of General Nathanael Greene,* vol. 2, ed. Richard K. Showman (Chapel Hill: University of North Carolina Press, 1980), p. 5; Joseph Galloway, *Selected Tracts,* vol. 1 (New York: Da Capo Press, 1974), pp. 387–89; John Adams to James Warren, 3 February 1777, *The Works of John Adams, Second President of the United States,* vol. 9 (Freeport, N.Y.: Books for Libraries Press, 1969), p. 451; Charles Stuart, "Record of the Campaign of 1777," *New Records of the American Revolution* (London: L. Kashnor, 1927), p. 48; Washington to Hancock, 22 January 1777, *Washington Papers,* vol. 8, pp. 125–26; Archibald Robertson, *Archibald Robertson: His Diaries and Sketches in America, 1762–1780,* ed. Harry Miller Lydenberg (New York: Arno Press, 1971), p. 122; Washington to Heath, 3 February 1777, *Washington Papers,* vol. 8, p. 230.

7. The quotation is from Joseph Plumb Martin, *Private Yankee Doodle: Being a Narrative of Some of the Adventures, Dangers, and Sufferings of a Revolutionary Soldier,* ed. George Scheer (Boston: Little, Brown, 1962), pp. 68–69. See also Nathanael Greene to George Weedon, 24 February 1777, *Greene Papers,* vol. 2, pp. 26–27; Nathanael Greene to John Adams, 13 April 1777, *Greene Papers,* vol. 2, pp. 55–56; Washington to Robert Morris, 12 February 1777, *Washington Papers,* vol. 8, p. 320.

8. For example, New Jersey militia commander Philemon Dickinson reported to Washington that his men captured a British soldier who said that although the British army in New Jersey had plenty of pork and peas, they lacked fish, meat, and flour. Moreover, their horses were getting very thin. Philemon Dickinson to Washington, 13 February 1777, *Washington Papers,* vol. 8, p. 324. See also Israel Putnam to Washington, 18 February 1777, *Washington Papers,* vol. 8, p. 363.

9. For an explanation of American militia, see John Shy, *A People Numerous and Armed: Reflections on the Military Struggle for American Independence* (New York: Oxford University Press, 1976). See also Rodney, 14 January 1777, *Diary,* p. 44; William Young, 13–17 January 1777, "Journal of Sergeant William Young," *Pennsylvania Magazine of History and Biography* 8 (1884): 267–69; John Cadwalader to the Pennsylvania Council of Safety, 15 January 1777, "Selections from the Military Papers of General John Cadwalader," *Pennsylvania Magazine of History and Biography* 32 (1908): 159–60; Timothy Matlack to Cadwalader, 21 January 1777, "Selections," p. 163; Peale, 6–20 January 1777, "Journal," pp. 284–86; Washington to Hancock, 19 January 1777, *Washington Papers,* vol. 8, pp. 102–3; Washington to John Augustine Washington, 24 February 1777, *Washington Papers,* vol. 8, p. 439; Washington, "Returns of the American Forces in New Jersey," 15 March 1777, *Washington Papers,* vol. 8, p. 576.

10. See, for instance, Washington to Hancock, 2 September 1776, *The Papers of George Washington: Revolutionary War Series,* vol. 6, ed. Philander Chase and Frank Grizzard Jr. (Charlottesville: University Press of Virginia, 1994), pp. 199–200; Nathanael Greene to Jacob Greene [?], 28 September 1776, *The Papers of General Nathanael Greene,* vol. 1, ed. Richard K. Showman (Chapel Hill: University of North Carolina Press, 1976), p. 303.

11. New Jersey was a case in point. See Washington to William Livingston, 24 January 1777, *Washington Papers,* vol. 8, p. 147; William Livingston to Hancock, 7 September 1777, *The Papers of William Livingston,* vol. 2, *July 1777–December 1778,* ed. Carl E. Prince and Dennis P. Ryan (Trenton, N.J.: New Jersey Historical Commission, 1980), p. 65.

12. Washington to a Committee of the Continental Congress, 12 April 1777, *Washington Papers,* vol. 9, pp. 126–27.

13. Washington to Patrick Henry, 31 May 1777, *Washington Papers,* vol. 9, p. 573; Washington to Hancock, 25 July 1777, *The Papers of George Wash-*

ington: Revolutionary War Series, vol. 10, ed. Frank Grizzard Jr. (Charlottesville: University Press of Virginia, 2000), pp. 410–12.

14. Washington, "Return of the American Forces in New Jersey," 15 March 1777, *Washington Papers*, vol. 8, p. 576.

15. See, for instance, Nathanael Greene to Jacob Greene, 2 February 1777, *Greene Papers*, vol. 2, p. 18; John Adams to Abigail Adams, 28 March 1777, *Letters of Delegates*, vol. 6, p. 504.

16. Washington to John Armstrong, 5 March 1777, *Washington Papers*, vol. 8, p. 515.

17. Washington to Henry, 17 May 1777, *Washington Papers*, vol. 9, pp. 451–52.

18. John Adams to Abigail Adams, 2 February 1777, *Letters of Delegates*, vol. 6, p. 194; James Duane to Certain Members of the New York Delegation, 2 May 1777, *Letters of Delegates to Congress, 1774–1789*, vol. 7, ed. Paul Smith (Washington, D.C.: Library of Congress, 1981), p. 17; Washington to Hancock, 26 January 1777, *Washington Papers*, vol. 8, pp. 161–62; Washington to Hancock, 28 February 1777, *Washington Papers*, vol. 8, pp. 463–64; William Duer to Washington, 2 March 1777, *Washington Papers*, vol. 8, p. 479; James Varnum to Washington, 1–4 April 1777, *Washington Papers*, vol. 9, pp. 42–43; Samuel Blachley Webb to Washington, 25 January 1777, *Washington Papers*, vol. 8, p. 159; Washington to Alexander McDougall, 6 March 1777, *Washington Papers*, vol. 8, p. 524; Washington to Hancock, 21 May 1777, *Washington Papers*, vol. 9, pp. 492–93.

19. Washington, 6 July 1777, "General Orders," *Washington Papers*, vol. 10, p. 205.

20. Washington, "Circular Instructions to the Brigade Commanders," 26 May 1777, *Washington Papers*, vol. 9, pp. 532–33; Washington to Hancock, 19 January 1777, *Washington Papers*, vol. 8, pp. 102–3; John Peebles, 8 April 1777, *John Peebles' American War: The Diary of a Scottish Grenadier, 1776–1782*, ed. Ira D. Gruber (Mechanicsburg, Pa.: Stackpole Books, 1998), p. 107; Washington, "Circular to Eleven States," 31 January 1777, *Washington Papers*, vol. 8, pp. 196–97; Washington to John Sullivan, 7 June 1777, *Washington Papers*, vol. 9, p. 640; Washington to Richard Henry Lee, 1 June 1777, *Washington Papers*, vol. 9, p. 581.

21. Washington, 8 May 1777, "General Orders," *Washington Papers*, vol. 9, p. 368; Washington, 3 April 1777, "General Orders," *Washington Papers*, vol. 9, pp. 51–52; Washington, 10 April 1777, "General Orders," *Washington Papers*, vol. 9, p. 109; Washington, 12 April 1777, "General Orders," *Washington Papers*, vol. 9, p. 126; Washington, 8 May 1777, "General Orders," *Washington Papers*, vol. 9, p. 368; Washington, 31 May 1777, "General Orders," *Washington Papers*, vol. 9, pp. 567–68; John Muhlenberg, 1 June 1777, "Orderly Book of Gen. John Peter Gabriel Muhlenberg," *Pennsylvania Magazine of History and Biography* 33 (1909): 268–69; Muhlenberg, 7 July 1777,

"Orderly Book," vol. 34, p. 167; Washington to McDougall, 23 May 1777, *Washington Papers,* vol. 9, p. 506; Washington, 1 June 1777, "General Orders," *Washington Papers,* vol. 9, pp. 577–78; Washington, 6 July 1777, "General Orders," *Washington Papers,* vol. 10, p. 205; Muhlenberg, 7 July 1777, "Orderly Book," vol. 34, p. 167; Washington, 1 June 1777, "General Orders," *Washington Papers,* vol. 9, pp. 577–78; Chevalier Dubuysson, "His Memoir," *Lafayette's Letters and Papers,* vol. 1, p. 81.

22. John Adams to Nathanael Greene, 9 May 1777, *Greene Papers,* vol. 2, pp. 74–75; Nathanael Greene to ———, 20 May 1777, *Greene Papers,* vol. 2, p. 88; Alexander Hamilton to Adam Stephen, 13 March 1777, *The Papers of Alexander Hamilton,* vol. 1, ed. Harold Syrett (New York: Columbia University Press, 1961), pp. 204–5; Washington to Robert Harrison, 20 January 1777, *Washington Papers,* vol. 8, p. 115; William Shippen Jr. to Washington, 25 January 1777, *Washington Papers,* vol. 8, p. 158; Washington to Horatio Gates, 28 January 1777, *Washington Papers,* vol. 8, p. 172; Washington to Shippen, 28 January 1777, *Washington Papers,* vol. 8, p. 174; Washington to Shippen, 6 February 1777, *Washington Papers,* vol. 8, p. 264; Washington to New York Convention, 10 February 1777, *Washington Papers,* vol. 8, p. 299; Citizens of Hanover, Pennsylvania, to Washington, 12 February 1777, *Washington Papers,* vol. 8, p. 317; Continental Congress Medical Committee to Washington, 13 February 1777, *Washington Papers,* vol. 8, p. 323; Washington to Jonathan Trumbull, 3 March 1777, *Washington Papers,* vol. 8, pp. 505–6; Richard Henry Lee to Washington, 27 February 1777, *Washington Papers,* vol. 8, p. 455; Henry to Washington, 29 March 1777, *Washington Papers,* vol. 9, pp. 12–13.

23. John Adams to Abigail Adams, 22 May 1777, *Letters of Delegates,* vol. 7, p. 103.

24. Muhlenberg, 15 July 1777, "Orderly Book," vol. 34, p. 35; Washington to John Parke Custis, 22 January 1777, *Washington Papers,* vol. 8, pp. 123–24; Washington to Hancock, 5 April 1777, *Washington Papers,* vol. 9, p. 69; Washington, 28 April 1777, "General Orders," *Washington Papers,* vol. 9, p. 290; Washington, 15 June 1777, "General Orders," *Washington Papers,* vol. 10, p. 42; Council of War, 12 June 1777, *Washington Papers,* vol. 10, p. 10; Washington, 13 June 1777, "General Orders," *Washington Papers,* vol. 10, p. 20; Thomas Burke, "Notes on Debates," 12–19 February 1777, *Letters of Delegates,* vol. 6, pp. 263–64; Roger Sherman to Jonathan Trumbull, 6 March 1777, *Letters of Delegates,* vol. 6, pp. 404–5.

25. Washington to Hancock, 11 February 1777, *Washington Papers,* vol. 8, p. 305; Charles Carroll of Carrollton to Charles Carroll Sr., 13 June 1777, *Letters of Delegates,* vol. 7, p. 189; Washington to Richard Henry Lee, 17 May 1777, *Washington Papers,* vol. 9, p. 454; Nathanael Greene to Hancock, 1 July 1777, *Greene Papers,* vol. 2, p. 109; John Adams to Nathanael Greene, 7 July 1777, *Greene Papers,* vol. 2, pp. 111–13; Nathanael Greene to Hancock, 19

July 1777, *Greene Papers,* vol. 2, pp. 123–25; Sullivan to Hancock, 1 July 1777, *Letters and Papers of Major-General John Sullivan,* vol. 1, ed. Otis G. Hammond (Concord, N.H.: New Hampshire Historical Society, 1930), p. 403; Resolve of Congress, 7 July 1777, *Sullivan Papers,* vol. 1, p. 407; Eliphalet Dyer to Joseph Trumbull, 7 July 1777, *Letters of Delegates,* vol. 7, pp. 312–14.

26. Board of War to Washington, 8 July 1777, *Letters of Delegates,* vol. 7, pp. 318–20.

27. John Adams to Warren, 7 July 1777, *Letters of Delegates,* vol. 7, p. 308.

28. Washington to Continental Congress Executive Committee, 7 January 1777, *Washington Papers,* vol. 8, pp. 5–6; Washington to Schuyler, 27 January 1777, *Washington Papers,* vol. 8, p. 166; Washington to James Bowdoin, 28 February 1777, *Washington Papers,* vol. 8, p. 462; Washington to Gates, 5 February 1777, *Washington Papers,* vol. 8, p. 248; Washington to Hancock, 22 January 1777, *Washington Papers,* vol. 8, p. 126; Heath to Washington, 30 June 1777, *Washington Papers,* vol. 10, p. 153; Washington to Jonathan Trumbull, 2 July 1777, *Washington Papers,* vol. 10, p. 173; Washington to Jonathan Trumbull, 23 March 1777, *Washington Papers,* vol. 8, p. 622.

29. Washington to James Mease, 10 January 1777, *Washington Papers,* vol. 8, p. 36; Washington to Thomas Mifflin, 31 January 1777, *Washington Papers,* vol. 8, pp. 203–4; Martin, *Yankee Doodle,* pp. 76–77; Mifflin to Washington, 9 March 1777, *Washington Papers,* vol. 8, pp. 545–46; Mifflin to Washington, 27 May 1777, *Washington Papers,* vol. 9, p. 543; John Adams to John Avery Jr., 21 March 1777, *Adams's Works,* vol. 9, pp. 457–58; Washington to Mifflin, 13 March 1777, *Washington Papers,* vol. 8, p. 567; Washington, 19 February 1777, "General Orders," *Washington Papers,* vol. 8, p. 367; Washington to Hancock, 3 May 1777, *Washington Papers,* vol. 9, p. 334; Washington to Richard Peters, 30 June 1777, *Washington Papers,* vol. 10, pp. 155–56; Washington to Peters, 12 July 1777, *Washington Papers,* vol. 10, pp. 258–59; Washington to Duer, 14 January 1777, *Washington Papers,* vol. 8, pp. 63–64; New York Committee of Safety to Washington, 22 January 1777, *Washington Papers,* vol. 8, p. 130; Mease to Washington, 22 July 1777, *Washington Papers,* vol. 10, pp. 357–58; Jonathan Trumbull to Washington, 4 May 1777, *Washington Papers,* vol. 9, p. 342; Robertson, 28 April 1777, *His Diaries,* pp. 129–30.

30. Washington to Chevalier Anmours, 19 June 1777, *Washington Papers,* vol. 10, p. 70. However, Washington was initially discouraged because early reports indicated that the militia had not fought very well, but he changed his mind and became convinced that the British suffered heavily in the raid. See Washington to Hancock, 28 April 1777, *Washington Papers,* vol. 9, pp. 293–94.

31. Washington to McDougall, 2 April 1777, *Washington Papers,* vol. 9, p. 49; Washington to Hancock, 28 April 1777, *Washington Papers,* vol. 9, pp. 293–94. See Ellery to Cooke, 24 April 1777, *Letters of Delegates,* vol. 6, p.

647; John Adams to Abigail Adams, 24 May 1777, *Letters of Delegates,* vol. 7, p. 113; Sherman to Jonathan Trumbull, 26 May 1777, *Letters of Delegates,* vol. 7, p. 133.

32. Nathanael Greene to John Adams, 3 March 1777, *Greene Papers,* vol. 2, pp. 28–31; Charles-Albert de Moré de Pontgibaud, *A French Volunteer of the War of Independence,* trans. and ed. Robert B. Douglas (New York: D. Appleton, 1898), p. 65; Washington to a Committee of the Continental Congress, 12 April 1777, *Washington Papers,* vol. 9, pp. 126–28; Instructions to Major General John Sullivan, 15 May 1777, *Washington Papers,* vol. 9, pp. 436–37; Washington to Henry, 31 May 1777, *Washington Papers,* vol. 9, p. 573; Washington to Schuyler, 16 June 1777, *Washington Papers,* vol. 10, pp. 53–54; Washington to Benedict Arnold, 17 June 1777, *Washington Papers,* vol. 10, pp. 58–60.

33. Washington to Jonathan Trumbull, 11 May 1777, *Washington Papers,* vol. 9, p. 392.

34. The quotation is from Washington to Hancock, 31 May 1777, *Washington Papers,* vol. 9, p. 571. See also Washington to Schuyler, 12 March 1777, *Washington Papers,* vol. 8, p. 560. See Pennsylvania Board of War to Washington, 19 April 1777, *Washington Papers,* vol. 9, pp. 213–14; Jonathan Trumbull to Washington, 4 May 1777, *Washington Papers,* vol. 9, pp. 342–43; McDougall to Washington, 7 May 1777, *Washington Papers,* vol. 9, p. 363; Washington to Schuyler, 19 January 1777, *Washington Papers,* vol. 8, pp. 101–2; Washington to Continental Congress Executive Committee, 27 February 1777, *Washington Papers,* vol. 8, pp. 452–53; Washington to Gates, 19 February 1777, *Washington Papers,* vol. 8, p. 370; Hamilton to New York Committee of Correspondence, 5 April 1777, *Hamilton Papers,* vol. 1, p. 219; Washington to McDougall, 20 March 1777, *Washington Papers,* vol. 8, p. 603; Nathaniel Sackett to Washington, 7 April 1777, *Washington Papers,* vol. 9, p. 81; Washington to Hancock, 18 April 1777, *Washington Papers,* vol. 9, pp. 201–2; Washington to Joseph Spencer, 11 March 1777, *Washington Papers,* vol. 8, p. 554; Washington to McDougall, 10 May 1777, *Washington Papers,* vol. 9, p. 379; Washington to Joseph Trumbull, 12 May 1777, *Washington Papers,* vol. 9, p. 407; Washington to Hancock, 8 June 1777, *Washington Papers,* vol. 9, p. 645.

35. Hamilton to John Jay, 2 June 1777, *Hamilton Papers,* vol. 1, p. 262; Nathanael Greene, "Proceedings of a Council of General Officers," 12 June 1777, *Greene Papers,* vol. 2, p. 106.

36. Washington to Hancock, 8 June 1777, *Washington Papers,* vol. 9, p. 645.

37. The quotation is from Peebles, 24 February 1777, *American War,* pp. 95–98. See also James Murray to Elizabeth Smyth, *Letters from America, 1773 to 1780: Being the Letters of a Scots Officer, Sir James Murray, to His Home During the War of American Independence,* ed. Eric Robson (Manchester:

Manchester University Press, 1951), pp. 39–41; Peebles, 23 February 1777, *American War,* pp. 95–98.

38. For example, Lord Francis Rawdon wrote home, "The rebels are so broken and dispirited that I am sometimes tempted to think we shall not have another campaign." See Lord Francis Rawdon to Earl of Huntingdon, 28 November 1776, Historical Manuscripts Commission, *Report on the Manuscripts of the Late Reginald Rawdon Hastings, Esq.,* vol. 3, ed. Francis Bickley (London: His Majesty's Stationery Office, 1934), p. 188; Henry Clinton to Duke of Newcastle, 11 July 1777, *Henry Clinton Papers,* Clements Library (hereafter cited as CL), vol. 21, no. 39.

39. William Harcourt to Earl Harcourt, 18 January 1777, *The Harcourt Papers,* vol. 11 (Oxford: James Parker and Co., 1880), pp. 203–4.

40. Johann Ewald, *Diary of the American War: A Hessian Journal,* ed. and trans. by Joseph P. Tustin (New Haven, Conn.: Yale University Press, 1979), pp. 50–51; Stephan Popp, 7–12 June 1777, "Popp's Journal, 1777–1783," ed. Joseph G. Rosengarten, *Pennsylvania Magazine of History and Biography* 26 (1902): 6; Philipp Waldeck, 1–8 January 1777, *A Hessian Report on the People, the Land, the War as Noted in the Diary of Chaplain Philipp Waldeck,* ed. Bruce E. Burgoyne (Bowie, Md.: Heritage Books, 1995), pp. 29–30; Platte Grenadier Battalion Journal, 4 January 1777, *Enemy Views: The American Revolutionary War as Recorded by the Hessian Participants,* ed. Bruce E. Burgoyne (Bowie, Md.: Heritage Books, 1996), p. 140; George Inman, "George Inman's Narrative of the American Revolution," *Pennsylvania Magazine of History and Biography* 7 (1893): 240; Henry Stirke, "A British Officer's Revolutionary War Journal, 1776–1778," *Maryland Historical Magazine* 61 (1961): 167; Friedrich von Muenchhausen, 17 April 1777, *At General Howe's Side, 1776–1778,* trans. by Ernst Kipping (Monmouth Beach, N.J.: Philip Freneau Press, 1974), p. 11; Charles Stuart to Lord Bute, 29 March 1777, *A Prime Minister and His Son: From the Correspondence of the 3rd Earl of Bute and of Lt.-General the Hon. Sir Charles Stuart, K.B.,* ed. E. Stuart Wortley (New York: Dutton, 1925), pp. 101–2; Ewald, *Hessian Journal,* p. 55. For good analyses of British logistics, see R. Arthur Bowler, *Logistics and the Failure of the British Army in America, 1775–1783* (Princeton, N.J.: Princeton University Press, 1975); and David Syrett, *Shipping and the American War, 1775–1783: A Study of British Transport Organization* (London: Athlone Press, 1970); Allan Maclean to Alexander Cummings, 30 March 1777, *Prime Minister and His Son,* p. 104.

41. See, for example, Maclean to Cummings, 30 March 1777, *Prime Minister and His Son,* pp. 105–7.

42. For biographies on Howe, see Troyer Steele Anderson, *The Command of the Howe Brothers During the American Revolution* (New York: Oxford University Press, 1936); and Ira D. Gruber, *The Howe Brothers and the American Revolution* (New York: Norton, 1972).

43. Howe to Germain, 24 April 1777, *Documents of the American Revolu-*

tion, vol. 14, ed. K. G. Davies (Dublin: Irish University Press, 1976), pp. 72–73.

44. Johann Conrad Dohla, 28 February 1778, *A Hessian Diary of the American Revolution,* ed. and trans. Bruce E. Burgoyne (Norman: University of Oklahoma Press, 1990), pp. 71–72; George Osborn to Germain, 15 May 1777, *Documents,* vol. 14, pp. 82–83; John Bowater to Lord Denbigh, 22 May 1777, *The Lost War: Letters from British Officers During the American Revolution,* ed. Marion Balderston and David Syrett (New York: Horizon Press, 1975), p. 126; Rawdon to Earl of Huntingdon, 5 August 1776, *Hastings Manuscripts,* vol. 3, p. 179. The king agreed. See King George III, "Remarks on the Requisitions and Observations," *The Correspondence of King George the Third from 1760 to December 1783,* vol. 3, ed. John Fortescue (London: Macmillan, 1928), p. 445.

45. Howe to Germain, 31 December 1776, Historical Manuscripts Commission, *Report on the Manuscripts of Mrs. Stopford-Sackville, of Drayton House, Northhamptonshire,* vol. 2 (Boston: Gregg Press, 1972), p. 54; Dohla, 28 February 1778, *Hessian Diary,* pp. 70–71; Carl Leopold Baurmeister, 20 July–17 October 1777, *Revolution in America: Confidential Letters and Journals 1774–1784 of Adjutant General Major Baurmeister of the Hessian Forces,* trans. by Bernhard A. Uhlendorf (New Brunswick, N.J.: Rutgers University Press, 1957), p. 100.

46. Provincial Strength in America, 7 July 1777, *Clinton Papers,* CL, vol. 21, no. 28.

47. Johann Bardeleben, 12 January–19 April 1777, *Enemy Views,* pp. 141–47.

48. Howe to Germain, 10 August 1776, *Stopford-Sackville Manuscripts,* vol. 2, p. 38.

49. Howe to Germain, 30 November 1776, *Stopford-Sackville Manuscripts,* vol. 2, pp. 49–50.

50. Howe undoubtedly got much of his evidence of large-scale loyalist sentiment in Pennsylvania from Joseph Galloway. See Galloway, *Selected Tracts,* vol. 1, pp. 360–61. He also planned to recruit many of these loyalists into the British army and use them to garrison Pennsylvania. See Howe to Germain, 2 April 1777, *Stopford-Sackville Manuscripts,* vol. 2 (Boston: Gregg Press, 1972), pp. 63–65.

51. William Howe, *Narrative of Lieut. Gen. Sir William Howe, in a Committee of the House of Commons* (London: H. Baldwin, 1781), pp. 11, 18; Howe to Germain, 20 December 1776, *Stopford-Sackville Manuscripts,* vol. 2, pp. 52–53; Germain to Howe, 18 October 1776, *Stopford-Sackville Manuscripts,* vol. 2, pp. 42–43.

52. The quote is from Howe to Germain, 20 January 1777, *Documents,* vol. 14, p. 33. See also Henry Clinton, 6 July 1777, Minutes of a Conversation with Sir Howe, *Clinton Papers,* CL, vol. 21, no. 26; Howe to Germain, 2 April

1777, *Stopford-Sackville Manuscripts,* vol. 2, pp. 63–65. Indeed, he was merely building on what he said the previous year. See Howe to Germain, 26 April 1776, *Stopford-Sackville Manuscripts,* vol. 2, p. 30.

53. Howe to Germain, 20 January 1777, *Documents,* vol. 14, p. 33; Henry Clinton, 6 July 1777, Minutes of a Conversation with Sir William Howe, *Clinton Papers,* CL, vol. 21, no. 26; Henry Clinton, 8 July 1777, Conversation with General Howe, *Clinton Papers,* CL, vol. 21, no. 29.

54. The quotation is from Howe to Germain, 2 April 1777, *Stopford-Sackville Manuscripts,* vol. 2, pp. 64. See also, Howe to Germain, 20 January 1777, *Documents,* vol. 14, p. 33; Germain to Howe, 14 January 1777, *Stopford-Sackville Manuscripts,* vol. 2, pp. 56–57; Howe, *Howe's Narrative,* pp. 12–14; Howe to Germain, 2 April 1777, *Stopford-Sackville Manuscripts,* vol. 2, pp. 63–66.

55. Germain to Howe, 3 March 1777, *Documents,* vol. 14, pp. 46–47; Germain to Howe, 19 April 1777, *Documents,* vol. 14, pp. 69–71.

56. Germain wrote to Howe about the New York City campaign, "It is the first military operation with which no fault could be found in the planning of it, nor in the conduct of any officer to whom you entrusted a command." Germain to Howe, 18 October 1776, *Stopford-Sackville Manuscripts,* vol. 2, pp. 42–43. Later Germain wrote to Howe, "It has been the occasion of great concern to me that I have not been able to gratify your wishes to the utmost and send you greater reinforcements." See Germain to Howe, 19 April 1777, *Documents,* vol. 14, pp. 69–71.

57. Germain to Howe, 18 May 1777, *Stopford-Sackville Manuscripts,* vol. 2, pp. 66–67. See also Horace Walpole, 15 May 1777, *The Last Journals of Horace Walpole,* vol. 2 (New York: AMS Press, 1973), p. 27; John Burgoyne to Germain, 28 February 1777, *George Germain Papers,* CL, vol. 5.

58. Or so he testified later. See Howe, *Howe's Narrative,* pp. 19–20.

59. Howe, *Howe's Narrative,* p. 15; Howe to Germain, 5 June 1777, *Stopford-Sackville Manuscripts,* vol. 2, p. 68; Howe to Germain, 16 July 1777, *Stopford-Sackville Manuscripts,* vol. 2, pp. 72–73; Howe to Germain, 16 July 1777, *King George III's Correspondence,* vol. 3, p. 462; Howe, "Sir William Howe's Army, Campaign of 1777," *Stopford-Sackville Manuscripts,* vol. 2, p. 88.

60. The classic biography of Clinton is William B. Willcox, *Portrait of a General: Sir Henry Clinton in the War of Independence* (New York: Knopf, 1964). See also Walpole, 28 February 1777, *Last Journals,* vol. 2, p. 10; Henry Clinton to Lord Hugh Percy, 12 July 1777, *Clinton Papers,* CL, vol. 21, no. 40.

61. Henry Clinton, *The American Rebellion: Sir Henry Clinton's Narrative of His Campaigns, 1775–1782,* ed. William Willcox (Hamden, Conn.: Archon Books, 1971), pp. 59–67.

62. The quote is from Henry Clinton to Duke of Newcastle, 11 July 1777, *Clinton Papers,* CL, vol. 21, no. 39. See also Howe to Henry Clinton, 18 No-

vember 1777, *Clinton Papers,* CL, vol. 27, no. 9; Henry Clinton, 6 July 1777, Minutes of a Conversation with Sir William Howe, *Clinton Papers,* CL, vol. 21, no. 26; Henry Clinton, 8 July 1777, Conversation with General Howe, *Clinton Papers,* CL, vol. 21, no. 29; Henry Clinton, 13 July 1777, Conversation with Sir William Howe, *Clinton Papers,* CL, vol. 21, no. 42; Henry Clinton to Edward Harvey, 11 July 1777, *Clinton Papers,* CL, vol. 21, no. 38; Clinton, *American Rebellion,* pp. 59–67; Howe, *Howe's Narrative,* pp. 21–23.

63. Howe to Germain, 24 April 1777, *Documents,* vol. 14, pp. 72–73; Howe to Germain, 3 June 1777, *Documents,* vol. 14, pp. 102–3; Howe to Henry Clinton, 9 July 1777, *Clinton Papers,* CL, vol. 21, no. 35.

64. Howe to Germain, 5 July 1777, *Documents,* vol. 14, pp. 127–28.

65. Harrison to Sullivan, 11 June 1777, *Sullivan Papers,* vol. 1, p. 380; Washington to Putnam, 12 June 1777, *Washington Papers,* vol. 10, pp. 16–17; Nathanael Greene, 12 June 1777, "Proceedings of a Council of General Officers," *Greene Papers,* vol. 2, p. 106; Washington to Schuyler, 16 June 1777, *Washington Papers,* vol. 10, pp. 53–54; Washington to Sullivan, 12 June 1777, *Sullivan Papers,* vol. 1, p. 385; Washington to Hancock, 15 June 1777, *Washington Papers,* vol. 10, pp. 27–28.

66. For a biography of Sullivan, see Charles P. Whittemore, *A General of the Revolution: John Sullivan of New Hampshire* (New York: Columbia University Press, 1961).

67. Sullivan to Meshech Weare, 12 June 1777, *Sullivan Papers,* vol. 1, pp. 387–88; Washington to Sullivan, 14 June 1777, *Sullivan Papers,* vol. 1, p. 389.

68. Washington to Arnold, 17 June 1777, *Washington Papers,* vol. 10, p. 59.

69. Washington to Sullivan, 17 June 1777, *Sullivan Papers,* vol. 1, p. 392; Tench Tilghman to Sullivan, 18 June 1777, *Sullivan Papers,* vol. 1, p. 393; Washington to Arnold, 17 June 1777, *Washington Papers,* vol. 10, pp. 58–60; Washington to Arnold, 17 June 1777, *Washington Papers,* vol. 10, p. 59; Washington to Sullivan, 17 June 1777, *Sullivan Papers,* vol. 1, p. 292; Arnold to Washington, 16 June 1777, *Washington Papers,* vol. 10, pp. 48–49; Philemon Dickinson to Washington, 18 June 1777, *Washington Papers,* vol. 10, p. 66; Washington to Joseph Reed, 23 June 1777, *Washington Papers,* vol. 10, pp. 113–15; Francis Lightfoot Lee to Richard Henry Lee, 17 June 1777, *Letters of Delegates,* vol. 7, pp. 202–3.

70. Howe, *Howe's Narrative,* pp. 15–16; Howe to Germain, 5 July 1777, *Documents,* vol. 14, pp. 127–28.

71. Peebles, 22 June 1777, *American War,* p. 117; John Andre, *Major Andre's Journal: Operations of the British Army Under Lieutenant Generals Sir William Howe and Sir Henry Clinton, June 1777 to November 1778* (Tarrytown, N.Y.: William Abbatt, 1930), pp. 25–30; John Montresor, 10–24 June 1777, "Extracts from the Journals and Note-Books of Capt. John Montresor," *Collections of the New-York Historical Society,* 1881, pp. 421–24; Muenchhausen, 18–22 June 1777, *At Howe's Side,* pp. 18–19.

72. Cresswell, 20–23 June 1777, *Journal,* pp. 238–43; Ewald, 8–25 June 1777, *Hessian Journal,* pp. 63–68; JR, 12–24 June 1777, *Enemy Views,* p. 151; Platte Grenadier Battalion Journal, 22 June 1777, *Enemy Views,* p. 157; Howe to Germain, 5 July 1777, *Documents,* vol. 14, pp. 127–28.

73. For a biography of Greene, see Elswyth Thane, *The Fighting Quaker: Nathanael Greene* (New York: Hawthorn Books, 1972).

74. Washington to John Glover and McDougall, 20 June 1777, *Washington Papers,* vol. 10, pp. 83–84; Washington to Putnam, 20 June 1777, *Washington Papers,* vol. 10, p. 88; Washington to Sullivan, 21 June 1777, *Sullivan Papers,* vol. 1, p. 395; Washington to Hancock, 22 June 1777, *Washington Papers,* vol. 10, pp. 104–5; Washington to Heath, 23 June 1777, *Washington Papers,* vol. 10, p. 110; Washington to Reed, 23 June 1777, *Washington Papers,* vol. 10, pp. 113–15; Washington to Hancock, 25 June 1777, *Washington Papers,* vol. 10, pp. 123–25; Washington to Sullivan, 23 June 1777, *Washington Papers,* vol. 10, p. 116.

75. Muenchhausen, 24–26 June 1777, *At Howe's Side,* pp. 19–20; Howe to Germain, 5 July 1777, *Documents,* vol. 14, pp. 128–29.

76. Andre, 25–30 June 1777, *Andre's Journal,* pp. 31–33; Montresor, 26–30 June 1777, "Extracts," pp. 424–26.

77. Andre, 25–30 June 1777, *Andre's Journal,* pp. 31–33; Muenchhausen, 24–26 June 1777, *At Howe's Side,* pp. 19–20; Ewald, 26 June 1777, *Hessian Journal,* pp. 69–70.

78. Howe to Germain, 7 July 1777, *Stopford-Sackville Manuscripts,* vol. 2, pp. 70–72.

79. Baurmeister, 31 August 1777, *Baurmeister's Letters and Journals,* p. 93.

80. Bowalter to Lord Denbigh, 23 July 1777, *Lost War,* p. 138; Muenchhausen, 13 July 1777, *At Howe's Side,* p. 21; Hugh Gaine, 23–25 July 1777, *Journals of Hugh Gaine, Printer* (New York: Arno Press, 1970), p. 41; Howe, *Howe's Narrative,* p. 21; Richard Howe to Philip Stephens, 28 August 1777, *Naval Documents of the American Revolution,* vol. 9, ed. William James Morgan (Washington, D.C.: Naval Historical Center, Department of the Navy, 1982), p. 835.

81. For a sampling, see Nathanael Greene to McDougall, 29 July 1777, *Greene Papers,* vol. 2, pp. 126–27; Sullivan to Washington, 12 August 1777, *Sullivan Papers,* vol. 1, pp. 428–29; Putnam to Washington, 31 July 1777, *Washington Papers,* vol. 10, pp. 469–70; Reed to Washington, 7 August 1777, *Defences of Philadelphia in 1777,* ed. Worthington Chauncey Ford (New York: Da Capo Press, 1971), pp. 20–24; Washington to Hancock, 21 August 1777, *The Writings of George Washington,* vol. 9, ed. John Fitzpatrick (Washington, D.C.: Government Printing Office, 1933), pp. 107–10.

82. Washington to Putnam, 22 July 1777, *Washington Papers,* vol. 10, p. 361.

83. Washington to George Clinton, 1 July 1777, *Washington Papers,* vol.

10, p. 163; Washington to Hancock, 2 July 1777, *Washington Papers,* vol. 10, pp. 168–70; Washington to Jonathan Trumbull, 4 July 1777, *Washington Papers,* vol. 10, pp. 174–75; David Forman to Washington, 6 July 1777, *Washington Papers,* vol. 10, pp. 207–9; Washington to Hancock, 7 July 1777, *Washington Papers,* vol. 10, pp. 215–16; Washington to Hancock, 10 July 1777, *Washington Papers,* vol. 10, pp. 240–41.

84. Washington to Benjamin Lincoln, 24 July 1777, *Washington Papers,* vol. 10, p. 385; John Fellows to Washington, 24 July 1777, *Washington Papers,* vol. 10, pp. 384–85; Howe to Burgoyne, 20 July 1777, *Clinton Papers,* CL, vol. 22, no. 4; Washington to Putnam, 25 July 1777, *Washington Papers,* vol. 10, pp. 414–15; Washington to Mifflin, 28 July 1777, *Washington Papers,* vol. 10, pp. 447–48; Washington to Hancock, 31 July 1777, *Washington Papers,* vol. 10, p. 468; Washington to Gates, 30 July 1777, *Washington Papers,* vol. 10, p. 459.

85. Washington to Putnam, 1 August 1777, *Washington Papers,* vol. 10, pp. 481–82.

86. Washington to John Langdon, 4 August 1777, *Washington Papers,* vol. 10, p. 501.

87. Washington to Hancock, 21 August 1777, *Washington Writings,* vol. 9, pp. 107–11; Washington to John Page, 21 August 1777, *Washington Writings,* vol. 9, pp. 112–13; Washington to William Livingston, 21 August 1777, *Washington Writings,* vol. 9, p. 114; Washington to Putnam, 22 August 1777, *Washington Writings,* vol. 9, p. 115.

CHAPTER 3. BARBAROUS BUSINESS IN A BARBAROUS COUNTRY

1. For British troop strength, see Army Returns, 13 October 1777, *George Germain Papers,* CL, vol. 5.

2. James Murray to Elizabeth Smyth, 1 September 1777, *Letters from America, 1773 to 1780: Being the Letters of a Scots Officer, Sir James Murray, to His Home During the War of American Independence,* ed. Eric Robson (Manchester: Manchester University Press, 1951), p. 47.

3. For a collection of perspectives, see Francis Downman, *The Services of Lieut. Colonel Francis Downman, R.A. in France, North America, and the West Indies, Between the Years 1758 and 1784,* ed. F. A. Whinyates (Woolwich: Royal Artillery Institution, 1898), pp. 27–29; Carl Leopold Baurmeister, 31 August–17 October 1777, *Revolution in America: Confidential Letters and Journals 1774–1784 of Adjutant General Major Baurmeister of the Hessian Forces,* trans. by Bernhard A. Uhlendorf (New Brunswick, N.J.: Rutgers University Press, 1957), pp. 93–99; Thomas Sullivan, 3–16 August 1777, "Before and After the Battle of Brandywine: Extracts from the Journal of Sergeant Thomas Sullivan of H.M. Forty-Ninth Regiment of Foot," *Pennsylvania Mag-*

azine of History and Biography 31 (1907): 407–8; Richard Howe to Philip Stephens, 28 August 1777, *Naval Documents of the American Revolution,* vol. 9, ed. William James Morgan (Washington, D.C.: Naval Historical Center, Department of the Navy, 1992), pp. 835–37; Friedrich von Muenchhausen, 4–17 August 1777, *At General Howe's Side, 1776–1778,* trans. Ernst Kipping (Monmouth Beach, N.J.: Philip Freneau Press, 1974), pp. 23–24; John Montresor, 23 July–20 August 1777, "Extracts from the Journals and Note-Books of Capt. John Montresor," *Collections of the New-York Historical Society,* 1881, pp. 429–42; William Paca to Samuel Chase, 26 August 1777, *Naval Documents,* vol. 9, p. 821; Carl Friedrich Rueffer, 26 July–22 August 1777, *Enemy Views: The American Revolutionary War as Recorded by the Hessian Participants,* ed. Bruce E. Burgoyne (Bowie, Md.: Heritage Books, 1996), pp. 167–69.

4. Heinrich Carl Philipp von Feilitzsch, 6 August 1777, *Enemy Views,* pp. 164–65.

5. See, for example, Baurmeister, 20 July–17 October 1777, *Baurmeister's Letters and Journals,* pp. 97–99; Anonymous, "A Contemporary British Account of General Sir William Howe's Military Operations in 1777," *Proceedings of the American Antiquarian Society,* April 1930, p. 75.

6. Andrew Hamond, "Narrative of Captain Andrew Snape Hamond," *Naval Documents,* vol. 9, p. 363; William Howe, *Narrative of Lieut. Gen. Sir William Howe, in a Committee of the House of Commons* (London: H. Baldwin, 1781), pp. 71–75, 85–87.

7. Howe, *Howe's Narrative,* pp. 23–25. See also Joseph Galloway, *Selected Tracts,* vol. 1 (New York: Da Capo Press, 1974), pp. 377–79; Richard Howe to Philip Stephens, 20 February 1777, *Documents of the American Revolution,* vol. 14, ed. K. G. Davies (Dublin: Irish University Press, 1976), p. 39.

8. Hamond, "Narrative of Captain Andrew Snape Hamond," *Naval Documents,* vol. 9, p. 363.

9. Archibald Robertson, 23–27 August 1777, *Archibald Robertson: His Diaries and Sketches in America, 1762–1780,* ed. Harry Miller Lydenberg (New York: Arno Press, 1971), pp. 142–43; John Peebles, 23–25 August 1777, *John Peebles' American War: The Diary of a Scottish Grenadier, 1776–1782,* ed. Ira D. Gruber (Mechanicsburg, Pa.: Stackpole Books, 1998), p. 127; John Andre, 25 August 1777, *Major Andre's Journal: Operations of the British Army Under Lieutenant Generals Sir William Howe and Sir Henry Clinton, June 1777 to November 1778* (Tarrytown, N.Y.: William Abbatt, 1930), pp. 36–37; Baurmeister, 31 August 1777, *Baurmeister's Letters and Journals,* pp. 94–95; Muenchhausen, 22–27 August 1777, *At Howe's Side,* pp. 24–26; Montresor, 25–31 August 1777, "Extracts," pp. 442–45; Johann Ewald, 22–26 August 1777, *Diary of the American War: A Hessian Journal,* trans. and ed. Joseph P. Tustin (New Haven, Conn.: Yale University Press, 1979), pp. 73–75; Hamond, 25 August 1777, "Journal of HMS *Roebuck,*" *Naval Documents,* vol. 9, p.

810; Anthony Hunt, 25 August 1777, "Journal of HMS *Sphynx*," *Naval Documents*, vol. 9, p. 810; John Henry, 25 August 1777, "Journal of HMS *Vigilant*," *Naval Documents*, vol. 9, pp. 810–11; Richard Howe to Philip Stephens, 28 August 1777, *Naval Documents*, vol. 9, p. 835; Hamond, 21–26 August 1777, "Narrative of Captain Andrew Snape Hamond," *Naval Documents*, vol. 9, p. 857.

10. Robertson, 28–30 August 1777, *His Diaries*, p. 133; Loftus Cliffe to Jack Cliffe, 24 October 1777, *Loftus Cliffe Papers*, CL; Peebles, 28 August 1777, *American War*, p. 128; Downman, *Services*, pp. 30–31; Andre, 26–28 August 1777, *Andre's Journal*, pp. 37–38; Baurmeister, 20 July–17 October 1777, *Baurmeister's Letters and Journals*, p. 100; Ambrose Serle, 26 August 1777, *The American Journal of Ambrose Serle, Secretary to Lord Howe, 1776–78*, ed. Edward H. Tatum (San Marino, Calif.: The Huntington Library, 1940), p. 246; Muenchhausen, 27 August–1 September 1777, *At Howe's Side*, pp. 24–27; Anonymous, "Contemporary British Account," pp. 75–76; Montresor, 25–31 August 1777, "Extracts," pp. 442–45; Ewald, 28–31 August 1777, *Hessian Journal*, pp. 75–77; Henry Stirke, 25–28 August 1777, "A British Officer's Revolutionary War Journal, 1776–1778," *Maryland Historical Magazine* 61 (1961): 167–68; Rueffer, 26 August 1777, *Enemy Views*, p. 169; Charles Stuart to Lord Bute, September 1777, *New Records of the American Revolution* (London: L. Kashnor, 1927), pp. 45–46.

11. Murray to Smyth, 1 September 1777, *Murray's Letters*, pp. 47–48.

12. Peebles, 1 September 1777, *American War*, p. 129; Downman, *Services*, pp. 30–31; Andre, 26 August–2 September 1777, *Andre's Journal*, pp. 37–42; Baurmeister, 20 July–17 October 1777, *Baurmeister's Letters and Journals*, pp. 94–99; Charles Stuart to Lord Bute, 31 August 1777, *A Prime Minister and His Son: From the Correspondence of the 3rd Earl of Bute and of Lt.-General the Hon. Sir Charles Stuart, K.B.*, ed. E. Stuart Wortley (New York: Dutton, 1925), pp. 115–16; Serle, 26–28 August 1777, *American Journal*, p. 246; Muenchhausen, 22 August–1 September 1777, *At Howe's Side*, pp. 24–27; Montresor, 25–31 August 1777, "Extracts," pp. 442–45; Ewald, 28–31 August 1777, *Hessian Journal*, pp. 75–77.

13. Howe, *Howe's Narrative*, p. 25; Howe to Lord George Germain, 30 August 1777, Historical Manuscripts Commission, *Report on the Manuscripts of Mrs. Stopford-Sackville, Of Drayton House, Northhamptionshire*, vol. 2 (Boston: Gregg Press, 1972), pp. 74–75.

14. Peebles, 3 September 1777, *American War*, p. 130; Downman, *Services*, p. 32; Andre, 3 September 1777, *Andre's Journal*, pp. 42–43; Baurmeister, 20 July–17 October 1777, *Baurmeister's Letters and Journals*, p. 102; Muenchhausen, 3 September 1777, *At Howe's Side*, p. 28; Montresor, 3 September 1777, "Extracts," pp. 445–46; Ewald, 3 September 1777, *Hessian Journal*, pp. 77–78; Stirke, 3 September 1777, "British Officer's Journal," p. 168; Hesse-Cassel Jaeger Corps Journal, 3 September 1777, *Enemy Views*, p. 170.

15. Andrew Snape Hamond, "Autobiography of Sir Andrew Snape Hamond," *Naval Documents,* vol. 9, p. 984.

16. Robertson, 7–10 September 1777, *His Diaries,* pp. 145–46; Peebles, 8 September 1777, *American War,* pp. 131–32; Downman, *Services,* p. 32; Andre, 6 September 1777, *Andre's Journal,* pp. 43–44; Baurmeister, 20 July–17 October 1777, *Baurmeister's Letters and Journals,* p. 103; Muenchhausen, 4–9 September 1777, *At Howe's Side,* pp. 28–30; Anonymous, 4–10 September 1777, "Contemporary British Account," pp. 77–78; Montresor, 4–10 September 1777, "Extracts," pp. 447–49; Ewald, 4–10 September 1777, *Hessian Journal,* pp. 78–81; Henry Stirke, 5–9 September 1777, "British Officer's Journal," 168–69; Howe to Germain, 10 October 1777, *Howe's Narrative,* p. 97; Rueffer, 8–9 September 1777, *Enemy Views,* p. 172.

17. John Adams to Abigail Adams, 24 August 1777, *Letters of Delegates to Congress, 1774–1789,* vol. 7, ed. Paul Smith (Washington, D.C.: Library of Congress, 1981), pp. 538–39.

18. Ibid.; James McMichael, 24 August 1777, "Diary of Lieutenant James McMichael, of the Pennsylvania Line, 1776–1778," *Pennsylvania Magazine of History and Biography* 16 (1892): 147; Marquis de Lafayette, "Memoir of 1776," *Lafayette in the Age of the American Revolution: Selected Letters and Papers, 1776–1790,* vol. 1, ed. Stanley J. Idzerda (Ithaca, N.Y.: Cornell University Press, 1979), pp. 91–92; Alexander Graydon, *Memoirs of His Own Time with Reminiscences of the Men and Events of the Revolution,* ed. John Stockton Littell (Philadelphia: Lindsay and Blakiston, 1846), pp. 290–91; Robert Kirkwood, 19 August 1777, *The Journal and Order Book of Captain Robert Kirkwood of the Delaware Regiment of the Continental Line,* ed. Joseph Brown Turner (Port Washington, N.Y.: Kennikat Press, 1970), p. 150; George Washington to Thomas Mifflin, 28 July 1777, *The Papers of George Washington: Revolutionary War Series,* vol. 10, ed. Frank Grizzard Jr. (Charlottesville: University Press of Virginia, 2000), pp. 447–48; Washington, 23 August 1777, "General Orders," *The Writings of George Washington,* vol. 9, ed. John Fitzpatrick (Washington, D.C.: Government Printing Office, 1933), pp. 124–27; John Adams to Abigail Adams, 23 August 1777, *Letters of Delegates,* vol. 7, p. 533; Richard Henry Lee to Thomas Jefferson, 25 August 1777, *Letters of Delegates,* vol. 7, p. 551.

19. Nathanael Greene to Jacob Greene, 13 July 1777, *The Papers of General Nathanael Greene,* vol. 2, ed. Richard K. Showman (Chapel Hill: University of North Carolina Press, 1980), p. 119; Alexander Hamilton to John Jay, 13 July 1777, *The Papers of Alexander Hamilton,* vol. 1, ed. Harold Syrett (New York: Columbia University Press, 1961), p. 285; Philip Schuyler to Washington, 14 July 1777, *Washington Papers,* vol. 10, pp. 279–80; Schuyler to Washington, 26 July 1777, *Washington Papers,* vol. 10, p. 430; Schuyler to Washington, 28 July 1777, *Washington Papers,* vol. 10, p. 450; Schuyler to Washington, 4 August 1777, *Washington Papers,* vol. 10, p. 506.

20. Washington to Schuyler, 15 July 1777, *Washington Papers,* vol. 10, p. 290.

21. Washington to Schuyler, 22 July 1777, *Washington Papers,* vol. 10, pp. 363–65; Washington to Schuyler, 24 July 1777, *Washington Papers,* vol. 10, pp. 396–97; Washington to New York Council of Safety, 4 August 1777, *Washington Papers,* vol. 10, pp. 503–4.

22. See Washington to Schuyler, 10 July 1777, *Washington Papers,* vol. 10, p. 244; Washington to John Hancock, 12 July 1777, *Washington Papers,* vol. 10, pp. 252–54; Washington to Richard Peters, 12 July 1777, *Washington Papers,* vol. 10, pp. 258–59; Washington to Schuyler, 12 July 1777, *Washington Papers,* vol. 10, pp. 261–62; Washington to Hancock, 18 July 1777, *Washington Papers,* vol. 10, p. 320; Washington to Benjamin Lincoln, 24 July 1777, *Washington Papers,* vol. 10, p. 385; Washington to Schuyler, 24 July 1777, *Washington Papers,* vol. 10, pp. 396–97; Washington to Hancock, 3 August 1777, *Washington Papers,* vol. 10, pp. 492–93; Washington to New York Council of Safety, 4 August 1777, *Washington Papers,* vol. 10, pp. 503–4; Washington to Hancock, 17 August 1777, *Washington Papers,* vol. 10, p. 649; Hancock to Washington, *Letters of Delegates,* vol. 7, p. 492.

23. Charles Conaway, *The Revolution Remembered: Eyewitness Accounts of the War for Independence,* ed. John C. Dann (Chicago: University of Chicago Press, 1980), p. 171; Nathanael Greene to Catharine Greene, 10 September 1777, *Greene Papers,* vol. 2, pp. 154–56; Washington to John Armstrong, 25 August 1777, *Washington Writings,* vol. 9, p. 130; Washington to John Thompson, 28 August 1777, *Washington Writings,* vol. 9, pp. 140–42; Washington to John Cadwalader, 28 August 1777, *Washington Writings,* vol. 9, pp. 142–43; Washington to William Smallwood, 30 August 1777, *Washington Writings,* vol. 9, pp. 147–48; Washington to Thomas Johnson, 3 September 1777, *Washington Writings,* vol. 9, pp. 174–75; Washington to Caesar Rodney, 10 September 1777, *Washington Writings,* vol. 9, pp. 202–3; William Livingston to Hancock, 5 September 1777, *The Papers of William Livingston,* vol. 2, *July 1777–December 1778,* ed. Carl E. Prince and Dennis P. Ryan (Trenton, N.J.: New Jersey Historical Commission, 1980), p. 62; William Livingston to Hancock, 7 September 1777, *Livingston Papers,* vol. 2, p. 65; Chase to Johnson, 23 August 1777, *Letters of Delegates,* vol. 7, p. 534; John Adams to Abigail Adams, 26 August 1777, *Letters of Delegates,* vol. 7, p. 554; Thomas McKean to Washington, 8 October 1777, *The Papers of George Washington: Revolutionary War Series,* vol. 11, ed. Philander Chase and Edward Lengel (Charlottesville: University Press of Virginia, 2001), pp. 442–45.

24. Washington to Cadwalader, 28 August 1777, *Washington Writings,* vol. 9, pp. 142–43; Washington to William Maxwell, 1 September 1777, *Washington Writings,* vol. 9, pp. 153–56; Washington to William Livingston, 1 September 1777, *Washington Writings,* vol. 9, pp. 159–60; Washington to Maxwell, 2 September 1777, *Washington Writings,* vol. 9, p. 162; Washington

to Hancock, 5 September 1777, *Washington Writings,* vol. 9, pp. 186–87; Washington, 7 September 1777, "General Orders," *Washington Writings,* vol. 9, p. 192; Washington to William Heath, 7 September 1777, *Washington Writings,* vol. 9, pp. 194–95; Washington to Jonathan Trumbull, 8 September 1777, *Washington Writings,* vol. 9, pp. 196–97.

25. Nathanael Greene to Jacob Greene, 31 August 1777, *Greene Papers,* vol. 2, p. 149; Hamilton to Gouverneur Morris, 1 September 1777, *Hamilton Papers,* vol. 1, p. 321; Washington, 5 September 1777, "General Orders," *Washington Writings,* vol. 9, pp. 180–82.

26. Washington to Maxwell, 3 September 1777, *Washington Writings,* vol. 9, pp. 171–72; Washington to Hancock, 3 September 1777, *Washington Writings,* vol. 9, pp. 172–73; George Ewing, *The Military Journal of George Ewing (1754–1824): A Soldier of Valley Forge* (Yonkers, N.Y.: privately printed by Thomas Ewing, 1928), p. 21; Joseph Clark, "Diary of Joseph Clark," *Proceedings of the New Jersey Historical Society* 7 (1853–55): 97–98; Jacob Nagle, *The Nagle Journal: A Diary of the Life of Jacob Nagle, Sailor, from the Year 1775 to 1841,* ed. John C. Dann (New York: Weidenfeld and Nicolson, 1988), pp. 6–7.

27. Nathanael Greene to Catharine Greene, 10 September 1777, *Greene Papers,* vol. 2, pp. 154–56; McMichael, 8 September 1777, "McMichael's Diary," p. 149; Washington to Hancock, 9 September 1777, *Washington Writings,* vol. 9, pp. 197–98; Washington to Israel Putnam, 10 September 1777, *Washington Writings,* vol. 9, pp. 201–2.

28. Downman, *Services,* p. 33; Baurmeister, 20 July–17 October 1777, *Baurmeister's Letters and Journals,* pp. 107–9; Thomas Sullivan, 11 September 1777, "Before and After Brandywine," pp. 413–14; Ewald, 11 September 1777, *Hessian Journal,* pp. 81–82; George Weedon to John Page, 11 September 1777, George Weedon–John Page Correspondence, Chicago Historical Society (hereafter cited as CHS); Patrick Ferguson, *The Fate of a Nation: The American Revolution Through Contemporary Eyes,* ed. William P. Cumming and Hugh Rankin (London: Phaidon Press, 1975), pp. 176–77; Wilhelm Knyphausen to Germain, 21 October 1777, *Documents,* vol. 14, pp. 238–39; Rueffer, 11 September 1777, *Enemy Views,* p. 176.

29. Downman, *Services,* p. 33; Andre, 11 September 1777, *Andre's Journal,* p. 45; Baurmeister, 20 July–17 October 1777, *Baurmeister's Letters and Journals,* pp. 107–9; Joseph Townsend, *The Battle of Brandywine: Joseph Townsend* (New York: Arno Press, 1969), p. 19; Thomas Sullivan, 11 September 1777, "Before and After Brandywine," pp. 413–14; Ewald, 11 September 1777, *Hessian Journal,* pp. 81–82; Weedon to Page, 11 September 1777, Weedon-Page Correspondence, CHS; Knyphausen to Germain, 21 October 1777, *Documents,* vol. 14, pp. 238–39.

30. Robertson, 11 September 1777, *His Diaries,* pp. 146–47; Peebles, 11 September 1777, *American War,* pp. 132–34; Baurmeister, 20 July–17 October

1777, *Baurmeister's Letters and Journals,* p. 110; Muenchhausen, 11 September 1777, *At Howe's Side,* pp. 31–32; Montresor, 11 September 1777, "Extracts," pp. 449–51; Ewald, 11 September 1777, *Hessian Journal,* pp. 83–84; Howe, 10 October 1777, "Howe's Report on the Battle of Brandywine" *The First American Civil War: First Period, 1775–1778,* vol. 2, ed. Henry Belcher (London: Macmillan, 1911), pp. 249–50; Hesse-Cassel Jaeger Corps Journal, 11 September 1777, *Enemy Views,* pp. 173–74.

    31. Townsend, *Brandywine,* pp. 21–25.

    32. Ewald, 11 September 1777, *Hessian Journal,* pp. 83–86.

    33. Townsend, *Brandywine,* pp. 21–25; Robertson, 11 September 1777, *His Diaries,* pp. 146–47; Peebles, 11 September 1777, *American War,* pp. 132–34; Andre, 11 September 1777, *Andre's Journal,* pp. 46–47; Baurmeister, 31 August–17 October 1777, *Baurmeister's Letters and Journals,* pp. 110–12; Muenchhausen, 11 September 1777, *At Howe's Side,* pp. 31–32; Montresor, 11 September 1777, "Extracts," pp. 449–51; Howe, 10 October 1777, "Howe's Report on the Battle of Brandywine," *First American Civil War,* vol. 2, pp. 249–50; Hesse-Cassel Jaeger Corps Journal, 11 September 1777, *Enemy Views,* pp. 173–74; Stuart to Lord Bute, September 1777, *New Records,* pp. 46–47; Stuart, "Record of the Campaign of 1777," *New Records,* p. 49.

    34. John Sullivan to Hancock, 25 October 1777, *Letters and Papers of Major-General John Sullivan,* vol. 1, ed. Otis G. Hammond (Concord, N.H.: New Hampshire Historical Society, 1930), p. 549.

    35. Charles Cotesworth Pinckney, 14 November 1820, "The Battles of Brandywine and Germantown," *The Historical Magazine* 10 (1866): 202–3; Weedon to Page, 11 September 1777, Weedon-Page Correspondence, CHS; Sullivan to Washington, 11 September 1777, *Sullivan Papers,* vol. 1, p. 451; Sullivan to Hancock, 6 October 1777, *Sullivan Papers,* vol. 1, pp. 475–77; Washington to Sullivan, 24 October 1777, *Sullivan Papers,* vol. 1, pp. 541–42; Washington to Theodorick Bland, 11 September 1777, *Washington Writings,* vol. 9, p. 205; Washington to Hancock, 11 September 1777, *Washington Writings,* vol. 9, p. 207; Ferguson, 11 September 1777, *Fate of a Nation,* pp. 174–76.

    36. Sullivan to Washington, 11 September 1777, *Sullivan Papers,* vol. 1, p. 453.

    37. Sullivan to Hancock, 6 October 1777, *Sullivan Papers,* vol. 1, pp. 475–77; Sullivan to Hancock, 27 September 1777, *Sullivan Papers,* vol. 1, pp. 462–65; Sullivan, 27 September 1777, *Sullivan Papers,* vol. 1, pp. 472–74; Thomas Conway's Statement, 20 September 1777, *Sullivan Papers,* vol. 1, pp. 555–56.

    38. Smallwood to Washington, 15 August 1777, *Washington Papers,* vol. 10, pp. 626–27; Andre, 11 September 1777, *Andre's Journal,* pp. 46–47; Baurmeister, 20 July–17 October 1777, *Baurmeister's Letters and Journals,* pp. 110–12; Lafayette, "Memoir of 1776," *Lafayette's Letters and Papers,* vol. 1, pp. 94–95; Montresor, 11 September 1777, "Extracts," pp. 449–51; Howe, 10

October 1777, "Howe's Report on the Battle of Brandywine," *First American Civil War*, vol. 2, pp. 249–50; Samuel Smith, "The Papers of General Samuel Smith," *Historical Magazine* 7 (1870): 85–86; Sullivan to Hancock, 27 September 1777, *Sullivan Papers*, vol. 1, pp. 464–65.

39. For a biography on Stephen, see Harry M. Ward, *Major General Adam Stephen and the Cause of American Liberty* (Charlottesville: University Press of Virginia, 1989).

40. Anonymous, 2 October 1777, "The Actions at Brandywine and Paoli, Described by a British Officer," *Pennsylvania Magazine of History and Biography* 29 (1905): 368.

41. Andre, 11 September 1777, *Andre's Journal*, pp. 46–47; Baurmeister, 20 July–17 October 1777, *Baurmeister's Letters and Journals*, pp. 110–12; Muenchhausen, 11 September 1777, *At Howe's Side*, pp. 31–32; Montresor, 11 September 1777, "Extracts," pp. 449–51; Stirke, 11 September 1777, "British Officer's Journal," p. 170; Hesse-Cassel Jaeger Corps Journal, 11 September 1777, *Enemy Views*, pp. 173–74; Stuart, "Record of the Campaign of 1777," *New Records*, p. 49; Enoch Anderson, *Personal Recollections of Captain Enoch Anderson* (New York: Arno Press, 1971), pp. 36–37; Weedon to Page, 11 September 1777, Weedon-Page Correspondence, CHS; Clark, "Clark's Diary," p. 99; Henry Lee, *Memoirs of the War in the Southern Department of the United States*, vol. 1 (Philadelphia: Bradford and Inskeep, 1812), p. 16; "Report of a Court of Enquiry," 1 November 1777, *Greene Papers*, vol. 2, pp. 188–89.

42. For a biography of Stirling, see Paul David Nelson, *William Alexander, Lord Stirling* (University: University of Alabama Press, 1987).

43. Peebles, 11 September 1777, *American War*, pp. 132–34; Baurmeister, 20 July–17 October 1777, *Baurmeister's Letters and Journals*, pp. 110–12; Lafayette, "Memoir of 1776," *Lafayette's Letters and Papers*, vol. 1, pp. 94–95; Muenchhausen, 11 September 1777, *At Howe's Side*, pp. 31–32; Heinrich Carl Philipp von Feilitzsch, 11 September 1777, *Enemy Views*, pp. 172–73; Ebenezer Elmer, 11 September 1777, "Journal of Ebenezer Elmer," *Pennsylvania Magazine of History and Biography* 35 (1911): 104–5; Sullivan to Hancock, 27 September 1777, *Sullivan Papers*, vol. 1, pp. 464–65; Thomas Conway's Statement, 20 September 1777, *Sullivan Papers*, vol. 1, pp. 555–56; Charles Pinckney's Statement, 24 September 1777, *Sullivan Papers*, vol. 1, p. 557; François Louis Teissèdre de Fleury's Statement, 23 February 1778, *Letters and Papers of Major-General John Sullivan*, vol. 2, ed. Otis G. Hammond (Concord, N.H.: New Hampshire Historical Society, 1931), p. 25.

44. Observers disagree on whether Stephen's or Stirling's division retreated first. See, for example, Elmer, 11 September 1777, "Elmer's Journal," pp. 104–5; Weedon to Page, 11 September 1777, Weedon-Page Correspondence, CHS.

45. Baurmeister, 20 July–17 October 1777, *Baurmeister's Letters and Journals*, pp. 110–12; Lafayette, "Memoir of 1776," *Lafayette's Letters and Pa-*

pers, vol. 1, pp. 94–95; Joseph Bloomfield, 11 September 1777, *Citizen Soldier: The Revolutionary War Journal of Joseph Bloomfield,* ed. Mark E. Lender and James Kirby Martin (Newark, N.J.: New Jersey Historical Society, 1982), pp. 127–28; Ewald, 11 September 1777, *Hessian Journal,* p. 86; Howe, 10 October 1777, "Howe's Report on the Battle of Brandywine," *First American Civil War,* vol. 2, pp. 249–50; Stirke, 11 September 1777, "British Officer's Journal," p. 170; Andre, 11 September 1777, *Andre's Journal,* pp. 46–47; Anderson, *Recollections,* pp. 36–37; Weedon to Page, 11 September 1777, Weedon-Page Correspondence, CHS; Clark, "Clark's Diary," p. 99; Henry Lee, *Memoirs of the War,* vol. 1, p. 16.

46. Pinckney, 14 November 1820, "Battles," p. 203; Loftus Cliffe to Jack Cliffe, 24 October 1777, *Cliffe Papers,* CL; Nathanael Greene to Henry Merchant, 25 July 1778, *Greene Papers,* vol. 2, p. 471; Andre, 11 September 1777, *Andre's Journal,* pp. 46–47; Montresor, 11 September 1777, "Extracts," pp. 449–51; Ewald, 11 September 1777, *Hessian Journal,* pp. 86–87; Howe, 10 October 1777, "Howe's Report on the Battle of Brandywine," *First American Civil War,* vol. 2, pp. 249–50; Weedon to Page, 11 September 1777, Weedon-Page Correspondence, CHS; Elmer, 11 September 1777, "Elmer's Journal," pp. 104–5; Sullivan, 27 September 1777, *Sullivan Papers,* vol. 1, pp. 472–74; Thomas Burke to Richard Caswell, 17 September 1777, *Letters of Delegates,* vol. 7, p. 680.

47. Knyphausen to Germain, 21 October 1777, *Documents,* vol. 14, pp. 240–41; Johann Carl Buettner, *Narrative of Johann Carl Buettner in the American Revolution* (New York: Benjamin Blom, 1971), pp. 49–50; Baurmeister, 20 July–17 October 1777, *Baurmeister's Letters and Journals,* p. 109; Thomas Sullivan, 11 September 1777, "Before and After Brandywine," pp. 416–17; Ewald, 11 September 1777, *Hessian Journal,* pp. 82–83; Ferguson, *Fate of a Nation,* p. 177; Burke to Caswell, 17 September 1777, *Letters of Delegates,* vol. 7, pp. 679–80.

48. Lafayette, "Memoir of 1776," *Lafayette's Letters and Papers,* vol. 1, p. 95; Kirkwood, 12 September 1777, *Journal and Order Book,* p. 168; John Muhlenberg, 12–13 September 1777, "Orderly Book of Gen. John Peter Gabriel Muhlenberg," *Pennsylvania Magazine of History and Biography* 34 (1910): 464–65; Washington to Hancock, 11 September 1777, *Washington Writings,* vol. 9, p. 208; Washington to Smallwood, 12 September 1777, *Washington Writings,* vol. 9, pp. 210–11; William Livingston to Hancock, 17 September 1777, *Livingston Papers,* vol. 2, pp. 74–75; William Livingston to Silas Newcomb, 20 September 1777, *Livingston Papers,* vol. 2, pp. 76–77; William Harcourt to Earl Harcourt, 7 October 1777, *The Harcourt Papers,* vol. 11 (Oxford: James Parker and Co., 1880), p. 219; Muenchhausen, 11 September 1777, *At Howe's Side,* p. 32.

49. Nathanael Greene to Catharine Greene, 14 September 1777, *Greene Papers,* vol. 2, pp. 162–63; Anderson, *Recollections,* p. 38; Resolve of Congress,

14 September 1777, *Sullivan Papers,* vol. 1, p. 452; Action of Congress, 16 September 1777, *Sullivan Papers,* vol. 1, pp. 452–53; Adam Stephen to Sullivan, 20 September 1777, *Sullivan Papers,* vol. 1, pp. 455–56; Sullivan to Hancock, 27 September 1777, *Sullivan Papers,* vol. 1, pp. 460–61; Burke to Sullivan, 12 October 1777, *Sullivan Papers,* vol. 1, pp. 534–36; Sullivan to Hancock, 12 October 1777, *Sullivan Papers,* vol. 1, pp. 537–38; Resolve of Congress, 20 October 1777, *Sullivan Papers,* vol. 1, p. 540; Washington to Hancock, 11 September 1777, *Washington Writings,* vol. 9, pp. 207–8; Washington to Hancock, 15 September 1777, *Washington Writings,* vol. 9, pp. 227–29; Washington to Thomas Nelson, 27 September 1777, *Washington Writings,* vol. 9, p. 272; Burke to Caswell, 17 September 1777, *Letters of Delegates,* vol. 7, p. 680.

50. Baurmeister, 20 July–17 October 1777, *Baurmeister's Letters and Journals,* pp. 112–13; Stephen Kemble, 13 September and 11 October 1777, *Journals of Lieut.-Col. Stephen Kemble, 1773–1789; and British Army Orders: Gen. Sir William Howe, 1775–1778; Gen. Sir Henry Clinton, 1778; and Gen. Daniel Jones, 1778* (Boston: Gregg Press, 1972), pp. 135, 494; Howe, *Howe's Narrative,* p. 26; Howe to Germain, 10 October 1777, *Howe's Narrative,* p. 100; Montresor, 12–15 September 1777, "Extracts," pp. 451–52; Ewald, 12–15 September 1777, *Hessian Journal,* pp. 87–88.

51. Ewald, *Hessian Journal,* p. 87; Loftus Cliffe to Jack Cliffe, 24 October 1777, *Cliffe Papers,* CL; Charles Cornwallis, *Howe's Narrative,* pp. 95–96; William Hale, 21 October 1777, *Some British Soldiers in America,* ed. W. H. Wilkin (London: Hugh Rees, 1914), p. 231; Charles Grey, *Howe's Narrative,* p. 96; Stuart, "Record of the Campaign of 1777," *New Records,* p. 49; Harcourt to Earl Harcourt, 7 October 1777, *Harcourt Papers,* vol. 11, p. 219.

52. Townsend, *Brandywine,* p. 26.

53. Washington to Hancock, 19 September 1777, *Washington Writings,* vol. 9, pp. 237–39; Washington to Hancock, 23 September 1777, *Washington Writings,* vol. 9, pp. 257–59; McMichael, 13–28 September 1777, "McMichael's Diary," pp. 150–52; Washington to Charles Stewart, 13 September 1777, *Washington Writings,* vol. 9, pp. 214–15; Washington to Hancock, 13 September 1777, *Washington Writings,* vol. 9, p. 215; Washington to Armstrong, 14 September 1777, *Washington Writings,* vol. 9, pp. 220–21; Washington to Smallwood, 14 September 1777, *Washington Writings,* vol. 9, pp. 222–23; Washington to Hancock, 15 September 1777, *Washington Writings,* vol. 9, pp. 229–30; Washington to Hancock, 16 September 1777, *Washington Writings,* vol. 9, p. 230; Washington to Nelson, 27 September 1777, *Washington Writings,* vol. 9, pp. 272–73.

54. Montresor, 12–15 September 1777, "Extracts," pp. 451–52; Ewald, 12–15 September 1777, *Hessian Journal,* pp. 87–88; Howe, *Howe's Narrative,* p. 26.

55. Baurmeister, 20 July–17 October 1777, *Baurmeister's Letters and Journals,* p. 114.

56. Montresor, 17–20 September 1777, "Extracts," pp. 453–56.

57. "Proceedings of a Council of General Officers," 23 September 1777, *Greene Papers,* vol. 2, p. 164; Thomas Paine to Benjamin Franklin, 16 May 1778, "Military Operations Near Philadelphia in the Campaign of 1777–8," *Pennsylvania Magazine of History and Biography* 2 (1878): 283; William Beatty, 16–17 September 1777, "Journal of Capt. William Beatty," *Maryland Historical Magazine* 3 (1907): 110; Washington to Maxwell, 17 September 1777, *Washington Writings,* vol. 9, pp. 231–32; Washington to Hancock, 19 September 1777, *Washington Writings,* vol. 9, pp. 237–39; Nagle, *Nagle Journal,* p. 10; Washington to Hancock, 18 September 1777, *Washington Writings,* vol. 9, pp. 236–37; Washington, 20 September 1777, "General Orders," *Washington Writings,* vol. 9, pp. 243–44; Washington to Smallwood, 19 September 1777, *Washington Writings,* vol. 9, p. 240; Timothy Pickering, 16 September 1777, *The Life of Timothy Pickering,* vol. 1, ed. Octavius Pickering (Boston: Little, Brown, 1867), pp. 159–60.

58. Anthony Wayne to Washington, 19 September 1777, *Life and Correspondence of Joseph Reed,* vol. 1, ed. William B. Reed (Philadelphia: Lindsay and Blakiston, 1847), p. 313n.

59. For a biography of Wayne, see Paul David Nelson, *Anthony Wayne: Soldier of the Early Republic* (Bloomington: Indiana University Press, 1985). See also ibid., pp. 312–13n; Samuel Hay to William Irvine, 29 September 1777, "Papers Relating to the Paoli Massacre," *Pennsylvania Magazine of History and Biography* 1 (1877): 313–15; Washington to Wayne, 18 September 1777, *Washington Writings,* vol. 9, p. 235; Wayne, 2 November 1777, "Paoli Papers," pp. 310–18; Mordecai Gist to Washington, 15 September 1777, *Washington Papers,* vol. 11, pp. 235–36; Smallwood to Washington, 15 September 1777, *Washington Papers,* vol. 11, pp. 240–42.

60. The quotation is from Anonymous, "Paoli Papers," pp. 311–12. See also Wayne to Washington, 2 September 1777, *Washington Papers,* vol. 11, p. 131.

61. Robertson, *His Diaries,* pp. 148–49; Loftus Cliffe to Jack Cliffe, 24 October 1777, *Cliffe Papers,* CL; Andre, 20 September 1777, *Andre's Journal,* pp. 49–51; Baurmeister, 20 July–17 October 1777, *Baurmeister's Letters and Journals,* pp. 115–16; Muenchhausen, 20–21 September 1777, *At Howe's Side,* p. 34; Anonymous, 2 October 1777, "Actions," pp. 368–69; Howe to Germain, 10 October 1777, *Howe's Narrative,* pp. 101–2; Lieutenant Hunter, "Paoli Papers," pp. 310–11; Frank Moore, 22 September 1777, "Paoli Papers," pp. 312–13.

62. Hay, 20 September 1777, "Letter from Samuel Hay," *Historical Magazine* 3 (1859): 349–50; William Hutchinson, *Revolution Remembered,* pp. 149–50; Benjamin Tallmadge, *Memoir of Col. Benjamin Tallmadge* (New York: Thomas Holman, 1858), p. 22; Wayne to Washington, 2 November 1777, "Paoli Papers," pp. 316–18; Hay to Irvine, 29 September 1777, "Paoli Papers," pp. 313–15; Wayne to George Wayne, 19 September 1777, *Reed's Life,* vol. 1, p. 313n.

63. Robertson, 21–25 September 1777, *His Diaries*, pp. 149–50; Downman, *Services*, pp. 34–35; Andre, 21–25 September 1777, *Andre's Journal*, pp. 51–52; Baurmeister, 20 July–17 October 1777, *Baurmeister's Letters and Journals*, pp. 116–17; Muenchhausen, 20–25 September 1777, *At Howe's Side*, pp. 34–36; Anonymous, 13–25 September 1777, "Contemporary British Account," pp. 80–83; Montresor, 21–25 September 1777, "Extracts," pp. 456–68; Howe to Germain, 10 October 1777, *Howe's Narrative*, pp. 101–3; Feilitzsch, 21–25 September 1777, *Enemy Views*, p. 180; Hesse-Cassel Jaeger Corps Journal, 16–25 September 1777, *Enemy Views*, pp. 181–82.

64. Washington to Sullivan, 20 September 1777, *Sullivan Papers*, vol. 1, p. 454; Washington to Hancock, 23 September 1777, *Washington Writings*, vol. 9, pp. 257–60; Washington to John Augustine Washington, 18 October 1777, *Washington Writings*, vol. 9, p. 397.

65. "Proceedings of a Council of General Officers," 23 September 1777, *Greene Papers*, vol. 2, pp. 163–65; Muhlenberg, 20–22 September 1777, "Orderly Book," vol. 34, pp. 470–73; Beatty, 17–30 September 1777, "Beatty's Journal," p. 110; Washington to Hancock, 18 September 1777, *Washington Writings*, vol. 9, pp. 236–37; Washington, 20 September 1777, "General Orders," *Washington Writings*, vol. 9, pp. 243–44; Washington to Sullivan, 21 September 1777, *Washington Writings*, vol. 9, p. 245; Washington to Alexander McDougall, 22 September 1777, *Washington Writings*, vol. 9, pp. 246–47; Washington to Philemon Dickinson, 22 September 1777, *Washington Writings*, vol. 9, p. 246; Washington to Wayne, 23 September 1777, *Washington Writings*, vol. 9, p. 252; Washington to Hancock, 23 September 1777, *Washington Writings*, vol. 9, pp. 257–60; Washington to Lord Alexander Stirling, 25 September 1777, *Washington Writings*, vol. 9, pp. 265–66; Washington to Clement Biddle, 26 September 1777, *Washington Writings*, vol. 9, p. 269.

66. Sarah Fisher, 21 September 1777, "'A Diary of Trifling Occurrences': Philadelphia, 1776–1778," *Pennsylvania Magazine of History and Biography* 82 (1958): 448.

67. Hamilton to Hancock, 18 September 1777, *Hamilton Papers*, vol. 1, p. 326; Washington to Hamilton, 22 September 1777, *Hamilton Papers*, vol. 1, p. 333; Robert Proud, 29 September 1777, "Letters of Robert Proud," *Pennsylvania Magazine of History and Biography* 34 (1910): 72–73; Fisher, 21–26 September 1777, "Diary," pp. 448–50; Paine to Franklin, 16 May 1778, *The Complete Writings of Thomas Paine*, ed. Philip S. Foner (New York: Citadel Press, 1945), p. 1144; Burke to Caswell, 20 September 1777, *Letters of Delegates to Congress, 1774–1789*, vol. 8, ed. Paul Smith (Washington, D.C.: Library of Congress, 1981), p. 5; Charles Carroll of Carrollton to Charles Carroll Sr., 29 September 1777, *Letters of Delegates*, vol. 8, p. 26; Hancock to Dorothy Hancock, 1 October 1777, *Letters of Delegates*, vol. 8, p. 38.

68. Peebles, 26 September 1777, *American War*, p. 138; Downman, *Services*, pp. 36–38; Muenchhausen, 26 September 1777, *At Howe's Side*, p. 36;

Anonymous, 26 September 1777, "Contemporary British Account," p. 83; Montresor, 26–29 September 1777, "Extracts," pp. 458–61; Fisher, 21–26 September 1777, "Diary," pp. 448–50; Ewald, 31 [*sic*] September 1777, *Hessian Journal*, p. 92.

69. Howe, *Howe's Narrative*, p. 32.

70. Ibid., p. 26.

71. John Adams to Abigail Adams, 30 September 1777, *Letters of Delegates*, vol. 8, p. 27; Elbridge Gerry to James Warren, 6 October 1777, *Letters of Delegates*, vol. 8, p. 66.

72. Washington to Horatio Gates, 24 September 1777, *Washington Writings*, vol. 9, pp. 263–64; Kirkwood, 26 October and 5 November 1777, *Journal and Order Book*, pp. 217–18, 228–29.

73. Armstrong to Thomas Wharton, 26 September 1777, *Reed's Life*, vol. 1, p. 317.

74. "Proceedings of a Council of General Officers," 28 September 1777, *Greene Papers*, vol. 2, pp. 167–69; Washington to Hancock, 29 September 1777, *Washington Writings*, vol. 9, pp. 284–85.

75. Christopher Marshall, 4 October 1777, *Extracts from the Diary of Christopher Marshall, 1774–1781*, ed. William Duane (New York: Arno Press, 1969), p. 132; Sullivan to Meshech Weare, 25 October 1777, *Sullivan Papers*, vol. 1, pp. 542–43; Smallwood to ———, 9 October 1777, "Unpublished Papers Relating to the Battle of Germantown," *Pennsylvania Magazine of History and Biography* 1 (1877): 401–2; Washington to Hancock, 5 October 1777, *Washington Writings*, vol. 9, pp. 308–9; Stephen Moylan to Washington, 1 October 1777, *George Washington Papers at the Library of Congress, 1741–1799*, series 4, General Correspondence, 1697–1799; Alexander Dandridge to Wayne, 1 October 1777, *Washington Papers at Library of Congress*.

76. McMichael, 3 October 1777, "McMichael's Diary," p. 152; Sullivan to Weare, 25 October 1777, *Sullivan Papers*, vol. 1, pp. 542–43; "Order of Battle," 3 October 1777, "Unpublished Papers for Germantown," pp. 399–400; Washington to Hancock, 5 October 1777, *Washington Writings*, vol. 9, pp. 308–9; Washington to Jonathan Trumbull, 8 October 1777, *Washington Writings*, vol. 9, pp. 329–30.

77. Joseph Plumb Martin, *Private Yankee Doodle: Being a Narrative of Some of the Adventures, Dangers, and Sufferings of a Revolutionary Solder*, ed. George Scheer (Boston: Little, Brown, 1962), p. 72; Ewing, *Military Journal*, p. 23; Clark, "Clark's Diary," pp. 100–101; Kirkwood, 3 October 1777, *Journal and Order Book*, pp. 189–90; Sullivan to Weare, 25 October 1777, *Sullivan Papers*, vol. 1, pp. 545–47; John Lacey, "Memoirs of Brigadier-General John Lacey, of Pennsylvania," *Pennsylvania Magazine of History and Biography* 26 (1902): 106.

78. Howe, *Howe's Narrative*, pp. 27–28; Howe to Henry Clinton, 8 October 1777, *Henry Clinton Papers*, CL, vol. 25, no. 38; Ewald, 3–4 October 1777, *Hessian Journal*, pp. 92–93.

79. According to Ewald, Knyphausen visited Howe and told him about Ewald's encounter, and Howe reportedly responded, "That cannot be!" See Ewald, 3–4 October 1777, *Hessian Journal,* pp. 92–93.

80. Paul David Nelson, *General James Grant: Scottish Soldier and Royal Governor of East Florida* (Gainesville: University Press of Florida, 1993), pp. 122–23; Hesse-Cassel Jaeger Corps Journal, 4 October 1777, *Enemy Views,* p. 183; Howe to Germain, 10 October 1777, *Documents,* vol. 14, p. 207; Grey, 10 October 1777, *Howe's Narrative,* p. 108; Howe, *Howe's Narrative,* pp. 27–28; Andre, 4 October 1777, *Andre's Journal,* pp. 54–55; Ewald, 3–4 October 1777, *Hessian Journal,* pp. 92–93; Robertson, 4 October 1777, *His Diaries,* pp. 151–52; Baurmeister, 20 July–17 October 1777, *Baurmeister's Letters and Journals,* p. 119.

81. Martin Hunter, *Fate of a Nation,* pp. 187–88.

82. Ibid.; "Contemporary Account of the Battle of Germantown," *Pennsylvania Magazine of History and Biography* 11 (1887): 330; Loftus Cliffe to Jack Cliffe, 24 October 1777, *Cliffe Papers,* CL; Pickering, 4 October 1777, *Pickering's Life,* vol. 1, p. 168; Baurmeister, 20 July–17 October 1777, *Baurmeister's Letters and Journals,* p. 119; Tallmadge, *Memoir,* p. 23; Joseph Blackwell to William Edmonds, 10 October 1777, *A Salute to Courage: The American Revolution as Seen Through Wartime Writings of Officers of the Continental Army and Navy,* ed. Dennis Ryan (New York: Columbia University Press, 1979), p. 102; Andre, 4 October 1777, *Andre's Journal,* pp. 54–55; Anderson, *Recollections,* p. 45; Howe, 4 October 1777, "Howe's Report on the Battle of Germantown," *First American Civil War,* vol. 2, p. 274; Beatty, 4 October 1777, "Beatty's Journal," pp. 110–11; Sullivan to Weare, 25 October 1777, *Sullivan Papers,* vol. 1, pp. 544–45; "Battle of Germantown from a British Account," *Pennsylvania Magazine of History and Biography* 11 (1887): 112; Washington to Hancock, 5 October 1777, *Washington Writings,* vol. 9, pp. 309–10; Howe to Germain, 10 October 1777, *Documents,* vol. 14, p. 207; Wayne, 6 October 1777, *Reed's Life,* vol. 1, pp. 320–21; Harcourt to Earl Harcourt, 7 October 1777, *Harcourt Papers,* vol. 11, p. 220; Muenchhausen, 4 October 1777, *At Howe's Side,* pp. 38–39.

83. Pinckney, 14 November 1820, "Battles," p. 203; Pickering, 4 October 1777, *Pickering's Life,* vol. 1, pp. 168–70; Tallmadge, *Memoir,* p. 23; Baurmeister, 20 July–17 October 1777, *Baurmeister's Letters and Journals,* p. 120; Ewald, 5 October 1777, *Hessian Journal,* p. 96; Sullivan to Weare, 25 October 1777, *Sullivan Papers,* vol. 1, pp. 545–47; Henry Lee, *Memoirs of the War,* vol. 1, pp. 29–30; "Battle of Germantown from a British Account," pp. 112–14; Washington to Hancock, 5 October 1777, *Washington Writings,* vol. 9, pp. 309–10; Howe to Germain, 10 October 1777, *Documents,* vol. 14, pp. 207–08.

84. Pinckney, 14 November 1820, "Battles," p. 203; McDougall to Nathanael Greene, 14 February 1778, *Greene Papers,* vol. 2, p. 284; Andre, 4

October 1777, *Andre's Journal,* pp. 54–55; Martin, 4 October 1777, *Yankee Doodle,* pp. 72–73; Walter Stewart to Gates, 12 October 1777, "Unpublished Papers for Germantown," p. 400; Washington to Hancock, 5 October 1777, *Washington Writings,* vol. 9, pp. 309–10; Howe to Germain, 10 October 1777, *Documents,* vol. 14, p. 208; Sullivan to Weare, 25 October 1777, *Sullivan Papers,* vol. 1, pp. 545–47; Stirke, 4 October 1777, "British Officer's Journal," p. 172; John Watson, *Annals of Philadelphia, and Pennsylvania, in the Olden Time,* vol. 2 (Philadelphia: Edwin S. Stuart, 1884), p. 48.

85. Wayne to Gates, 21 November 1777, *Horatio Gates Papers, 1726–1828,* reel 6 (Sanford, N.C.: Microfilming Corporation of America, 1978); Pickering, 4 October 1777, *Pickering's Life,* vol. 1, pp. 168–70; Watson, *Annals,* vol. 2, p. 48; Stewart to Gates, 12 October 1777, "Unpublished Papers for Germantown," p. 400; Howe to Germain, 10 October 1777, *Documents,* vol. 14, p. 208; McMichael, 4 October 1777, "McMichael's Diary," p. 153; Martin, *Yankee Doodle,* p. 73; Clark, "Clark's Diary," pp. 100–101; Henry Miller, "A Memoir of General Henry Miller," *Pennsylvania Magazine of History and Biography* 12 (1888): 427; Wayne, 6 October 1777, *Reed's Life,* vol. 1, pp. 320–21; Andre, 4 October 1777, *Andre's Journal,* pp. 55–57; Report of a Court of Enquiry, 1 November 1777, *Greene Papers,* vol. 2, pp. 188–89.

86. Lacey, "Lacey's Memoirs," p. 106; Sullivan to Weare, 25 October 1777, *Sullivan Papers,* vol. 1, pp. 545–47; Smallwood to ——, 9 October 1777, "Unpublished Papers for Germantown," p. 402; Howe to Germain, 10 October 1777, *Documents,* vol. 14, pp. 207–8; Andre, 4 October 1777, *Andre's Journal,* pp. 55–57; Baurmeister, 20 July–17 October 1777, *Baurmeister's Letters and Journals,* pp. 120–21; Pickering to Rebecca Pickering, 13 October 1777, *Pickering's Life,* vol. 1, p. 176.

87. Armstrong to Gates, n.d., James Wilkinson, *Memoirs of My Own Times,* vol. 1 (New York: AMS Press, 1973), pp. 353–54; Hesse-Cassel Jaeger Corps Journal, 4 October 1777, *Enemy Views,* pp. 183–84; Feilitzsch, 4 October 1777, *Enemy Views,* p. 184; Armstrong to Wharton, 5 October 1777, *Reed's Life,* vol. 1, pp. 322–23; Lacey, "Lacey's Memoirs," p. 106; Howe to Germain, 10 October 1777, *Documents,* vol. 14, pp. 207–8; Washington to Gates, 20 February 1777, *The Papers of George Washington: Revolutionary War Series,* vol. 8, ed. Dorothy Twohig (Charlottesville: University Press of Virginia, 1998), p. 378.

88. McMichael, 4 October 1777, "McMichael's Diary," p. 153.

89. "Contemporary Account of Germantown," p. 331; Tallmadge, *Memoir,* p. 23; Andre, 4 October 1777, *Andre's Journal,* pp. 55–57; Muenchhausen, 4 October 1777, *At Howe's Side,* pp. 38–39; Paine to Franklin, 16 May 1778, "Military Operations," p. 289; Howe to Germain, 10 October 1777, *Documents,* vol. 14, p. 208; McDougall to Nathanael Greene, 14 February 1778, *Greene Papers,* vol. 2, p. 284; Lacey, "Lacey's Memoirs," p. 106; Sullivan to

Weare, 25 October 1777, *Sullivan Papers,* vol. 1, pp. 445–47; Washington to Hancock, 5 October 1777, *Washington Writings,* vol. 9, pp. 309–10; Simeon Vanartsdalen to John Bogart, 13 October 1777, *The John Bogart Letters* (New Brunswick, N.J.: Rutgers College, 1914), pp. 13–14; Miller, "Miller's Memoir," p. 427.

90. Howe to Germain, 10 October 1777, *Documents of the American Revolution,* vol. 13, ed. K. G. Davies (Dublin: Irish University Press, 1976), p. 187; Washington to Jonathan Trumbull, 8 October 1777, *Washington Writings,* vol. 9, pp. 329–30; Tallmadge, *Memoir,* p. 22; Andre, 4 October 1777, *Andre's Journal,* p. 57; Weedon to Page, 8 October 1777, Weedon-Page Correspondence, CHS; Lacey, "Lacey's Memoirs," pp. 106–7; Kirkwood, 6 October 1777, *Journal and Order Book,* p. 193; Kirkwood, 13 October 1777, *Journal and Order Book,* pp. 204–5; Paine to Franklin, 16 May 1778, "Military Operations," p. 289; Sullivan to Weare, 25 October 1777, *Sullivan Papers,* vol. 1, p. 547; Wayne to Gates, 21 November 1777, *Gates Papers;* Wilkinson, *Wilkinson's Memoirs,* vol. 1, p. 352; Report of a Court of Enquiry, 1 November 1777, *Greene Papers,* vol. 2, pp. 188–89; Kirkwood, 20 November 1777, *Journal and Order Book,* pp. 248–49.

91. Muenchhausen, 4 October 1777, *At Howe's Side,* pp. 38–39; Ewald, 19 October 1777, *Hessian Journal,* p. 96; Howe, *Howe's Narrative,* pp. 27–28; Grey, *Howe's Narrative,* p. 108; Howe to Germain, 10 October 1777, *Documents,* vol. 14, p. 207.

92. Henry Lee, *Memoirs of the War,* vol. 1, p. 29.

CHAPTER 4. THE DELAWARE RIVER

1. Minutes of the Pennsylvania Navy Board, 6 June 1777, *Naval Documents of the American Revolution,* vol. 9, ed. William James Morgan (Washington, D.C.: Naval Historical Center, Department of the Navy, 1992), p. 45; Anonymous, "A Contemporary British Account of General Sir William Howe's Military Operations in 1777," *Proceedings of the American Antiquarian Society,* April 1930, p. 84.

2. George Washington to Owen Biddle, 14 April 1777, *The Papers of George Washington: Revolutionary War Series,* vol. 9, ed. Dorothy Twohig (Charlottesville: University Press of Virginia, 1999), p. 158; Philip Schuyler to Washington, 22 April 1777, *Letters of Delegates to Congress, 1774–1789,* vol. 6, ed. Paul Smith (Washington, D.C.: Library of Congress, 1980), p. 635; John Adams to Abigail Adams, 8 June 1777, *Letters of Delegates to Congress, 1774–1789,* vol. 7, ed. Paul Smith (Washington, D.C.: Library of Congress, 1981), p. 175; Phillippe-Charles-Jean-Baptiste Tronson du Coudray, July 1777, "Du Coudray's 'Observations on the Delaware Forts,'" *Pennsylvania Magazine of History and Biography* 24 (1900): 343–47; Washington to John Hancock, 13

June 1777, *The Papers of George Washington: Revolutionary War Series,* vol. 10, ed. Frank Grizzard Jr. (Charlottesville: University Press of Virginia, 2000), p. 27; Pennsylvania Supreme Executive Council to Washington, 18 July 1777, *Washington Papers,* vol. 10, pp. 322–23; Washington to Hancock, 22 July 1777, *Washington Papers,* vol. 10, p. 357; Anthony Wayne to Washington, 6 August 1777, *Defences of Philadelphia in 1777,* ed. Worthington Chauncey Ford (New York: Da Capo Press, 1971), pp. 19–20; Joseph Reed to Washington, 7 August 1777, Ford, *Defences of Philadelphia,* pp. 24–28; Nathanael Greene to Washington, 7 August 1777, *The Papers of General Nathanael Greene,* vol. 2, ed. Richard K. Showman (Chapel Hill: University of North Carolina Press, 1980), pp. 135–37; Washington to Hancock, 10 August 1777, *Washington Papers,* vol. 10, pp. 569–74; Washington to Silas Newcomb, 11 August 1777, *Washington Papers,* vol. 10, p. 587; Hancock to Washington, 17 August 1777, *Washington Papers,* vol. 10, p. 650; Washington to Hancock, 15 August 1777, *Washington Papers,* vol. 10, pp. 616–17.

3. Pennsylvania Supreme Executive Council to Washington, 18 July 1777, *Washington Papers,* vol. 10, pp. 322–23; Minutes of the Pennsylvania Navy Board, 8 September 1777, *Naval Documents,* vol. 9, p. 897; Continental Marine Committee to John Hazelwood, 23 September 1777, *Naval Documents,* vol. 9, p. 969; Continental Marine Committee to Hazelwood, 26 September 1777, *Letters of Delegates to Congress, 1774–1789,* vol. 8, ed. Paul Smith (Washington, D.C.: Library of Congress, 1981), p. 21; Hazelwood, 20 September 1777, *Naval Documents,* vol. 9, p. 945.

4. Washington to Hancock, 23 September 1777, *The Writings of George Washington,* vol. 9, ed. John Fitzpatrick (Washington, D.C.: Government Printing Office, 1933), p. 259.

5. Henry Lee, *Memoirs of the War in the Southern Department of the United States,* vol. 1 (Philadelphia: Bradford and Inskeep, 1812), p. 26; Washington to Samuel Smith, 23 September 1777, *Washington Writings,* vol. 9, pp. 260–61; Washington to Hazelwood, 23 September 1777, *Washington Writings,* vol. 9, pp. 255–56; Washington to Hancock, 23 September 1777, *Washington Writings,* vol. 9, p. 259; Washington to Hancock, 13 September 1777, *Washington Writings,* vol. 9, p. 215; Washington to Thomas Wharton, 13 September 1777, *Washington Writings,* vol. 9, pp. 216–17; Samuel Smith to Washington, 2 October 1777, *Naval Documents of the American Revolution,* vol. 10, ed. Michael Crawford (Washington, D.C.: Naval Historical Center, Department of the Navy, 1996), pp. 16–17.

6. Francis Downman, *The Services of Lieut. Colonel Francis Downman, R.A. in France, North America, and the West Indies, Between the Years 1758 and 1784,* ed. F. A. Whinyates (Woolwich: Royal Artillery Institution, 1898), pp. 36–38; Archibald Robertson, 27–29 September, *Archibald Robertson: His Diaries and Sketches in America, 1762–1780,* ed. Harry Miller Lydenberg (New York: Arno Press, 1971), pp. 150–51; John Peebles, 27 September 1777,

John Peebles' American War: The Diary of a Scottish Grenadier, 1776–1782, ed. Ira Gruber (Mechanicsburg, Pa.: Stackpole Books, 1998), pp. 138–39; William Bradford to Wharton, 3 October 1777, *Naval Documents,* vol. 10, p. 29; John Montresor, 27 September 1777, "Extracts from the Journals and Note-Books of Capt. John Montresor," *Collections of the New-York Historical Society,* 1881, p. 459; Robert Morton, 27 September 1777, "The Diary of Robert Morton," *Pennsylvania Magazine of History and Biography* 1 (1877): 8; Hesse-Cassel Jaeger Corps Journal, 27–28 September 1777, *Enemy Views: The American Revolutionary War as Recorded by the Hessian Participants,* ed. Bruce E. Burgoyne (Bowie, Md.: Heritage Books, 1996), p. 182; William Howe to Lord George Germain, 10 October 1777, *Documents of the American Revolution,* vol. 14, ed. K. G. Davies (Dublin: Irish University Press, 1976), p. 206; Hazelwood to Charles Alexander, 26 September 1777, *Naval Documents,* vol. 9, p. 970.

7. Henry Yeager, *The Revolution Remembered: Eyewitness Accounts of the War for Independence,* ed. John C. Dann (Chicago: University of Chicago Press, 1980), p. 159; Samuel Smith to Washington, 2 October 1777, *Naval Documents,* vol. 10, pp. 16–17; Samuel Smith to Washington, 3 October 1777, *Naval Documents,* vol. 10, p. 28; Bradford to Wharton, 3 October 1777, *Naval Documents,* vol. 10, p. 29; Washington to Lewis Nicola, 29 September 1777, *Washington Writings,* vol. 9, pp. 283–84; Howe to Germain, 10 October 1777, *Documents,* vol. 14, pp. 206–7.

8. Samuel Smith, "The Papers of General Samuel Smith," *Historical Magazine* 7 (1870): 86.

9. Samuel Smith to Washington, 2 October 1777, *Naval Documents,* vol. 10, pp. 16–17; Washington to Samuel Smith, 1 October 1777, *Washington Writings,* vol. 9, pp. 292–93; Samuel Smith to Washington, 27 September 1777, *Naval Documents,* vol. 9, pp. 974–75; Samuel Smith, *Memoirs of Samuel Smith: Soldier of the Revolution, 1776–1786* (New York: privately printed, 1860), p. 86; Bradford to Wharton, 3 October 1777, *Naval Documents,* vol. 10, p. 29.

10. Washington to Hancock, 7 October 1777, *Washington Writings,* vol. 9, p. 321; Washington to James Varnum, 7 October 1777, *Washington Writings,* vol. 9, pp. 326–27; Washington to Hancock, 8 October 1777, *Washington Writings,* vol. 9, p. 332; Washington to John Armstrong, 8 October 1777, *Washington Writings,* vol. 9, pp. 337–38; Washington to James Potter, 9 October 1777, *Washington Writings,* vol. 9, pp. 344–45; Washington to Thomas McKean, 10 October 1777, *Washington Writings,* vol. 9, pp. 346–47; Potter to Washington, 5 November 1777, Ford, *Defences of Philadelphia,* p. 85; Washington to Armstrong, 27 March 1778, *The Writings of George Washington,* vol. 11, ed. John Fitzpatrick (Washington, D.C.: Government Printing Office, 1934), p. 159.

11. Hazelwood to Washington, 10 October 1777, *Naval Documents,* vol.

10, p. 110; John Linzee, 4 October 1777, "Journal of HMS *Pearl,*" *Naval Documents,* vol. 10, p. 39; Andrew Hamond, 11 October 1777, "Master's Log of HMS *Roebuck,*" *Naval Documents,* vol. 10, p. 121; Bradford to Wharton, 13 October 1777, *Naval Documents,* vol. 10, p. 146; Hamond, 13 October 1777, "Master's Journal of HMS *Roebuck,*" *Naval Documents,* vol. 10, p. 147; John Henry, 13 October 1777, "Journal of HM Armed Ship *Vigilant,*" *Naval Documents,* vol. 10, pp. 147–48; Henry Bellew, 14 October 1777, "Journal of HMS *Liverpool,*" *Naval Documents,* vol. 10, p. 165; Samuel Smith to Washington, 14 October 1777, *Naval Documents,* vol. 10, pp. 164–65.

12. Downman, *Services,* pp. 41–42.

13. Ibid., pp. 40–42; Peebles, 14–15 October 1777, *American War,* pp. 142–43; Howe to Henry Clinton, 9 October 1777, Henry Clinton Papers, CL, vol. 25, no. 35; Bradford to Wharton, 8 October 1777, *Naval Documents,* vol. 10, p. 74; Bradford to Wharton, 11 October 1777, *Naval Documents,* vol. 10, p. 120; Bradford to Wharton, 15 October 1777, *Naval Documents,* vol. 10, p. 177; Washington to Hazelwood, 11 October 1777, *Naval Documents,* vol. 10, p. 118; Hazelwood to Washington, 12 October 1777, *Naval Documents,* vol. 10, pp. 128–29; Hazelwood to Washington, 15 October 1777, *Naval Documents,* vol. 10, p. 178; Samuel Smith to Washington, 18 October 1777, *Naval Documents,* vol. 10, p. 205; Friedrich von Muenchhausen, 8–9 October 1777, *At General Howe's Side, 1776–1778,* trans. Ernst Kipping (Monmouth Beach, N.J.: Philip Freneau Press, 1974), p. 40; Montresor, 6–17 October 1777, "Extracts," pp. 462–68.

14. Hazelwood to Washington, 10 October 1777, *Naval Documents,* vol. 10, p. 110; Hazelwood to Washington, 12 October 1777, *Naval Documents,* vol. 10, pp. 128–29; Bradford and Hazelwood to Wharton, 11 October 1777, *Naval Documents,* vol. 10, p. 120; Washington to Christopher Greene, 14 October 1777, *Naval Documents,* vol. 10, p. 162; Alexander Hamilton to Christopher Greene, 15 October 1777, *Naval Documents,* vol. 10, p. 175; Hazelwood to Benjamin Eyre, 15 October 1777, *Naval Documents,* vol. 10, p. 177; Hazelwood to Washington, 15 October 1777, *Naval Documents,* vol. 10, p. 178; Samuel Smith to Washington, 18 October 1777, *Naval Documents,* vol. 10, p. 205; Washington to Hazelwood, 19 October 1777, *Naval Documents,* vol. 10, p. 214; Washington to Hazelwood, 21 October 1777, *Naval Documents,* vol. 10, pp. 233–34; Washington to Samuel Smith, 22 October 1777, *Washington Writings,* vol. 9, p. 416; Smith, "Smith's Papers," pp. 88–89.

15. Richard Howe to Philip Stephens, 25 October 1777, *Naval Documents,* vol. 10, pp. 289–93.

16. Ibid.; Thomas Paine to Benjamin Franklin, 16 May 1778, *The Complete Writings of Thomas Paine,* ed. Philip S. Foner (New York: Citadel Press, 1945), p. 1148; Henry, 22 October 1777, "Journal of HM Armed Ship *Vigilant,*" *Naval Documents,* vol. 10, pp. 239–40; Linzee, 22 October 1777, "Journal of

HMS *Pearl*," *Naval Documents*, vol. 10, p. 240; Hazelwood to Washington, 23 October 1777, *Naval Documents*, vol. 10, p. 248; "Court-Martial of Captain John Reynolds," 26 November 1777, *Naval Documents*, vol. 10, pp. 603–7; Smith, "Smith's Papers," p. 89.

17. Howe to Germain, 31 December 1776, Historical Manuscripts Commission, *Report on the Manuscripts of Mrs. Stopford-Sackville, of Drayton House, Northhamptonshire*, vol. 2 (Boston: Gregg Press, 1972), p. 54; Downman, *Services*, pp. 43–44; Johann Ewald, 21 October 1777, *Diary of the American War: A Hessian Journal*, trans. and ed. Joseph P. Tustin (New Haven, Conn.: Yale University Press, 1979), p. 97; William Howe, *Narrative of Lieut. Gen. Sir William Howe, in a Committee of the House of Commons* (London: H. Baldwin, 1781), pp. 28–29; William Harcourt to Earl Harcourt, 26 October 1777, *The Harcourt Papers*, vol. 11 (Oxford: James Parker and Co., 1880), pp. 221–22; Johann Conrad Dohla, 10 August 1777, *A Hessian Diary of the American Revolution*, ed. and trans. Bruce E. Burgoyne (Norman: University of Oklahoma Press, 1990), p. 44.

18. Ewald, 22 October 1777, *Hessian Journal*, p. 98.

19. Ibid., pp. 97–104; James Robertson to Lord Bute, 13 November 1777, *A Prime Minister and His Son: From the Correspondence of the 3rd Earl of Bute and of Lt.-General the Hon. Sir Charles Stuart, K.B.*, ed. E. Stuart Wortley (New York: Dutton, 1925), p. 117.

20. Ebenezer David to Nicholas Brown, 5 November 1777, *A Rhode Island Chaplain in the Revolution: Letters of Ebenezer David to Nicholas Brown, 1775–1778*, ed. Jeannette Black and William Greene Roelker (London: Kennikat Press, 1972), pp. 52–54; Jeremiah Greenman, 22–23 October 1777, *Diary of a Common Soldier in the American Revolution, 1775–1783: An Annotated Edition of the Military Journal of Jeremiah Greenman*, ed. Robert C. Bray and Paul E. Bushnell (DeKalb: Northern Illinois University Press, 1978), pp. 82–84; Henry Lee, *Memoirs of the War*, vol. 1, pp. 31–33; Nathanael Greene to Christopher Greene, 26 October 1777, *Greene Papers*, vol. 2, p. 181.

21. David to Brown, 5 November 1777, *Rhode Island Chaplain*, pp. 52–54; Johann Carl Buettner, *Narrative of Johann Carl Buettner in the American Revolution* (New York: Benjamin Blom, 1971), pp. 51–53; Greenman, 22–23 October 1777, *Diary of a Common Soldier*, pp. 82–84; Ewald, 22 October 1777, *Hessian Journal*, pp. 97–99; Carl Friedrich Rueffer, *Enemy Views*, pp. 227–29.

22. Downman, *Services*, pp. 43–44; Buettner, *Buettner's Narrative*, pp. 51–53; Ewald, 22 October 1777, *Hessian Journal*, p. 99; Smith, *Soldier of the Revolution*, pp. 9–10; Rueffer, *Enemy Views*, pp. 227–29.

23. Council of General Officers, 29 October 1777, *Greene Papers*, vol. 2, pp. 184–86; Nathanael Greene to John Clark, 5 November 1777, *Greene Papers*, vol. 2, p. 191; James McMichael, 18 October 1777, "Diary of Lieutenant James McMichael, of the Pennsylvania Line, 1776–1778," *Pennsylvania Magazine of History and Biography* 16 (1892): 154.

24. Continental Navy Board of the Middle Department to Washington, 25 October 1777, *Naval Documents,* vol. 10, p. 282; John Muhlenberg, 13 October 1777, "Orderly Book of Gen. John Peter Gabriel Muhlenberg," *Pennsylvania Magazine of History and Biography* 33 (1909): 77; Washington to Hancock, 10–11 October 1777, *Washington Writings,* vol. 9, pp. 350–52; Washington to James Mease, 15 October 1777, *Washington Writings,* vol. 9, pp. 374–75; Eliphalet Dyer to Joseph Trumbull, 8 October 1777, *Letters of Delegates,* vol. 8, p. 75; James Duane to George Clinton, 10 October 1777, *Letters of Delegates,* vol. 8, p. 94; Cornelius Harnett to Richard Caswell, 10 October 1777, *Letters of Delegates,* vol. 8, p. 97.

25. Council of General Officers, 29 October 1777, *Greene Papers,* vol. 2, pp. 182–88; Washington to Henry Laurens, 17 November 1777, *The Writings of George Washington,* vol. 10, ed. John Fitzpatrick (Washington, D.C.: Government Printing Office, 1933), pp. 73–77; Potter to Washington, 3 November 1777, *Naval Documents,* vol. 10, p. 384; Henry Lee to Washington, 3 November 1777, *Naval Documents,* vol. 10, pp. 388–89; Washington to Hazelwood, 4 November 1777, *Naval Documents,* vol. 10, p. 394; John Laurens to Henry Laurens, 14 November 1777, *The Army Correspondence of Colonel John Laurens in the Years 1777–8* (New York: Bradford Club, 1868), pp. 77–78; Washington to John Gill, 6 October 1777, *Washington Writings,* vol. 9, pp. 317–18; Washington to Hancock, 16 October 1777, *Washington Writings,* vol. 9, p. 382; Washington to Potter, 3 November 1777, *Washington Writings,* vol. 9, pp. 496–97; Potter to Washington, 30 October 1777, Ford, *Defences of Philadelphia,* p. 69; Clark to Washington, 3 November 1777, "Letters from Major John Clark, Jr., to Gen. Washington," *Bulletin of the Historical Society of Pennsylvania* 1 (1845–47): 5–6; John Laurens to Henry Laurens, 7 November 1777, *The Papers of Henry Laurens,* vol. 12 (Columbia: University of South Carolina Press, 1990), pp. 32–35.

26. Samuel Smith to Washington, 26 October 1777, Ford, *Defences of Philadelphia,* pp. 56–57.

27. Henry d'Arendt to Washington, 24 October 1777, *Naval Documents,* vol. 10, pp. 263–64; Hazelwood to d'Arendt and Samuel Smith, 26 October 1777, *Naval Documents,* vol. 10, pp. 308–9; Washington to Samuel Smith, 4 November 1777, *Washington Writings,* vol. 10, pp. 7–8; Washington to John Green, 28 October 1777, *Washington Writings,* vol. 9, p. 458; Washington to Samuel Smith, 28 October 1777, *Washington Writings,* vol. 9, pp. 458–59; Samuel Smith, "Smith's Papers," p. 89; Samuel Smith to Washington, 26 October 1777, Ford, *Defences of Philadelphia,* pp. 56–57; François Louis Teissèdre de Fleury, 2–3 November 1777, Ford, *Defences of Philadelphia,* pp. 74–76.

28. Smith came out and by and large accused Hazelwood of cowardice, but the record is not clear as to why Robinson and his officers stalked out of the meeting. In a letter to Robinson, Washington merely stated, "The matters between you and him, I mean the Navy officers under different denominations, is

so delicate in its nature that I would with reluctance suppose it to exist—I trust it is done away, and that in future, there will be the happiest understanding and participation of councils between the whole." See Washington to Isaiah Robinson, 25 October 1777, *Naval Documents,* vol. 10, p. 285; Hazelwood to Washington, 26 October 1777, *Naval Documents,* vol. 10, p. 307; Pennsylvania State Navy Board to Wharton, 30 October 1777, *Naval Documents,* vol. 10, pp. 359–60; Varnum to Washington, 6 November 1777, Ford, *Defences of Philadelphia,* pp. 88–89; Smith, "Smith's Papers," p. 89.

29. Washington to William Livingston, 6 November 1777, *Washington Writings,* vol. 10, pp. 21–22; Washington to Philemon Dickinson, 30 October 1777, *Washington Writings,* vol. 9, pp. 468–69; David Forman to Washington, 26 October 1777, Ford, *Defences of Philadelphia,* pp. 54–56; Forman to Washington, 28 October 1777, Ford, *Defences of Philadelphia,* pp. 65–67; Forman to Washington, 7 November 1777, Ford, *Defences of Philadelphia,* pp. 88–93; Livingston to Newcomb, 5 November 1777, *The Papers of William Livingston,* vol. 2, *July 1777–December 1778,* ed. Carl E. Prince and Dennis P. Ryan (Trenton, N.J.: New Jersey Historical Commission, 1980), pp. 99–100; Washington to Livingston, 11 February 1777, *The Papers of George Washington: Revolutionary War Series,* vol. 8, ed. Dorothy Twohig (Charlottesville: University Press of Virginia, 1998), pp. 308–9; Washington to Livingston, 1 November 1777, *Washington Writings,* vol. 9, pp. 485–86.

30. Hamilton to Washington, 12 November 1777, *The Papers of Alexander Hamilton,* vol. 1, ed. Harold Syrett (New York: Columbia University Press, 1961), p. 360.

31. Hamilton to Horatio Gates, 5 November 1777, *Hamilton Papers,* vol. 1, pp. 351–52; Hamilton to Washington, 6 November 1777, *Hamilton Papers,* vol. 1, pp. 353–55; Hamilton to Washington, 10 November 1777, *Hamilton Papers,* vol. 1, pp. 356–60; Hamilton to Washington, 12 November 1777, *Hamilton Papers,* vol. 1, pp. 360–62; Hamilton to Washington, 15 November 1777, *Hamilton Papers,* vol. 1, pp. 363–64; Washington to Israel Putnam, 4 November 1777, *Washington Writings,* vol. 10, pp. 2–3; Washington to Putnam, 9 November 1777, *Washington Writings,* vol. 10, pp. 28–29; Washington to John Augustine Washington, 26 November 1777, *Washington Writings,* vol. 10, pp. 112–14.

32. Nathanael Greene to Catharine Greene, 20 May 1777, *Greene Papers,* vol. 2, p. 85.

33. Varnum to Washington, 8 November 1777, *Naval Documents,* vol. 10, pp. 434–35; Washington to Varnum, 4 November 1777, *Washington Writings,* vol. 10, pp. 5–6; Washington to Varnum, 1 November 1777, *Washington Writings,* vol. 9, pp. 488–89; Varnum to Washington, 3 November 1777, Ford, *Defences of Philadelphia,* p. 78; Varnum to Washington, 6 November 1777, Ford, *Defences of Philadelphia,* pp. 88–89; Samuel Smith to Washington, 9 November 1777, Ford, *Defences of Philadelphia,* p. 105; Washington to Varnum, 28 October 1777, *Washington Writings,* vol. 9, pp. 455–57.

34. Officer at Fort Mercer to John Hughes, 6 November 1777, *Naval Documents,* vol. 10, p. 421; Varnum to Washington, 6 November 1777, Ford, *Defences of Philadelphia,* pp. 86–88; Washington to Hazelwood, 25 October 1777, *Naval Documents,* vol. 10, p. 284; Washington to Hazelwood, 28 October 1777, *Naval Documents,* vol. 10, p. 333; Hazelwood to Wharton, 29 October 1777, *Naval Documents,* vol. 10, pp. 343–44; David to Brown, 11 November 1777, *Rhode Island Chaplain,* p. 64; Varnum to Washington, 8 November 1777, Ford, *Defences of Philadelphia,* pp. 434–35; Jonathan Rumford to Potter, 11 November 1777, *Naval Documents,* vol. 10, p. 468; John Laurens to Henry Laurens, 9 November 1777, *John Laurens's Correspondence,* p. 73; Washington to Varnum, 7 November 1777, *Washington Writings,* vol. 10, pp. 16–17; Washington to Henry Laurens, 11 November 1777, *Washington Writings,* vol. 10, p. 39; Adam Comstock to Washington, 27 October 1777, Ford, *Defences of Philadelphia,* pp. 59–60; Samuel Smith to Washington, 3 November 1777, Ford, *Defences of Philadelphia,* pp. 78–79.

35. Downman, *Services,* p. 46.

36. Ibid.; Sarah Fisher, "'A Diary of Trifling Occurrences': Philadelphia, 1776–1778," *Pennsylvania Magazine of History and Biography* 82 (1958): 454–55; Heinrich Carl Philipp von Feilitzsch, *Enemy Views,* pp. 231–33.

37. Peebles, 28 October 1777, *American War,* p. 146; William Cornwallis to Richard Howe, 30 October 1777, *Naval Documents,* vol. 10, p. 359; Richard Howe to William Cornwallis, 30 October 1777, *Naval Documents,* vol. 10, p. 360; William Cornwallis to Richard Howe, 31 October 1777, *Naval Documents,* vol. 10, pp. 363–64; Ambrose Serle, *The American Journal of Ambrose Serle, Secretary to Lord Howe, 1776–78,* ed. Edward Tatum (San Marino, Calif.: Huntington Library, 1940), pp. 261–63; Muenchhausen, 28 October–14 November 1777, *At Howe's Side,* pp. 42–43; Montresor, 24 October–5 November 1777, "Extracts," pp. 470–73.

38. Much of this description of the fort, as well as the quotation, is taken from Joseph Plumb Martin, *Private Yankee Doodle: Being a Narrative of Some of the Adventures, Dangers, and Sufferings of a Revolutionary Soldier,* ed. George Scheer (Boston: Little, Brown, 1962), pp. 85–94. Quotation is found on p. 85. See also De Fleury, 13–14 November 1777, Ford, *Defences of Philadelphia,* pp. 123–25.

39. Smith, "Smith's Papers," p. 90; Samuel Smith to Washington, 9 November 1777, Ford, *Defences of Philadelphia,* p. 105; Varnum to Washington, 10 November 1777, Ford, *Defences of Philadelphia,* pp. 110–11; Samuel Smith to Washington, 11 November 1777, Ford, *Defences of Philadelphia,* pp. 11–12; Varnum to Washington, 11 November 1777, Ford, *Defences of Philadelphia,* p. 116; Samuel Smith to Varnum, 11 November 1777, Ford, *Defences of Philadelphia,* p. 117; De Fleury to Washington, 12 November 1777, Ford, *Defences of Philadelphia,* p. 120; Samuel Smith to Washington, 12 November 1777, Ford, *Defences of Philadelphia,* pp. 121–22.

40. Henry Lee, *Memoirs of the War*, vol. 1, p. 41; Washington to Varnum, 12 November 1777, *Washington Writings*, vol. 10, pp. 48–50; Washington to Varnum, 13 November 1777, *Washington Writings*, vol. 10, pp. 58–60; Washington to Varnum, 15 November 1777, *Washington Writings*, vol. 10, pp. 68–70; Simeon Thayer to Varnum, 14 November 1777, Ford, *Defences of Philadelphia*, p. 127; Varnum to Washington, 14 November 1777, Ford, *Defences of Philadelphia*, p. 126.

41. Downman, *Services*, p. 50; James Parker, 15 November 1777, *Naval Documents*, vol. 10, pp. 500–501; Linzee, 15 November 1777, "Journal of HMS *Pearl*," *Naval Documents*, vol. 10, p. 507; Richard Howe to Philip Stephens, 23 November 1777, *Naval Documents*, vol. 10, pp. 583–88; Montresor, 10–15 November, "Extracts," pp. 474–77.

42. Hamond, *Naval Documents*, vol. 10, p. 1190.

43. Downman, *Services*, pp. 50–52; Henry, 15 November 1777, *Naval Documents*, vol. 10, p. 508; Richard Howe to Philip Stephens, 23 November 1777, *Naval Documents*, vol. 10, pp. 583–88; Muenchhausen, 14–26 November 1777, *At Howe's Side*, pp. 43–44; Anonymous, "Contemporary Account," p. 91; Montresor, 10–15 November, "Extracts," pp. 474–77.

44. Greenman, 15 November 1777, *Diary of a Common Soldier*, p. 86; De Fleury, 15 November 1777, *Naval Documents*, vol. 10, pp. 503–4; Martin, *Yankee Doodle*, pp. 90–92; Hazelwood to Wharton, *Naval Documents*, vol. 10, pp. 645–47.

45. David to Brown, 23 November 1777, *Rhode Island Chaplain*, pp. 67–69; De Fleury, 15 November 1777, *Naval Documents*, vol. 10, pp. 503–4; Hazelwood to Washington, 15 November 1777, *Naval Documents*, vol. 10, pp. 504–5; Varnum to Washington, 16 November 1777, *Naval Documents*, vol. 10, pp. 514–15.

46. Martin, *Yankee Doodle*, p. 92.

47. Ibid.; Varnum to Washington, 16 November 1777, *Naval Documents*, vol. 10, pp. 514–15.

48. Peebles, 22 November 1777, *American War*, p. 150.

49. The quotation is from Serle, *American Journals*, p. 264. For descriptions of the assault, see Downman, *Services*, pp. 50–52; Henry, 15 November 1777, *Naval Documents*, vol. 10, p. 508; Richard Howe to Philip Stephens, 23 November 1777, *Naval Documents*, vol. 10, pp. 583–88; Muenchhausen, 14–26 November 1777, *At Howe's Side*, pp. 43–44; Anonymous, "Contemporary Account," p. 91; Montresor, 10–15 November, "Extracts," pp. 474–77.

50. Peebles, 22 November 1777, *American War*, p. 150; John Andre, 20–30 November 1777, *Major Andre's Journal: Operations of the British Army Under Lieutenant Generals Sir William Howe and Sir Henry Clinton, June 1777 to November 1778* (Tarrytown, N.Y.: William Abbatt, 1930), pp. 65–67; Howe to Germain, 28 November 1777, *Naval Documents*, vol. 10, p. 625;

James Parker, 1 December 1777, *Naval Documents,* vol. 10, p. 645; JR, 12 November 1777, *Enemy Views,* p. 233.

51. However, in a 26 November 1777 letter to his brother, Washington claimed that once Fort Mifflin fell, he lost all hope of holding on to Fort Mercer, but his subsequent decisions contradict this. See Washington to John Augustine Washington, 26 November 1777, *Washington Writings,* vol. 10, pp. 112–14.

52. Washington to Nathanael Greene, 22 November 1777, *Greene Papers,* vol. 2, p. 205; John Heard to Washington, 18 November 1777, *A Salute to Courage: The American Revolution as Seen Through Wartime Writings of Officers of the Continental Army and Navy,* ed. Dennis Ryan (New York: Columbia University Press, 1979), pp. 109–10; Washington to Varnum, 19 November 1777, *Washington Writings,* vol. 10, pp. 85–86; Washington to Henry Laurens, 23 November 1777, *Washington Writings,* vol. 10, pp. 100–101; Clark to Washington, 18 November 1777, "Clark's Letters," p. 13; David to Brown, 23 November 1777, *Rhode Island Chaplain,* pp. 67–69; Washington to Henry Laurens, 17 November 1777, *Washington Writings,* vol. 10, pp. 73–77.

53. Varnum to Washington, 17 November 1777, *Naval Documents,* vol. 10, p. 521; Bradford to Wharton, 22 November 1777, *Naval Documents,* vol. 10, pp. 568–69; Hazelwood to Wharton, 1 December 1777, *Naval Documents,* vol. 10, pp. 645–47; Varnum to Washington, 19 November 1777, Ford, *Defences of Philadelphia,* pp. 153–54; Varnum to Washington, 20 November 1777, Ford, *Defences of Philadelphia,* pp. 156–57; Varnum to Washington, 21 November 1777, Ford, *Defences of Philadelphia,* pp. 157–58; Christopher Greene to Livingston, 23 November 1777, *Livingston Papers,* vol. 2, pp. 121–22.

54. Arthur St. Clair, Henry Knox, and Johann Kalb to Hazelwood, 18 November 1777, *Naval Documents,* vol. 10, p. 533; Washington to Hazelwood, 19 November 1777, *Naval Documents,* vol. 10, p. 542; Council of War Held on Board the Pennsylvania Navy Sloop *Speedwell,* 19 November 1777, *Naval Documents,* vol. 10, pp. 543–44; Bradford to Wharton, 22 November 1777, *Naval Documents,* vol. 10, pp. 568–69; Hazelwood to Wharton, 1 December 1777, *Naval Documents,* vol. 10, pp. 645–47; Morton, 21 November 1777, "Morton's Diary," pp. 29–30.

55. Nathanael Greene to Washington, 24 November 1777, *Greene Papers,* vol. 2, p. 209.

56. Nathanael Greene to Washington, 21 November 1777, *Greene Papers,* vol. 2, pp. 202–3; Nathanael Greene to Washington, 22 November 1777, *Greene Papers,* vol. 2, pp. 204–5; Joseph Ellis to Nathanael Greene, 24 November 1777, *Greene Papers,* vol. 2, p. 207; Nathanael Greene to Washington, 24 November 1777, *Greene Papers,* vol. 2, pp. 208–9; Washington to Nathanael Greene, 24 November 1777, *Greene Papers,* vol. 2, pp. 210–12.

57. Henry Stirke, 22–27 November 1777, "A British Officer's Revolutionary War Journal, 1776–1778," *Maryland Historical Magazine* 61 (1961): 175; Hesse-Cassel Jaeger Corps Journal, 25–26 November 1777, *Enemy Views*, p. 237.

58. The various generals' views on a proposed attack on Philadelphia are in Ford, *Defences of Philadelphia*, pp. 178–97. See also Clark to Washington, 22 November 1777, "Clark's Letters," pp. 15–16; Washington to Nathanael Greene, 25 November 1777, *Greene Papers*, vol. 2, p. 217; Nathanael Greene to Washington, 26 November 1777, *Greene Papers*, vol. 2, pp. 218–19; Washington to Nathanael Greene, Varnum, and Jedediah Huntington, 28 November 1777, *Greene Papers*, vol. 2, p. 224; Council of War, 8 November 1777, *Washington Writings*, vol. 10, pp. 23–24.

59. Howe, *Howe's Narrative*, p. 29.

60. Morton, 15 November 1777, "Morton's Diary," p. 28.

61. Downman, *Services*, pp. 51–52; Serle, 15–23 November 1777, *American Journal*, pp. 263–64.

CHAPTER 5. WINTER QUARTERS

1. Archibald Robertson, 3–8 December 1777, *Archibald Robertson: His Diaries and Sketches in America, 1762–1780,* ed. Harry Miller Lydenberg (New York: Arno Press, 1971), pp. 158–61; John Peebles, 1–8 December 1777, *John Peebles' American War: The Diary of a Scottish Grenadier, 1776–1782,* ed. Ira D. Gruber (Mechanicsburg, Pa.: Stackpole Books, 1998), pp. 153–55; Carl Leopold Baurmeister, 16 December 1777, *Revolution in America: Confidential Letters and Journals 1774–1784 of Adjutant General Major Baurmeister of the Hessian Forces,* trans. Bernhard A. Uhlendorf (New Brunswick, N.J.: Rutgers University Press, 1957), pp. 134–38; Friedrich von Muenchhausen, 3–6 December 1777, *At General Howe's Side, 1776–1778,* trans. Ernst Kipping (Monmouth Beach, N.J.: Philip Freneau Press, 1974), p. 45; Johann Ewald, 2–9 December 1777, *Diary of the American War: A Hessian Journal,* trans. and ed. Joseph P. Tustin (New Haven, Conn.: Yale University Press, 1979), pp. 108–10; Heinrich Carl Philipp von Feilitzsch, 4–8 December 1777, *Enemy Views: The American Revolutionary War as Recorded by the Hessian Participants,* ed. Bruce E. Burgoyne (Bowie, Md.: Heritage Books, 1996), pp. 239–40.

2. William Howe to Lord George Germain, 13 December 1777, Historical Manuscripts Commission, *Report on the Manuscripts of Mrs. Stopford-Sackville, of Drayton House, Northhamptonshire,* vol. 2 (Boston: Gregg Press, 1972), pp. 85–86; Howe to Henry Clinton, 12 December 1777, *Henry Clinton Papers,* CL, vol. 28, no. 25; Robertson, 3–8 December 1777, *His Diaries,* pp. 158–61; Peebles, 1–8 December 1777, *American War,* pp. 153–55; John Andre,

3–6 December 1777, *Major Andre's Journal: Operations of the British Army Under Lieutenant Generals Sir William Howe and Sir Henry Clinton, June 1777 to November 1778* (Tarrytown, N.Y.: William Abbatt, 1930), pp. 67–70; Muenchhausen, 7–8 December 1777, *At Howe's Side*, p. 45; Joseph Reed to Thomas Wharton, 10 December 1777, *Life and Correspondence of Joseph Reed,* vol. 1, ed. William Reed (Philadelphia: Lindsay and Blakiston, 1847), pp. 350–53; Ewald, 2–9 December 1777, *Hessian Journal*, pp. 108–10.

3. Benjamin Tallmadge, *Memoir of Col. Benjamin Tallmadge* (New York: Thomas Holman, 1858), p. 25; Henry Dearborn, 5–8 December 1777, *Revolutionary War Journals of Henry Dearborn, 1775–1783* (Freeport, N.Y.: Books for Libraries Press, 1969), pp. 115–17; Lewis Morris to his dad, 3 December 1777, "Letters of General Lewis Morris," *Collections of the New-York Historical Society,* 1875, p. 453; Joseph Plumb Martin, *Private Yankee Doodle: Being a Narrative of Some of the Adventures, Dangers, and Sufferings of a Revolutionary Solder,* ed. George Scheer (Boston: Little, Brown, 1962), pp. 75, 98–99; William Beatty, 1–5 December 1777, "Journal of Capt. William Beatty," *Maryland Historical Magazine* 3 (1907): 111; George Washington to Henry Laurens, 10 December 1777, *The Writings of George Washington,* vol. 10, ed. John Fitzpatrick (Washington, D.C.: Government Printing Office, 1933), pp. 142–45; John Laurens to Henry Laurens, 10 December 1777, *The Papers of Henry Laurens,* vol. 12 (Columbia: University of South Carolina Press, 1990), pp. 137–40.

4. William Howe, *Narrative of Lieut. Gen. Sir William Howe, in a Committee of the House of Commons* (London: H. Baldwin, 1781), pp. 30–31; Howe to Henry Clinton, 18 December 1777, *Clinton Papers, CL,* vol. 28, no. 40; Howe to Germain, 22 October 1777, *Stopford-Sackville Manuscripts,* vol. 2, pp. 78–79; Howe to Germain, 30 November 1777, *Stopford-Sackville Manuscripts,* vol. 2, pp. 80–81.

5. King George III to Frederick Lord North, 18 February 1778, *The Correspondence of King George the Third with Lord North from 1768 to 1783,* vol. 2, ed. W. Bodham Donne (London: John Murray, 1867), p. 136; North to King George III, January 1778, *The Correspondence of King George the Third from 1760 to December 1783,* vol. 4, ed. John Fortescue (London: Macmillan, 1928), p. 13; Germain to Howe, 11 December 1777, *Stopford-Sackville Manuscripts,* vol. 2, pp. 83–84; Germain to Howe, 4 February 1778, *Stopford-Sackville Manuscripts,* vol. 2, pp. 92–93.

6. Many of the generals' views on a winter campaign are in *Defences of Philadelphia in 1777,* ed. Worthington Chauncey Ford (New York: Da Capo Press, 1971), pp. 218–95. See also Nathanael Greene to Washington, December 1777, *The Papers of General Nathanael Greene,* vol. 2, ed. Richard K. Showman (Chapel Hill: University of North Carolina Press, 1980), pp. 225–36; Marquis de Lafayette, 3 December 1777, "Memorandum on a Winter Campaign," *Lafayette in the Age of the American Revolution, Selected Let-*

ters and Papers, 1776–1790, vol. 1, ed. Stanley J. Idzerda (Ithaca, N.Y.: Cornell University Press, 1979), pp. 173–76; Elbridge Gerry to John Adams, 3 December 1777, *Letters of Delegates to Congress, 1774–1789,* vol. 8, ed. Paul Smith (Washington, D.C.: Library of Congress, 1981), p. 373; Robert Morris' Committee Notes, 4 December 1777, *Letters of Delegates,* vol. 8, pp. 377–78; Committee at Headquarters to Washington, 10 December 1777, *Letters of Delegates,* vol. 8, pp. 399–400; James Lovell to Samuel Adams, 20 December 1777, *Letters of Delegates,* vol. 8, p. 451.

7. For the various views and opinions of Washington's generals on the subject, see Ford, *Defenses of Philadelphia,* pp. 218–44, 281–95; Nathanael Greene to Washington, December 1777, *Greene Papers,* vol. 2, pp. 225–28; Washington to Reed, 2 December 1777, *Washington Writings,* vol. 10, pp. 133–34. Later some of them apparently changed their minds. See *The Papers of George Washington: Revolutionary War Series,* vol. 12, ed. Philander Chase (Charlottesville: University Press of Virginia, 2002), p. 500n.

8. Washington, 17 December 1777, "General Orders," *Washington Writings,* vol. 10, pp. 167–68; Washington to Henry Laurens, 22 December 1777, *Washington Writings,* vol. 10, pp. 187–88; William Smallwood to Washington, 1 December 1777, Ford, *Defences of Philadelphia,* pp. 228–29.

9. Albigence Waldo, 11–14 December 1777, "Diary of Surgeon Albigence Waldo, of the Connecticut Line," *Pennsylvania Magazine of History and Biography* 21 (1897): 305–7.

10. John Laurens to Henry Laurens, 23 December 1777, *The Army Correspondence of Colonel John Laurens in the Years 1777–8* (New York: Bradford Club, 1867), pp. 95–97; Martin, *Yankee Doodle,* p. 99; Samuel Smith, *Memoirs of Samuel Smith: Soldier of the Revolution, 1776–1786* (New York: privately printed, 1860), pp. 11–12; Washington to Henry Laurens, 14 December 1777, *Washington Writings,* vol. 10, pp. 156–57; Ewald, 11 December 1777, *Hessian Journal,* p. 110.

11. E. Wayne Carp, *To Starve the Army at Pleasure: Continental Army Administration and American Political Culture, 1775–1783* (Chapel Hill: University of North Carolina Press, 1984), p. 55. This was more than enough food to feed Washington's army, but in all likelihood the faulty American logistical system led to a feast-or-famine situation for the troops.

12. For an analysis of American logistics, see Carp, *To Starve the Army.* See also Tallmadge, *Memoir,* p. 25; Washington to Board of War, 2–3 January 1778, *Washington Writings,* vol. 10, pp. 250–54; Nathanael Greene to Christopher Greene, 5 January 1778, *Greene Papers,* vol. 2, pp. 247–48; James Varnum to Nathanael Greene, 16 February 1778, *Greene Papers,* vol. 2, p. 280; Nathanael Greene to William Greene, 7 March 1778, *Greene Papers,* vol. 2, p. 301; John Laurens to Henry Laurens, 1 January 1778, *John Laurens's Correspondence,* p. 97; Waldo, 18–21 December 1777, "Waldo's Diary," pp. 308–9; John Sullivan to Washington, 24 January 1778, *Letters and Papers of*

Major-General John Sullivan, vol. 2, ed. Otis G. Hammond (Concord, N.H.: New Hampshire Historical Society, 1931), p. 17; Washington, 18 December 1777, "General Orders," *Washington Writings,* vol. 10, pp. 169–71; Washington, 25 December 1777, "General Orders," *Washington Writings,* vol. 10, pp. 205–6; Peter S. Duponceau, 13 June 1836, "Autobiographical Letters of Peter S. Duponceau," *Pennsylvania Magazine of History and Biography* 40 (1916): 180; Francis Dana to Gerry, 16 February 1778, *Letters of Delegates to Congress, 1774–1789,* vol. 9, ed. Paul Smith (Washington, D.C.: Library of Congress, 1982), pp. 108–9; Nathanael Greene to Jacob Greene, 3 January 1778, *Greene Papers,* vol. 2, p. 244; Alexander Hamilton to George Clinton, 13 February 1778, *The Papers of Alexander Hamilton,* vol. 1, ed. Harold Syrett (New York: Columbia University Press, 1961), p. 426; Washington to Henry Laurens, 23 December 1777, *Washington Writings,* vol. 10, pp. 192–98.

13. Washington to Henry Laurens, 22 December 1777, *Washington Writings,* vol. 10, 183.

14. Washington to James Mease, 16 May 1778, *The Writings of George Washington,* vol. 11, ed. John Fitzpatrick (Washington, D.C.: Government Printing Office, 1934), p. 398.

15. Nathanael Greene to Jacob Greene, 3 January 1778, *Greene Papers,* vol. 2, pp. 242–43; Washington to Israel Putnam, 6 February 1778, *Washington Writings,* vol. 10, p. 423; Washington to William Buchanan, 7 February 1778, *Washington Writings,* vol. 10, pp. 427–28; Washington to Mease, 17 April 1778, *Washington Writings,* vol. 10, pp. 269–70; Committee at Camp to Henry Laurens, 12 February 1778, *Letters of Delegates,* vol. 9, pp. 79–82; Washington to Henry Laurens, 23 December 1777, *Washington Writings,* vol. 10, pp. 192–98.

16. The quotation is from Nathanael Greene to Alexander McDougall, 25 January 1778, *Greene Papers,* vol. 2, p. 261. See also Washington to Nathanael Greene, 12 February 1778, *Greene Papers,* vol. 2, p. 281; Washington to Nathanael Greene, 16 February 1778, *Greene Papers,* vol. 2, pp. 287–88; Nathanael Greene to Washington, 17 February 1778, *Greene Papers,* vol. 2, pp. 288–90; Nathanael Greene to Henry Knox, 29 February 1778, *Greene Papers,* vol. 2, p. 293; John Laurens to Henry Laurens, 17 February 1778, *John Laurens's Correspondence,* pp. 126–28; Washington to Henry Laurens, 11 November 1777, *Washington Writings,* vol. 10, pp. 36–39; Washington to Board of War, 11 November 1777, *Washington Writings,* vol. 10, pp. 39–40; Washington, November 1777, "Powers to Officers Collecting Clothing, etc.," *Washington Writings,* vol. 10, pp. 124–25; "Washington to Officers Ordered to Remove Provisions from the Country Near the Enemy," December 1777, *Washington Writings,* vol. 10, pp. 162–63; Washington to Henry Champion, 7 February 1778, *Washington Writings,* vol. 10, pp. 425–26; Washington to Champion, 9 March 1778, *Washington Writings,* vol. 11, pp. 54–55.

17. Washington to William Woodford, 21 February 1778, *Washington*

Writings, vol. 10, pp. 490–91; Washington to Board of Artillery Officers, 2 March 1778, *Washington Writings,* vol. 11, pp. 15–18; Washington to George Weedon, 15 March 1778, *Washington Writings,* vol. 11, pp. 87–88; Washington to Peter Muhlenberg, 10 April 1778, *Washington Writings,* vol. 11, pp. 233–34; Washington to Sullivan, 14 February 1778, *Sullivan Papers,* vol. 2, p. 22; Varnum to Sullivan, 27 May 1778, *Sullivan Papers,* vol. 2, p. 60.

18. General Officers to Washington, 10 November 1777, *Greene Papers,* vol. 2, p. 193.

19. Although next spring Washington put the total number of resigning officers at 200 to 300. See Washington to Henry Laurens, 24 March 1778, *Washington Writings,* vol. 11, pp. 138–39.

20. Nathanael Greene to William Greene, 7 March 1778, *Greene Papers,* vol. 2, pp. 301–2; Washington to Gerry, 25 December 1777, *Washington Writings,* vol. 10, p. 201; Washington to Richard Caswell, 25 December 1777, *Washington Writings,* vol. 10, pp. 201–2; Washington, 16 May 1778, "General Orders," *Washington Writings,* vol. 11, p. 399; Washington to Samuel Parsons, 16 January 1778, *Washington Writings,* vol. 10, pp. 309–10; Washington, 18 May 1778, *Washington Writings,* vol. 11, pp. 412–13; Thomas Burke to Caswell, 9 April 1778, *Letters of Delegates,* vol. 9, pp. 394–95; Waldo, 25–29 December 1777, "Waldo's Diary," pp. 312–15.

21. Jonathan Dickinson Sergeant to Lovell, 20 November 1777, *Letters of Delegates,* vol. 8, p. 296.

22. For the classic and influencial reappraisal of the Conway Cabal, see Bernhard Knollenberg, *Washington and the Revolution: A Reappraisal: Gates, Conway, and the Continental Congress* (New York: Macmillan Company, 1941). See also Jonathan Gregory Rossie, *The Politics of Command in the American Revolution* (Syracuse, N.Y.: Syracuse University Press, 1975), pp. 174–202. For examples of discontent with Washington, see Benjamin Rush to John Adams, 1 October 1777, *Letters of Benjamin Rush,* vol. 1, ed. L. H. Butterfield (Princeton, N.J.: Princeton University Press, 1951), pp. 154–57; Charles Carroll of Carrollton to Charles Carroll Sr., 5 October 1777, *Letters of Delegates,* vol. 8, p. 50; Henry Laurens to John Laurens, 16 October 1777, *Letters of Delegates,* vol. 8, p. 125; Lovell to Joseph Whipple, 21 November 1777, *Letters of Delegates,* vol. 8, p. 302; Thomas McKean to George Read, 12 February 1778, *Letters of Delegates,* vol. 9, p. 85.

23. Rush to John Adams, 21 October 1777, *Rush Letters,* vol. 1, p. 160.

24. Alexander Graydon, *Memoirs of His Own Time with Reminiscences of the Men and Events of the Revolution,* ed. John Stockton Littell (Philadelphia: Lindsay and Blakiston, 1846), pp. 299–300; Samuel Adams to Samuel Savage, 26 October 1777, *Letters of Delegates,* vol. 8, p. 188.

25. Horatio Gates to James Wilkinson, 23 February 1778, *Horatio Gates Papers, 1726–1828,* reel 6 (Sanford, N.C.: Microfilming Corporation of America, 1978); Lord Alexander Stirling to Wilkinson, 6 January 1778, *Gates Pa-*

pers, reel 6; Wilkinson to Stirling, 4 February 1778, *Memoirs of My Own Times,* vol. 1 (New York: AMS Press, 1973), pp. 383–84; Wilkinson, 4 February 1778, *Memoirs of My Own Times,* vol. 1, p. 384; Washington to Thomas Conway, 9 November 1777, *Washington Writings,* vol. 10, p. 29; Abraham Clark to Stirling, 15 January 1778, *Letters of Delegates,* vol. 8, pp. 597–98; Stirling to Washington, August–September 1777, *The Papers of George Washington: Revolutionary War Series,* vol. 11, ed. Philander Chase and Edward Lengel (Charlottesville: University Press of Virginia, 2001), p. 105.

26. Washington to Richard Henry Lee, 17 October 1777, *The Writings of George Washington,* vol. 9, ed. John Fitzpatrick (Washington, D.C.: Government Printing Office, 1933), pp. 388.

27. John Adams to Nathanael Greene, 2 June 1777, *Greene Papers,* vol. 2, p. 103; Nathanael Greene to Jacob Greene, 3 January 1778, *Greene Papers,* vol. 2, pp. 243–44; John Laurens to Henry Laurens, 3 January 1778, *John Laurens's Correspondence,* pp. 102–4; Chevalier Dubuysson, "His Memoir," *Lafayette's Letters and Papers,* vol. 1, p. 79; Lafayette to Washington, 14 October 1777, *Lafayette's Letters and Papers,* vol. 1, p. 122; Graydon, *Memoirs of His Own Time,* p. 301 n; Washington to John Hancock, 9 May 1777, *The Papers of George Washington: Revolutionary War Series,* vol. 9, ed. Dorothy Twohig (Charlottesville: University Press of Virginia, 1999), p. 370; Sullivan to John Adams, 10 November 1777, *Letters and Papers of Major-General John Sullivan,* vol. 1, ed. Otis Hammond (Concord, N.H.: New Hampshire Historical Society, 1930), p. 577; Richard Henry Lee to Washington, 20 October 1777, *Letters of Delegates,* vol. 8, pp. 152–53.

28. Nathanael Greene to Susanna Livingston, 11 November 1777, *Greene Papers,* vol. 2, p. 195; John Clark to Nathanael Greene, 10 January 1778, *Greene Papers,* vol. 2, p. 250; Nathanael Greene to McDougall, 5 February 1778, *Greene Papers,* vol. 2, p. 275; John Laurens to Henry Laurens, 28 January 1778, *John Laurens's Correspondence,* p. 113; Lafayette to Adrienne de Noailles de Lafayette, 29 October 1778, *Lafayette's Letters and Papers,* vol. 1, p. 138; Protest of General Officers to Congress, 31 December 1777, *Sullivan Papers,* vol. 1, pp. 606–7; Richard Henry Lee to Washington, 20 October 1777, *Letters of Delegates,* vol. 8, pp. 152–53.

29. Nathanael Greene to Jacob Greene, 3 January 1778, *Greene Papers,* vol. 2, p. 243; Nathanael Greene to McDougall, 25 January 1778, *Greene Papers,* vol. 2, p. 260; Nathanael Greene to McDougall, 5 February 1778, *Greene Papers,* vol. 2, p. 275; McDougall to Nathanael Greene, 28 February 1778, *Greene Papers,* vol. 2, p. 295; Nathanael Greene to Jacob Greene, 3 January 1778, *Greene Papers,* vol. 2, p. 243; John Laurens to Henry Laurens, 3 January 1778, *John Laurens's Correspondence,* pp. 102–4; Lafayette, "Memoir of 1779," *Lafayette's Letters and Papers,* vol. 1, pp. 171–72; Hamilton to George Clinton, 13 February 1778, *Hamilton Papers,* vol. 1, p. 428; Washington to Thomas Nelson, 8 February 1778, *Washington Writings,* vol. 10, p. 432;

Washington to Patrick Henry, 28 March 1778, *Washington Writings*, vol. 11, pp. 164–65; Tench Tilghman to John Cadwalader, 18 January 1778, "Selections from the Military Papers of General John Cadwalader," *Pennsylvania Magazine of History and Biography* 32 (1908): 168–69.

30. Abraham Clark to Stirling, 15 January 1778, *Letters of Delegates*, vol. 8, pp. 597–98; Gerry to Washington, 13 January 1778, *Letters of Delegates*, vol. 8, p. 576; Nathaniel Folsom to Josiah Bartlet, 2 January 1778, *Letters of Delegates*, vol. 8, p. 517; Eliphalet Dyer to Joseph Trumbull, 15 December 1777, *Letters of Delegates*, vol. 8, p. 414; Henry Laurens to John Rutledge, 1 December 1777, *Letters of Delegates*, vol. 8, pp. 358–59; William Williams to Joseph Trumbull, 28 November 1777, *Letters of Delegates*, vol. 8, p. 343; Henry Laurens to Gates, 28 November 1777, *Letters of Delegates*, vol. 8, pp. 335–36; Dyer to Joseph Trumbull, 28 November 1777, *Letters of Delegates*, vol. 8, pp. 332–33; James Duane to Philip Schuyler, 22 November 1777, *Letters of Delegates*, vol. 8, p. 304; Richard Henry Lee to Washington, 20 November 1777, *Letters of Delegates*, vol. 8, p. 293; Richard Henry Lee to Washington, 20 October 1777, *Letters of Delegates*, vol. 8, pp. 152–53.

31. Henry Laurens to Lafayette, 12 January 1778, *Lafayette's Letters and Papers*, vol. 1, pp. 231–32.

32. Conway's letter is quoted in John Fitzgerald to Washington, 16 February 1778, *Washington Writings*, vol. 10, pp. 528–29n. See also Henry Laurens to Lafayette, 12 January 1778, *Lafayette's Letters and Papers*, vol. 1, pp. 231–32; John Laurens to Henry Laurens, 28 January 1778, *John Laurens's Correspondence*, p. 113; John Laurens to Henry Laurens, 9 June 1778, *John Laurens's Correspondence*, p. 180; Henry Laurens to Lafayette, 6 December 1777, *Lafayette's Letters and Papers*, vol. 1, p. 178; Lafayette to Henry Laurens, 26 January 1778, *Lafayette's Letters and Papers*, vol. 1, p. 254; Henry Laurens to Benjamin Huger, 15 November 1777, *Correspondence of Henry Laurens of South Carolina* (New York: privately printed for the Zenger Club, 1861), p. 63; Washington to Henry Laurens, 10 November 1777, *Washington Writings*, vol. 10, p. 33; Washington to Henry Laurens, 31 January 1778, *Washington Writings*, vol. 10, pp. 410–11; Henry Laurens to John Laurens, 16 October 1777, *Letters of Delegates*, vol. 8, p. 125; Henry Laurens to Congress, 12 December 1777, *Letters of Delegates*, vol. 8, p. 408; Henry Laurens to Jonathan Trumbull, 23 December 1777, *Letters of Delegates*, vol. 8, pp. 465–66; Henry Laurens to John Laurens, 8 January 1777, *Letters of Delegates*, vol. 8, pp. 545–49; Henry Laurens to Lafayette, 28 January 1778, *Letters of Delegates*, vol. 8, p. 677; Henry Laurens to John Laurens, 3 February 1778, *Letters of Delegates*, vol. 9, p. 18; Henry Laurens to Lafayette, 24 March 1778, *Letters of Delegates*, vol. 9, pp. 330–32.

33. Gates to Washington, 19 February 1778, *Gates Papers*, reel 6.

34. The quotation is from Washington to Fitzgerald, 28 February 1778, *Washington Writings*, vol. 10, pp. 528–29. See also Gates to Washington, 19

February 1778, *Gates Papers,* reel 6; Thomas Mifflin to Gates, 28 November 1777, *Memoirs of My Own Times,* vol. 1, p. 374; Gates to Washington, 23 January 1778, *Gates Papers,* reel 6; Gates to Wilkinson, 23 February 1778, *Gates Papers,* reel 6; Gates to Conway, 3 December 1777, *Gates Papers,* reel 6; Gates to Mifflin, 4 December 1777, *Gates Papers,* reel 6; Wilkinson, *Memoirs of My Own Times,* vol. 1, pp. 372–73; Washington to Gates, 4 January 1778, *Washington Writings,* vol. 10, pp. 263–65; Washington to Gates, 9 February 1778, *Washington Writings,* vol. 10, pp. 437–41; Washington to Gates, 24 February 1778, *Washington Writings,* vol. 10, pp. 508–9; Henry Laurens to John Laurens, 3 February 1778, *Letters of Delegates,* vol. 9, p. 18; George Lux to Nathanael Greene, 28 April 1778, *Greene Papers,* vol. 2, p. 367.

35. Nathanael Greene to Jacob Greene, 3 January 1778, *Greene Papers,* vol. 2, p. 243; John Clark to Nathanael Greene, 10 January 1778, *Greene Papers,* vol. 2, pp. 249–50; John Laurens to Henry Laurens, 1 January 1778, *John Laurens's Correspondence,* pp. 100–101; Henry Laurens to Lafayette, 5 June 1778, *Lafayette's Letters and Papers,* vol. 1, pp. 69–70; Gates to Henry Laurens, 27 May 1778, *Henry Laurens's Correspondence,* p. 111; Conway to Gates, 18 (?) November 1777, *Gates Papers,* reel 6; Conway to Gates, 4 January 1778, *Gates Papers,* reel 6; Washington to Conway, 16 November 1777, *Washington Writings,* vol. 10, pp. 71–72; Washington to Conway, 30 December 1777, *Washington Writings,* vol. 10, pp. 226–28; Washington to Henry Laurens, 2 January 1778, *Washington Writings,* vol. 10, pp. 249–50; Washington to Gouverneur Morris, 18 May 1778, *Washington Writings,* vol. 11, p. 414; Henry Laurens to John Laurens, 28 January 1778, *Letters of Delegates,* vol. 8, p. 678; Henry Laurens to Washington, 28 April 1778, *Letters of Delegates,* vol. 9, p. 516; Henry Laurens to Rutledge, 3 June 1778, *Letters of Delegates to Congress, 1774–1789,* vol. 10, ed. Paul Smith (Washington, D.C.: Library of Congress, 1983), p. 19; Conway to Washington, 5 November 1777, George Washington Papers at the Library of Congress, *http://memory. loc.gov/ammem/gwhtml/;* Conway to Washington, 10 January 1778, George Washington Papers at the Library of Congress; Conway to Washington, 27 January 1778, George Washington Papers at the Library of Congress; Conway to Washington, 23 July 1778, George Washington Papers at the Library of Congress; King George III to North, 6 March 1778, *George III and Lord North's Correspondence,* vol. 2, p. 143.

36. Wilkinson to Stirling, 4 February 1778, *Memoirs of My Own Times,* vol. 1, pp. 383–84.

37. Abraham Clark to Stirling, 15 January 1778, *Letters of Delegates,* vol. 8, pp. 597–98.

38. Wilkinson to Gates, 22 February 1778, *Memoirs of My Own Times,* vol. 1, p. 385.

39. John Clark to Nathanael Greene, 10 January 1778, *Greene Papers,* vol. 2, pp. 249–50; Conway, 3 January 1778, *Sullivan Papers,* vol. 2, pp. 1–2; Sul-

livan to Henry Laurens, 20 January 1778, *Sullivan Papers,* vol. 2, pp. 14–16; Gates to Wilkinson, 28 February 1778, *Gates Papers,* reel 6; Conway to Gates, 4 January 1778, *Gates Papers,* reel 6; Lord Alexander to Wilkinson, 6 January 1778, *Gates Papers,* reel 6; Wilkinson, *Memoirs of My Own Times,* vol. 1, pp. 339–40, 372–73, 384–85, 388–95; Wilkinson to Stirling, 4 February 1778, *Memoirs of My Own Times,* vol. 1, pp. 383–84; Washington to Stirling, 21 March 1778, *Washington Writings,* vol. 11, p. 125.

40. Nathanael Greene to Smallwood, *Greene Papers,* vol. 2, p. 316.

41. The quotation is from Washington to Landon Carter, 30 May 1778, *Washington Writings,* vol. 11, pp. 493–94. See also Hamilton to George Clinton, 13 February 1778, *Hamilton Papers,* vol. 1, p. 428; Washington to Nelson, 8 February 1778, *Washington Writings,* vol. 10, p. 432; Washington to Fitzgerald, 28 February 1778, *Washington Writings,* vol. 10, pp. 528–29; Henry Laurens to John Laurens, 3 February 1778, *Letters of Delegates,* vol. 9, p. 18; Dyer to Williams, 10 March 1778, *Letters of Delegates,* vol. 9, p. 257; Timothy Pickering to Alexander Scammell, 7 February 1778, *The Life of Timothy Pickering,* vol. 1, ed. Octavius Pickering (Boston: Little, Brown, 1867), pp. 206–7.

42. James Murray to Elizabeth Smyth, 29 November 1777 and 5 March 1778, *Letters from America, 1773 to 1780: Being the Letters of a Scots Officer, Sir James Murray, to His Home During the War of American Independence,* ed. Eric Robson (Manchester: Manchester University Press, 1951), pp. 50–54; Peebles, 17 December 1777–17 March 1778, *American War,* pp. 161–71; Johann Heinrichs, "Extracts from the Letter-Book of Captain Johann Heinrichs of the Hessian Jager Corps, 1778–1780," *Pennsylvania Magazine of History and Biography* 22 (1898): 139–40; Johann Conrad Dohla, 21 November 1777, *A Hessian Diary of the American Revolution,* ed. and trans. Bruce E. Burgoyne (Norman: University of Oklahoma Press, 1990), pp. 65–68; Muenchhausen, 21 January 1778, *At Howe's Side,* p. 47; Ewald, 16 February 1778, *Hessian Journal,* pp. 119–20; Stephen Kemble, 29 March 1778, *Journals of Lieut.-Col. Stephen Kemble, 1773–1789; and British Army Orders: Gen. Sir William Howe, 1775–1778; Gen. Sir Henry Clinton, 1778; and Gen. Daniel Jones, 1778* (Boston: Gregg Press, 1972), p. 561; Andrew Hamond, "Autobiography of Sir Andrew S. Hamond," *Naval Documents of the American Revolution,* vol. 10, ed. Michael Crawford (Washington, D.C.: Naval Historical Center, Department of the Navy, 1996), p. 1191; Howe to Germain, 19 January 1778, *Documents of the American Revolution,* vol. 13, ed. K. G. Davies (Dublin: Irish University Press, 1976), p. 227; State of Troops in North America Under Sir William Howe, 20 January 1778, *Documents,* vol. 13, p. 253; William John Hale, 20 January 1778, *Some British Soldiers in America,* ed. W. H. Wilkin (London: Hugh Rees, 1914), pp. 234–42.

43. Peebles, 23 March–1 May 1778, *American War,* pp. 171–77; John Charles Philip von Krafft, 5–17 April 1778, *Von Krafft's Journal* (New York:

New-York Historical Society, 1882), pp. 32–34; Ewald, 16 February 1778, *Hessian Journal,* pp. 119–20; Hale, 20 January 1778, *Some British Soldiers,* pp. 234–42.

44. The quotation is from Muenchhausen, 25 March 1778, *At Howe's Side,* p. 49. See also An Account of the Number of Deserted Soldiers, Galleymen, etc., 25 March 1778, *George Germain Papers,* CL, vol. 7; Peter Dubois, 18 December 1777, *Clinton Papers,* CL, vol. 28, no. 39; Howe to Henry Clinton, 5 March 1777, *Clinton Papers,* CL, vol. 31, no. 42; Simeon Vanartsdalen to John Bogart, 6 December 1777, *The John Bogart Letters* (New Brunswick, N.J.: Rutgers College, 1914), p. 14; Francis Downman, *The Services of Lieut. Colonel Francis Downman, R.A. in France, North America, and the West Indies, Between the Years 1758 and 1784,* ed. F. A. Whinyates (Woolwich: Royal Artillery Institution, 1898), p. 53; Dohla, 21 November 1777, *Hessian Diary,* pp. 65–68; Muenchhausen, 23 December 1777–24 March 1778, *At Howe's Side,* pp. 46–49; Germain to King George III, 8 May 1778, *King George III's Correspondence,* vol. 4, p. 137; Howe, *Howe's Narrative,* p. 30; Charles Grey, *Howe's Narrative,* p. 106; Howe to Germain, 19 April 1778, *Stopford-Sackville Manuscripts,* vol. 2, p. 107; Hesse-Cassel Jaeger Corps Journal, 30 December 1777, *Enemy Views,* pp. 243–44; Howe to Germain, 5 March 1777, *Documents of the American Revolution,* vol. 15, ed. K. G. Davies (Dublin: Irish University Press, 1976), pp. 52–54.

45. King George III to North, 18 February 1778, *George III and Lord North's Correspondence,* vol. 2, p. 136; King George III to North, 13 January 1778, *George III and Lord North's Correspondence,* vol. 2, p. 119; Howe to Germain, 19 April 1778, *Stopford-Sackville Manuscripts,* vol. 2, pp. 107–8; Howe to Germain, 16 January 1778, *Documents,* vol. 15, p. 29; Germain to Howe, 18 February 1778, *Stopford-Sackville Manuscripts,* vol. 2, pp. 93–94; Germain to William Knox, Historical Manuscripts Commission, *Report on Manuscripts in Various Collections,* vol. 6 (Dublin: John Falconer, 1909), p. 143; Minute of Cabinet, 17 January 1778, *King George III's Correspondence,* vol. 4, pp. 20–21.

46. For an overall explanation of British occupation, see Frederick Bernays Weiner, "The Military Occupation of Philadelphia, in 1777–1778," *Proceedings of the American Philosophpical Society* 111 (1967): 310–13. See also Peebles, 17 December 1777 and 4 February 1778, *American War,* pp. 155, 163; Account of Prohibited Goods Imported into Philadelphia, 27 May 1777, *Clinton Papers,* CL, vol. 35, no. 14; A State of the Circumstances of Philadelphia, December 1777, *Germain Papers,* CL, vol. 6; Heinrichs, 18 January 1778, "Heinrichs' Extracts," pp. 139–40; Baurmeister, 20 January 1778, *Letters and Journals,* p. 150; Ambrose Serle, 24 November 1777, *The American Journal of Ambrose Serle, Secretary to Lord Howe, 1776–78,* ed. Edward H. Tatum (San Marino, Calif.: Huntington Library, 1940), p. 265; John Montresor, 28 March 1778, "Extracts from the Journals and Note-Books of Capt. John Montresor,"

Collections of the New-York Historical Society, 1881, p. 483; Ewald, *Hessian Journal,* pp. 117–18; Robert Morton, 22 November 1777, "The Diary of Robert Morton," *Pennsylvania Magazine of History and Biography* 1 (1877): 30; Hale, 20 January 1778, *Some British Soldiers,* pp. 234–42; John Simcoe, *Simcoe's Military Journal: A History of the Operations of a Partisan Corps, Called the Queen's Rangers Commanded by Lieut. Col. J. G. Simcoe, During the War of the American Revolution* (New York: Bartlett and Welford, 1844), pp. 36–37.

47. John McCasland, *The Revolution Remembered: Eyewitness Accounts of the War for American Independence,* ed. John Dann (Chicago: University of Chicago Press, 1980), p. 156; Francis Murray to Washington, 13 February 1778, *A Salute to Courage: The American Revolution as Seen Through Wartime Writings of Officers of the Continental Army and Navy,* ed. Dennis Ryan (New York: Columbia University Press, 1979), p. 119; Washington to James Potter, 21 December 1777, *Washington Writings,* vol. 10, p. 182; Washington to John Jameson, 24 December 1777, *Washington Writings,* vol. 10, p. 199; Washington to John Armstrong, 28 December 1777, *Washington Writings,* vol. 10, pp. 215–16; Washington to Wharton, 1 January 1778, *Washington Writings,* vol. 10, p. 246; Washington to William Stewart, 22 January 1778, *Washington Writings,* vol. 10, pp. 336–37; Washington to John Lacey, 23 January 1778, *Washington Writings,* vol. 10, pp. 340–41; Washington to Jameson, 1 February 1778, *Washington Writings,* vol. 10, pp. 412–13; Washington to Wharton, 12 February 1778, *Washington Writings,* vol. 10, pp. 452–53; Instructions to Captain Stephen Chambers, 27 February 1778, *Washington Writings,* vol. 10, pp. 522–23; Washington to Armstrong, 27 March 1778, *Washington Writings,* vol. 11, p. 159; Armstrong to Wharton, 30 December 1777, "Letters of General John Armstrong to Thomas Wharton, President of Pennsylvania, 1777," *Pennsylvania Magazine of History and Biography* 38 (1914): 208–9; Committee at Camp to Henry Laurens, 20 February 1778, *Letters of Delegates,* vol. 9, p. 144; Washington to Lacey, 11 May 1778, *Washington Writings,* vol. 11, p. 374; John Clark to Washington, 30 December 1777, "Letters from Major John Clark, Jr., to Gen. Washington," *Bulletin of the Historical Society of Pennsylvania* 1 (1845–47): 34.

48. For a biography of Steuben, see John M. Palmer, *General Von Steuben* (Port Washington, N.Y.: Kennikat Press, 1966). See also John Laurens to Henry Laurens, 28 February 1778, *John Laurens's Correspondence,* pp. 131–33; John Laurens to Henry Laurens, 9 March 1778, *John Laurens's Correspondence,* pp. 137–38; Hamilton to William Duer, 18 June 1778, *Hamilton Papers,* vol. 1, pp. 497–99; Lewis L'estarjette to Henry Laurens, 5 September 1777, *Steuben Papers,* Kraus-Thomson Organization Limited, roll 1; Baron von Steuben, 6 December 1777, *Steuben Papers;* Henry Beekman Livingston to Robert Livingston, 25 March 1778, *Steuben Papers;* Washington to Henry Laurens, 27 February 1778, *Washington Writings,* vol. 10, p. 519; Washington, 28 March

1778, "General Orders," *Washington Writings*, vol. 11, p. 163; Benjamin Franklin to Washington, 4 September 1777, *The Papers of Benjamin Franklin*, vol. 24, ed. William Willcox (New Haven, Conn.: Yale University Press, 1984), pp. 499–500.

49. Washington to Henry Laurens, 30 April 1778, *Washington Writings*, vol. 11, pp. 328–31; Washington, 4 May 1778, "General Orders," *Washington Writings*, vol. 11, pp. 346–47; Washington to Brigadiers and Officers Commanding Brigades, 19 March 1778, *Washington Writings*, vol. 11, p. 108.

50. John Laurens to Henry Laurens, 28 February 1778, *John Laurens's Correspondence*, pp. 131–33; John Laurens to Henry Laurens, 25 March 1778, *John Laurens's Correspondence*, p. 147; Martin, *Yankee Doodle*, p. 118; George Ewing, *The Military Journal of George Ewing (1754–1824): A Soldier of Valley Forge* (Yonkers, N.Y.: privately printed by Thomas Ewing, 1928), p. 34; Lafayette to Lazare-Jean Theveneau de Francy, 10 April 1778, *Lafayette in the Age of the American Revolution: Selected Letters and Papers, 1776–1790*, vol. 2, ed. Stanley J. Idzerda (Ithaca, N.Y.: Cornell University Press, 1979), p. 21; Lafayette to Henry Laurens, 14 April 1778, *Lafayette's Letters and Papers*, vol. 2, p. 26; Scammell to Sullivan, 8 April 1778, *Sullivan Papers*, vol. 2, pp. 32–33; Henry Beekman Livingston to Robert Livingston, 25 March 1778, *Steuben Papers*; Steuben to the Continental Congress, 27 May 1778, *Steuben Papers*; William Fleury, *The Fate of a Nation: The American Revolution Through Contemporary Eyes*, ed. William P. Cumming and Hugh Rankin (London: Phaidon Press, 1975), p. 201; Peter du Ponceau, *Fate of a Nation*, p. 201.

51. Richard Peters to Pickering, 9 June 1778, *Steuben Papers*.

52. John Laurens to Henry Laurens, 1 April 1778, *John Laurens's Correspondence*, p. 152; Hamilton to Duer, 18 June 1778, *Hamilton Papers*, vol. 1, pp. 497–99; Scammell to Sullivan, 8 April 1778, *Sullivan Papers*, vol. 2, pp. 32–33; Conway to Gates, 21 April 1778, *Steuben Papers*; Scammell to Pickering, 21 April 1778, *Steuben Papers*; Jacob Morgan to George Bryan, 30 May 1778, *Steuben Papers*; Duponceau, 3 June 1836, "Duponceau's Letters," p. 178; Henry Laurens to Steuben, 5 May 1778, *Letters of Delegates*, vol. 9, p. 605.

53. Nathanael Greene to William Greene, 7 March 1778, *Greene Papers*, vol. 2, p. 301; Dana (by order of the Committee of Conference) to Henry Laurens, 25 February 1778, *Steuben Papers*; Washington to Gerry, 25 December 1777, *Washington Writings*, vol. 10, pp. 200–201; Washington to Henry Laurens, 1 January 1778, *Washington Writings*, vol. 10, pp. 243–45; Washington to Committee of Congress with the Army, 29 January 1778, *Washington Writings*, vol. 10, pp. 362–94; Daniel Roberdeau to Wharton, 26 December 1777, *Letters of Delegates*, vol. 8, p. 482; Committee on Emergency Provisions to Wharton, 30 December 1777, *Letters of Delegates*, vol. 8, p. 499; Committee on Emergency Provisions to Thomas Johnson, 31 December 1777, *Letters of Delegates*, vol. 8, pp. 507–8; Henry Laurens to Nicholas Cooke, 3 January

1778, *Letters of Delegates,* vol. 8, p. 520; Henry Laurens to Jonathan Trumbull, 3 January 1778, *Letters of Delegates,* vol. 8, p. 524; Reed to Henry Laurens, 12 February 1778, *Reed's Life,* vol. 1, pp. 360–63; Committee at Camp to Henry Laurens, 6 February 1778, *Letters of Delegates,* vol. 9, pp. 36–38; Committee at Camp to Henry Laurens, 25 February 1778, *Letters of Delegates,* vol. 9, pp. 168–74.

54. Nathanael Greene to Knox, 26 February 1778, *Greene Papers,* vol. 2, p. 294; Nathanael Greene to Weedon, 7 March 1778, *Greene Papers,* vol. 2, pp. 304–5; Dana (by order of the Committee of Conference) to Henry Laurens, 25 February 1778, *Steuben Papers;* Washington to Henry Laurens, 1 January 1778, *Washington Writings,* vol. 10, pp. 243–45; Washington to Henry, 19 April 1778, *Washington Writings,* vol. 11, pp. 278–79; Committee at Camp to Henry Laurens, 28 January 1778, *Letters of Delegates,* vol. 8, p. 676; Committee at Camp to Henry Laurens, 29 January 1778, *Letters of Delegates,* vol. 8, p. 680; Dana to Gerry, 29 January 1778, *Letters of Delegates,* vol. 8, p. 681; Committee at Camp to Henry Laurens, 12 February 1778, *Letters of Delegates,* vol. 9, pp. 79–82; Reed to Jonathan Bayard Smith, 13 February 1778, *Letters of Delegates,* vol. 9, pp. 92–93; Duer to Francis Lightfoot Lee, 14 February 1778, *Letters of Delegates,* vol. 9, pp. 97–98; Committee at Camp to Henry Laurens, 25 February 1778, *Letters of Delegates,* vol. 9, pp. 168–74; Reed to Jonathan Bayard Smith, 19 February 1778, *Letters of Delegates,* vol. 9, p. 141; Jonathan Bayard Smith to Reed, 25 February 1778, *Letters of Delegates,* vol. 9, pp. 176–77.

55. Nathanael Greene to the Inhabitants of the United States, 28 March 1778, *Greene Papers,* vol. 2, p. 324; Nathanael Greene to Clement Biddle, 30 March 1778, *Greene Papers,* vol. 2, p. 327; Nathanael Greene to Charles Pettit, 11 April 1778, *Greene Papers,* vol. 2, p. 335; Nathanael Greene, to John Davis, 29 April 1778, *Greene Papers,* vol. 2, p. 369; Washington to Johnson, 21 March 1778, *Washington Writings,* vol. 11, pp. 123–24; Washington to Thomas Wheaton, 11 May 1778, *Washington Writings,* vol. 11, pp. 369–70.

CHAPTER 6. A BRAND-NEW WAR

1. For an analysis of American foreign policy during the war, see Jonathan R. Dull, *A Diplomatic History of the American Revolution* (New Haven, Conn.: Yale University Press, 1985).

2. The best explanation for British strategic thinking in 1777–78 is Piers Mackesy, *The War for America, 1775–1783* (Lincoln: University of Nebraska Press, 1964), pp. 180–89. See also Lord George Germain to Henry Clinton, 8 March 1778, Historical Manuscripts Commission, *Report on the Manuscripts of Mrs. Stopford-Sackville, of Drayton House, Northhamptionshire,* vol. 2 (Boston: Gregg Press, 1972), pp. 96–99; Germain to Lords of Admiralty, 8

March 1778, *Documents of the American Revolution,* vol. 15, ed. K. G. Davies (Dublin: Irish University Press, 1976), p. 57.

3. King George III to Lord Frederick North, 4 December 1777, *The Correspondence of King George the Third with Lord North from 1768 to 1783,* vol. 2, ed. W. Bodham Donne (London: John Murray, 1867), p. 92; Henry Clinton, *The American Rebellion: Sir Henry Clinton's Narrative of His Campaigns, 1775–1782,* ed. William Willcox (Hamden, Conn.: Archon Books, 1971), pp. 86–87; North to King George III, 20 March 1778, *The Correspondence of King George the Third from 1760 to December 1783,* vol. 3, ed. John Fortescue (London: Macmillan, 1928), p. 431; Minute of Cabinet, 17 January 1778, *The Correspondence of King George the Third from 1760 to December 1783,* vol. 4, ed. John Fortescue (London: Macmillan, 1928), pp. 20–21; King George III to North, 3 March 1778, *King George III's Correspondence,* vol. 4, p. 46; Germain to Henry Clinton, 8 March 1778, *Stopford-Sackville Manuscripts,* vol. 2, pp. 95–99; Germain to Lords of Admiralty, 8 March 1778, *Documents,* vol. 15, p. 57; Memorial of Lord William Campbell and Others to Germain, August 1777, *Documents of the American Revolution,* vol. 14, ed. K. G. Davies (Dublin: Irish University Press, 1976), pp. 182–84.

4. King George III to North, 3 February 1778, *George III and Lord North's Correspondence,* vol. 2, p. 131; Germain to Henry Clinton, 21 March 1778, *Documents,* vol. 15, pp. 73–74. Lord North was an exception. See North to King George III, 20 March 1778, *King George III's Correspondence,* vol. 3, p. 431.

5. Secret Instructions for General Sir Henry Clinton, 21 March 1778, *Documents,* vol. 15, pp. 74–76; State of the Rank and File Fit for Duty, 20 May 1778, *Henry Clinton Papers,* CL, vol. 35, no. 1; Germain to Henry Clinton, 4 May 1778, *Documents,* vol. 15, pp. 114–15; King George III to North, 31 January 1778, *George III and Lord North's Correspondence,* vol. 2, p. 126; King George III to North, 9 February 1778, *George III and Lord North's Correspondence,* vol. 2, p. 133; King George III to North, 23 March 1778, *George III and Lord North's Correspondence,* vol. 2, p. 148; King George III to North, 17 March 1778, *George III and Lord North's Correspondence,* vol. 2, pp. 152–53; Henry Clinton, *American Rebellion,* pp. 86–87; King George III to North, 3 March 1778, *King George III's Correspondence,* vol. 4, p. 46.

6. King George III to North, 31 January 1778, *George III and Lord North's Correspondence,* vol. 2, pp. 125–26; North to the Duke of Newcastle, 3 March 1778, *Clinton Papers,* CL, vol. 31, no. 36; Draft Bill Read in the House of Commons, 19 February 1778, *Clinton Papers,* CL, vol. 31, no. 20; Carl Leopold Baurmeister, 18 April 1778, *Revolution in America: Confidential Letters and Journals 1774–1784 of Adjutant General Major Baurmeister of the Hessian Forces,* trans. Bernhard Uhlendorf (New Brunswick, N.J.: Rutgers University Press, 1957), p. 163; Friedrich von Muenchhausen, 19 April 1778, *At General Howe's Side, 1776–1778,* trans. Ernst Kipping (Monmouth Beach,

N.J.: Philip Freneau Press, 1974), p. 51; King George III to North, February 1778, *King George III's Correspondence*, vol. 4, p. 35; Lord Frederick Carlisle to Reverend Elkins, October 1778, Historical Manuscripts Commission, *The Manuscripts of the Earl of Carlisle, 15th Report, Appendix, Part VI* (London: Eyre and Spottiswoode, 1897), pp. 377–79; Germain to Henry Clinton, 8 March 1778, *Stopford-Sackville Manuscripts*, vol. 2, pp. 94–95; Germain to William Knox, 23 July 1778, Historical Manuscripts Division, *Report on Manuscripts in Various Collections*, vol. 6 (Dublin: John Falconer, 1909), p. 144.

7. The quotation is from Ambrose Serle, 18 May 1778, *The American Journal of Ambrose Serle, Secretary to Lord Howe, 1776–78,* ed. Edward H. Tatum (San Marino, Calif.: Huntington Library, 1940), pp. 293–94. See also Francis Downman, *The Services of Lieut. Colonel Francis Downman, R.A. in France, North America, and the West Indies, Between the Years 1758 and 1784,* ed. F. A. Whinyates (Woolwich: Royal Artillery Institution, 1898), p. 60; John Peebles, 18 May 1778, *John Peebles' American War: The Diary of a Scottish Grenadier, 1776–1782,* ed. Ira D. Gruber (Mechanicsburg, Pa.: Stackpole Books, 1998), pp. 181–83; Baurmeister, 18 May–21 June 1778, *Baurmeister's Letters and Journals,* pp. 177–78; Muenchhausen, 15–18 May 1778, *At Howe's Side,* p. 52; John Andre, "Major Andre's Story of the 'Mischianza,'" *Century Magazine,* n.s., 25 (1894): 687–88; Johann Ernst Prechtel, 18 May 1778, *Enemy Views: The American Revolutionary War as Recorded by the Hessian Participants,* ed. Bruce E. Burgoyne (Bowie, Md.: Heritage Books, 1996), pp. 255–56; John Montresor, 24 May 1778, "Extracts from the Journals and Note-Books of Capt. John Montresor," *Collections of the New-York Historical Society,* 1881, p. 493; William John Hale, 20 April 1778, *Some British Soldiers in America,* ed. W. H. Wilkin (London: Hugh Rees, 1914), p. 250.

8. Baurmeister, 18 May–21 June 1778, *Baurmeister's Letters and Journals,* p. 174; Serle, 24 April 1778, *American Journal,* p. 287; Muenchhausen, 4–5 April 1778, *At Howe's Side,* p. 50; Montresor, 7 May 1778, "Extracts," p. 490; John Simcoe, *Simcoe's Military Journal: A History of the Operations of a Partisan Corps, Called the Queen's Rangers Commanded by Lieut. Col. J. G. Simcoe, During the War of the American Revolution* (New York: Bartlett and Welford, 1844), p. 54; Hesse-Cassel Jaeger Corps Journal, 1 April–7 May 1778, *Enemy Views,* p. 259; William Howe to Germain, 11 May 1778, *Documents,* vol. 15, p. 120; John Henry to the Lords of Admiralty, 18 June 1778, *Documents of the American Revolution,* vol. 13, ed. K. G. Davies (Dublin: Irish University Press, 1976), p. 313; Hale, 9 May 1778, *Some British Soldiers,* p. 252; George Washington to John Lacey, 3 May 1778, *The Writings of George Washington,* vol. 11, ed. John Fitzpatrick (Washington, D.C.: Government Printing Office, 1934), p. 345; Washington to William Maxwell, 7 May 1778, *Washington Writings,* vol. 11, pp. 357–58; Washington to Israel Shreve, 7 May 1778, *Washington Writings,* vol. 11, pp. 358–59.

9. Archibald Robertson, 19 May 1778, *Archibald Robertson: His Diaries and Sketches in America, 1762–1780,* ed. Harry Miller Lydenberg (New York: Arno Press, 1971), pp. 172–73; Peebles, 20 May 1778, *American War,* p. 183; John Charles Phillip von Krafft, 20 May 1778, *Von Krafft's Journal* (New York: New-York Historical Society, 1882), pp. 35–36; Downman, *Services,* pp. 59–60; Baurmeister, 18 May–21 June 1778, *Baurmeister's Letters and Journals,* pp. 175–78; Serle, 20 May 1778, *American Journal,* p. 295; Muenchhausen, 19–20 May 1778, *At Howe's Side,* pp. 52–54; Johann Ewald, 19 May 1778, *Diary of the American War: A Hessian Journal,* trans. and ed. Joseph P. Tustin (New Haven, Conn.: Yale University Press, 1979), pp. 129–30; Simcoe, *Simcoe's Journal,* pp. 60–61; Stephen Kemble, 18 June 1778, *Journals of Lieut.-Col. Stephen Kemble, 1773–1789; and British Army Orders: Gen. Sir William Howe, 1775–1778; Gen. Sir Henry Clinton, 1778; and Gen. Daniel Jones, 1778* (Boston: Gregg Press, 1972), p. 152; William Howe, *Narrative of Lieut. Gen. Sir William Howe, in a Committee of the House of Commons* (London: H. Baldwin, 1781), pp. 30–31; Hale, 15 June 1778, *Some British Soldiers,* p. 253.

10. Henry Clinton to William Phillips, 11 December 1777, *Clinton Papers,* CL, vol. 28, no. 22; Horace Walpole, 28 February 1777, *The Last Journals of Horace Walpole,* vol. 2 (New York: AMS Press, 1973), p. 10; Clinton, *American Rebellion,* pp. 83–86; North to King George III, 12 January 1778, *King George III's Correspondence,* vol. 4, p. 10.

11. Clinton, *American Rebellion,* pp. 86–90; Henry Clinton to Germain, 24 May 1778, *Clinton Papers,* CL, vol. 35, no. 6; Henry Clinton, May 1778, *Clinton Papers,* CL, vol. 35, no. 17; Henry Clinton, May 1778, *Clinton Papers,* CL, vol. 35, no. 18; Henry Clinton, Richard Howe, and Joseph Galloway, May 1778, *Clinton Papers,* CL, vol. 35, no. 19; Montresor, 9 May 1778, "Extracts," pp. 490–91; Henry Clinton to Germain, 23 May 1778, *Documents,* vol. 15, p. 126; Henry Clinton to Germain, 5 June 1778, *Documents,* vol. 15, pp. 132–33.

12. Johann Heinrichs, 14 April 1778, "Extracts from the Letter-Book of Captain Johann Heinrichs of the Hessian Jager Corps, 1778–1780," *Pennsylvania Magazine of History and Biography* 22 (1898): 143–46; Charles Cornwallis to Germain, 17 June 1778, *Correspondence of Charles, First Marquis Cornwallis,* vol. 1, ed. Charles Ross (London: John Murray, 1859), p. 33; Germain to Cornwallis, 6 August 1778, *Cornwallis's Correspondence,* vol. 1, p. 34; John Bowater to Lord Denbigh, 4 January 1778, *The Lost War: Letters from British Officers During the American Revolution,* ed. Marion Balderston and David Syrett (New York: Horizon Press, 1975), p. 156; Baurmeister, 24 March 1778, *Baurmeister's Letters and Journals,* p. 158; Serle, 26 May–1 June 1778, *American Journal,* pp. 298–302; Muenchhausen, 14 April and 23 May 1778, *At Howe's Side,* pp. 50–54; Montresor, 13 June 1778, "Extracts," p. 498; Simcoe, *Simcoe's Journal,* p. 60; Heinrich Carl Philipp von Feilitzsch, 15 April–15 May 1778, *Enemy Views,* p. 258.

13. Serle, 25 April–4 June 1778, *American Journal,* pp. 287–304; An Account of the Number of Persons Who Have Taken the Oath of Allegiance at Philadelphia, 17 June 1778, *George Germain Papers,* CL, vol. 7; Henry Clinton, Richard Howe, and Galloway, May 1778, *Clinton Papers,* CL, vol. 35, no. 19; Joseph Galloway, *Selected Tracts,* vol. 1 (New York: Da Capo Press, 1974), pp. 379–82.

14. Carlisle to Lady Carlisle, 27 May 1778, *Carlisle Manuscripts,* p. 335; Henry Clinton, May 1778, *Clinton Papers,* CL, vol. 35, no. 18; Carlisle Commission to Germain, 15 June 1778, *Clinton Papers,* CL, vol. 35, no. 42; Carlisle to Lady Carlisle, 8 June 1778, *Carlisle Manuscripts, 15th Report, Appendix, Part VI,* p. 336; Carlisle to Lady Carlisle, 14 June 1778, *Carlisle Manuscripts, 15th Report, Appendix, Part VI,* p. 341; Carlisle to Lord Gower, June 1778, *Carlisle Manuscripts, 15th Report, Appendix, Part VI,* pp. 341–42; Carlisle to Duchess of ———, 18 June 1778, *Carlisle Manuscripts, 15th Report, Appendix, Part VI,* p. 344; Carlisle to Lady Carlisle, 21 June–7 July 1778, *Carlisle Manuscripts, 15th Report, Appendix, Part VI,* p. 345; Carlisle to Elkins, October 1778, *Carlisle Manuscripts, 15th Report, Appendix, Part VI,* pp. 381–84; William Eden to Germain, 19 June 1778, *Stopford-Sackville Manuscripts,* vol. 2, p. 115; Commissioners for Restoring Peace to Germain, 7 May 1778, *Documents,* vol. 15, p. 116.

15. King George III to North, 23 August 1778, *George III and Lord North's Correspondence,* vol. 2, p. 207; Washington to John Banister, 21 April 1778, *Washington Writings,* vol. 11, pp. 287–89; Washington to William Livingston, 22 April 1778, *Washington Writings,* vol. 11, pp. 295–97; Washington to Henry Laurens, 30 April 1778, *Washington Writings,* vol. 11, pp. 326–27; Washington to John Augustine Washington, May 1778, *Washington Writings,* vol. 11, pp. 500–501; Samuel Chase to Thomas Johnson, 20 April 1778, *Letters of Delegates to Congress, 1774–1789,* vol. 9, ed. Paul Smith (Washington, D.C.: Library of Congress, 1982), pp. 451–53; Henry Laurens to Jonathan Trumbull, 20 April 1778, *Letters of Delegates,* vol. 9, pp. 458–59; Richard Henry Lee's Draft Letter to the Carlisle Commission, 16 June 1778, *Letters of Delegates to Congress, 1774–89,* vol. 10, ed. Paul Smith (Washington, D.C.: Library of Congress, 1983), p. 105; Charles Thomson's Notes, 16 June 1778, *Letters of Delegates,* vol. 10, pp. 111–12; Henry Laurens to the Carlisle Commissioners, 17 June 1778, *Letters of Delegates,* vol. 10, pp. 122–23; Josiah Barlett to William Whipple, 20 June 1778, *Letters of Delegates,* vol. 10, p. 143; Carlisle Commission to Germain, 7 July 1778, *Clinton Papers,* CL, vol. 36, no. 36.

16. Robertson, 6–17 June 1778, *His Diaries,* p. 173; Peebles, 23 May–18 June 1778, *American War,* pp. 184–89; Krafft, 24 May–16 June 1778, *Von Krafft's Journal,* pp. 37–40; Henry Clinton, *American Rebellion,* p. 90; Johann Conrad Dohla, 9 June 1778, *A Hessian Diary of the American Revolution,* ed. and trans. Bruce E. Burgoyne (Norman: University of Oklahoma Press, 1990), p. 75; Andre, 18 June 1778, *Major Andre's Journal: Operations of the British*

Army Under Lieutenant Generals Sir William Howe and Sir Henry Clinton, June 1777 to November 1778 (Tarrytown, N.Y.: William Abbatt, 1930), p. 74; Baurmeister, 18 May–21 June 1778, *Baurmeister's Letters and Journals,* pp. 174–81; Serle, 18 June 1778, *American Journal,* p. 311; Montresor, 24 May–22 June 1778, "Extracts," pp. 493–500; Ewald, 22 May–4 June 1778, *Hessian Journal,* pp. 130–31; Sarah Fisher, 29 May–18 June 1778, "'A Diary of Trifling Occurrences': Philadelphia, 1776–1778," *Pennsylvania Magazine of History and Biography* 82 (1958): 462–65; Carlisle to Lady Carlisle, 21 June–7 July 1778, *Carlisle Manuscripts, 15th Report, Appendix, Part VI,* p. 344; Carlisle to Elkins, October 1778, *Carlisle Manuscripts, 15th Report, Appendix, Part VI,* p. 381.

17. Robertson, 24–27 June 1778, *His Diaries,* p. 176; Henry Clinton to Germain, 5 July 1778, *The Lee Papers,* vol. 2 (New York: New-York Historical Society, 1873), pp. 461–73; Henry Clinton's Journal Through New Jersey, 18 June–1 July 1778, *Clinton Papers,* CL, no. 35, vol. 49; Ewald, 18–27 June 1778, *Hessian Journal,* pp. 132–35; Simcoe, *Simcoe's Journal,* pp. 63–68; Andrew Bell, 17–27 June 1778, "Copy of a Journal by Andrew Bell," *Proceedings of the New Jersey Historical Society* 6 (1851): 15–17; Peebles, 18–27 June 1778, *American War,* pp. 189–92; Krafft, 18–27 June 1778, *Von Krafft's Journal,* pp. 41–47; Andre, 20–27 June 1778, *Andre's Journal,* pp. 75–78; Baurmeister, 7 July 1778, *Baurmeister's Letters and Journals,* pp. 183–85; Clinton, *American Rebellion,* pp. 90–91.

18. James McMichael, 6 May 1778, "Diary of Lieutenant James McMichael, of the Pennsylvania Line, 1776–1778," *Pennsylvania Magazine of History and Biography* 16 (1892): 158–59; John Laurens to Henry Laurens, 7 May 1778, *The Army Correspondence of Colonel John Laurens in the Years 1777–8* (New York: Bradford Club, 1867), pp. 169–70; Joseph Bloomfield, 6 May 1778, *Citizen Soldier: The Revolutionary War Journal of Joseph Bloomfield,* ed. Mark E. Lender and James Kirby Martin (Newark, N.J.: New Jersey Historical Society, 1982), p. 134; George Ewing, 30 April 1778, *The Military Journal of George Ewing (1754–1824): A Soldier of Valley Forge* (Yonkers, N.Y.: privately printed by Thomas Ewing, 1928), pp. 43–46.

19. Washington to William Heath, 22 January 1778, *The Writings of George Washington,* vol. 10, ed. John Fitzpatrick (Washington, D.C.: Government Printing Office, 1933), pp. 335–36; Washington to Thomas Nelson, 8 February 1778, *Washington Writings,* vol. 10, pp. 431–33; Washington to John Armstrong, 27 March 1778, *Washington Writings,* vol. 11, pp. 157–59; Washington to Alexander McDougall, 31 March 1778, *Washington Writings,* vol. 11, pp. 178–79; Washington to Jonathan Trumbull, 31 March 1778, *Washington Writings,* vol. 11, pp. 182–84; Washington to William Livingston, 14 April 1778, *Washington Writings,* vol. 11, pp. 256–57.

20. Washington's Thoughts upon a Plan of Operation for Campaign 1778, April [?] 1778, *Washington Writings,* vol. 11, pp. 182–94.

21. Ibid.; Washington to General Officers, 20 April 1778, *The Papers of General Nathanael Greene,* vol. 2, ed. Richard Showman (Chapel Hill: University of North Carolina Press, 1980), p. 348.

22. Washington to Jonathan Trumbull, 31 March 1778, *Washington Writings,* vol. 11, pp. 182–84; Washington to Nathanael Greene, 5 May 1778, *Greene Papers,* vol. 2, p. 376; Washington to Board of War, 1 May 1778, *Washington Writings,* vol. 11, pp. 333–34; Washington to McDougall, 1 May 1778, *Washington Writings,* vol. 11, p. 335; Washington to Heath, 5 May 1778, *Washington Writings,* vol. 11, pp. 349–51; Washington to McDougall, 5 May 1778, *Washington Writings,* vol. 11, pp. 351–53; John Penn to Theodorick Bland, 1 December 1777, *Letters of Delegates to Congress, 1774–1789,* vol. 8, ed. Paul Smith (Washington, D.C.: Library of Congress, 1981), p. 364; William Ellery to Whipple, 21 December 1777, *Letters of Delegates,* vol. 8, p. 456.

23. General Officers to Washington, 9 May 1778, *Greene Papers,* vol. 2, p. 382.

24. Ibid., pp. 383–84.

25. Nathanael Greene to Washington, 3 May 1778, *Greene Papers,* vol. 2, pp. 372–73; Council of War, 8 May 1778, *Greene Papers,* vol. 2, pp. 378–80; General Officers to Washington, 9 May 1778, *Greene Papers,* vol. 2, pp. 381–85; Nathanael Greene to Griffin Greene, 25 May 1778, *Greene Papers,* vol. 2, p. 406.

26. Washington to David Mason, 4 April 1778, *Washington Writings,* vol. 11, pp. 210–11; Washington to Heath, 8 April 1778, *Washington Writings,* vol. 11, pp. 226–27; Washington to Henry Laurens, 10 April 1778, *Washington Writings,* vol. 11, pp. 235–41; Washington to Thomas Wharton, 11 April 1778, *Washington Writings,* vol. 11, p. 248; Washington to Heath, 27 April 1778, *Washington Writings,* vol. 11, pp. 320–21; Washington to Commissioners of Indian Affairs, 13 March 1778, *Washington Writings,* vol. 11, pp. 76–77; Washington to Committee of Congress with the Army, 29 January 1778, *Washington Writings,* vol. 10, pp. 400–401; Washington to McDougall, 11 May 1778, *Washington Writings,* vol. 11, p. 373; Washington to Philip Schuyler, 15 May 1778, *Washington Writings,* vol. 11, pp. 390–91; Washington to Samuel French, 17 May 1778, *Washington Writings,* vol. 11, p. 408; Washington to John Augustine Washington, 10 June 1778, *The Writings of George Washington,* vol. 12, ed. John Fitzpatrick (Washington, D.C.: Government Printing Office, 1934), pp. 42–43; Committee at Camp to Wharton, 28 February 1778, *Letters of Delegates to Congress,* vol. 9, pp. 180–81; Henry Laurens to Rawlins Lowndes, 17 May 1778, *Letters of Delegates,* vol. 9, p. 700; Richard Peters to Timothy Pickering, 9 June 1778, *Steuben Papers,* Kraus-Thomson Organization Limited, roll 1.

27. John Laurens to Henry Laurens, 14 June 1778, *John Laurens's Correspondence,* p. 186; John Laurens to Henry Laurens, 15 June 1778, *John Lau-*

rens's Correspondence, p. 190; Alexander Hamilton to William Duer, 18 June 1778, *The Papers of Alexander Hamilton,* vol. 1, ed. Harold Syrett (New York: Columbia University Press, 1961), p. 500; Marquis de Lafayette to Henry Laurens, 14 April 1778, *Lafayette in the Age of the American Revolution: Selected Letters and Papers, 1776–1790,* vol. 2, ed. Stanley J. Idzerda (Ithaca, N.Y.: Cornell University Press, 1979), p. 26; Washington to Henry Laurens, 24 March 1778, *Washington Writings,* vol. 11, pp. 138–39; Washington to Stephen Moylan, 11 April 1778, *Washington Writings,* vol. 11, p. 244; Washington to Officer Commanding the Second Continental Dragoons, 14 April 1778, *Washington Writings,* vol. 11, p. 269; Washington to Moylan, 29 April 1778, *Washington Writings,* vol. 11, pp. 322–23; Washington to Committee of Congress with the Army, 29 January 1778, *Washington Writings,* vol. 10, pp. 400–401.

28. Washington to Richard Henry Lee, 26 April 1777, *The Papers of George Washington, Revolutionary War Series,* vol. 9, ed. Dorothy Twohig (Charlottesville: University Press of Virginia, 1999), p. 258; Washington to Henry Laurens, 24 March 1778, *Washington Writings,* vol. 11, pp. 138–39; Washington to Committee of Congress with the Army, 29 January 1778, *Washington Writings,* vol. 10, pp. 400–401; Washington to George Clinton, 12 March 1778, *Washington Writings,* vol. 11, p. 68; Washington to Robert Livingston, 12 March 1778, *Washington Writings,* vol. 11, pp. 69–70; Washington to McDougall, 7 October 1777, *The Writings of George Washington,* vol. 9, ed. John Fitzpatrick (Washington, D.C.: Government Printing Office, 1933), p. 322; Washington to Henry Laurens, 16 March 1778, *Washington Writings,* vol. 11, pp. 90–92; Washington to Gouverneur Morris, 29 May 1778, *Washington Writings,* vol. 11, p. 484.

29. Nathanael Greene to William Smallwood, 16 March 1778, *Greene Papers,* vol. 2, p. 316; George Lux to Nathanael Greene, 28 April 1778, *Greene Papers,* vol. 2, p. 367; John Sullivan to Washington, 9 March 1777, *The Papers of George Washington, Revolutionary War Series,* vol. 8, ed. Dorothy Twohig (Charlottesville: University Press of Virginia, 1998), p. 547; Washington to Sullivan, 15 March 1777, *Washington Papers,* vol. 8, p. 580; Sullivan to Washington, February 1778, *Letters and Papers of Major-General John Sullivan,* vol. 2, ed. Otis G. Hammond (Concord, N.H.: New Hampshire Historical Society, 1931), p. 21; Sullivan to Washington, February 1778, *Sullivan Papers,* vol. 2, p. 18; Washington to Sullivan, 14 February 1778, *Sullivan Papers,* vol. 2, p. 22; Sullivan to Washington, 2 March 1778, *Sullivan Papers,* vol. 2, pp. 25–26; Eliphalet Dyer to Sullivan, 23 October 1777, *Letters of Delegates,* vol. 8, p. 163.

30. For a biography of Lee, see John Richard Alden, *General Charles Lee: Traitor or Patriot?* (Baton Rouge: Lousiana State University Press, 1951). The quotation is from Charles Lee to Henry Laurens, 17 April 1778, *Lee Papers,* vol. 2, p. 390. See also Bowalter to Denbigh, 23 July 1777, *Lost War,* p. 138; Serle, 5 June 1778, *American Journal,* pp. 305–6; Nicholas Cresswell, 2 July

1777, *The Journal of Nicholas Cresswell, 1774–1777* (Port Washington, N.Y.: Kennikat Press, 1968), p. 246; Philipp Waldeck, 26 September 1777, *A Hessian Report on the People, the Land, the War as Noted in the Diary of Chaplain Philipp Waldeck,* ed. Bruce E. Burgoyne (Bowie, Md.: Heritage Books, 1995), pp. 43–44; Hale, 19 December 1776, *Some British Soldiers,* p. 218.

31. Nathanael Greene to Griffin Greene, 25 May 1778, *Greene Papers,* vol. 2, p. 406; Charles Lee to Washington, 13 April 1778, "Plan of an Army, Etc.," *Lee Papers,* vol. 2, pp. 383–89; Washington to Charles Lee, 22 April 1778, *Lee Papers,* vol. 2, p. 391; Charles Lee to Henry Laurens, 13 May 1778, *Lee Papers,* vol. 2, pp. 392–93; Charles Lee to Washington, 13 June 1778, *Lee Papers,* vol. 2, pp. 399–402; Elias Boudinot, "Exchange of Major-General Charles Lee," *Pennsylvania Magazine of History and Biography* 15 (1891): 27–33; Charles Carroll of Carrollton to Charles Carroll Sr., 17 May 1778, *Letters of Delegates,* vol. 9, p. 691; Henry Laurens to John Laurens, 17 June 1778, *Letters of Delegates,* vol. 10, p. 126.

32. Washington to Nathanael Greene, 17 May 1778, *Greene Papers,* vol. 2, pp. 392–93; Nathanael Greene to Griffin Greene, 25 May 1778, *Greene Papers,* vol. 2, p. 408; Nathanael Greene to Gouverneur Morris, 1 June 1778, *Greene Papers,* vol. 2, p. 423; John Laurens to Henry Laurens, 27 May 1778, *John Laurens's Correspondence,* pp. 175–77; James Varnum to Sullivan, 27 May 1778, *Sullivan Papers,* vol. 2, p. 60; Washington to Nathanael Greene, 16 May 1778, *Washington Writings,* vol. 11, pp. 397–98; Washington to Henry Laurens, 18 May 1778, *Washington Writings,* vol. 11, pp. 415–16; Washington to Sullivan, 20 May 1778, *Washington Writings,* vol. 11, pp. 428–29; Washington to Smallwood, 23 May 1778, *Washington Writings,* vol. 11, pp. 435–36; Washington to Henry Laurens, 23 May 1778, *Washington Writings,* vol. 11, p. 444; Washington to Philemon Dickinson, 28 May 1778, *Washington Writings,* vol. 11, pp. 468–69; Washington to George Clinton, 29 May 1778, *Washington Writings,* vol. 11, pp. 473–74; Washington to Gouverneur Morris, 29 May 1778, *Washington Writings,* vol. 11, pp. 483–86; Washington to Smallwood, 1 June 1778, *Washington Writings,* vol. 12, p. 2.

33. The quotation is from Washington to Philemon Dickinson, 28 May 1778, *Washington Writings,* vol. 11, pp. 468–69. See also Washington to Philemon Dickinson, 24 May 1778, *Washington Writings,* vol. 11, pp. 445–46; Washington to Horatio Gates, 25 May 1778, *Washington Writings,* vol. 11, p. 447; Washington to Maxwell, 25 May 1778, *Washington Writings,* vol. 11, pp. 448–49; Washington to Richard Henry Lee, 25 May 1778, *Washington Writings,* vol. 11, pp. 450–52; Washington to George Clinton, 29 May 1778, *Washington Writings,* vol. 11, pp. 473–74; Washington to Gates, 29 May 1778, *Washington Writings,* vol. 11, pp. 476–77; Washington to Gouverneur Morris, 29 May 1778, *Washington Writings,* vol. 11, pp. 483–86.

34. Washington to Gouverneur Morris, 29 May 1778, *Washington Writings,* vol. 11, p. 485.

35. The quotation is from Henry Dearborn, 20 May 1778, *Revolutionary War Journals of Henry Dearborn, 1775–1783* (Freeport, N.Y.: Books for Libraries Press, 1969), p. 121. See also John Laurens to Henry Laurens, 27 May 1777, *John Laurens's Correspondence,* p. 174; Charles-Albert de Moré de Pontgibaud, *A French Volunteer of the War of Independence,* trans. and ed. Robert B. Douglass (New York: D. Appleton, 1898), pp. 73–76; Joseph Plumb Martin, *Private Yankee Doodle: Being a Narrative of Some of the Adventures, Dangers, and Sufferings of a Revolutionary Soldier,* ed. George Scheer (Boston: Little, Brown, 1962), pp. 118–22; Ewing, 18–21 May 1778, *Military Journal,* pp. 52–54; Washington to Lafayette, 18 May 1778, *Lafayette's Letters and Papers,* vol. 2, pp. 53–54; Marquis de Lafayette, *Memoirs of General Lafayette Embracing Details of His Public and Private Life* (Hartford, Conn.: Barber and Robinson, 1825), pp. 120–25; Anthony Wayne to Sharp Delaney, 21 May 1778, "Letter of General Anthony Wayne," *Pennsylvania Magazine of History and Biography* 11 (1887): 115.

36. William Hutchinson, *The Revolution Remembered: Eyewitness Accounts of the War for Independence,* ed. John Dann (Chicago: University of Chicago Press, 1980), p. 154; Christopher Marshall, 23–25 June 1778, *Extracts from the Diary of Christopher Marshall, 1774–1781,* ed. William Duane (New York: Arno Press, 1969), p. 189; John Laurens to Henry Laurens, 16 June 1778, *John Laurens's Correspondence,* p. 191; Washington to Henry Laurens, 18 June 1778, *Washington Writings,* vol. 12, pp. 82–83; Washington to Henry Laurens, 18 June 1778, *Washington Writings,* vol. 12, p. 83; Washington to Henry Jackson, 18 June 1778, *Washington Writings,* vol. 12, p. 88; Washington to Charles Lee, 18 June 1778, *Washington Writings,* vol. 12, p. 85; Robert Morris to Alexander Clough, 18 June 1778, *Letters of Delegates,* vol. 10, p. 138; Council of War, 17 June 1778, *Greene Papers,* vol. 2, pp. 434–36.

37. The quote is from Hamilton to Boudinot, 5 July 1778, *Lee Papers,* vol. 2, p. 468. See also Dearborn, 23–26 June 1778, *Dearborn's Journals,* pp. 124–25; Washington to Henry Laurens, 1 July 1778, *Lee Papers,* vol. 2, pp. 441–42; William Beatty, 5–27 June 1778, "Journal of Capt. William Beatty," *Maryland Historical Magazine* 3 (1907): 112–13; Washington to Gates, 20 June 1778, *Washington Writings,* vol. 12, p. 95; Washington to Henry Laurens, 20 June 1778, *Washington Writings,* vol. 12, pp. 96–97; Washington to William Livingston, 21 June 1778, *Washington Writings,* vol. 12, p. 100; Washington to Henry Laurens, 22 June 1778, *Washington Writings,* vol. 12, pp. 108–9; Washington, 22 June 1778, "General Orders," *Washington Writings,* vol. 12, p. 106; William Lloyd, *Revolution Remembered,* pp. 123–24; Council of War, 24 June 1778, *Greene Papers,* vol. 2, pp. 445–46; Charles Lee's Testimony, 9 August 1778, *Lee Papers,* vol. 3 (New York: New-York Historical Society, 1874), pp. 174–77.

38. Hamilton to Washington, 26 June 1778, *Lee Papers,* vol. 2, p. 420.

39. Nathanael Greene to Washington, 24 June 1778, *Greene Papers,* vol. 2,

p. 447; Lafayette to Washington, 24 June 1778, *Lafayette's Letters and Papers,* vol. 2, pp. 85–86; Hamilton to Boudinot, 5 July 1778, *Lee Papers,* vol. 2, pp. 468–69; Washington to Lafayette, 25 June 1778, *Lee Papers,* vol. 2, pp. 413–15; Lafayette to Washington, 26 June 1778, *Lee Papers,* vol. 2, pp. 416–24; Washington to Henry Laurens, 1 July 1778, *Lee Papers,* vol. 2, pp. 441–42; Martin, *Yankee Doodle,* pp. 122–24.

40. Charles Lee to Washington, 25 June 1778, *Lee Papers,* vol. 2, pp. 417–18; Lafayette to Washington, 26 June 1778, *Lee Papers,* vol. 2, pp. 418–19; Washington to Charles Lee, 26 June 1778, *Lee Papers,* vol. 2, pp. 421–22.

41. The quotation is from Wayne's Testimony, 4 July 1778, *Lee Papers,* vol. 3, p. 5. See also Hamilton to Washington, 26 June 1778, *Lee Papers,* vol. 2, pp. 424–25; Charles Lee to Washington, 27 June 1778, *Lee Papers,* vol. 2, p. 425; Washington to Henry Laurens, 28 June 1778, *Lee Papers,* vol. 2, pp. 427–28; Washington to Henry Laurens, 1 July 1778, *Lee Papers,* vol. 2, p. 443; Charles Scott's Testimony, 4 July 1778, *Lee Papers,* vol. 3, pp. 2–3; Fitzgerald's Testimony, 4 July 1778, *Lee Papers,* vol. 3, pp. 5–6; Hamilton's Testimony, 4 July 1778, *Lee Papers,* vol. 3, pp. 8–10; Maxwell's Testimony, 18 July 1778, *Lee Papers,* vol. 3, p. 89; Captain Edwards's Testimony, 25 July 1778, *Lee Papers,* vol. 3, p. 161; Charles Lee's Testimony, 9 August 1778, *Lee Papers,* vol. 3, pp. 174–77; Captain Mercer's Testimony, 19 July 1778, *Lee Papers,* vol. 3, pp. 101–4.

42. Wayne's Testimony, 4 July 1778, *Lee Papers,* vol. 3, p. 5; Lafayette to Washington, 26 June 1778, *Lee Papers,* vol. 2, p. 425; Washington to Henry Laurens, 1 July 1778, *Lee Papers,* vol. 2, p. 443; Washington to John Augustine Washington, 4 July 1778, *Lee Papers,* vol. 2, p. 459; Charles Scott's Testimony, 4 July 1778, *Lee Papers,* vol. 3, pp. 2–3; Fitzgerald's Testimony, 4 July 1778, *Lee Papers,* vol. 3, pp. 5–6; Hamilton's Testimony, 4 July 1778, *Lee Papers,* vol. 3, pp. 8–10; Maxwell's Testimony, 18 July 1778, *Lee Papers,* vol. 3, p. 89; Captain Edwards's Testimony, 25 July 1778, *Lee Papers,* vol. 3, p. 161; Charles Lee's Testimony, 9 August 1778, *Lee Papers,* vol. 3, pp. 174–77; Captain Mercer's Testimony, 19 July 1778, *Lee Papers,* vol. 3, pp. 101–4.

43. William Grayson's Testimony, 11 July 1778, *Lee Papers,* vol. 3, pp. 34–37; Jeremiah Olney's Testimony, 22 July 1778, *Lee Papers,* vol. 3, pp. 126–27, 130–32; Captain Cumpiton's Testimony, 23 July 1778, *Lee Papers,* vol. 3, pp. 140–41; Dearborn, 28 June 1778, *Dearborn's Journals,* p. 126; John Laurens to Henry Laurens, 30 June 1778, *Lee Papers,* vol. 3, pp. 431–32; Lafayette's Testimony, 5 July 1778, *Lee Papers,* vol. 3, pp. 10–17; Grayson's Testimony, 11 July 1778, *Lee Papers,* vol. 3, pp. 34–37; John Laurens's Testimony, 13 July 1778, *Lee Papers,* vol. 3, pp. 51–55; Mercer's Testimony, 19 July 1778, *Lee Papers,* vol. 3, pp. 101–5; Jackson's Testimony, 21 July 1778, *Lee Papers,* vol. 3, pp. 120–23; Eleazer Brooks's Testimony, 23 July 1778, *Lee Papers,* vol. 3, pp. 143–44; Edwards's Testimony, 25 July 1778, *Lee Papers,* vol. 3, pp. 161–65; Charles Lee's Testimony, 9 August 1778, *Lee Papers,* vol. 3, pp. 178–80; Martin, *Yankee Doodle,* pp. 124–27.

44. John Laurens to Henry Laurens, 30 June 1778, *Lee Papers*, vol. 2, pp. 431–32; Lafayette's Testimony, 5 July 1778, *Lee Papers*, vol. 3, pp. 10–17; Wayne's Testimony, 6 July 1778, *Lee Papers*, vol. 3, pp. 17–20; Richard Butler's Testimony, 12 July 1778, *Lee Papers*, vol. 3, pp. 42–44; Benjamin Fishbourne's Testimony, 12 July 1778, *Lee Papers*, vol. 3, pp. 46–48; David Rhea's Testimony, 12 July 1778, *Lee Papers*, vol. 3, pp. 50–51; Maxwell's Testimony, 18 July 1778, *Lee Papers*, vol. 3, pp. 89–91; Mercer's Testimony, 19 July 1778, *Lee Papers*, vol. 3, pp. 101–7; Jackson's Testimony, 21 July 1778, *Lee Papers*, vol. 3, pp. 120–23; Olney's Testimony, 22 July 1778, *Lee Papers*, vol. 3, pp. 126–27; Eleazer Oswald's Testimony, 22 July 1778, *Lee Papers*, vol. 3, pp. 130–32; Brooks's Testimony, 23 July 1778, *Lee Papers*, vol. 3, pp. 143–46; Edwards's Testimony, 25 July 1778, *Lee Papers*, vol. 3, pp. 163–65.

45. John Laurens to Henry Laurens, 30 June 1778, *Lee Papers*, vol. 2, pp. 431–32; Wayne's Testimony, 6 July 1778, *Lee Papers*, vol. 3, pp. 22–24; Scott's Testimony, 6 July 1778, *Lee Papers*, vol. 3, pp. 27–28; Joseph Cilley's Testimony, 11 July 1778, *Lee Papers*, vol. 3, pp. 32–33; Grayson's Testimony, 11 July 1778, *Lee Papers*, vol. 3, pp. 34–37; John Laurens's Testimony, 13 July 1778, *Lee Papers*, vol. 3, pp. 51–55; Hamilton's Testimony, 13 July 1778, *Lee Papers*, vol. 3, pp. 57–59; Mercer's Testimony, 19 July 1778, *Lee Papers*, vol. 3, pp. 105–10; Edwards's Testimony, 25 July 1778, *Lee Papers*, vol. 3, pp. 163–65; Charles Lee's Testimony, 9 August 1778, *Lee Papers*, vol. 3, pp. 178–82.

46. James McHenry's Journal, *A Salute to Courage: The American Revolution as Seen Through Wartime Writings of Officers of the Continental Army and Navy*, ed. Dennis Ryan (New York: Columbia University Press, 1979), p. 129; Cilley to Thomas Bartlett, 3 July 1778, *Salute to Courage*, pp. 132–33; Dearborn, 28 June 1778, *Dearborn's Journals*, p. 126; John Laurens to Henry Laurens, 30 June 1778, *Lee Papers*, vol. 2, pp. 432–33; Wayne and Scott to Washington, 30 June 1778, *Lee Papers*, vol. 2, pp. 438–40; Wayne's Testimony, 6 July 1778, *Lee Papers*, vol. 3, pp. 18–22; Lafayette's Testimony, 5 July 1778, *Lee Papers*, vol. 3, pp. 10–17; David Forman's Testimony, 6 July 1778, *Lee Papers*, vol. 3, pp. 25–27; Scott's Testimony, 6 July 1778, *Lee Papers*, vol. 3, pp. 28–29; Grayson's Testimony, 11 July 1778, *Lee Papers*, vol. 3, pp. 37–39; Alexander Stewart's Testimony, 11 July 1778, *Lee Papers*, vol. 3, pp. 40–42; William Smith's Testimony, 15 July 1778, *Lee Papers*, vol. 3, pp. 83–88; Mercer's Testimony, 19 July 1778, *Lee Papers*, vol. 3, p. 114; Oswald's Testimony, 22 July 1778, *Lee Papers*, vol. 3, pp. 133–35; Brooks's Testimony, 23–24 July 1778, *Lee Papers*, vol. 3, pp. 149–56; Edwards's Testimony, 25 July 1778, *Lee Papers*, vol. 3, pp. 165–66; Charles Lee's Testimony, 9 August 1778, *Lee Papers*, vol. 3, pp. 182–84, 194–97.

47. Clinton, *American Rebellion*, pp. 90–93; Henry Clinton to Germain, 5 July 1778, *Lee Papers*, vol. 2, pp. 463–64; Andre, 28 June 1778, *Andre's Journal*, pp. 78–79; Simcoe, *Simcoe's Journal*, pp. 68–72.

48. McHenry's Journal, *Salute to Courage*, p. 129; Dearborn, 28 June

1778, *Dearborn's Journals,* pp. 126–27; John Laurens to Henry Laurens, 30 June 1778, *Lee Papers,* vol. 2, pp. 432–33; Richard Meade's Testimony, 13 July 1778, *Lee Papers,* vol. 3, pp. 62–64; John Fitzgerald's Testimony, 14 July 1778, *Lee Papers,* vol. 3, pp. 67–68; Robert Harrison's Testimony, 14 July 1778, *Lee Papers,* vol. 3, pp. 71–73; Tench Tilghman's Testimony, 14 July 1778, *Lee Papers,* vol. 3, pp. 79–81; Beatty, 28 June 1778, "Beatty's Journal," p. 113; Martin, *Yankee Doodle,* pp. 127–31; Marinus Willett, *A Narrative of the Military Accounts of Colonel Marinus Willett,* ed. William Willet (New York: New York Times and Arno Press, 1969), pp. 68–70.

49. John Laurens to Henry Laurens, 30 June 1778, *Lee Papers,* vol. 2, pp. 432–33; Wayne's Testimony, 6 July 1778, *Lee Papers,* vol. 3, p. 24; Hamilton's Testimony, 13 July 1778, *Lee Papers,* vol. 3, pp. 59–60; Meade's Testimony, *Lee Papers,* vol. 3, pp. 62–64; Harrison's Testimony, 14 July 1778, *Lee Papers,* vol. 3, pp. 75–76; Dr. M'Henry's Testimony, 14 July 1778, *Lee Papers,* vol. 3, p. 78; Tilghman's Testimony, 14 July 1778, *Lee Papers,* vol. 3, pp. 81–82; Dr. Griffiths's Testimony, 15 July 1778, *Lee Papers,* vol. 3, pp. 82–83; Mercer's Testimony, 19 July 1778, *Lee Papers,* vol. 3, pp. 112–14; Brooks's Testimony, 23 July 1778, *Lee Papers,* vol. 3, pp. 147–48; Major Shaw's Testimony, 24 July 1778, *Lee Papers,* vol. 3, p. 159; Charles Lee's Testimony, 9 August 1778, *Lee Papers,* vol. 3, pp. 188–90; Lafayette, *Lafayette's Memoirs,* pp. 126–27.

50. Martin, *Yankee Doodle,* pp. 127–31; Washington to Henry Laurens, 1 July 1778, *Lee Papers,* vol. 2, pp. 443–45; Charles Lee's Testimony, 9 August 1778, *Lee Papers,* vol. 3, pp. 188–90; Hale, 4 July 1778, *Some British Soldiers,* pp. 257–61; McHenry's Journal, *Salute to Courage,* pp. 129–30.

51. Peebles, 28 June 1778, *American War,* pp. 193–95; Henry Clinton, *American Rebellion,* pp. 94–96; Andre, 28 June 1778, *Andre's Journal,* pp. 80–81; Henry Clinton, "Sir Henry Clinton's Review of Simcoe's Journal," ed. Howard H. Peckham, *William and Mary Quarterly,* 2d ser., 21 (1941): 363–64, 368; Forbes Champagne to Lord Rawdon, 29 June 1778, *Clinton Papers,* CL, vol. 36, no. 10; Anonymous, 28 June 1778, "Notes on the Battle of Monmouth," *Pennsylvania Magazine of History and Biography* 14 (1890): 46–47.

52. Clinton, *American Rebellion,* pp. 94–96; Ewald, 28 June 1778, *Hessian Journal,* p. 136; Hale, 4 July 1778, *Some British Soldiers,* pp. 257–61; McHenry's Journal, *Salute to Courage,* pp. 129–30; Cilley to Bartlett, *Salute to Courage,* pp. 132–33; Dearborn, 28 June 1778, *Dearborn's Journals,* pp. 127–29; John Laurens to Henry Laurens, 30 June 1778, *Lee Papers,* vol. 2, pp. 433–34; Henry Clinton to Germain, 5 July 1778, *Lee Papers,* vol. 2, pp. 464–65; Washington to Henry Laurens, 1 July 1778, *Lee Papers,* vol. 2, pp. 444–45; Wayne to his wife, 1 July 1778, *Lee Papers,* vol. 2, pp. 448–49; Martin, *Yankee Doodle,* pp. 127–33; Pontgibaud, *French Volunteer,* pp. 77–78; McHenry, 1 July 1778, "The Battle of Monmouth," *Magazine of American History* 3 (1879): 357–59.

53. Washington to Henry Laurens, 1 July 1778, *Lee Papers,* vol. 2, pp. 445–46; Henry Clinton to Germain, 5 July 1778, *Lee Papers,* vol. 2, pp. 465–66.

54. Cilley to Bartlett, 3 July 1778, *Salute to Courage,* pp. 132–33.

55. Washington to Charles Lee, 30 June 1778, *Lee Papers,* vol. 2, p. 437.

56. Henry Clinton, *American Rebellion,* p. 96; Washington to Gates, 3 July 1778, *Washington Writings,* vol. 12, pp. 148–49; Henry Clinton to Germain, 5 July 1778, *Documents,* vol. 13, p. 319; McHenry, 1 July 1778, "Notes on the Battle of Monmouth," *Pennsylvania Magazine of History and Biography* 14 (1890): 359–60; Charles Lee to Washington, 30 June 1778, *Lee Papers,* vol. 2, pp. 435–38; Wayne and Scott to Washington, 30 June 1778, *Lee Papers,* vol. 2, pp. 438–40; Lafayette, *Lafayette's Memoirs,* pp. 129–30.

57. Clinton, *American Rebellion,* p. 96.

58. Ibid., p. 98n.

59. Ibid., p. 97.

CHAPTER 7. CONCLUSIONS

1. Ambrose Serle, 1 June 1778, *The American Journal of Ambrose Serle, Secretary to Lord Howe, 1776–78,* ed. Edward H. Tatum (San Marino, Calif.: Huntington Library, 1940), pp. 300–302; William Howe, *Narrative of Lieut. Gen. Sir William Howe, in a Committee of the House of Commons* (London: H. Baldwin, 1781), pp. 20–21.

Bibliography

ARCHIVAL SOURCES

Chicago Historical Society. George Weedon–John Page Correspondence. Cited as CHS.

Clements Library, University of Michigan. Papers of Loftus Cliffe, Henry Clinton, George Germain, Nicholas Fish, William and Richard Howe, William Knox, and the Schoff Revolutionary War Collection. Cited as CL.

PRIMARY SOURCES

Adams, John. *Diary and Autobiography of John Adams.* Vol. 2. Edited by L. H. Butterfield. Cambridge, Mass.: Belknap Press, 1961.

———. *The Works of John Adams, Second President of the United States.* Vol. 9. Freeport, N.Y.: Books for Libraries Press, 1969.

Anderson, Enoch. *Personal Recollections of Captain Enoch Anderson.* New York: Arno Press, 1971.

Andre, John. *Major Andre's Journal: Operations of the British Army Under Lieutenant Generals Sir William Howe and Sir Henry Clinton, June 1777 to November 1778.* Tarrytown, N.Y.: William Abbatt, 1930.

———. "Major Andre's Story of the 'Mischianza.'" *Century Magazine,* n.s., 25 (1894): 684–91.

Anonymous. "The Actions at Brandywine and Paoli, Described by a British Officer." *Pennsylvania Magazine of History and Biography* 29 (1905): 368–69.

———. "A Contemporary British Account of General Sir William Howe's Military Operations in 1777." *Proceedings of the American Antiquarian Society,* April 1930, pp. 69–92.

———. "Notes on the Battle of Monmouth." *Pennsylvania Magazine of History and Biography* 14 (1890): 46–47.

Armstrong, John. "Letters of General John Armstrong to Thomas Wharton, President of Pennsylvania, 1777. *Pennsylvania Magazine of History and Biography* 38 (1914): 206–10.

Balderston, Marion, and David Syrett, eds. *The Lost War: Letters from British Officers During the American Revolution.* New York: Horizon Press, 1975.

"Battle of Germantown from a British Account." *Pennsylvania Magazine of History and Biography* 11 (1887): 112–14.

"Battle of Monmouth." *Pennsylvania Magazine of History and Biography* 2 (1878): 147–48.

Baurmeister, Carl Leopold. *Revolution in America: Confidential Letters and Journals 1774–1784 of Adjutant General Major Baurmeister of the Hessian Forces.* Translated by Bernhard A. Uhlendorf. New Brunswick, N.J.: Rutgers University Press, 1957.

Beatty, William. "Journal of Capt. William Beatty." *Maryland Historical Magazine* 3 (1907): 104–19.

Bell, Andrew. "Copy of a Journal by Andrew Bell." *Proceedings of the New Jersey Historical Society* 6 (1851): 15–19.

Bloomfield, Joseph. *Citizen Soldier: The Revolutionary War Journal of Joseph Bloomfield.* Edited by Mark E. Lender and James Kirby Martin. Newark, N.J.: New Jersey Historical Society, 1982.

Bogart, John. *The John Bogart Letters.* New Brunswick, N.J.: Rutgers College, 1914.

Boudinot, Elias. "Exchange of Major-General Charles Lee." *Pennsylvania Magazine of History and Biography* 15 (1891): 26–34.

———. *The Life, Public Services, Addresses and Letters of Elias Boudinot.* Vol. 1. Edited by J. J. Boudinot. New York: Houghton, Mifflin, 1896.

Brown, Marian R., and Ralph A. Brown, eds. *Europeans Observe the American Revolution.* New York: Julian Messner, 1976.

Buettner, Johann Carl. *Narrative of Johann Carl Buettner in the American Revolution.* New York: Benjamin Blom, 1971.

Burgoyne, Bruce E., ed. *Enemy Views: The American Revolutionary War as Recorded by the Hessian Participants.* Bowie, Md.: Heritage Books, 1996.

Cadwalader, John. "Selections from the Military Papers of General John Cadwalader." *Pennsylvania Magazine of History and Biography* 32 (1908): 149–74.

Clark, John. "Letters from Major John Clark, Jr., to Gen. Washington." *Bulletin of the Historical Society of Pennsylvania* 1 (1845–47): 1–36.

Clark, Joseph. "Diary of Joseph Clark." *Proceedings of the New Jersey Historical Society* 7 (1853–55): 95–110.

Clinton, Henry. *The American Rebellion: Sir Henry Clinton's Narrative of His Campaigns, 1775–1782.* Edited by William Willcox. Hamden, Conn.: Archon Books, 1971.

———. "Sir Henry Clinton's Review of Simcoe's Journal." Edited by Howard H. Peckman. *William and Mary College Quarterly Historical Magazine,* 2d ser., 21 (1941): 363–64, 368.

"Contemporary Account of the Battle of Germantown." *Pennsylvania Magazine of History and Biography* 11 (1887): 330–32.

Cooper, Samuel. "Extracts from the Letters of Samuel Cooper." *Pennsylvania Magazine of History and Biography* 10 (1886): 33–42.

Cornwallis, Charles. *Correspondence of Charles, First Marquis Cornwallis.* Vol. 1. Edited by Charles Ross. London: John Murray, 1859.

Cresswell, Nicholas. *The Journal of Nicholas Cresswell, 1774–1777.* Port Washington, N.Y.: Kennikat Press, 1968.

Dann, John C., ed. *The Revolution Remembered: Eyewitness Accounts of the War for Independence.* Chicago: University of Chicago Press, 1980.

David, Ebenezer. *A Rhode Island Chaplain in the Revolution: Letters of Ebenezer David to Nicholas Brown, 1775–1778.* Edited by Jeannette Black and William Greene Roelker. London: Kennikat Press, 1972.

Davies, K. G., ed. *Documents of the American Revolution.* Vols. 13–15. Dublin: Irish University Press, 1976.

Dearborn, Henry. *Revolutionary War Journals of Henry Dearborn, 1775–1783.* Freeport, N.Y.: Books for Libraries Press, 1969.

Dohla, Johann Conrad. *A Hessian Diary of the American Revolution.* Edited and translated by Bruce E. Burgoyne. Norman: University of Oklahoma Press, 1990.

Donne, W. Bodham, ed. *The Correspondence of King George the Third with Lord North from 1768 to 1783.* Vol. 2. London: John Murray, 1867.

Downman, Francis. *The Services of Lieut. Colonel Francis Downman, R.A. in France, North America, and the West Indies, Between the Years 1758 and 1784.* Edited by F. A. Whinyates. Woolwich: Royal Artillery Institution, 1898.

DuCoudray, Philippe-Charles-Jean-Baptiste Tronson. "Du Coudray's 'Observations on the Delaware River Forts.'" *Pennsylvania Magazine of History and Biography* 24 (1900): 343–47.

Duponceau, Peter S. "Autobiographical Letters of Peter S. Duponceau." *Pennsylvania Magazine of History and Biography* 40 (1916): 172–86.

Elmer, Ebenezer. "Journal of Ebenezer Elmer." *Pennsylvania Magazine of History and Biography* 35 (1911): 103–07.

Ewald, Johann. *Diary of the American War: A Hessian Journal.* Translated and edited by Joseph P. Tustin. New Haven, Conn.: Yale University Press, 1979.

Ewing, George. *The Military Journal of George Ewing (1754–1824): A Soldier of Valley Forge.* Yonkers, N.Y.: privately printed by Thomas Ewing, 1928.

Fisher, Sarah. "'A Diary of Trifling Occurrences': Philadelphia, 1776–1778." *Pennsylvania Magazine of History and Biography* 82 (1958): 411–65.

Ford, Worthington Chauncey, ed. *Defences of Philadelphia in 1777.* New York: Da Capo Press, 1971.

———. *Journals of the Continental Congress, 1774–1789.* 34 vols. Washington, D.C.: Government Printing Office, 1904–37.

Fortescue, John, ed. *The Correspondence of King George the Third from 1760 to December 1783.* Vols. 3–4. London: Macmillan, 1928.

Franklin, Benjamin. *The Papers of Benjamin Franklin.* Vol. 24. Edited by William Willcox. New Haven, Conn.: Yale University Press, 1984.

Gaine, Hugh. *The Journals of Hugh Gaine, Printer.* New York: Arno Press, 1970.

Galloway, Grace Growden. "Diary of Grace Growden Galloway." *Pennsylvania Magazine of History and Biography* 55 (1931): 32–94.

Galloway, Joseph. *Letters to a Nobleman, on the Conduct of the War in the Middle Colonies.* London, 1780.

———. *Selected Tracts.* Vols. 1–2. New York: Da Capo Press, 1974.

Gates, Horatio. *Horatio Gates Papers, 1726–1828.* Sanford, N.C.: Microfilming Corporation of America, 1978.

Glover, John. *General John Glover's Letterbook, 1776–1777.* Edited by Russell W. Knight. Salem, Mass.: Essex Institute, 1976.

Graydon, Alexander. *Memoirs of His Own Time with Reminiscences of the Men and Events of the Revolution.* Edited by John Stockton Littell. Philadelphia: Lindsay and Blakiston, 1846.

Greene, Nathanael. *The Papers of General Nathanael Greene.* Vols. 1–2. Edited by Richard K. Showman. Chapel Hill: University of North Carolina Press, 1976–80.

Greenman, Jeremiah. *Diary of a Common Soldier in the American Revolution, 1775–1783: An Annotated Edition of the Military Journal of Jeremiah Greenman.* Edited by Robert C. Bray and Paul E. Bushnell. DeKalb: Northern Illinois University Press, 1978.

Hamilton, Alexander. *The Papers of Alexander Hamilton.* Vol. 1. Edited by Harold Syrett. New York: Columbia University Press, 1961.

Harcourt, William Edward. *The Harcourt Papers.* Vol. 11. Oxford: James Parker and Co., 1880.

Haslewood, John. "Journal of a British Officer During the American Revolution." Edited by Louise Phelps Kellogg. *Mississippi Valley Historical Review* 7 (1920): 51–58.

Hay, Samuel. "Letter from Samuel Hay." *Historical Magazine* 3 (September and November 1859): 283–84 and 349–50.

Hazard, Ebenezer. "Ebenezer Hazard's Diary: New Jersey During the Revolution." Edited by Fred Shelley. *Proceedings of the New Jersey Historical Society* 90 (1952): 169–80.

Heath, William. *Memoirs of Major-General William Heath, by Himself.* Edited by William Abbott. New York: William Abbott, 1901.

Heinrichs, Johann. "Extracts from the Letter-Book of Captain Johann Heinrichs of the Hessian Jager Corps, 1778–1780." *Pennsylvania Magazine of History and Biography* 22 (1898): 137–70.

Historical Manuscripts Commission. *The Manuscripts of the Earl of Carlisle, 15th Report, Appendix, Part VI.* London: Eyre and Spottiswoode, 1897.

———. *Report on the Manuscripts of Mrs. Stopford-Sackville, of Drayton House, Northhamptonshire.* Vol. 2. Boston: Gregg Press, 1972.

———. *Report on Manuscripts in Various Collections.* Vol. 6. Dublin: John Falconer, 1909.

———. *Report on the Manuscripts of the Late Reginald Rawdon Hastings, Esq.* Vol. 3. Edited by Francis Bickley. London: His Majesty's Stationery Office, 1934.

Howe, William. *Narrative of Lieut. Gen. Sir William Howe, in a Committee of the House of Commons.* London: H. Baldwin, 1781.

Inman, George. "George Inman's Narrative of the American Revolution." *Pennsylvania Magazine of History and Biography* 7 (1893): 237–48.

Irvine, William. "Selections from the Military Papers of Brig. Gen. William Irvine." *Pennsylvania Magazine of History and Biography* 40 (1916): 108–12.

Jones, Caleb. *Orderly Book of the "Maryland Loyalists Regiment," June 18th, 1778, to October 12th, 1778.* Edited by Paul Leicester Ford. Brooklyn, N.Y.: Historical Printing Club, 1891.

Kemble, Stephen. *Journals of Lieut.-Col. Stephen Kemble, 1773–1789; and British Army Orders: Gen. Sir William Howe, 1775–1778; Gen. Sir Henry Clinton, 1778; and Gen. Daniel Jones, 1778.* Boston: Gregg Press, 1972.

Kidder, Frederic. *History of the First New Hampshire Regiment in the War of the Revolution.* Albany, N.Y.: Joel Munsell, 1868.

Kirkwood, Robert. *The Journal and Order Book of Captain Robert Kirkwood of the Delaware Regiment of the Continental Line.* Edited by Joseph Brown Turner. Port Washington, N.Y.: Kennikat Press, 1970.

Knox, Henry. *Henry Knox Papers.* Vols. 3–4. Boston: New England Historic Genealogical Society, 1960.

Krafft, John Charles Philip von. *Von Krafft's Journal.* New York: New-York Historical Society, 1882.

Lacey, John. "Memoirs of Brigadier-General John Lacey, of Pennsylvania." *Pennsylvania Magazine of History and Biography* 26 (1902): 101–11, 265–70.

Lafayette, Marquis de. *Lafayette in the Age of the American Revolution: Selected Letters and Papers, 1776–1790.* Vols. 1–2. Edited by Stanley J. Idzerda. Ithaca, N.Y.: Cornell University Press, 1979.

———. *Memoirs of General Lafayette Embracing Details of His Public and Private Life.* Hartford, Conn.: Barber and Robinson, 1825.

Laurens, Henry. *Correspondence of Henry Laurens of South Carolina.* New York: privately printed for the Zenger Club, 1861.

———. *The Papers of Henry Laurens.* Vols. 12–13. Columbia: University of South Carolina Press, 1990–92.

Laurens, John. *The Army Correspondence of Colonel John Laurens in the Years 1777–8.* New York: Bradford Club, 1867.

Lee, Charles. *The Lee Papers.* Vols. 2–3. New York: New-York Historical Society, 1873–74.

Lee, Henry. *Memoirs of the War in the Southern Department of the United States.* Vol. 1. Philadelphia: Bradford and Inskeep, 1812.

Letters of Brunswick and Hessian Officers During the American Revolution. Translated by William L. Stone. New York: Da Capo Press, 1970.

Livingston, William. *The Papers of William Livingston.* Vol. 2, *July 1777– December 1778.* Edited by Carl E. Prince and Dennis P. Ryan. Trenton, N.J.: New Jersey Historical Commission, 1980.

MacKenzie, Frederick. *Diary of Frederick MacKenzie.* Vol. 1. Cambridge, Mass.: Harvard University Press, 1930.

Marshall, Christopher. *Extracts from the Diary of Christopher Marshall, 1774–1781.* Edited by William Duane. New York: Arno Press, 1969.

Martin, Joseph Plumb. *Private Yankee Doodle: Being a Narrative of Some of the Adventures, Dangers, and Sufferings of a Revolutionary Soldier.* Edited by George Scheer. Boston: Little, Brown, 1962.

McDonald, Alexander. *Letter-Book of Captain McDonald.* New York: New-York Historical Society, 1882.

McHenry, James. "The Battle of Monmouth." *Magazine of American History* 3 (1879): 355–63.

McMichael, James. "Diary of Lieutenant James McMichael, of the Pennsylvania Line, 1776– 1778." *Pennsylvania Magazine of History and Biography* 16 (1892) 129–59.

Miller, Henry. "A Memoir of General Henry Miller." *Pennsylvania Magazine of History and Biography* 12 (1888) 425–31.

Monroe, James. *The Writings of James Monroe.* Vol. 1. Edited by Stanislaus Murray Hamilton. New York: G. P. Putnam's Sons, 1898.

Montresor, John. "Extracts from the Journals and Note-Books of Capt. John Montresor." In *Collections of the New-York Historical Society, 1881,* pp. 1–520.

Moody, James. *Lieut. James Moody's Narrative of His Exertions and Sufferings in the Cause of Government, Since the Year 1776.* New York: Arno Press, 1968.

Morris, Lewis. "Letters to General Lewis Morris." In *Collections of the New-York Historical Society, 1875,* pp. 433–534.

Morris, Margaret. *Private Journal Kept During the Revolutionary War: Margaret Morris.* New York: Arno Press, 1969.

Morton, Robert. "The Diary of Robert Morton." *Pennsylvania Magazine of History and Biography* 1 (1877) 1–39.

Moylan, Stephen. "Correspondence of Colonel Stephen Moylan." *Pennsylvania Magazine of History and Biography* 37 (1913): 341–60.

Muhlenberg, John. "Orderly Book of Gen. John Peter Gabriel Muhlenberg." *Pennsylvania Magazine of History and Biography* 33, 34, 35 (1909–11).

Muenchhausen, Friedrich von. *At General Howe's Side, 1776–1778.* Translated by Ernst Kipping. Monmouth Beach, N.J.: Philip Freneau Press, 1974.

Murray, James. *Letters from America, 1773 to 1780: Being the Letters of a Scots Officer, Sir James Murray, to His Home During the War of American Independence.* Edited by Eric Robson. Manchester: Manchester University Press, 1951.

Nagle, Jacob. *The Nagle Journal: A Diary of the Life of Jacob Nagle, Sailor, from the Year 1775 to 1841.* Edited by John C. Dann. New York: Weidenfeld and Nicolson, 1988.

Naval Documents of the American Revolution. Vols. 9–10. Edited by William James Morgan and Michael Crawford. Washington, D.C.: Naval Historical Center, Department of the Navy, 1982–96.

New Records of the American Revolution. London: L. Kashnor, 1927.

Nice, John. "Extracts from the Diary of Captain John Nice." *Pennsylvania Magazine of History and Biography* 16 (1892): 399–411.

"Notes on the Battle of Monmouth." *Pennsylvania Magazine of History and Biography* 14 (1890): 46–49.

Paine, Thomas. *The Complete Writings of Thomas Paine.* Edited by Philip S. Foner. New York: Citadel Press, 1945.

———. "Military Operations Near Philadelphia in the Campaign of 1777–8." *Pennsylvania Magazine of History and Biography* 2 (1878): 283–96.

"Papers Relating to the Paoli Massacre." *Pennsylvania Magazine of History and Biography* 1 (1877): 310–19.

Peale, Charles Willson. "Journal by Charles Willson Peale." *Pennsylvania Magazine of History and Biography* 38 (1914): 271–86.

Peebles, John. *John Peebles' American War: The Diary of a Scottish Grenadier, 1776–1782.* Edited by Ira D. Gruber. Mechanicsburg, Pa.: Stackpole Books, 1998.

Pickering, Octavius, ed. *The Life of Timothy Pickering.* Vol. 1. Boston: Little, Brown, 1867.

Pinckney, Charles Cotesworth. "The Battles of Brandywine and Germantown." *Historical Magazine* 10 (1866): 202–4.

Pontgibaud, Charles-Albert de Moré de. *A French Volunteer of the War of Independence.* Translated and edited by Robert B. Douglas. New York: D. Appleton, 1898.

Popp, Stephan. "Popp's Journal, 1777–1783." Edited by Joseph G. Rosengarten. *Pennsylvania Magazine of History and Biography* 26 (1902): 245–54.

Prechtel, Johann Ernst. *A Hessian Officer's Diary of the American Revolution.* Edited and translated by Bruce E. Burgoyne. Bowie, Md.: Heritage Books, 1994.

Proud, Robert. "Letters of Robert Proud." *Pennsylvania Magazine of History and Biography* 34 (1910): 62–73.

Reed, William B., ed. *Life and Correspondence of Joseph Reed.* Vol. 1. Philadelphia: Lindsay and Blakiston, 1847.

Ritter, Jacob. *Memoirs of Jacob Ritter.* Philadelphia: T. E. Chapman, 1844.

Robertson, Archibald. *Archibald Robertson: His Diaries and Sketches in America, 1762–1780.* Edited by Harry Miller Lydenberg. New York: Arno Press, 1971.

Rodney, Thomas. *Diary of Captain Thomas Rodney, 1776–1777.* New York: Da Capo Press, 1974.

Rush, Benjamin. *Letters of Benjamin Rush.* Vol. 1. Edited by L. H. Butterfield. Princeton, N.J.: Princeton University Press, 1951.

Ryan, Dennis, ed. *A Salute to Courage: The American Revolution as Seen Through Wartime Writings of Officers of the Continental Army and Navy.* New York: Columbia University Press, 1979.

Serle, Ambrose. *The American Journal of Ambrose Serle, Secretary to Lord Howe, 1776–78.* Edited by Edward H. Tatum. San Marino, Calif.: Huntington Library, 1940.

Simcoe, John. *Simcoe's Military Journal: A History of the Operations of a Partisan Corps, Called the Queen's Rangers Commanded by Lieut. Col. J. G. Simcoe, During the War of the American Revolution.* New York: Bartlett and Welford, 1844.

Smith, Paul, ed. *Letters of Delegates to Congress, 1774–1789.* Vols. 6–10. Washington, D.C.: Library of Congress, 1980–83.

Smith, Samuel. *Memoirs of Samuel Smith: Soldier of the Revolution, 1776–1786.* New York: privately printed, 1860.

Smith, Samuel. "The Papers of General Samuel Smith." *Historical Magazine* 7 (1870): 81–92.

Steuben, Friedrich Wilhelm Augustus von. *Steuben Papers.* Kraus-Thomson Organization Limited. Roll no. 1.

Stevens, Enos. "A Fragment of the Diary of Lieutenant Enos Stevens, Tory, 1777–78." *The New England Quarterly* 11 (1938): 374–88.

Stirke, Henry. "A British Officer's Revolutionary War Journal, 1776–1778." *Maryland Historical Magazine* 61 (1961): 150–75.

Sullivan, John. *Letters and Papers of Major-General John Sullivan.* Vols.1–2. Edited by Otis G. Hammond. Concord, N.H.: New Hampshire Historical Society, 1930–31.

Sullivan, Thomas. "Before and After the Battle of Brandywine: Extracts from the Journal of Sergeant Thomas Sullivan of H.M. Forty-Ninth Regiment of Foot." *Pennsylvania Magazine of History and Biography* 31 (1907): 406–18.

Tallmadge, Benjamin. *Memoir of Col. Benjamin Tallmadge.* New York: Thomas Holman, 1858.

Townsend, Joseph. *The Battle of Brandywine: Joseph Townsend.* New York: Arno Press, 1969.

"Unpublished Papers Relating to the Battle of Germantown." *Pennsylvania Magazine of History and Biography* 1 (1877): 399–403.

Waldeck, Philipp. *A Hessian Report on the People, the Land, the War as Noted in the Diary of Chaplain Philipp Waldeck.* Edited by Bruce E. Burgoyne. Bowie, Md.: Heritage Books, 1995.

Waldo, Albigence. "Diary of Surgeon Albigence Waldo, of the Connecticut Line." *Pennsylvania Magazine of History and Biography* 21 (1897): 299–323.

Walpole, Horace. *The Last Journals of Horace Walpole.* Vol. 2. New York: AMS Press, 1973.

Washington, George. *George Washington Papers at the Library of Congress, 1741–1799.* Series 4. General Correspondence, 1697–1799, or http://memory.loc.gov/ammem/gwhtml/.

————. *The Papers of George Washington: Revolutionary War Series.* Vols. 6, 8–12. Edited by Philander Chase, Frank Grizzard Jr., Dorothy Twohig, and Edward Lengel. Charlottesville: University Press of Virginia, 1994–2002.

————. *The Writings of George Washington.* Vols. 9–12. Edited by John Fitzpatrick. Washington, D.C.: Government Printing Office, 1933–34.

Wayne, Anthony. "Letter of General Anthony Wayne." *Pennsylvania Magazine of History and Biography* 11 (1887): 115–16.

Wilkin, W. H., ed. *Some British Soldiers in America.* London: Hugh Rees, 1914.

Wilkinson, James. *Memoirs of My Own Times.* Vol. 1. New York: AMS Press, 1973.

Wister, Sally. "Journal of Sally Wister." *Pennsylvania Magazine of History and Biography* 9 (1885): 318–33, 463–78.

Wortley, E. Stuart, ed. *A Prime Minister and His Son: From the Correspondence of the 3rd Earl of Bute and of Lt.-General the Hon. Sir Charles Stuart, K.B.* New York: Dutton, 1925.

Young, William. "Journal of Sergeant William Young." *Pennsylvania Magazine of History and Biography* 8 (1884): 255–78.

SECONDARY SOURCES

Alden, John Richard. *General Charles Lee: Traitor or Patriot?* Baton Rouge: Louisiana State University Press, 1951.

Anderson, Troyer Steele. *The Command of the Howe Brothers During the American Revolution.* New York: Oxford University Press, 1936.

Baker, William. *Itinerary of George Washington from June 15, 1775, to December 23, 1783.* Lambertville, N.J.: Hunterdon House, 1970.

Belcher, Henry. *The First American Civil War: First Period, 1775–1778.* Vol. 2. London: Macmillan, 1911.

Berg, Fred Anderson. *Encyclopedia of Continental Army Units: Battalions, Regiments and Independent Corps.* Harrisburg, Pa.: Stackpole Books, 1972.

Bernier, Olivier. *Lafayette: Hero of Two Worlds.* New York: Dutton, 1983.

Bill, Alfred Hoyt. *New Jersey and the Revolutionary War.* Princeton, N.J.: D. Van Nostrand, 1964.

————. *Valley Forge: The Making of an Army.* New York: Harper and Brothers, 1952.

Billias, George Allan, ed. *George Washington's Generals.* New York: William Morrow, 1964.

————. *George Washington's Opponents.* New York: William Morrow, 1969.

Boatner, Mark Mayo III. *Encyclopedia of the American Revolution.* New York: David McKay, 1974.

Bowler, R. Arthur. *Logistics and the Failure of the British Army in America, 1775–1783.* Princeton, N.J.: Princeton University Press, 1975.

Bowman, Allen. *The Morale of the American Revolutionary Army.* Fort Washington, N.Y.: Kennikat Press, 1943.

Brownlow, Donald Grey. *A Documentary History of the Battle of Germantown.* Germantown, Pa.: The Germantown Historical Society, 1955.

Callahan, North. *Henry Knox: George Washington's General.* New York: Rinehart and Co., 1958.

Carp, E. Wayne. *To Starve the Army at Pleasure: Continental Army Administration and American Political Culture, 1775–1783.* Chapel Hill: University of North Carolina Press, 1984.

Conway, Stephen. "To Subdue America: British Officers and the Conduct of the Revolutionary War." *William and Mary Quarterly* 43 (1986): 380–407.

Cornwallis-West, G. *The Life and Letters of Admiral Cornwallis.* London: Robert Holden and Co., 1927.

Cumming, William P., and Hugh Rankin. *The Fate of a Nation: The American Revolution Through Contemporary Eyes.* London: Phaidon Press, 1975.

Curtis, Edward E. *The Organization of the British Army in the American Revolution.* New Haven, Conn.: Yale University Press, 1926.

Davis, Burke. *George Washington and the American Revolution.* New York: Random House, 1975.

Dickinson, H. T., ed. *Britain and the American Revolution.* London: Longman, 1998.

Doughty, Robert A., Ira D. Gruber, et al. *American Military History and the Evolution of Warfare in the Western World.* Lexington, Mass.: Heath, 1996.

Dull, Jonathan R. *A Diplomatic History of the American Revolution.* New Haven, Conn.: Yale University Press, 1985.

Dupuy, R. Ernest, Gay Hammerman, and Grace P. Hayes. *The American Revolution: A Global War.* New York: David McKay, 1977.

Fowler, William, Jr., and Wallace Coyle, eds. *The American Revolution: Changing Perspectives.* Boston: Northeastern University Press, 1979.

Frantz, John B., and William Pencak, eds. *Beyond Philadelphia: The American Revolution in the Pennsylvania Hinterland.* University Park: Pennsylvania State University Press, 1998.

Freeman, Douglas Southall. *George Washington: A Biography.* Vols. 4–5. London: Scribner, 1951–52.

Gruber, Ira D. *The Howe Brothers and the American Revolution.* New York: Norton, 1972.

Hargreaves, Reginald. *The Bloodybacks: The British Serviceman in North America and the Caribbean 1655–1783.* New York: Walker and Company, 1968.

Hibbert, Christopher. *Redcoats and Rebels: The American Revolution Through British Eyes.* New York: Avon Books, 1990.

Higginbotham, Don. "The Early American Way of War: Renaissance and Appraisal." *William and Mary Quarterly,* 3d ser., 44 (1987): 230–73.

———. *George Washington and the American Military Tradition.* Athens: University of Georgia Press, 1985.

———. *War and Society in Revolutionary America: The Wider Dimensions of the Conflict.* Columbia: University of South Carolina Press, 1988.

———. *The War of American Independence: Military Attitudes, Policies, and Practice, 1763–1789.* Bloomington: Indiana University Press, 1971.

Hudson, James A. *Logistics of Liberty: American Services and Supply in the Revolutionary War and After.* Newark: University of Delaware Press, 1991.

Jackson, John W. *The Pennsylvania Navy, 1775–1781: The Defense of the Delaware.* New Brunswick, N.J.: Rutgers University Press, 1974.

———. *Valley Forge: Pinnacle of Courage.* Gettysburg, Pa.: Thomas Publications, 1992.

———. *With the British Army in Philadelphia, 1777–1778.* San Rafael, Calif.: Presidio Press, 1979.

Jensen, Merrill. *The Articles of Confederation.* Madison: University of Wisconsin Press, 1940.

Kaplan, Roger. "The Hidden War: British Intelligence Operations during the American Revolution." *William and Mary Quarterly,* 3d ser., 47 (1990): 115–38.

Ketchum, Richard M. *Saratoga: Turning Point of America's Revolutionary War.* New York: Henry Holt, 1997.

Kite, Elizabeth. *Brigadier-General Louis Lebegue Duportail: Commandant of Engineers in the Continental Army, 1777–1783.* Philadelphia: Dolphin Press, 1933.

Knollenberg, Bernhard. *Washington and the Revolution: A Reappraisal: Gates, Conway, and the Continental Congress.* New York: Macmillan, 1941.

Kohn, Richard H. *Eagle and Sword: The Federalists and the Creation of the Military Establishment of America, 1783–1802.* New York: Free Press, 1975.

Kwasny, Mark V. *Washington's Partisan War, 1775–1783.* Kent, Ohio: Kent State University Press, 1996.

Leiby, Adrian C. *The Revolutionary War in the Hackensack Valley: The Jersey Dutch and Neutral Ground, 1775–1783.* New Brunswick, N.J.: Rutgers University Press, 1992.

Lloyd, T. O. *The British Empire, 1558–1983.* Oxford: Oxford University Press, 1984.

Lundin, Leonard. *Cockpit of the Revolution: The War for Independence in New Jersey.* Princeton, N.J.: Princeton University Press, 1940.

Mackesy, Piers. *The War for America, 1775–1783.* Lincoln: University of Nebraska Press, 1964.

Martin, James Kirby, and Mark Edward Lender. *A Respectable Army: The Military Origins of the Republic, 1763–1789.* Arlington Heights, Ill.: Harlan Davidson, 1982.

Middlekauff, Robert. *The Glorious Cause: The American Revolution, 1763–1789.* New York: Oxford University Press, 1982.

Miller, John C. *Triumph of Freedom, 1775–1783.* Boston: Little, Brown, 1948.

Millett, Allan, and Peter Maslowski. *For the Common Defense: A Military History of the United States of America.* New York: Free Press, 1984.

Millis, Walter. *Arms and Men: A Study in American Military History.* New York: Putnam, 1956.

Mitchell, Joseph B. *Military Leaders in the American Revolution.* McLean, Va.: EPM Publications, 1967.

Montross, Lynn. *The Story of the Continental Army, 1775–1783.* New York: Barnes and Noble, 1952.

Morris, Richard B., ed. *The Era of the American Revolution.* New York: Harper Torchbooks, 1965.

Muhlenberg, Henry A. *The Life of Major-General Peter Muhlenberg of the Revolutionary Army.* Philadelphia: Carey and Hart, 1849.

Nelson, Paul David. *Anthony Wayne: Soldier of the Early Republic.* Bloomington: Indiana University Press, 1985.

———. *General James Grant: Scottish Soldier and Royal Governor of East Florida.* Gainesville: University Press of Florida, 1993.

———. *William Alexander, Lord Stirling.* University: University of Alabama Press, 1987.

Palmer, Dave Richard. *The Way of the Fox: American Strategy in the War for America, 1775–1783.* Westport, Conn.: Greenwood Press, 1975.

Palmer, David Richard, and Albert Sidney Britt III. *The Art of War in the 17th and 18th Centuries.* West Point, N.Y.: United States Military Academy, 1972.

Palmer, John M. *General Von Steuben.* Port Washington, N.Y.: Kennikat Press, 1966.

Purcell, L. Edward. *Who Was Who in the American Revolution.* New York: Facts on File, 1993.

Quarles, Benjamin. *The Negro in the American Revolution.* Chapel Hill: University of North Carolina Press, 1961.

Randall, Willard Sterne. *George Washington: A Life.* New York: Henry Holt, 1997.

Reid, Stuart, and Richard Hook. *British Redcoat, 1740–1793.* London: Reed International Books, 1996.

Robson, Eric. *The American Revolution: In Its Political and Military Aspects, 1763–1783.* London: Batchworth Press, 1955.

Rossie, Jonathan Gregory. *The Politics of Command in the American Revolution.* Syracuse, N.Y.: Syracuse University Press, 1975.

Royster, Charles. *Light-Horse Harry Lee and the Legacy of the American Revolution.* New York: Knopf, 1981.

———. *A Revolutionary People at War: The Continental Army and American Character, 1775–1783.* New York: Norton, 1981.

Saxe, Maurice. *Reveries, or Memoirs upon the Art of War.* Westport, Conn.: Greenwood Press, 1971.

Schaffel, Kenneth. "The American Board of War, 1776–1781." *Military Affairs* 50 (1986): 185–89.

Scheer, George F., and Hugh R. Rankin. *Rebels and Redcoats*. New York: World Publishing, 1957.

Shea, William. *The Virginia Militia in the Seventeenth Century*. Baton Rouge: Louisiana State University Press, 1983.

Shy, John. *A People Numerous and Armed: Reflections on the Military Struggle for American Independence*. New York: Oxford University Press, 1976.

Siebert, Wilbur Henry. *The Loyalists of Pennsylvania*. Boston: Gregg Press, 1972.

Smith, Paul H. *Loyalists and Redcoats: A Study in British Revolutionary Policy*. Chapel Hill: University of North Carolina Press, 1964.

Smith, Samuel Stelle. *The Battle of Brandywine*. Monmouth Beach, N.J.: Philip Freneau Press, 1976.

———. *Fight for the Delaware, 1777*. Monmouth Beach, N.J.: Philip Freneau Press, 1970.

Syrett, David. *Shipping and the American War, 1775–1783: A Study of British Transport Organization*. London: Athlone Press, 1970.

Thane, Elswyth. *The Fighting Quaker: Nathanael Greene*. New York: Hawthorn Books, 1972.

Tuchman, Barbara W. *The March of Folly: From Troy to Vietnam*. New York: Ballantine, 1984.

Van Dorn, Carl. *Secret History of the American Revolution*. New York: Viking, 1941.

Ward, Harry M. *Charles Scott and the "Spirit of '76."* Charlottesville: University Press of Virginia, 1988.

———. *Duty, Honor or Country: General George Weedon and the American Revolution*. Philadelphia: American Philosophical Society, 1979.

———. *Major General Adam Stephen and the Cause of American Liberty*. Charlottesville: University Press of Virginia, 1989.

———. *"Unite or Die": Intercolony Relations 1690–1763*. London: Kennikat Press, 1971.

Watson, John. *Annals of Philadelphia, and Pennsylvania, in the Olden Time*. Vol. 2. Philadelphia: Edwin S. Stuart, 1884.

Weigley, Russell. *The American Way of War: A History of United States Military Strategy and Policy*. Bloomington: Indiana University Press, 1973.

Weiner, Frederick Bernays. "The Military Occupation of Philadelphia, in 1777–1778." *Proceedings of the American Philosophical Society* 111 (1967): 310–13.

Whittemore, Charles P. *A General of the Revolution: John Sullivan of New Hampshire*. New York: Columbia University Press, 1961.

Wickwire, Franklin, and Mary Wickwire. *Cornwallis: The American Adventure*. Boston: Houghton Mifflin, 1970.

Willcox, William B. "British Strategy in America, 1778." *Journal of Modern History* 19 (1947): 97–121.

———. *Portrait of a General: Sir Henry Clinton in the War of Independence*. New York: Knopf, 1964.

Willett, Marinus. *A Narrative of the Military Accounts of Colonel Marinus Willett*. Edited by William Willett. New York: N.Y. Times and Arno Press, 1969.

Wood, Gordon S. *The Radicalism of the American Revolution*. New York: Knopf, 1992.

Wright, John W. "The Rifle in the American Revolution." *Historical Review* 29 (1924): 293–99.

Index

Abercrombie, Robert, 98–99, 105, 188
Abington Hill, 189
Adams, John, 17, 20, 57–58
Agnew, James, 68, 74, 75, 99, 102, 103, 104, 106, 234
Albany, New York, 29, 32, 33, 34, 45, 54, 58, 59, 128, 163, 190
Alexander, William. *See* Stirling, Lord
Allen, Andrew, 90
Allentown, New Jersey, 196
Amboy, New Jersey, 23, 24, 25, 26, 36, 40, 41, 42, 43, 44, 46
American Indians, 4, 58, 201, 246, 247
Amherst, Jeffrey, 181, 190
Amiens, Peace of, 241
Amphitrite, 19
Andre, John, 187, 239
Andrew Doria, 129, 139
Ansbach-Bayreuth, 28
Armstrong, John, 68, 76, 81, 96, 103, 104, 140, 149, 150, 173, 199, 235, 239
Army, American
 and Battle of Brandywine, 63–80
 and Battle of Germantown, 93–107
 and Battle of Monmouth Courthouse, 212–24
 cavalry, 202
 Continentals, 14
 desertions from, 15–16
 discipline, 15–16
 drilling of, 16, 174–76
 and eighteenth-century warfare, 71–72
 evaluation of, 179, 232–33
 logistics, 19–21, 23, 89, 92, 124, 149, 153–55, 177–79, 198, 201
 march to Morristown, 6–8
 and militia (*see* Militia)
 and New Jersey incursions, 38–40, 41–42, 43
 officer corps, 17–18, 179, 202, 235–37
 parade through Philadelphia, 57–58
 recruitment of, 14–15
 riflemen, 41–43, 55, 59, 62, 72, 76, 84, 92, 138, 141, 146, 195, 209, 211,
 213, 218, 223
 and smallpox, 16–17
 winter quarters at Valley Forge, 148–56
 and winter skirmishing in New Jersey, 10–12
Army, British
 atrocities and plundering, 10, 54, 195
 and Battle of Brandywine, 63–80
 and Battle of Germantown, 93–107
 and Battle of Monmouth Courthouse, 212–24
 composition of, 27–28
 desertion from, 192, 195
 and eighteenth-century warfare, 71–72
 evaluation of, 231–32
 Germans, 7–8, 10, 25, 27–28, 41, 103, 118, 120–23
 grenadiers, 23–24, 27, 68, 87, 90, 118, 120, 216, 218, 234
 landing at Elk River, 53
 light infantry, 27, 37, 68, 73, 74, 85, 87, 99, 100, 145, 146, 216, 218, 219, 223, 232, 234
 logistics, 108, 172
 and New Jersey incursions, 36–37, 40–41, 42–44
 and occupation of Philadelphia, 169–73
 officer corps, 25, 27, 169, 191–92, 223, 234–35
 preparations for amphibious assault on Philadelphia, 44–45
 sea voyage to Maryland, 50–53
 and subordinate commanders, 233–35
 and winter skirmishing in New Jersey, 23–26
Arnold, Benedict, 18, 38, 39, 59, 60, 121, 158, 160, 208, 239
Augusta, HMS, 119, 120, 123, 129, 134, 147

Baltimore, Maryland, 246
Barren Hill, 188–89, 206–8, 234, 236
Basking Ridge, New Jersey, 204
Bennington, Battle of, 61

327